Humanizing Humanity

Humanizing Humanity

Bidyut Chakrabarty

B L O O M S B U R Y
NEW DELHI • LONDON • OXFORD • NEW YORK • SYDNEY

BLOOMSBURY INDIA
Bloomsbury Publishing India Pvt. Ltd
Second Floor, LSC Building No. 4, DDA Complex, Pocket C – 6 & 7,
Vasant Kunj, New Delhi, 110070

BLOOMSBURY, BLOOMSBURY ACADEMIC INDIA and the Diana logo are trademarks of Bloomsbury Publishing Plc

First published in India 2024
This edition published 2024

Bloomsbury Academic India
An imprint of Bloomsbury Publishing Plc

ISBN: HB: 978-93-56409-13-2 eBook: 978-93-56409-75-0
2 4 6 8 10 9 7 5 3 1

Typeset at Manipal Technologies Limited
Printed and bound in India by Replika Press Pvt. Ltd

To

Those who are relentlessly battling for humanizing humanity against the forces seeking to dehumanize humanity.

Contents

Preface and Acknowledgements

Humanizing Humanity is a long analytical assessment of ideational visions of three leading thinkers of Indian nationalism who stand out for being innovative. The text is an elaboration of how they developed their politico-ideological priorities in a context when the nationalist campaign became far more complex due to the rising sociocultural ideas supportive of the demands of the peripheral classes. Rabindranath Tagore (1861–1941), Mohandas Karamchand Gandhi (1869–1948) and Bhimrao Ramji Ambedkar (1891–1956) carved a new space in the nationalist approach to humanity which did not receive adequate attention in the past. While dwelling on the principal theme, the book is an attempt to comprehend one of the critical ideas that has gained momentum in contemporary scholarship, namely humanism, which is being attacked politico-ideologically perhaps due to radical metamorphosis in global thinking. It is also required to clarify that my purpose is not to suggest that concern for humanism is completely absent. This is not at all the case, since the goal is to draw on the ideas of past thinkers to reiterate that, as a phenomenon, humanism continues to be pertinent in contemporary thinking.

Since the purpose is to understand an ideational genre, the book concentrates on the texts articulated by three of the top ideologues who provided significant inputs to meaningfully understand sociocultural prejudices as a deterrent to human progress. This is a unique approach in the study of nationalist thought since the theme is conceptualized with reference to the prevalent socio-economic and politico-cultural context in which nationalist ideas were viewed differently. For instance, Gandhi did not appear to be as enthusiastic as Ambedkar to destabilize the existent inter-personal relationships due to the caste system. Being an advocate for the annihilation of caste, Ambedkar never appreciated Gandhi's defence for *varnashrama* as it was one of the justifying conceptual parameters for caste division in India. Similarly, Tagore questioned Gandhi when he characterized the 1934 Bihar earthquake as God's caprice since it was likely to mislead the Indians. It was justified by Gandhi by saying that perhaps the fear of God was likely to restrain Indians from being casteist. For Tagore, the argument was far-fetched because caste prejudices were too well-entrenched to be ignored so easily. Their approaches to earthquakes were governed by their concerns for humanity although they differed radically in their assessment of a geological metamorphosis.

Of the texts I have published so far, this book stands out because it is an offshoot of my politico-ideological priorities. I am of the firm opinion that Tagore, Gandhi and Ambedkar reinterpreted some of the serious constraints inhibiting humanity to flourish naturally. What is striking is the fact that despite being raised in nearly the same political milieu, their grasp on social issues was different and innovative in nature. A study of their writings reveals that their primary aim was to creatively interpret the milieu to understand what went wrong in India which helped the British to strike roots. Although their aims were nearly similar, they were linked with one another because their primary goal was to ensure India's political emancipation.

There is one point which may not be politically plausible. Nonetheless, this was too important to put away. Both Gandhi and Tagore were swayed by the British rule at the outset; they were however disenchanted because the system of governance that the foreign rulers consolidated became gradually brutal and oppressive. Gandhi organized nonviolent resistance to remove the British rule, while Tagore fiercely critiqued the colonisers with his condemnation of sociocultural prejudices segmenting human beings due to their religious and caste identities. Contrarily, Ambedkar, by being drawn to the principal values of Enlightenment, espoused the cause of the socioculturally and politico-economically peripheral sections of society; they were marginalized simply because of the accident of birth. It was the process of dehumanization of humanity, argued Ambedkar, to sustain interests of a few who wielded socio-political authority.

A book is an outcome of a creative blending of many efforts; the author is, of course, the main architect. My family, Sanchita, Urna and Pablo, always stood by me along with members of my extended family, Mini, Tinku, Debiporna and Sreeja. Without their constant support, it would not have been possible to concentrate on my academic accomplishments. I am grateful to my colleagues at Visva-Bharati, especially Professor Amrit Sen of the English Department and Dr Nimai Saha, Visva-Bharati's Liberarian, for being just a phone call away.

I owe a great deal to my students in various parts of the globe because of their powerful observations on my focus areas of study when preparing course curriculums. Their contribution is significant for allowing me to think about different challenging aspects of Indian nationalism which made me think of monographs on various themes of the campaign in

India against foreign hegemony during the nineteenth and twentieth centuries.

An author derives satisfaction when their students are provoked to raise new questions which also propel them to undertake research in areas of their interests. If that happens, an author will have achieved their academic objectives.

Bidyut Chakrabarty
Visva-Bharati
Santiniketan, India
September 2023

Introduction

I

History is full of instances to demonstrate how human beings deviate from the core values of humanity which invariably results in the exploitation of one section by another. Deployment of forces for subjugating the hapless for the empowered does not seem to be undesirable or ethically debased. Exploitation is hence considered a justified mode of privileging the privileged at the cost of the underprivileged. Such an activity is animalistic at one level since physically powerful animals dominate their less powerful counterparts in forests. This is a natural law justifying the killing of carnivorous animals of those which are, under no circumstances, threats to the survival of the former. In real terms, if a lion prays a deer for mere survival, it cannot be considered unfair as it is done for survival. At another level, it does not seem fair since the stronger prevails over the weakest. This poses a difficult moral question to those seeking to understand the growth of humanity amidst crises. As history demonstrates, the weaker continues to remain a victim of the stronger, which is not ethically justified, but the voice of opposition is not strong enough—at least at the outset—to challenge such a dehumanizing endeavour, presumably because of fear of adverse repercussion. Human history also shows that although the voice is feeble at the beginning of the rise of those deploying force, it grows stronger every day, finally leading to the decimation of the forces seeking to undermine fundamental human values. In other words, history proceeds with a tug-of-war between the oppressed and oppressor or between the rebels and those perpetrating unfair authority designs. Many examples exist to vindicate how humanity survives through a dialectical interaction between forces representing justice and fairness and those indulging in efforts to the contrary.

The purpose of this exercise is not to focus on events like some decisive revolutions in human history which radically altered the prevalent system of conceptualizing humanity; instead, it is devoted to manifold philosophical endeavours that transformed human thinking by empowering human beings to zealously participate in activities against the evil forces despite adverse consequences. To be precise, the only aim of this project is to understand human history with reference to the ideational visions directing the victims, in particular, to reinvigorate them under threatening circumstances. Fundamental here is the point that history develops out of constant friction between the exploiters and the exploited. This is a manifestation of how Hegelian dialectics works: the battle between thesis and anti-thesis culminating in synthesis manifests in both the radicalization of humanity and the concomitant processes, showing how it originates and prevails over many competing modes of thinking.

Implied here is the dialectical interaction between the ideas and the context, which means contextual metamorphosis—visible and invisible—remains critical to the changing ideational priorities. In clear terms, the argument here is not novel because ideas or texts are dialectically connected with the prevalent socio-economic, politico-cultural, and ideological contexts. What is insisted here is the importance of the prevalent socio-economic and politico-ideological context in shaping a mentality or mindset, which Plato articulated by saying that each philosopher is a child of his time, establishing a dialectical interconnection between ideas and the existent context. A caveat should be added here since ideational transformation also occurs at regular intervals, indicating that nothing is sacrosanct in human civilization except those values which hold the 'heartbeat' of society. Linked with this argument is also the claim that efforts towards dehumanizing remain integral to civilization as dehumanization and humanity are dialectically intertwined. It works at two levels—those of ideas and practice. The former articulates how the latter is conceptualized and spread out.

Keeping the vision in mind, the exercise is directed to understand how the contextual changes lead to ideational transformation seeking to prevail humanity over forces to the contrary. Many thinkers attract attention immediately and endeavour to establish a new mode of thinking, challenging what is held as axiomatic. Implicit here is also the point that tasks undertaken by ideational leaders to combat those committed to the prevalent socio-economic and politico-cultural visions are not easy. Here lies the justification of the exercise seeking to defend the emerging views and ideas contrary to the 'widely' accepted priorities. The articulation of a new vision involves a fierce debate between those in support of and those opposed to what appear to have destabilised the prevalent conceptual approaches to humanity. Intrinsic here is the point that debates involving arguments and counterarguments are integral to the blossoming of new and explanatory ideas. There are thus two sets of thinkers: one for change and the other for status quo. There is, of course, another group of thinkers who, by not belonging to either of the groups, prefer to take another line of thinking in which the old vision, instead of being rejected in its entirety, is also appreciated to the extent it helps them understand its new counterpart. Their approach is instead cautionary, presumably because they are not fully confident of the new ideas, nor are they persuaded to believe that their earlier counterparts are as decadent as they are shown to be. A cursory look at the evolution of politico-ideological thought cutting across geographical boundaries reveals that humanizing ideational visions draw upon the historical context and question those branded as 'conservative'. The process manifests how the Hegelian trio creates a synthesis from the struggle between thesis and anti-thesis.

Conceptual Points

There are three core conceptual points which deserve attention: first, as it is challenging to develop a grand theory of humanizing humanity, it is incumbent on the analysts to remember that models, by being context-driven, provide a context-specific approach to the phenomenon, which also contains ideas with transcendental importance. For instance, the Enlightenment philosophy—notwithstanding its roots in the Western context—helps build ideational visions elsewhere since it also has politico-ideological inputs for humanity. Secondly, human beings confront difficulties which are diverse in character and texture. Hence, the one-size-fits- all formula will never work for several reasons. Therefore, what is required is a grasp of the conceptual premises concerning the equally diverse contexts. Otherwise, the endeavour towards reconceptualizing human reality is futile. Reemphasized here is the view that conceptualizing contrarian visions involves not just reassessing the realities but also comprehending them in new conceptual prisms. Finally, a careful analysis of the intellectual exercises underlines that humanizing humanity is an effort undertaken by many in different phases and the unfolding of society in various spatial locations.

Complementing the above point is the claim that those engaged in humanizing humanity follow different conceptual paths. For Karl Marx (1818–1883) the annihilation of a section of people who were despised as exploiters or bourgeois in his lexicon of the proletariat or appallingly disprivileged was the only mode of taking humanity out of the vicious circle of exploitation. In contrast, Mohandas Karamchand Gandhi, also known as Mahatma, always discouraged a divisive mindset. Instead, he was in favour of universal humanism regardless of socio-economic schism. His idea of 'trusteeship' testifies to his political idioms since he conceptualized the rich as 'trustees' of wealth for the poor; these trustees are made so by divine power since they are adequately equipped to utilize their wealth for human welfare. Associated with this argument is the view that many thinkers not only lay out a conceptual blueprint but also provide a roadmap for protection from dehumanization in the future. Along with their ideational vision, these thinkers also pay attention to the means of doing so; for instance, the leading lights of Greek thought, Plato and Aristotle, among others, evolved models for democracy which, despite being different from the Lincolnian idea, were means of governance for guiding humanity in accordance to what they deemed appropriate for their politico-ideological objectives. This is also applicable to Niccolo Machiavelli (1469–1527) who in his *The Prince* (published in 1532), provided a model of statecraft with an identical goal of serving humanity in a situation when Italy was passing through severe crises which threatened its existence as a polity. His model is, for obvious reasons, inadequate in the contemporary world. However, his idea that a ruler needs to combine the agility and strength of a lion and the cunning of a jackal continues to remain relevant even after nearly four hundred years. One of the most glaring examples of how Machiavellian conceptualization influenced a twentieth-century thinker of India is Bhimrao Ramji Ambedkar (1891–1956) who, while justifying his approach to humanity, also insisted on the development of a strong state to implement some of his schemes for not only creating an egalitarian society but also for its protection from those who held contrarian views. Not only did he question the foundational basis of Hinduism, but he also demonstrated how the privileged sustained their hegemony by deliberately distorting the axiomatic values of Hinduism.

Conceptualizing humanizing humanity is both an easy and a difficult task at the same time; easy because the exercise entails an assessment of the path-breaking ideas of a selective set of thinkers who undertook the task during their life by confronting the dominant socio-economic situation and politico-ideological priorities governing human existence. Their texts are readily available in the public domain. It is a difficult task on two counts; on the one hand, humanizing the exercise must be weaved around conceptual preferences supporting humanizing humanity concerning the context to reiterate the well-established dictum that they are dialectically entwined. On the other hand, since the task attempts to delve into the intellectual/conceptual unfolding of ideational priorities tuned to collective well-being, one must draw on the processes culminating in articulating novel visions. The exercise is the development of context-specific ideas with transcendental significance, and by not being confined to a specific genre of thought, the endeavour is also directional. It establishes that the conceptual understanding of humanizing humanity maps out different politico-ideological preferences within one rubric of thought—human welfare regardless of chasm around caste, class, and ethnicity axes.

There is no denying that humanizing humanity is a politico-ideological exercise. A careful study of the ideological priorities of thinkers reveals that they are an articulation of their idea of 'political', which, in conventional parlance, means a mode of capturing power and authority. The well-defined ideational priorities, however, show that, for them, political does not denote so; instead, it is a design to metamorphose the prevalent power relationship governing human behaviour. Illustrative here is the conceptualization of *Leviathan* by Thomas Hobbes which he articulated in his book, *Leviathan*, published in 1651. Allegorically, *Leviathan* is an imaginary figure with unbelievable strength, physical and intellectual. According to Hobbes, amid the chaos confronting England in the middle of the seventeenth century, what was required was a powerful state to bring back peace and normalcy to protect humanity from being decimated. The text is, on the one hand, a persuasive analysis of how governance deteriorated in England, which led to the rise and consolidation of forces contrary to core human values, and, on the other hand, a seriously pursued endeavour for building a system of government capable of providing just and fair governance in place of indiscipline and misgovernance.

Critical Conceptual Parameters

There are two conceptual parameters—grand theory and dehumanization—which deserve to be elaborated to avoid confusion. A grand theory is an all-embracing ideational mode that helps us understand the unfolding of ideas and humanity, and sociocultural features. It appears to have lost its credence since it is challenging to conceptualize specific socio-economic contexts and politico-ideological visions by being dependent on grand theories. They are too general to capture the distinctive nature of the context and sociocultural concepts. In other words, the grand theories do not seem to be as effective as was assumed in the past when social reality was not as complex. Nonetheless, many ideologues in the West argued for grand theories. In a widely circulated collection of essays written by leading thinkers, Quentin Skinner identified the core arguments in favour of this genre. He borrows the idea of C. Wright Mills' characterization of 'a trans-historical straitjacket', and argues that there could be 'a systematic theory of the nature of man and society [because] human nature remains more or less similar across societies'.[1] To reinforce the argument, he further suggested that the idea of a grand theory 'not only served to direct social scientist to look for regularities as the only acceptable basis for explaining social phenomena, It also required them to believe that there was no reason in principle why human actions should not be viewed and explained in just the same way as natural events. The result was that 'man as a subject for science came to seem not just a possible but the only respectable goal for social disciplines.'[2]

The idea is justified by Karl Popper (1902–1994) who in his *The Open Society and its Enemies* (1945) argued, as per Skinner, that a belief which is rationally grounded and 'hence scientifically respectable, [shall be] an ingredient of a grand theory [except] if and only if it has been submitted to a "crucial experiment" designed to falsify it, and has [thus] succeeded in passing the test'.[3] Skinner was perfect in his interpretation of Karl Popper's idea of grand theory because he too established his theoretical premise in its favour by mentioning that his conceptualization is based on the fact that the principal aim of a philosopher is

> to quest for answers for decay of humanity and devise designs for combatting some of the difficulties faced by our civilization – a civilization which might be perhaps described as aiming at humaneness and reasonableness, at equality and freedom; a civilization which is still in its fancy, as it were, and which continues to grow in spite of the fact that it has been so often betrayed by so many of the intellectual leaders of mankind. [*The Open Society and its Enemies*] attempts to show that this civilization has not yet fully recovered from the shock of its birth—the transition from the tribal or 'closed society', with its submission to magical forces, to the 'open society' which sets free the critical powers of man.[4]

The approach is persuasive because Popper endeavours to highlight those basic human tendencies which are tuned to human betterment. Being aware that contrarian tendencies are hindering this task, he believes that notwithstanding such attempts, human society progresses by seeking to attain goals for its well-being. Such tendencies are undoubtedly universal, and human beings instinctively pursue their growth. For Popper, a grand theory seems inconceivable with reference to the object of humanity which is the same regardless of historical ages, namely, the containment of evil forces and engagement in activities for progress. In Popperian conceptualization of a grand theory, the transcendental goal of humanity is the most critical, as is evident when one dissects his notion of history. As he adumbrates,

> we interpret history, with an eye to those problems inhibiting the natural growth of humanity. Hence, we can interpret history of power politics, for instance, from the point of view of our fight for the open society, for a rule of reason, for justice, freedom, equality, and for the control of international crime. Although history has no ends, we can impose those ends of ours upon it; and although history has no meaning, we can give it a meaning.[5]

According to him, humans are the only agents of change and history is the imprint of this agency. History is thus not independent of human endeavour, and human beings act when their future is at stake. On this assumption, Popper argues that as history moves by being sensitive to a particular mode of argumentation, there are enough reasons to justify the contention that a grand theory does not seem to be an aberration. Hence, he pursues the point by firmly stating that

> instead of posing as prophets, we must become the makers of our fate. We must learn to do things as well as we can and to look out for our mistakes. And, when we have developed the idea that the history of power will be our judge, when we have given worrying whether or not history will justify us, then one day perhaps we may succeed in getting power under control. In this way we may even justify history, in our turn.[6]

From the point of view of historicism—to borrow from Popper's parlance—we have reasons to be influenced by the argument that grand theories are justified as the core goals of humanity remain the same across the globe. This is conclusive as characterize certain well-defined features characterize humanism. The contention is problematic since human experiences differ in sociocultural contexts, and their struggle to establish those core values may vary. This implies that a grand theory may not be an apt explanatory tool. Thus, one must be sensitive to contextual distinctiveness to comprehend how other ideas get systematised and propel many to act despite adverse conditions. The British rule in India is symbolic here. The most humanitarian liberal theorists, by being baptized in the philosophy of Enlightenment, espoused the cause of humanity. With the appearance of colonialism and the acceptance of the slave trade, these thinkers may have been disillusioned. Hence, grand theories could be valuable in conceptualizing certain broad human tendencies but are inadequate to grasp humanity.

Here lies the importance of contextual theories. One of the most convincing examples is Rabindranath Tagore (1861–1941), who, at the outset, uncritically accepted the grand theories that emerged out of the Western experiences of the philosophy of Enlightenment. He was also disenchanted with the philosophical theorization of humanity because it appeared to have been prejudiced against the colonized, presumably to selfishly argue that their ideas were transcendental. Tagore's critical essay, *The Crisis in Civilization* (1941), is a testimony here; it is an essay which historically traces Tagore's disappointment with the Western discourses that are hardly equipped to understand how the Enlightened sections of humanity become vicious to the extent of completely departing from the values on which the Western civilization rests.

Critical here is the claim that the application of grand theories is limited. The Popperian notion of historicism is no longer an effective tool for conceptualizing humanism in a single prism. In other words, it is improbable because the one-size-fits-all formula does not work in all circumstances. The arguments defending grand theories help us understand the less complex sociocultural realities; thus they are generally futile as far as complex social contexts are concerned. As humans are a product of their time, the grand theories cannot be satisfactory. This statement needs to be qualified because grand theories also uphold certain ideational priorities relevant to conceptualizing humanity as a collective. However, they appear to be less effective tools as soon as one is inclined to understand specific socio-economic and politico-cultural milieu. In conceptualizing humanizing humanity, what is preferred is a creative blending of both grand and contextual ideational visions to participate in the academic debate on whether one is theoretically well-equipped to comprehend historicism as a phenomenon by being dependent on one vision at the cost of another or by drawing on both in terms of their applicability to specific contexts.

The second concept which is critical to this study is dehumanization. It must be highlighted that humanization and dehumanization are dialectically entwined since the former is vacuous without the latter; or in other words, the apparent tendencies towards dehumanizing humanity contribute to the rise of those in favour of humanism. As history demonstrates, humans have been inherently keen to subjugate their brethren for partisan gains. As a result, many constructed identities gained salience. For instance, the idea of race is reflective of this act. Various new ideational theories arose to justify dehumanization of those born with a different skin colour. Edward Said, in his classical text, *Orientalism* (1978), argues that white Europeans redefined humanity to support their contention that people with black skin were inferior to them and needed to be civilized through coercion. Said emphasized this point by forcefully stating that

> Orientalism aided and was aided by general cultural pressures that tended to make more rigid and sense of difference between the European and Asiatic parts of the world. My [argument] is that Orientalism is fundamentally a political doctrine willed over the Orient because the Orient was weaker than the West, which elided the Orient's difference with its weakness.[7]

Explicit here is how a design of dehumanization is made to pursue the narrow aims of a section of humanity, which can force another to accept the hegemony of the former. This is the root of dehumanization, as argued by Said. Implicit here is also the viewpoint that approach to humanization is fractured for one section defends its grip over another because it was justified as morally correct by ignoring that forcing the vanquished to toe the line of the conquerors is tantamount to dehumanizing the ruled. Many European thinkers like Thomas Hobbes, Jean Jacques Rousseau, and Karl Marx, among others, raised their voices against those who justified designs of oppression as appropriate. This was the logic Edmund Burke (1729–1797), the British parliamentarian, endorsed while arguing that British colonialism in India was most desirable to civilize the 'barbarians of the East'. Colonialism was thus never identified as a deterrent to the growth of humanity regardless of their location and disparate sociocultural characteristics.

Many Indian thinkers and ideologues were opposed to the rule by foreigners, not only because it was an economically exploitative system—which Dadabhai Naoroji (1825–1917) had shown in his *Poverty and Un-British Rule in India* (1901)—but also due to its pernicious impact on India's natural unfolding as a sociocultural unit. Tagore, M.K. Gandhi and Aurobindo Ghose (1872–1950), among others, also developed a powerful critique of colonialism as an arrangement to dehumanize a section of humanity which was forcibly brought under colonial rule. Colonialism was a brutal system, and for its continuity, it also led to the creation of a different sociocultural design for the colonized. The Western definition of humanism was universal, and if there was a threat to this imposed conceptualization, it was to be coercively suppressed since it was a step towards dehumanizing those who were trained to be humanized. This is one aspect of dehumanization. The other was highlighted by BR Ambedkar in his texts questioning the division of humans according to birth. Opposed to caste distinction—another age-old system of dehumanization in India—

Ambedkar wrote extensively on how a section was being systematically dehumanized for fulfilling partisan goals of those reaping benefits by being dominantly placed in caste hierarchy by marking a large section of humanity as socioculturally inferior. In other words, they were ascribed an inferior identity by being born to lower caste parents.

With their stern critiques, humanizing thinkers in both Western and Indian intellectual traditions developed a genre of thinking which was unknown given the hegemonic grip of those who championed models of dehumanization by constructing conceptual designs in its favour. As mentioned earlier, the battle is dialectically construed, which means that the more support there is for dehumanization, the fiercer the counterattacks from many thinkers cutting across geographical boundaries will be. The effective challenge to racism led to the adoption of the Voting Rights Act of 1965, which guaranteed equal franchise to African-Americans in the US. Similarly, the relentless attacks on racism led to the Apartheid Legislation in 1991 in South Africa. In India, the rescinding of caste-driven discrimination following the adoption of the Constitution of the Republic of India is also another instance of how dehumanization was constitutionally abdicated. The concern for humanism continues to inspire many to take part in the struggle against forces supportive of dehumanization; this also helps build a powerful mode of thinking, developing an equally powerful counter-theoretical genre seeking to uproot the tendencies undermining core values of humanism.

Nature of the Text

Unlike the conventional modes of conceptualizing humanizing humanity, this text, by identifying the fundamental conceptual parameters of a selective set of ideational priorities, captures the trends in political thoughts that are critical in grasping how the phenomenon was articulated and developed. As it is difficult to dwell on the ideas of all the thinkers who devoted themselves to the cause of humanity, the text focuses on those thinkers who stand out for their significant contribution to humanizing humanity. It also draws on the idea of a new vista of knowledge for humanity, and the thinkers' ideas remain most significant in restating the importance of humanism in a global civilization. With their path-breaking ideas, they continue to remain useful to help build innovative designs for progress and development.

There are two cautionary notes which merit attention here: first, although the primary aim is to comprehend humanizing humanity, the present exercise concentrates on those texts which are conceptually different and politico-ideologically creative. Additionally, since it is a textual analysis of ideas, the author's efforts are directed to understand the ideational visions with reference to the prevalent socio-economic and politico-cultural context. It is important to remember those who developed *The Federalist Papers* to defend federalism in contrast with confederation in the US just before the inauguration of the US Constitution in 1787. Conceptually, this is the first serious attempt to formulate federalism as a design cementing a bond among immigrants from various parts of Europe; these papers were a challenge, at one level, and an innovative design of togetherness amidst sociocultural diversity, at another. By seeking to institutionalize the bond, the federalists, like Alexander Hamilton, John Jay and James Madison, provided a unique model which created a template of camaraderie among the settlers in the US despite being socioculturally different; a transcendental design, federalism continues to remain as effective as it was when the idea appeared in political lexicon in bringing socioculturally disparate people together for common well-being.

Human articulation of multifaceted ideas reinforces the claim that history is ideationally fractured around multiple socio-economic and politico-cultural axes. History, along with upholding the status-quoist ideas, also welcomes new visions that draw sustenance from contrarian ideas. History is thus both descriptive and analytical at the same time: descriptive since it is a narrative of how humanity progresses; analytical because it also provides an explanatory account of how we move from one generation to another. Thus, history is also a tool of conceptualizing and reconceptualizing civilizational unfolding of humanity. What triggers the thinkers to seek to explain the changing socio-economic realities and politico-ideological priorities is guided by their inert desire to provide explanations about what exists. The exercise is an outcome of a dialectical interactions between the thinkers and how they conceive the context in which they are born and raised. Fundamental here is the conceptual claim that the contextual transformation remains a significant determinant as far as ideas are concerned. While seeking to capture the criticality of the context, Rabindranath Tagore thus mentioned that,

> civilization, whose object is to afford humanity its greatest possible opportunity of complete manifestation, perishes when some selfish passion, in place of a moral ideal, is allowed to exploit its resources unopposed, for its own purposes. For the greed of acquisition and the living principle of creation are antagonist to each other.[8]

For Tagore, civilization is the context which contributes to the template in which challenging ideas are articulated. As a priest of universal humanism, he questioned how human selfishness gains ground in the wake of colonialism; and how it pushes out the humanitarian concerns as they stand in contradiction with the former. Such processes not only help us to understand the journey of human civilization, but also contribute to the building of alternative conceptual models of analysis. Furthermore, they also lay the foundation of the argument that human civilization is always in flux, which means that the idea of 'the end of civilization' does not bear truth. Tagore refers to the decisive role of human life as critical to civilizational changes. As he stated,

> life has brought with it the first triumph of freedom in the world of the inert, because it is an inner expression and not merely an external fact, because it must always exceed the limits of substance, never allowing its materials to clog its spirit, and yet ever keeping to the limits of its truth. Its accumulation must not suppress its harmony of growth, the harmony that unites the *in* and the *out*, the end and the means, the *what is* and the *what is to come*.[9]

Two important claims are made here and both are of immense theoretical significance. First, by attributing centrality to life, Tagore not only upholds that human life being a significant determinant of human civilization, but also reemphasizes its tremendous importance in steering specific paths for humanity. Critical of human greed, Tagore feels that it is impediment for humanity to flourish in its true manifestations. As greed is a 'passion and cannot create, … when any civilization,' recounts Tagore,

> gives the first place to greed, the soul relation between man and man is severed; and the more luxurious such a civilization grows in pomp and power, the poorer it becomes in truth of soul. [Illustrative here is] a picture [which] is a creation, because it is the harmony of many lines, related to one another. [Contrarily], … an engineer's plan is not a picture, because the lines there are bound to each other by some external necessity. When greed of success is the main nexus between man and man, … society becomes a huge plan and ceases to be a picture of the ideal. Man's spiritual relations are lost sight of; money becomes the prime mover; the capitalist the driver; and the rest of mankind merely fuel for the running of the machine.[10]

At the centre of his concern remains his heart-felt desire of humanizing humanity which was severely harmed when colonialism came into the frame in areas where the oppositional forces were ineffective to successfully combat the forces. Tagore's second claim draws out the adverse implications of colonial hegemony on humanity. An artist drawing a picture brings out their best when they are allowed to act free; otherwise, the creation shall never be their best since it evolves in an environment which is guided by a set of factors. The assessment is linked with his personal experience of being a colonial subject who is hardly free to carve out a path which is free because colonialism is meant to safeguard interests of a section of humanity at the expense of the other. To strengthen his argument, Tagore refers to the pernicious impact of capitalism on humanity in general, as it is nothing but a machine to augment wealth for the victorious. As soon as human civilization is divided between the vanquished and winners, human beings are demarcated as strong and weak, rich or wealthy and the poor or impoverished the forward and backward, the civilized and the uncivilized. Such an argument, despite being justified as plausible at a particular of human history, is parochial in nature and character. Tagore who is a humanist, raises his voice against the colonial state which is instinctively prejudiced against the colonized since its inception. Under no circumstance is this justified because 'the true expression of Man is possible ... when he realizes all creation in himself and himself in all creation. Otherwise, his truth is obscured'.[11] This is a context-driven realization because as long as human beings remain united, it is easier to contain forces seeking to destroy humanity. In other words, the scriptural reference to the idea that 'the man who knows others as himself is truly revealed' is evident at the glance of how human civilization moves forward. According to Tagore,

> in the beginning, we see man gathered into separate groups within barriers of mountain and ocean. As soon as man came into touch with man, the problems of his truth as a member of the human race demanded attention. ... Those of them who, having come into contact, hit out wildly against one another, none trusting the other, each trying to gain the advantage, have all disappeared from the face of the earth. And those, who have tried to realize the one Soul in the souls of all, have developed into great peoples.[12]

Fundamental here is a powerful conceptualization. Along with his condemnation for colonialism, he sharply argued for freedom for all or 'freedom of Universal Man'.[13] The sources of his claim are two-fold: first, by being drawn to *Isha Upanishad*, one of the important ancient texts considered to be most useful for humanity, Tagore defended his viewpoints scripturally; second, by assessing how human civilization develops, he also shows that his ideas have a solid empirical basis. The purpose is harmony among human beings not just for their physical existence, but also for their quest for truth. Implicit here is an important point which is both a sharp critique of those who are opposed to human harmony and a reiteration of his views championing the claim that togetherness is the root of human success. To empirically substantiate his contention, Tagore states that inflexibility is at the root of decline and debasement of human civilization, which he backed by saying,

> static regardless of civilizational change [which] … hindered the freedom of man and maintained dissensions [because] the moving principle of life unites [as] … it deals with the varied, and seeks unity in order to be able to deal truly.[14]

Based on understanding of *Upanishadic* ideals, he makes a persuasive argument suggesting how the creation of sociocultural boundaries harms well-knit collectivity. He refers to 'the Brahmins who had the static ideals of society in their change [which resulted in] the consolidation of different forms of ritualism and … sectarian barriers between clans and classes'.[15] When defending his claims. India underwent a sea-change once the forces opposed to Brahmin hegemony gained ground. History is witness to the processes leading to the crumbling of Brahmins' authority and their customary practices. Tagore argued that it was a manifestation of 'a swing in the Aryan civilization [due to] the pull of two opposite principles, that of self-preservation represented by the Brahmins, and that of self-expansion represented by the Kshatriya'.[16] An analytical dissection of the processes leading to the decline of Brahmins and the rise of Kshatriyas is not just a display of legitimizing their respective claims, but also an articulation of how two relatively well-off segments of society get entangled with the purpose of safeguarding their interests.

The study of India's ancient past reveals that humanizing humanity is a sectarian conceptual design, because it was meant to protect communities who were linked with one another due to their politico-ideological objectives. The point that humanizing humanity is an endeavour resulting in a battle between those in its favour and those who are opposed to it is essential here. History is full of examples of struggle between the rich and poor, between the conservatives and radicals, between the obscurantists or orthodox and those with contrarian views, and between classes with conflicting socio-economic interests. Thus, it can be said that struggle is one means for human progress which is documented by many thinkers all over the world; there is, however, another way, which shows accommodation of forces with nearly incompatible sociocultural and economic priorities for amity and peaceful existence of communities with identifiable differentiating characteristics. India is a good example. Despite being disparate around social, cultural, economic, and political axes, India survived independence and Partition. The argument that it was also possible because of the consolidation of a strong state is equally possible but one cannot rule out the critical role of civilizational togetherness in cementing a solid bond regardless of differences. A brief view of India's past since 1947 also reveals that one of the critical ingredients of civilizational unity is also concern for humanism. The idea that India stands paramount in the comity of nations due to the conscious collective efforts at humanizing humanity went deeper into the psyche of the majority who internalizes the feeling of being Indian. By expounding the compatible politico-ideological priorities, Indian thinkers contributed to the processes which led to the growth of collective well-being. Religion acted decisively in bifurcating India in 1947 and that it was hardly effective in sustaining the bond was proved beyond doubt with the rise of Bangladesh in 1971 when religious congruence among the people located in two different parts of Pakistan scarcely deterred the division of the country. So, religion did not appear to be strong enough to cement togetherness which meant that it was not adequate to contribute to humanizing humanity.

II

A perusal of the global intellectual traditions reveals that the efforts Tagore and his colleagues undertook did not seem to be unique. Many creative thinkers across the globe evolved their ideational priorities by being devout humanists, which means that they upheld views for humanizing humanity. Being a product of their time, these thinkers constructed models of defending humanism once it was virulently attacked by forces striking at the foundation of humanity. For instance, Thomas Hobbes' *Leviathan*, was a product of political instability in England which, the author thought, was likely to harm humanity. So, the tract emerged out of his concern for the need of political stability to safeguard humanity from difficulties. The chaotic England gave Hobbes an opportunity to conceptualize governance in a fashion which is contrary to monarchy or the prevalent administration. With his knowledge of the Puritan Revolution which began in 1641 with the objective of removing the Church controlled royal authority, Hobbes devised a design of governance articulating a new political vocabulary for the rising trading and commercial classes or, in common parlance, the bourgeoisie. It is thus argued that 'under the banner of Puritanism, were drawn the growing commercial and trading classes of England together with their allies among the gentry'.[17] In fact, it will not be an exaggeration to suggest that the Puritan Revolution was the first successful bourgeois revolution in England. One is tempted here to raise a question. Why did the Puritans couch their politico-ideological preferences in exclusively religious terms? For the Puritans, the faith was a relatively effective source for political mobilization in a context when typical bourgeois values did not appear to have gained salience in society. Here, Puritanism was a strategic vehicle for bringing the opposition together against monarchy, and in the absence of conceptually persuasive models of mobilization, religious beliefs instantly cemented a bond among those who opposed the royal authority. It was evident that monarchy ceased to be as effective, with the growth of parallel centres of power at the behest of the rising bourgeoisie. As the existence of human beings was at stake, Hobbes' *Leviathan* articulated perhaps the most powerful voice to humanize humanity. His arguments were thus context-driven as he began his treatise by saying that

> the passions that incline me to peace are the fear of death; desire of such things as are necessary to commodious living; and a hope by their industry to obtain them. And reason suggested [sic] convenient articles of peace, upon which men may be drawn to agreement.[18]

According to Hobbes, human beings were likely to join hands together as it was a shield for their survival. They were drawn to the idea of an agreement for peace and social tranquillity which hardly existed in a chaotic polity. For Hobbes, it was the state of nature where the law of nature was discriminatory and favoured those with power and authority. Two conceptually important claims are implied here: first, it is clear that the author dissociated himself from the existent authority; secondly, he also welcomed the new politico-ideological forces as they were protective of humanity which was being brutalized under the prevalent political dispensation. Although his admiration for the law of nature is visible since it deterred human beings to do 'which is destructive of his life, or taketh away the means of preserving the same',[19] he, however, was disenchanted with how the system governance deviated from these practices in the wake of the consolidation of monarchy and supportive forces. The *Leviathan* was the governing authority and it emerged out of voluntary abdication of one's rights. As per Hobbes, the surrender of rights to *Leviathan* meant protection of rights. In his words,

> whensoever a man transfereth his right, or renounceth it; it is either in consideration of some right reciprocally transferred to himself; or for some other he hopeth thereby. For it is a voluntary act and of the voluntary acts of every man, the object is some good to himself.[20]

Two points deserve attention: on the one hand, Hobbes was in favour of a complete surrender of one's rights to the authority which evolved out of an agreement among those who were inclined to renounce their rights for being safe and protected under *Leviathan*'s care. The surrender meant to ensure their well-being which was threatened under the present circumstances. On the other hand, surrender was also guided by the consideration that it was perhaps the best means to protect their existence as human beings. It was stated by the author when he mentioned that 'the end for which this renouncing, and transferring of right is introduced, is nothing else but the security of a man's person, in his life, and in the means of so preserving life, as not to be weary of it'.[21] Here too, Hobbes insisted that the surrender of rights and protection of life were mutually inclusive and it was possible once men happily transferred their right to the *Leviathan* out 'a contract'. With the contract in place, the *Leviathan* was held responsible for devising designs of governance appropriate for protecting humanity, by creating an environment in which 'injustice, ingratitude, arrogance, pride, iniquity ... are unlawful ... for it can never be that war shall preserve life and peace destroy it'.[22] There must be a warning here since the *Leviathan* was, according to Hobbes, not one person but 'a multitude of men [leading to the formation of] the *Leviathan*, ... so that, it be done with the consent of every one of that multitude in particular [which meant] ... the unity of the representer, not the unity of represented, that maketh the person one'.[23] In other words, the contract is between one group of people with another for the sake of common well-being, and the *Leviathan* represented the will of a collective betterment. Ideationally, Hobbes appears to have had the importance of parliament in mind; where decisions are made by a group of people through consultations.

The above dissection of Hobbes' views helps understand how one of the first contractualists conceptualized humanity. One discerns three points which are critical in figuring out how his views contributed to the conceptualization of humanizing humanity. First, being context-driven, Hobbes devised a contract as perhaps the most effective means in this regard. In a milieu of uncertainties, Hobbes made the second point by highlighting the importance of forming a collective consisting of those who were victims of circumstances Emphasized here was his concern for humanity which was being butchered due to the decline of a rule-driven governance because neither the Puritans nor the monarch was ready for a compromise. It was unlikely since Puritans represented new politico-ideological forces, while the monarchy nearly lost its viability and its foundation as it continued to draw on politically inept forces. Finally, to make the *Leviathan* as representative of the voice of the multitude, Hobbes stated that it was representative in character which further means that he was in favour of an authority of a section of people out of voluntary surrender of rights. In other words, the *Leviathan* was democratic, though in a limited sense. For Hobbes, the very nature of the constitution of the ruling authority set out hindrances for the *Leviathan.*

Guided by the fundamental proposition that *Leviathan* was a means to safeguard humanity, Hobbes was also one of the major proponents of humanizing humanity. Seeking to justify his primary objective, he pitched his argument at two levels; at the historical level, his conceptualization was pertinent in the context of the mid-seventeenth century when the Puritan Revolution created circumstances of hope and despair; hope since it fuelled momentum to a new social order led by the bourgeoisie in England, and despair because it was battle between two contrarian politico-ideological forces. This was a phase of history when human brutality was at its peak and Hobbes suggested a definite means of coming out of such circumstances Living in a time of civil wars, he regarded a strong government as an antidote to anarchy leading to decimation of humanity. The context-driven idea of *Leviathan* was thus a stepping stone for humanity to re-establish itself by being endowed with new values. Hobbes represented a new phase of humanity that reconceptualized the role of human beings. The design is not democratic enough if conceived in its contemporary sense, although it was certainly a significant step towards unshackling humanity from many of the constructed barriers in the nineteenth century. Hobbes' effort was a signal which received impetus in the writings of future philosophers, including Jean Jacques Rousseau who brought about the new phase of humanizing humanity in the wake of the 1789 French Revolution by advocating liberty, equality, and fraternity for all.

III

Jean-Jacques Rousseau was another champion of universal humanism which was brutally sacrificed by those wielding power and authority. His conceptualization of *Social Contract* was governed by this phenomenon. Philosophically, his doctrine 'finds its expression in the view that the State is based not on any original convention, not on any determinate power, but on the living and sustaining of its members'.[24] This was largely due to the rise of inequality which was nurtured by a section at the cost of another. Physical inequality manifested in differences in—age, health, bodily strength, and qualities of mind—is natural; what is however a deterrent to humanizing humanity was the artificially created 'moral and political inequality [consisting of] the different privileges which some men enjoy to the prejudice of others: such as that of being more rich, more honoured, more powerful or even in a position of to exact obedience'.[25] This resulted in what he articulated as 'man is born free, and everywhere he is in chains'.[26] In order to get out of uncertainties, he devised a model of Social Contract in which 'General Will' remained predominant. With the coming together of people following the execution of the Contract, what men lost was their 'natural liberty … and an unlimited right to everything [they try] to get and succeed in getting'.[27] Once the contract was in place, an individual obtained 'his civil liberty and proprietorship he possesses'.[28] Natural liberty was based on individual strength, while civil liberty was to be enjoyed by all, as long as the general well-being remained undisturbed. Here Rousseau's idea of General Will is of paramount importance since it was meant to protect all. Hence, despite being sovereign, the General Will 'cannot impose in respect of fetters that are useless to the community, nor can it even wish to do so'.[29] Furthermore, he also added that it 'helps to create and association which will defend and protect with the whole common force the person and goods of each associate, and in which each, while uniting himself with all, may still obey himself alone, and remain as free as before'.[30] He was concerned for humanity which was subject to atrocities; but the situation remained unaltered without taking efforts to devise a design for common well-being. The importance of institutional authority backed by morality tuned to ensure collective betterment is evident here. The General Will entailed a system of authority guided by a desire to contribute to the well-being of all. Here, Rousseau charted out the growth of the General Will which was the final stage of the consolidation of an instrument uprooting the sources of exploitation of one section by another. Historically speaking, argued Rousseau, the different forms of government

> owe their origin to the differing degrees of inequality which existed between individuals at the time of their institution. If there happened to be any one man among them preeminent in power, virtue, riches, or personal influence, he became sole magistrate, and the State assumed the form of monarchy. If several, nearly equal in point of eminence, stood above the rest, they were elected jointly, and formed an aristocracy. Again, among a people who had deviated less from a state nature, and between whose fortune or talents there was less disproportion, the supreme administration was retained in common, and a democracy was formed.[31]

A humanist to the core, Rousseau was one of the rare philosophers who privileged humanity over all else. His conceptualization of General Will is a testimony to this claim as it meant keeping the common interests in view. Of all the treatises, *The Social Contract*, was a harbinger of the 1789 French Revolution which was both a voice against oppression and a device leading to the institutionalization of democracy as a system of governance. There were powerful critics suggesting that Rousseau did not pay adequate attention to all sections of humanity, including the role of women in reconceptualizing equality in different phases of history.[32] However, what stands out was Rousseau's design for humanizing humanity to eradicate the sources of discrimination. Like that of Hobbes' *Leviathan*, the General Will helped build a society free from prejudices and inequality. Unlike Hobbes, he was not in favour of complete surrender of rights. Hence, he also suggested that the sovereignty rested with the community which was directly linked with the execution for liberty, equality, and fraternity of the 1789 French Revolution. Rousseau foresaw the processes that were finally crystalized in the outbreak of the Revolution which unshackled the control of aristocrats and established the hegemony of the bourgeoisie The French Revolution epitomized the rise of a new politico-ideological forces and decline of those who remained predominant socially, politically, and economically.

Rousseau's contribution was significant in humanizing humanity. *The Social Contract* was a powerful voice in this regard for three important reasons: first, by identifying the sources of inequality in conceptual terms, he helped understand how a society deteriorated. For Rousseau, it was linked to how historical processes unfolded at a particular juncture of history which explained the growth of monarchy, aristocracy, and democracy respectively. Second, guided by his concern for humanity, he provided a roadmap for evolving a system that lead humanity to carve out a new narrative of challenging hegemonic authority. It was a narrative highlighting how human efforts succeeded in completely decimating ruthless, torturous, and inhuman designs of a section of humanity. The treatise thus offered a design for resistance, and it was also a device to generate a zeal for reconceptualizing human existence in a completely different sociocultural and politico-ideological milieu. Finally, Rousseau's model led to the consolidation of an ideational universe which provided many thinkers in the context of India's nationalist struggle against the British with significant inputs to develop their distinct approaches. It does not seem strange that Indian nationalist thinkers, beginning with Rammohun Roy to Rabindranath Tagore, admired Rousseau for his steadfast commitment to universal humanism. Rousseau, however, was not an exception. The desire of humanizing humanity was a universally acknowledged area of concern inspiring many creative thinkers to not only articulate a new voice against dehumanizing of humanity but also a complementary design to completely weed out the forces in its favour.

As mentioned above, the conceptual paradigm provided is not free from critique by those who rightfully claimed that it was also a patriarchal design pursued to defend age-old prejudices. One of the most effective theoreticians who forcefully argued so is the political scientist Carole Pateman in her *The Sexual Contract* (1988). She argued that,

> men's freedom and women's subjection are created through the original contract—and the character of civil freedom cannot be understood without the missing half of the story that reveals how men's patriarchal right over women is established through contract. Civil freedom is not [thus] universal; [it is] masculine attribute and depends upon patriarchal right.[33]

Pateman establishes the point that a contract is a means through which modern patriarchy is constituted, which means that the effort towards defining contract as a design for humanizing humanity is self-defeating. The fact that women were never considered integral to the contract defends the claim. Despite not being part of the contract, women remain integral to human social existence although they do not have a space in civil society because, as Pateman argued, they 'naturally lack the capacities required to become civil individuals'.[34] Hence, she reinforced the point that 'contract is the specifically modern means of creating relationships of subordination'.[35] The argument that *Social Contract* is prejudiced is further pursued by Charles W. Mills who, in his *The Racial Contract*, highlighted the point that it was a design of permanently dividing the white race from the rest as inferior to the former. By quoting Malcolm X, the famous African-American ideologue who stated that the supposed contract was meant to highlight the contribution of the white race in consolidating human society by completely ignoring the critical role of the non-whites, Mills justified his contention that 'contract is nothing but an expression of racial subordination'.[36] The contract is exclusive and cannot be said to have taken into account the prevalent political and moral realities of the world. Those who fail to recognize the reality are, argued Mills, 'only continuing the epistemology of ignorance presumably to support what is clearly indefensible'.[37] Mills' attempt helps us understand the nature of the contract in a wider perspective. Moreover, this conceptual intervention directs our attention to the neglected human voice that was muzzled during the hegemony of the whites over the non-whites primarily in Africa and Asia. Both Pateman and Mills remain pioneers in reconceptualizing *The Social Contract* in a completely different theoretical format which allows us to view the phenomenon differently. Nonetheless, the specific point that is being made here to claim that endeavours towards humanizing humanity hardly lost its relevance for two complementary reasons: first, in a situation of political instability when human race was subject to inhuman brutality and also uncertainty, they devised a design for civilizing human; it was conceptualized by keeping in mind a specific section of humanity that hegemonized the rest of the world. So, it was a narrative of the supremacy of the men and of the whites, argue Pateman. The arguments developed by them do not overrule the claim that *Social Contract* was meant to protect humanity from being undermined, which substantiates the point that the conceptual design was a serious effort towards creating a space for humanity which was neither brutish nor prejudiced, but one that allowed human beings to lead a life of freedom, justice and fairness.

IV

Humanizing humanity involves two processes which work simultaneously. On the one hand, it is a design constructed by many thinkers with identical politico-ideological aims. Along with politico-ideological motivations, there also existed a system to translate the ideational priorities which are tuned to the protection of humanity into a reality. An adequately equipped institutional authority is thus required to preserve humanity from forces with evil designs.

As history reveals, humanity passes through many crises. To save humanity, a system of governance needed to be installed with identical goals. Focusing on The Federalist Papers, which constituted the politico-ideological foundation of the first democratic constitution in modern era, this section defends the importance of an institutionalized system of guiding humanity. Comprising of eighty-five letters to the people by Publius (a pseudonym), The Federalist Papers, published in the newspapers in New York City between 1787 and 1788, set out a form of governance which the framers of the US constitution readily accepted. The reason for this was not difficult to locate since Publius was a groups of leading US constitutionalists, Alexander Hamilton, James Madison and John Jay who defended democratic governance as perhaps the most effective means to sustain humanity in the war-torn US.

The purpose is not to dwell on the US constitutional history, but to identify those critical ideational values which are of tremendous significance in designing an institutional framework for humanizing humanity. There are three fundamental ideas which are paramount in The Federalist Papers: freedom, popular consent and responsible government. George Washington referred to these ideas when he said that 'The Federalist would merit the notice of posterity because in it are candidly and ably discussed the principles of freedom and the topics of government which will always be interesting to mankind so long as they shall be connected in civil society'.[38] The purpose was to contribute to a collective well-being. Two important claims critical to conceptually comprehending the efforts towards humanizing humanity even before the constitutional governance was in place in the decolonized US are evident her. First, the first US President drew attention to the institutional values which were complementary to the fulfilment of their politico-ideological preferences. In his opinion, the existence of the provinces as independent was contrary to those who dreamt of a socioculturally well-knit country after the war of independence. The second point, by insisting on a form of governance, was critically linked with the ideologically-inspired system of administration for fulfilling the objective for which the US raised its voice against the confederals. Condemning them as impediments for the grand goal helping humanity to prosper in a prejudice free milieu, the federalists undertook the task of justifying their politico-ideological inclinations as most appropriate.

The purpose is to elaborate the Federalist papers here to understand them as complementary to the goal of humanizing humanity. Hence, the primary focus is to highlight aspects of these texts which give inputs to substantiate the main theme of this exercise. As argued above, humanizing humanity remains a primary concern as articulated by the Federalists. Reverberating the ideas of Rousseau; John Jay, one of the prominent Federalists, suggested that for a strong government to grow, what was required was 'to surrender some of their natural rights in order to vest [the government] with requisite powers'.[39] It was further argued that 'the prosperity of the people of America depended on their continuing firmly united, and the wishes, prayers, and efforts of our best and wisest citizens have been constantly directed to that object'.[40] A united America was good for humanity, argued the Federalists and hence, they insisted that 'division of the States into distinct confederacies or sovereigns was, under no circumstances, conducive to the safety and happiness in the union'.[41] A united America was logically most appropriate because

> the Providence has been pleased to give this one connected country to one united people—a people descended from the same ancestors, speaking the same language, professing the same religion, attached to the same principles of government, very similar in their manners and customs, and who, by their joint counsels, arms and efforts, fighting side by side throughout a long bloody war, have notably established their general liberty and independence.[42]

A government is stronger once the governed remain socioculturally united. This was the fundamental assumption which helped the Federalists defend their claim for a united government for the newly emerged America. The Federalists who further pursued the argument by stressing that

> this country and this people seem to have been made for each other, and it appears as if it was the design of Providence that an inheritance so proper and convenient for a band of brethren, united to each other by the strongest ties, should never be split into a number of unsocial, jealous and alien sovereignties.[43]

A cursory look at the above argument reveals that the Federalists drew on the principles whose aim was to protect humanity from being derailed, if not diminished. Although, they expressed their conceptually unique ideas by interacting with the context in which they were born and raised, their design for humanizing humanity did not seem to have differed radically from one another. The Federalists played a historical role in ascertaining that the system of governance was equally important in executing the design into practice. Due to the sociocultural compatibility among the Americans, it was easier for them to defend federalism. This, however, did not preclude the conceptual possibility of creating human bond in a situation where the habitats were separated socioculturally. India is a good example. Despite being socioculturally disparate, India continues to remain a unified country. A brief interjection on the processes leading to the making of the Constitution of India does not seem to be overstretched. Just like the 1787 Philadelphia Convention which helped codify the provisions of the US Constitution, India's Constituent Assembly prepared the Constitution of India in three years (1946–1949). During the debates in the Assembly, not only did the members dwell on mechanisms for human well-being, they also considered various successful constitutional designs for protecting humanity. Three fundamental propositions deserve attention to understand the dialectical interconnection between humanizing humanity and ideational values which are critical to the institutional design for governance in India. First, the framers of the Constitution were guided by their concern for sociocultural amity which was a little disturbed following the communal events of 1947. Hence, it was most pertinent to the makers of the Constitution to provide a constitutional mechanism to permanently uproot the sources of communal disharmony. The purpose was to create conditions in which humanizing humanity was of paramount importance. Secondly, the Assembly members were equally sensitive to the diverse sociocultural texture of India as a country. Unlike the US or other countries, India was traditionally a diverse country on many counts. It was almost an impossible task to weave such a diverse population into one; given the fact that the sociocultural distinctiveness of communities was a matter of pride for them. This was a problem which helped the makers design a framework of governance for sustaining harmony among such diverse population. The idea of 'living together separately' gained ground and became an inspiring ideal for many countries with socioculturally diverse population. Finally, the framers of the Indian Constitution created a template to articulate democracy in its undiluted sense by ensuring *vox populi* in its real connotation. The battle for eradication of sociocultural barriers between human beings went on with the struggle for political freedom. Hence, it does not seem overstretched that unlike the Federalists, the Indian freedom fighters also adversely targeted the age-old customary practices dividing humanity. Unlike their American counterparts, the anti-colonial forces in India always clamoured for both political and sociocultural emancipation; there were many among the freedom fighters who undertook steps to link their political struggle for independence with their endeavour for emancipation from the deep seated caste-based prejudices separating human beings. Initially, the battle for sociocultural amity was confined to specific areas of the country; gradually however, it spread all over and the campaign not only created a new mindset but also helped build a constitutional design protecting those who remained socioculturally peripheral.

The text has two interrelated components: on the one hand, the aim is to evolve an argument with reference to the core ideas of those thinkers who played a critical role in devising ideas for humanization. As history shows, a section of human beings were victims of another for fulfilling partisan interests. It is therefore fair to argue that Hobbes and Rousseau from Europe, and Gandhi and Ambedkar from India, not only raised their voices against atrocities committed by the privileged, but also provided a politically effective design for creating equal opportunities for humanity as a whole regardless of socio-economic and politico-cultural differences. By drawing on the ideas of thinkers who evolved their voice in different sociocultural milieu, this book also argues that there are certain universal ideas which bind humanity together. Hence, the concern to construct a conceptual design for humanity in a situation of chaos and exploitation by the privileged sections corresponded with that of Gandhi and Ambedkar. Gandhi fought against the British for political freedom and he paid less attention to the battle that Ambedkar lodged against caste atrocities. Although Gandhi was, in general, peripheral when India's Constitution was being prepared for variety of reasons, Ambedkar was one of its principal architects. Furthermore, India's liberal constitution was largely due to Ambedkar's success in persuading his colleagues in the Assembly, and is now established beyond doubt. In doing so, there is no doubt that he was indebted to his academic mentor, John Dewey at Columbia where he successfully completed his doctoral studies. A cursory reading of Dewey's *Democracy and Education* (1916) reveals that Ambedkar was inspired by this text in articulating a libertarian voice complementary to the wider struggle the mainstream nationalists, including Gandhi, contemplated with the attainment of political freedom. Ambedkar also questioned the internalized caste-based prejudices. Broadly speaking, despite being raised in different sociocultural and politico-ideological milieus, Gandhi and Ambedkar, and their European and American colleagues, held similar concerns for humanity. As shown above, the chaotic conditions during the seventeenth-century England or eighteenth-century France led Hobbes and Rousseau to conceptually justify a social contract as perhaps the best means to humanize humanity. The situation was not so different in India in the context of colonialism, when the colonizers brutally executed various designs for sustaining their hegemony at the cost of core human values. By pursuing a battle for the establishment of a fair system of governance Gandhi appears to have had the same concern as Hobbes and Rousseau. Gandhi's design for human amity was not as pervasive as that of Ambedkar, since he was in favour of society-centric models of humanization. Ambedkar however opined that without a powerful state in place, Gandhi's espoused ideals for social amity remained distant. In other words, the differences between Gandhi and Ambedkar were fundamental because one was a proponent of society-driven mechanism for humanizing while Ambedkar insisted that society was hardly adequate for human emancipation. Hence, he argued for a strong state which was well-equipped with a equally strong set of laws to permanently eradicate discrimination based on sociocultural biases.

With the above introduction, this text focuses on the politico-ideological ideas of prominent Indian thinkers who carved out a new narrative for humanity. The text is based on two major and two peripheral arguments. The two major arguments relate to the claim that humanizing humanity is a universal endeavour and was explicit in the creative writings of many thinkers cutting across geographical and sociocultural boundaries. Hence, the ideas of Hobbes and Rousseau did not seem to be foreign when one is drawn to those of Gandhi and Tagore; they were linked together as they upheld the same concern for humanity. The peripheral arguments are devised by drawing on the specific contexts in which the concern for humanizing humanity gained precedence. This argument, despite not being central, is of paramount importance since it also helps us understand that sociocultural differences have significantly shaped their respective modes of thinking. The politico-ideological priorities of Gandhi, Tagore and Ambedkar are a testament to this claim. They conceptualized realities in terms of their own politico-ideological priorities to evolve ideational templates, and based on their respective existential experiences, their ideational universes differ from one another. With their meaningful intervention in reconceptualizing humanity, not only did they help build an alternative conceptualization, but also immensely contributed to the articulation of a voice which did not receive adequate politico-ideological attention in the past. What is strikingly similar is that despite having followed different ideational priorities, they always privileged their commitment to universal humanity. While Tagore and Gandhi seem to have held similar conceptual beliefs, Ambedkar redesigned the conventional approaches to humanizing humanity. His was a model which challenged the divisive sociocultural practices, and set in motion processes for reconceptualizing humanity. Nonetheless, by questioning the divisive practices and fiercely opposing the forces seeking to dehumanize humanity, Tagore, Gandhi and Ambedkar reinvented humanity in the nationalist context which will continue to remain relevant so long as human beings internalize 'togetherness' in its real connotation.

Part A

Rabindranath Tagore (1861–1941)

Humanism and humanization are conceptually complementary since the former is an end and the latter is a means. Many innovative thinkers made efforts to devise means to reach the end. This is not a linear path since the role of the prevalent socio-economic context and politico-ideological priorities provide inputs critical to the choice of the means. Two important issues need to be addressed here, neither end nor means are chosen independent of the prevalent context, and accordingly, ideational predilections evolved, which means that a thinker, by being sensitive to the contextual compulsions, is governed to a great extent by impulses rooted elsewhere. In other words, one must be careful in designing one's ideational model to pursue chosen goals. Implicit here is also the view that end and means are dialectically entwined, which considers the importance of factors other than the views of thinkers who are persuaded to carve a new path for humanity. There are three important components of an ideational vision; the context, the available intellectual inputs and the unique conceptual underpinning of thinkers seeking to see humanity through different lenses. It also makes comprehending specific politico-ideological preferences difficult because one's thought is an offshoot of factors which are not always fathomable within the available conventional yardstick. One needs to clearly understand the milieu in which one is raised to confirm ideational priorities are also rooted in the context; hence, it is not, at all, conceptually wrong to suggest that one's thought processes owe a great deal to the socio-economic environment along with the dominant mode of thinking. This is universally true. So, is the argument that Thomas Hobbes' *Leviathan* (1651) needs to be read in the background of nine years of the Puritan Revolution (1642–1651) in England. His elaboration of the state of nature was based on his experience of how the revolution unfolded and how social tranquillity was seriously disturbed during the period. The context was one of the critical factors for conceptualizing a strong authority or Leviathan. In so doing, he not only questioned the available theoretical wisdom of statecraft but also displayed the influence of the volatile circumstances creating uncertainties of various kinds. According to Hobbes, the only option was to establish law and order, which was possible only with a strong authority. The example of Leviathan is a testimony of the argument highlighting the criticality of the context in reconceptualizing designs for protecting humanity as a collective.

The claim that context was decisive in shaping human behaviour is universally applicable. Before the consolidation of the British authority, India was governed by those with feudal mindsets. It was one of the reasons why many public intellectuals—Rammohun Roy (1773–1833), Dwarkanath Tagore (1794–1846) and many leaders of Brahmo Samaj, Bankim Chandra Chattopadhyay (1838–1894)—welcomed the British rule due to their hope that the arrival of the colonizers was likely to bring radical sociocultural and politico-economic transformation in India. The idea continued to influence the politico-ideological priorities of those who then mattered in shaping public opinion against superstitious and customary practices in the name of religion. For instance, Rammohun Roy became one of the most powerful voices against the continuity of sati burning. Likewise, many well-entrenched prejudices against caste identities were severely challenged by Roy and his Brahmo disciples. A strong believer of *Deism*, which rejects revelation as a source of divine knowledge and asserts that empirical reason and observation of the natural world are exclusively logical, reliable and sufficient to determine the existence of a Supreme Being, Roy acted as a harbinger of new thought processes by abjuring those superstitious designs seeking to fulfil partisan goals of one section of Hindus at the cost of others.

The above discussion is made primarily to contextualize the politico-ideological priorities of Rabindranath Tagore. Born in a family of intellectual influence, Tagore was raised in an environment that saw attempts at hitting the foundation of these practices and beliefs. A representative of a Renaissance in Bengal, he not only helped unfold newer modes of thinking but also inspired the youth of Bengal, who appeared to have been disillusioned with nationalism. His role was most critical in comprehending radical sociocultural ideas, which acted decisively in designing newer conceptual paradigms; these not only persuaded many to rescind the sociocultural values but also led them to effectively challenge those justifying social conservatism. Tagore served two purposes: on the one hand, he built a conceptual model by drawing on both indigenous and Western discourses; on the other, he contributed to activism by being an opponent of prejudiced mindsets. Unlike his predecessors, Tagore was not an unconditional admirer of the

Raj; instead, he emphasized their role in supporting various campaigns against social orthodoxy. In other words, while Rammohun was highly appreciative of colonial rule and saw it as an opportunity to fight the forces championing orthodox sociocultural vision, Tagore was also impressed at the outset since colonial rule allowed Indians to have access to the libertarian Enlightenment texts. It was short-lived and was disillusioned. As a firm believer of universal humanism, it was contrary to his heart-felt belief, and manifested in the myriad critical texts and speeches he delivered to mobilize opinion against the British. Tagore's life sketch is a story of transformation.

The purpose of this chapter is to understand how Tagore pursued his sociocultural and politico-ideological goals simultaneously by being perhaps the most creative Indian writer during the tumultuous days of a sustained struggle between nationalists and the British to achieve freedom. He was encouraged in phases when Indian nationalism underwent a sea change: from Moderate nationalism to Gandhian mode of nonviolent resistance to colonial power via the New Nationalist phase when Lal-Bal-Pal (Lala Lajpat Rai, Bal Gangadhar Tilak and Bipin Chandra Pal) and Aurobindo Ghosh among others were predominant in the nationalist struggle. Tagore articulated his voice of protest by being a littérateur and a critical essayist.

By focusing on these two genres of articulations, this part is devoted to conceptualizing his approach to humanizing humanity. By dwelling on his creative writings, novels, short stories, plays and dance dramas, this chapter argues that it was Tagore who charted out a new nationalist course which was not confined to mere political emancipation but also focused on liberation from sociocultural prejudices which are divisive to humanity.

Contextualizing Tagore's Literary Texts

A literary text is an author's voice that is context-driven and a product of inputs, they internalize by being receptive to many conceptual packages. An author expresses their views, which are not independently constructed. Two major influences are always at work—the prevalent socio-economic ambience and, conceptual ideas acting critically in shaping their politico-ideological priorities. Bankim Chandra Chattopadhyay (1838–1894) was one of the famous littérateurs of Bengal who is also known for his significant contribution to Bangla as a language. Being heavily influenced by Enlightenment principles,

Bankim's literary texts were manifestations of how human beings should be viewed in the prism of liberalism. For instance, his novel *Bishbriksha* (Poison Tree) which was serialized in the renowned Bengal magazine, *Bangadarshan*, between 1872 and 1873, was about an illicit relationship between a zamindar, Nagendranath and a widow, Kundonandini. Nagendranath was not allowed to marry a widow by leaving his wife, Suryamukhi, nor was Kundonandini encouraged to violate the socially-dictated customs, although legally, it was not forbidden to wed a widow given the promulgation of the Hindu Widow's Remarriage Act 1856. The novel shows that Bankim was not favourably disposed towards widow remarriage, and hence, Kundonandini was allowed to consume poison to die. So, a socially conditioned Bankim, despite being drawn to Enlightenment philosophy, failed to go beyond the belief that he imbibed by being nurtured in a sociocultural environment which did not appear to have been as progressive as was expected following the legalization of widow remarriage. As demonstrated, a littérateur is not free from their own assessment of the situation, usually governed by contextual inputs and conceptual parameters. Rabindranath Tagore was not an exception. His approach to humanism was both restricted and open-ended: restricted because he, like Bankim, was equally sensitive to many of the well-entrenched sociocultural inputs regarding humanity; open-ended because he, in comparison with Bankim, was also ready to accept which, he thought, was unacceptable to humanity.

For a clear understanding of the influences that acted decisively in shaping Tagore's approach to humanity, his articulation of the possible sources of influence is significant. He was born in 1861, which was not historically significant, argued Tagore, although the decade of the 1860s provided him with many significant inputs, which later became critical in reassessing many of his derivative ideas. Hence, for Tagore, the decade was very distinctive for his ideational vision. As he claimed, he represented a confluence of three movements which figured prominently in Bengal's sociocultural life. First, one of the movements was in the domain of religion which Rammohun Roy led 'to open the channel of spiritual life which [was] obstructed for many years by the sands and debris of creeds that were formal and materialistic, fixed in external practices lacking spiritual significance'.[1] A born crusader, Roy carved a new narrative to reinvent humanity which was severely criticised by orthodox Hindus as he questioned their authority to interpret the ancient texts of India. Given his relentless battle against brutal sociocultural practices, he was thus identified by Tagore,

> as the great path-maker of this century who has removed ponderous obstacles that impeded our progress at every step, and initiated us into the present era of world-wide cooperation of humanity. ... In social ethics, he was an uncompromising interpreter of the truths of human relationship, tireless in his crusade against social wrongs and superstition [and] ... generous in his cooperation with any reformer ... who came to our aid in a genuine spirit of comradeship.[2]

Roy's ideas were an important marker in Tagore's model of humanizing humanity. Not only did he fight against divisive and sectarian sociocultural designs, he also welcomed reformers who had the same politico-ideological priorities as far as humanity was concerned. Primary to him was how to protect humanity from being brutalized by those who, by distorting religious dictums, deprived humans of their basic rights. It was a difficult task in circumstances when the opponents were too powerful to be defeated so easily. Despite terrible sufferings, his power of 'transmuting them to carry on further beneficent activities for the good of humanity',[3] was a significant source of inspiration to Tagore in reinventing the available politico-ideological designs for humanizing humanity.

The second important source which led Tagore to develop a new genre of voice were the writings of Bankim Chandra Chattopadhyay who revolutionized Bengali literature by changing the thematic core from the stories of Gods and Goddesses to the day-to-day experiences of Bengali households. The nature of expression changed from being very Sanskritized to a daily conversation register. According to Tagore, the literary style of the prevalent presentation took away life from Bengali literature. Condemning rigidity in the available literary style, Tagore admired Bankim as one who was 'brave enough to go against orthodoxy which believed in the security of tombstones and in that perfection which can only belong to the lifeless'.[4] It was he who 'lifted the deadweight of ponderous forms from our language and with a touch of his magic wand aroused our literature from her age-long sleep'.[5] Explicit here are two important claims which helped understand the language, further gaining popularity in Bengal. Tagore, inspired by Bankim, wrote in a language which was meaningful to his readers and gradually altered the nature of literature. The voice which the author raised reached a larger set of readers; second, since the language was lucid and easy to follow, the theme which the writer preferred to deal with had new readers who did not seem interested earlier in the literature, presumably because it delved on human experiences. The third significant source of Tagore's ideational universe was the changing nature of the nationalist campaign to an independent one. Two claims are simultaneously made here—one; based on the critique of Moderate Nationalism, Tagore shared the view of the New Nationalists, led by Lal-Bal-Pal and Aurobindo, and instilled a sense of belongingness among those involved in struggle against British colonialism. As Tagore explained, it was 'a voice of indignation at the humiliation heaped upon [the Indians] by those who were not oriental, and who had … the habit of sharply dividing people into good and bad according to how they conceived humanity'.[6] Highlighting this concern, Tagore questioned the British rule for not being indigenous and on their design of governance by segregating people based on its representatives. According to the poet, it was a dehumanizing system of administration as it survived on the belief that Indians were barbarians and needed the British to become civilized. He also realized that such an assessment of the governed by the rulers did not only strike at the foundation of humanity, which was always conceptualized as one by Tagore but also challenged that other civilizations had contributed to its development.

The above discussion of the sources of inspiration of Tagore is very useful to grasp how he evolved his own model of humanizing humanity. Underlying his assessment of the intellectual sources, it is clear that humanism has always remained his primary concern. As British rule silenced human voices for fulfilling the sectarian interests of a few at the cost of the majority, he raised cudgels against those opposed to efforts towards undermining foreign rule. In his texts, as will be shown below, he condemned the imposed governance because it was meant to humiliate Indians as inferior which justified the continuity of British hegemony and a force to evolve a design to establish the contention that humanity could never be one, but always divided into superior and inferior. We must add a note here to clarify that Tagore's notion of humanity being one never entailed oneness as a design for essentializing multifarious human identities due to inherent sociocultural differences for historical and socio-economic reasons.

Tagore enjoyed the 'freedom of the outcaste … [which helped him] … build [his] own world with [his] own thoughts and energy of mind'. This gave him adequate mental strength to develop 'a firm foundation of [his] ideas, including those which are complementary to [his] distinct nationalistic vision'.[7] It was one aspect of ideational priorities; the other aspect was an outcome of what he learnt from derivative discourses and his dialectical interaction with people he met during his travel in India and abroad. Tagore's model of humanizing humanity was an outcome of what he defined as 'the confluence of three movements, [mentioned above] all of which were revolutionary'. He was also particular in emphasizing that he was raised in a family that was unique in its sociocultural vision, he was opposed to blind borrowing which made building arguments relatively difficult which he explained by saying 'the language which belonged to the people had to be modulated according to the urging which I as an individual had'.[8] The root of this observation needs to be located in his upbringing in a family which was open to Hindu, Islamic and British sociocultural influences. Along with his exposure to multiple cultural impulses, he was also witness to the gradual transformations of India's socio-economic milieu from being predominantly pastoral to a life privileging 'the modern city-bred spirit of progress'.[9] In other words, it was a shift from 'the luscious green life of [Indian] village community'[10] to one encouraging the consolidation of a phase of human civilization in which humans were not part of a community but existed as nuclear units. Alarmed at the desecration of communities, Tagore felt that this was the first serious attack on humanity and the processes of dehumanizing humanity started unfolding because humans were forced to exist individually with the growth of urban civilization. Tagore was not critical of individualism per se; what disturbed him most was that individualism assisted in the consolidation of forces questioning the fundamental values on which humanism rested. He was intrigued when those supporting the Enlightenment values of care, concern and empathy for all upheld them selectively, which was a source of concern to Tagore, as it was the beginning of the consolidation of tendencies undermining the fundamental ideational vision of a collective.

Tagore's creative literary texts represent a search for innovative ways of protecting humanity from being dehumanized. For him, the expression, humanization did not simply mean political emancipation, but salvation from instruments of torture and brutality by a section of human beings onto others. In other words, freedom in its real connotation, remained unrealized if power was transferred from one set of rulers to another. According to Tagore, as long as others were not treated uniformly, freedom was futile. There were two implications of this claim: firstly, Tagore did not seem to have been persuaded to believe—like Gandhi—that the removal of foreign hegemony would lead to Indians likely to be free in the real sense of the term. Due to sociocultural shackles, Indians were hardly free, despite being free from colonial rule. Secondly, the mere withdrawal of British rule was, in his opinion, just a replacement of one kind of governance by another, which meant that there were hardly any substantial differences and the sociocultural foundation remained the same. Here lay the reason why Tagore differed radically from his colleagues who conceptualized political liberation in its narrow sense. One may find similarities in views between Tagore and Ambedkar because both of them thought that unless sociocultural prejudices were completely eradicated from society, freedom was elusive.

Tagore's conceptualization of dehumanizing humanity is not monochromatic but multidimensional, conforming to the idea of exploitation being intersectional. Based on the argument that human beings were exploited not merely by being poor but also by being lower castes, lower classes, and socio-economically marginalized, among others, which meant that poverty led humanity to suffer, which was further accentuated, for instance, by gender disparity due to hegemonic patriarchy. Muslim women suffered on two accounts: as Muslims, they, for instance, were subject to humiliation by those nurturing well-entrenched religious prejudices; the Muslim women confronted a situation where patriarchal biases resulted in further dehumanization. Following Kimberlé Crenshaw's formulation, one is now in a position to explain that intersectionality asserts that individuals simultaneously hold multiple social identities, such as race, gender, class, sexuality, disability and religion, among others. These identities intersect and interact, shaping an individual's experiences and position within society. Implicit here is also the claim that individuals can experience privilege or discrimination on the combination of their identities, rather than one aspect. In other words, intersectionality highlights that individuals are exploited, humiliated and deprived around many sociocultural and politico-ideological axes. Inequality thus needs to be understood accordingly. For instance, in colonial India, besides being marginalized because of well-entrenched sociocultural differences, humans were victims of the political preferences of those wielding power and authority. With the gaining of conceptual validity of intersectionality, it can be argued that systems of power and oppression are interconnected and cannot be addressed in isolation.

Structure of the Part

Given the fact that Tagore was a poet with strong politico-ideological views which he developed by being dialectically interactive with the inputs he received for the prevalent socio-economic milieu, it is obvious that he was bound to have been influenced, if not governed, by them while articulating his voice for humanity. Being a poet of the period in which he was raised, it does not seem inconceivable that while being critical of the British, he also accorded a voice to efforts challenging discrimination based on sociocultural prejudices around multiple levels of religion, gender, class and caste. A perusal of Tagore's texts reveals that he expressed his views not only in literary texts but also in many critical essays, which he regularly wrote in pursuit of his distinct ideational vision against attempts at dehumanizing humanity. By keeping this in mind, this part is divided into two chapters: Chapter 1 deals with his perception of intersectionality in his literary creations: novels, short stories, dance-drama and plays. Given the plethora of texts, it is difficult, if not impossible to deal with all of them in a chapter due to space limitations. Hence, for practical purposes, Chapter 2 focuses on a select set of his writings, both creative texts and critical essays, with a view to demonstrating how he conceptualized his design of humanizing humanity. While doing so, he not only developed a powerful mechanism against those seeking to dehumanize humanity but also emerged as one of the chief architects of a design for safeguarding humanity from being decimated.

1

Literary Insights and Universal Humanism

Rabindranath Tagore was one of those thinkers who dealt with how humanity was brutalized with the consolidation of British rule in India. Tagore who admired the colonizers for their initiative in mobilizing opinions against superstitious prejudices of one section against another; vehemently opposed foreign rule once it became a source of torture. A scan of his literary texts reveals that it was the underlying theme in almost all his writings. The poet raised a political voice which was complemented by his strong opposition to the well-entrenched sociocultural prejudices. There were two levels of his endeavour: at the political level, he attributed India's decadence to the British hegemony which the loyalists endorsed. This was one source of distress to the colonized; the other was linked to the customary practice of caste discrimination among Hindus. Additionally, religious schism also created a barrier between Hindus and Muslims, which was a source of agony for Tagore. The third source of his emotional discomfort was based on his insistence on gender equality in interpersonal relationships. In view of these, Tagore's texts demonstrate how the practice of dehumanization unfolded in Bengal around many axes; which are illustrative of how humans suffer on many counts. This is a conceptual advancement since Tagore was one of those creative thinkers who always raised cudgels against efforts towards demeaning humanity whether due to caste identity, religious identity or class identity. So, along with India's political independence—which he believed was a steppingstone to the beginning of his endeavour towards permanently removing sociocultural prejudices—he also strongly felt that it was likely to be compromised unless it was complemented by inculcating a sense of belongingness among all regardless of class, caste and religion.

By focusing on his creative writings, novels, plays, dance dramas and short stories, the aim of the chapter is to show that while exploring his literary prowess, Tagore also dealt with how humanization was regularly compromised due to well-entrenched mindsets justifying division of one caste group from another, along with religious and class differences. This chapter, through his literary texts, focuses on how he conceptualized humanizing humanity and how he dealt with this by combatting tendencies towards dehumanizing humanity.

There are two cautionary notes that should be emphasized to avoid being misunderstood. First, since the chapter is based on an analysis of selective creative tracts of Tagore, one may legitimately raise a question that because the argument is made on the basis of a specific set of sources, it may not have been as persuasive as it should have been. Second, Tagore's ideational vision was an outcome of his dialectical interaction with the prevalent socio-economic milieu and the nature of political governance he confronted as a member of a British colony. This is true at one level since his distinct ideational priority determined how he saw the reality around him. At another, given his literary prowess, it is logically appropriate to argue that as an author, he was well-equipped to generalize human feelings based on his conceptual yardstick. To capture the complex realities in which he expressed his ideas and feelings in the form of narratives, he may have dealt with specific instances which were articulations of a response based on his multifarious experiences by interacting with different people in various locations. The moot point here is that his ideas, by being an outcome of interactions with differently-textured humanity, were thus representative in character in the sense that they not only help us understand the sociocultural reasons for dehumanization but also act as possible means to tackle them. In his writings, we come across Tagore's inclination towards doing away with the roots of exploitation, humiliation, and torture of humans regardless of their sociocultural locations and identities.

Being imbued with the idea that for a sociocultural revolution to take place, a radical transformation of the prevalent mindset was required, which was neither an easy task nor could be accomplished instantaneously. Hence, his priority was to disseminate ideas conducive to his ideational vision through the characters in his literary texts. Since dehumanization was an outcome of processes based on multiple axes; one comes across in his writings characters who, he thought, perfectly articulated his ideational priorities. Furthermore, as he believed that the demeaning of humanity was clearly a result of multiple interrelated processes, he adequately focused on the historical dynamics of how they developed in Bengal. The prominent designs that Tagore developed while analyzing human behaviour were primarily context-driven, of course, with reference to the historical reasons contributing to the consolidation of the system.

As the chapter is directed to understand Tagore's approach to humanizing humanity, it is purely analytical in nature. The chapter dwells on the unfolding of conceptual designs pertinent to the context and beyond. It is thus not surprising that most of the ideas Tagore held while explaining the dehumanization of humanity remain relevant even today despite the fact that, with independence, India's socio-political fabric has undergone a sea change. In fact, many of the sociocultural prejudices defending the separation of humanity had hardly lost their salience in the changed political milieu. It is true that the form may not be the same now, although, in practice, they continue to be as demeaning as in the past with, occasional fiercer challenges to them by the victims.

Multiple Axes of Dehumanization

The fact that India was a British colony is an adequate description of how Indians were to be treated with colonial master as guardians. There were certain sections who were colonized accepted British rule as helpful for India's socio-economic and political progress; many of their counterparts—given their opposition to colonial hegemony—were subject to humiliation and deprivation as they never appeared to have been reliable to the British colonizers. Furthermore, many Indians in the hinterland and in villages were exploited by the sections supporting British who instinctively undertook those steps of the colonizers since it also protected their partisan interests in such circumstances.

To begin with, the chapter dwells on two of the most popular works of Tagore, *Gora* (1910) and *Ghare Baire* (1916). The former is probably the most-accurate articulation of intersectionality, while the latter is a narrative demonstrating how British rule provoked the nationalists to rise in unison against political designs.

Ghare Baire is a political novel and delves on how the nationalists challenged British authority in response to the partitioning Bengal in 1905. Historically known as the Swadeshi Movement (1905–1908), the Congress-led campaign raised various other issues to transform it into an onslaught against the British. Instead of dwelling on how colonialism contributed to the processes of dehumanizing humanity, Tagore introspected by focusing on the role of the nationalists in not being respectful to humanity. The impediment was human instinctive for safeguarding one's personal interests at the cost of the rest. *Ghare Baire* is, in other words, a narrative of how humanity was degraded as witnessed by Tagore in the *swadeshi* campaign in Bengal.

There are three protagonists, Nikhilesh, Sandip and Bimala. Nikhilesh was the landlord; Sandip was a *swadeshi* activist and Bimala was

Nikhilesh's wife. The narrative emerges out of dialogues amongst them regarding the nature and development of the campaign. The purpose was to revoke the first Partition of Bengal which was made between the people of East and West Bengal; so, it was a political design based on the British motives. As mentioned above, this was not Tagore's primary concern; his aim was to understand how humanity was demeaned by the nationalists who claimed themselves as saviours of humans.

At the outset of the novel, Bimala described her husband, Nikhilesh, as an epitome of virtues which were inconceivable then. For instance, Nikhilesh was averse to drinking because it was neither necessary for survival nor useful for a healthy existence which however was not appreciated by other members of the family because 'they thought [that] such purity only suited those who were not blessed by the goddess of wealth [and] only the expanses of the moon could contain blemishes with ease'.[1] For Nikhilesh, who was humane to the core, it was a most obnoxious habit to nurture since it was also a demonstration of the power of wealth, which the majority of those in his estates lacked. The claim was so electrifying that Bimala accepted her husband as 'the prince of her heart [and she was] his princess who was blessed to have found him [which] was a source of greater joy'.[2] Being someone who was respectful to humanity, Nikhilesh was only a rare human who never believed in graded humanity, argued Bimala. True to his belief, Nikhilesh stood out by not allowing his wife 'to revere him'[3] which was the common practice in gender-divided Bengal. Here, through Bimala, Tagore made a very perceptive comment which explains his inclinations. While highlighting that Bimala's husband never discriminated against her, she characterized this as 'his generosity of spirit'.[4] To sharply make his point, Tagore compared the behaviour of the greedy priest in temples with those individuals who believed that humans could only be subdued by force. Tagore expressed his views through Bimala who mentioned that

> at the holy place, the greedy priest grapples to get worshipped because he doesn't deserve it rightfully. In this world, only the weak demand reverence from their wives as their due [which] shapes both the worshipper and the worshipped.[5]

Respect and reverence for Nikhilesh were an outcome of Bimala's appreciation of those values which appeared to have lost their significance in contemporary Bengal. Although Nikhil was opposed to practices of gender discrimination which was commonly upheld, he was equally sensitive to those practices which were dismissed as 'orthodox and obscurantist' by his friends who were enlightened by Western discourses.

Tagore makes a profound point here by linking gender equality with care for humanism. Unfortunately, most of the practices that were accepted socioculturally, were at variance with the Western notion of gender parity. Nikhilesh, in all probability, personified Tagore, who—while believing in some of the core values of India's sociocultural and intellectual traditions—argued strongly for Enlightenment ideas which, he strongly felt, were complementary to humanity. In other words, Tagore was in favour of a creative blending of ideas from the East with those of the West which also confirms that he, by being appreciative of universal humanism, never undermined ideas for humanizing humanity because it was rooted in Western experiences. As gender equality was critical to humanity, Tagore always insisted that unless women were treated at par with their male counterparts, society could hardly move forward. This is further depicted in the novel. While admiring her husband for being so sensitive to gender equality, Bimala mentioned that 'my husband always claimed that men and women have equal rights over another and hence their love is also on an equal footing'.[6] However, being raised in an orthodox family, she was not able to appreciate this because she was taught that as a wife, her love meant

> devotion to her husband [which] is not an impediment to stop people from being equals [because] ... it is a mode of equalizing people by elevating them. Hence, the pleasure of becoming equal is ever-present in it and it never turns into a thing of indifference. Love is always giving, just like the lamp-oil [that helps] the flame to glow at its own cost.[7]

Two ideas emerge here; one, Bimala felt that being sincere to what she derived by being socialized in an orthodox family was not contrary to gender equality; or, that a devoted wife was not necessarily servile to her husband. Instead, love for each other was also a manifestation of equality not on the basis of unequal power relationships, but due to equal concern of a husband for his wife, and that human relations were not governed by the conceptualization that some were superior and some inferior. It drew on the fact that there should be no barricades. Tagore, by referring to Bimala–Nikhilesh's relationship, made a wider point by challenging the prevalent sociocultural imbalances present due to colonial hegemony complemented by well-entrenched customary practices. These were transferred from one generation to another by rigid processes of socialization. Second, Tagore was one those few thinkers in the nationalist phase who was keen to understand India's prevalent socio-economic realities taking into account ancient sources of wisdom too. Devotion was thus not equal to submission; rather, it was also a design of conceptualizing institutionalized interpersonal relationships in parameters which were usually dubbed as a mode of compartmentalizing human beings in the 'superior-inferior mould'. On the surface, the argument has substance because the term 'devotion' etymologically implies a relationship between two sets of individuals: one endowed with qualities which linked the other as a devotee to the former—a clearly defined interlinkage reflective of an unequal power relationship. In the novel, by being opposed to Bimala being a devotee, Nikhilesh set out his own thinking in this regard. Being aware that Bimala's conceptualization of not being at par with her husband was inculcated over centuries, he clarified his stance by saying that

> the entire society has squashed our women's minds from all sides and made them narrow in their perception [which resulted in the fact that] fate gambles with their lives—their lives depend on the turn of the dice, do they have any powers of their own.[8]

Gender discrimination was a problem, the root of which was in those well-entrenched social and customary practices. Implicit here are two conceptual points: women were just like clay which gets shaped by sociocultural forces considered to be significant in sustaining social balances, and as they lacked the ability to prepare a roadmap for themselves, they depended on fate which was neither logical nor persuasive since the progress of humanity was contingent on conscious efforts at achieving the unachievable. This was also a point of debate between Bimala and Nikhilesh. As Bimala was persuaded to believe that fate was a determinant and hence women suffered 'their misfortune', which did not please Nikhilesh as he always attributed gender inequality to the continuity of social practices linked with the desire of a select few to sustain their interests. It was thus artificially generated and in view of nearly zero opposition, the system continued. In response to Bimala's characterization of her widowed sister-in-law being a victim of her fate, Nikhilesh appeared disheartened because this was contrary to his claim that the customary practices to further cast out widows evolved purely out of consciously nurtured discriminatory practices against women. Furthermore, many women demanded to be treated differently which Bimala decried as it was not considered morally proper. Nikhilesh not only criticized Bimala, but also explained that it was a conscious design on the part of women 'to conquer their deprivation'.[9] Bimala was not persuaded and said that she had 'no sympathy for these thorns on the way, the cruel jibes and the artifice'.[10] This statement was an outcome of patriarchal prejudices prevalent in society; patriarchy was not only fuelled by men, women also had a significant role as it was translated into practices from which women were hardly immune. Hence, Bimala's caustic remarks did not appear to be unusual; but were organic to the mindset which steadily flourished. Here she selfishly argued her point to persuade Nikhilesh that women tended to be crafty as far as their interests were concerned. In contrast, being true to his commitment to universal humanism and gender parity, Nikhilesh highlighted the point that women were their own enemies because, as a social group, they hardly stood united, as Bimala's comment demonstrated. Selfishness was a deterrent, felt Tagore, which he showed when Nikhilesh mentioned that what Bimala insisted was directed by her instinctive desire of safeguarding her own interests; but she had none 'to spare for those whose lives have been ripped to shreds by the cruel arrows of society? Should the loser be made to pay a fine for losing?'[11] This is a perceptive comment Tagore made and it helped us understand women had a world of their own which rotated as per practices that evolved over generations; moreover, it was also a reiteration of the argument that gender equality remained elusive as long as women were not allowed to interact with the outside world. What is distinctive here is Tagore's criticism of the *parda* system of seclusion of women from the rest; it was allowed to survive given the superstitious belief that once they go out, they would no longer remain the same. Women were kept in chains, as it were. Nikhilesh, epitomizing Tagore's preferences, challenged the well-established practices and forced Bimala to venture out in the open to comprehend the world by herself because, as he believed, 'neither [she] nor [him] were made to play the game of life within this domestic chicanery [which he further substantiated by saying that] our love will be true only if we really know each other in the midst of truth'.[12] This was a revolutionary step because it was a break from the past and it also created a space of interaction between the inner and the outer world. It was a discovery for Bimala because she not only had the opportunity to delegitimize the claim that women were better off as domesticated entity but also challenged the axioms governing women vis-à-vis men. Not only was social design unfair, but it was also allowed to survive by developing complementary customary practices since women hardly had a choice in selecting their husbands, which Nikhilesh underlined to bolster his argument for gender parity and simultaneously questioned the sociocultural practices setting out this axiomatic roadmap for women. As Bimala had to take whoever she got as her husband, she was denied her freedom of choosing the man with whom she was entangled institutionally for life. Such a practice survived in a traditional society like India since husbands were shown to be divinely chosen which inculcated the sense that husbands were superior in the hierarchy. Hence, while being critical of marriage as a mechanism for sustaining such a mode of discrimination, Nikhilesh argued that husbands never became epistemological partners but were viewed as godly creations instead. As a result, wives 'ignore the man, but garland the God [because] in [their] imagination [they] create an ideal man and are happy to remain in a make-believe world'.[13] For Nikhilesh, it was a systemic feature which received encouragement from deliberately constructed sociocultural ethos governing relationships. Although it was a source of embarrassment for Nikhilesh, he tried to make Bimala aware by motivating her to think differently.[14]

Bimala was treated as an equal partner in many of Nikilesh's projects which was evident because he always consulted her before finalizing what he proposed to do for collective well-being. To substantiate, Bimala referred to her husband's investments in the development of a bank to inculcate a habit of saving among the villagers for rainy days and also when they required an extra amount for their special needs. Furthermore, by paying high interests on their savings, the villagers were drawn to the bank because it offered high interest on their savings.[14] Although it collapsed soon as those involved in running the bank were not as honest and sincere as Nikhilesh expected. Similarly, in the installation of a loom and a husking machine, Nikhilesh sought Bimala's advice; once Bimala approved the project, Nikhilesh undertook steps to execute his plan.[15] These two initiatives did not succeed, but were referred to defend the point that for Nikhilesh, Bimala always remained his first sounding board, and only with her consent, did he embark on the project. For the point of gender equality, this was significant because it demonstrated Nikhilesh's acceptance of Bimala as equal to him and, Bimala's participation in the discussion also proves that she was as capable as any of her male counterparts in successfully entering male domain areas. In contrast, the other protagonist, Sandip, who talked about women being superior to men was, as per Bimala, deceptive since what he claimed and his behaviour towards women were incongruent. Bimala was most impressed by Sandip's justification that it was natural under specific circumstances. For instance, while they were involved in the freedom struggle, they were not constrained by morality which led them to defend their deeds as proper. It was not inappropriate to resort to such means to fulfil their goal. As the politico-ideological objective was foremost, Sandip argued that 'this is not the time for us to differentiate between morality and immorality, between good and evil, between right and wrong; today unscrupulously and indifferently we have to be ruthless and unfettered'.[16] Bimala understood that Sandip always stood against righteousness since the attainment of goal was prior to the pursuit of moral values while being involved in a battle to liberate India. She was perhaps a victim of his 'habitual display of excellent histrionics, common to the business of impressing an audience'.[17] As she became closer to Sandip, she realized that the claim for gender equality was, for him, a coy to fulfil his partisan goals. This was not the case with Nikhilesh, because he, in various ways, had not only shown what he believed, but also helped his wife carve a space for herself during that time.

It was Nikhilesh who, by being committed to gender parity, was uncertain on occasions for he was intrigued if Bimala was 'driven by social pressures like the fixed ration of municipal water that one receives daily [or] ... did it stem from the deep well of her heart'.[18] Being critical of Sandip's modus operandi, Nikhilesh criticized him and his associates as they never bothered about 'justness of the means ... [but] were keen to arrive at [their] goal quickly through unfair means'.[19] This was not just a critique of those who launched and guided the campaign, but also a firm view on its nature which did not inspire Nikhilesh due to its inherent weakness. There are two levels of arguments here; one, he judged that Bimala's fascination for non-righteous individuals was one of the reasons for admiring Sandip whose notion of gender equality was deceitful. Secondly, Nikhilesh pursued one of the most sharp critiques of nationalism that flourished at the behest of Sandip and his colleagues by saying

> when you can't summon up the enthusiasm to serve the country by thinking of her merely as a country and its people as mere human beings, when you need to scream and shout out *mantras* and call her goddess and go into a trance, they you love the craze more than you love your motherland.[20]

Apart from characterizing Sandip's endeavours as vacant and misleading, Nikhilesh exposed serious limitations of his efforts that he undertook along with those of his compatriots. As one who believed in self-reliance as a factor enabling Indians to stand in competition with the British, he not only devised a new conceptual parameter but also endeavoured to put it in practice. The task was easier said than done as his firm dislike for Sandip and his comrades unfortunately helped build an image of Nikhilesh as a loyalist who was either 'scared of the police or [was] angling for a title'.[21] For the police, he was identified as one who was 'masquerading as a good soul because [he has] other hidden agenda'.[22] Nonetheless, he gradually understood that for Sandip, exalted ideas, like devotion to the country and acceptance of all as indivisible, were just a means to hide his exclusive intention. What caused serious agony to Nikhilesh was his realization that Bimala, being convinced by Sandip's pretentions, was not ready to listen to him. The reason, as he explained, was a manifestation of his 'insecurities' with reference to Sandip that could have been entirely false because 'the image of Sandip that comes to [his] minds [then] is warped by the searing of heat of anguish'.[23] A contrast between Sandip and Nikhilesh reveals how Tagore conceptualized humanity. There are two important features; one humanism denotes concern for humanity and as soon as this was compromised, Tagore raised his voice. In *Ghare Baire*, Nikhilesh was the protagonist of new nationalism which was not just vacuous slogans, but was coupled with constructive programmes. So, in Tagore's perception, humanization never meant a slogan-driven expression of one's love for the country; instead, it was an articulation of love, care, and compassion for the countrymen who were reduced beyond description. *Ghare Baire* was also about inter-personal relationships which—if based on selfish interests—was likely to be weakened soon, as it happened with Sandip and Bimala. Sandip's concern and care for Bimala was governed by his selfish urge; including the fulfilment of desires which were not socially acceptable. He made Bimala a supplier of funds, primarily for his own luxuries which did not go unnoticed by Amulyo, one of his close confidants in the campaign for pursuing political goals.

Tagore, by graphically illustrating three of the protagonists in the novel, highlighted his exclusive approach to humanizing humanity. A wordsmith per excellence, he demonstrated that humanism did not seem to matter to Sandip as it did to Nikhilesh. Sandip was a deceiver because in the open, he pretended to be a genuine devotee of India who was ready to do anything possible for humanity although he, in his private life, hardly restrained himself from enjoying comforts which he claimed to have abdicated till his nationalist goal was achieved. On the contrary, Nikhilesh was reticent and involved in tasks which, he thought, were of great use for self-reliance. He realised that one of the serious impediments of India being unable to compete with the British was the inability to produce goods for common consumption; once that was meaningfully addressed, it would be easier to effectively seal an important source of revenue for the foreign merchants. So, Nikhilesh had short and long-term goals; the former was linked with his effort towards creating a mindset supportive of the idea of India being self-reliant, and the latter was to develop an alternative system of production which was strong enough to stand the competition. It was a design to both empower the colonized and also instrumentalize his ideas for execution. When it dawned on Bimala that Sandip was misleading, it was too late to control the damage. Although she was uncertain about her assessment of Sandip at the beginning, she was persuaded to believe that he was deceitful following the extensive dialogue with Amulyo. While dwelling on how Bimala conceptualized the entire situation, Tagore developed a narrative by creatively blending emotions which was evident in his articulation of her feelings. As Bimala mentioned, 'when she realized, she felt miserable because Sandip took advantage of her being deeply in love with him. … Perhaps, this is', argued Bimala, 'a woman's nature [and thus] when our heart is involved in one arena, we lose all our senses of other spaces. … We are like flowing water—when we flow between two shores, we nurture with all our might and when we overflow the banks, we destroy with equal vehemence'.[24] Two ideas are central here which are also a reinforcement of Tagore's assessment of humanity from a woman's perspective. First, he looked at how a woman felt when she trusted someone. Sandip became a trustworthy companion which allowed Bimala—as she admitted—to ignore or undermine other relationships. Here Tagore saw Bimala as a representative of a feeling which was universal in character; a woman was ready to sacrifice everything for love which, despite not socially inappropriate, highlighted one aspect of humanity. Humanizing humanity did not therefore preclude such a possibility. Secondly, there is an interrelated point which Tagore offered, by reiterating the claim that women could simultaneously become both a source of happiness and pain. Once Bimala became intimate with Sandip, she was ecstatic; the same Bimala was devastated when her husband came back with a fatal head injury when he went to the riot-affected villages to quell the situation.

Representing three interrelated modes of conceptualizing humanity, Tagore laid out his approach to the phenomenon. In very complex interpersonal relationships, involving three individuals, it was not easy to disentangle differently textured responses of three people occupying different spaces. Being true to his ideational vision, Nikhilesh was never mesmerized by Sandip's troublemaking style while being involved in the campaign. Being critical of Sandip's description of a man, he further suggested that it was neither judicious nor explanatory because 'man is not just a logo, he's made of all sciences and he goes beyond them all, stretching himself to the eternity'.[25] Disturbed by Sandip's desire of demeaning humanity, Nikhilesh added that 'you are intent on … denigrating man, humiliating him [which] I see in the environment through my own pain; you are determined to torturously kill him'.[26] His failure was complemented by Bimala being magnetically drawn to Sandip who persuaded her to believe in modernity because it is not modern to revere control as the greater virtue and desire as lesser virtue. Sandip succeeded in inculcating the sense of being 'modern' by introducing her to 'contemporary English books [which taught her that] if she only takes refuge in the word "modern", she'd gain a lot of courage, because women need ... a holy man to push them out of the world that she has inherited'.[27] Sandip was a man who, in the name of serving India actually undertook many measures for filling his desires. He developed a conceptual model which was not humane; in view of Nikhilesh's blind faith in him and Bimala's unconditional devotion to him, the narrative shows how Sandip became close to them within a very short period. The narrative changed when Nikhilesh realized that he was responsible for his own agony when he assessed things around him by 'erasing all the colourful doodles [he has] splattered with the colours of many things [which made him realize that] ... the person whom Bimal's entire life can truly complement, is Sandip'.[28] Having been betrayed by life, Nikhilesh never lost faith in love for humanity; despite being deluded by the complexities of life, he remained optimistic which he expressed by saying that

> my love will not betray me—she's Truth, the Truth—that's why I see her again and again and will continue to see her always; I have seen her through my mistakes and through the mist of tears. In the midst of marketplace of life, I have seen her, lost her, and found her again and when I slip through death jaws, I will see her again. ... The star whose veil has slipped, is telling me—no, oh no, don't be afraid. Whatever is eternal will always be there.[29]

Fundamental here are two ideas which are critical to Tagore's approach to humanity: first, amidst uncertainties and frustration, love continued to remain a rejuvenating force for humanity which is a reiteration of an *Upanishadic* belief that

> when our self is illuminated with the light of love, then the negative aspect of its separateness with others loses its finality, and then our relationship with others is no longer that of competition and conflict, but of sympathy and cooperation.[30]

This is true and human beings cutting across historical phases of human civilization remain engaged in exploring how love was a riveting force as far as humanity was concerned. Illustrative in *Upanishads* was also the claim that despite being an account of multifaceted experiences of humanity over centuries, love was always a riveting tool reinforcing the claim that it created 'oneness' among socioculturally disparate human collective. The idea was also reiterated in the Western Enlightenment principles highlighting care, concern, and empathy for all. Nikhilesh thus repeated what had, so far, been appreciated in human discourses. Secondly, with his belief in love as a resilient force regardless of circumstances, Tagore rekindled faith in love in a context when humanity was sharply divided between colonizers and the colonized, exploiters and exploited. *Ghare Baire* is a micro account of interpersonal relationships that revolved around forces seeking to hamper humanity, but it remained as it was presumably because care, concern, and empathy hardly lost their significance in human civilization. In a divided human existence—as colonial India witnessed—divisive forces might appear to have triumphed which was deceptive because love, by being ingrained in humanity, continued to act decisively in developing and consolidating sociability among humans spatially as well as temporally. Sandip did not take into account poverty and the lack of Hindu–Muslim amity while setting out his political strategies. For instance, when Nikhilesh referred that Panchu—a petty vendor selling household items for survival—was deprived of even two meals a day, Sandip immediately said it was not his responsibility. In case of Muslims, his response was scary since he felt that no persuading would work, 'they have to be subdued and shown who was the boss in no uncertain terms [because] … today they bare their fangs at us; but one day we'll make them dance to our tune'.[31] Aghast with this statement, Nikhilesh lost his hope that the campaign, instead of bringing socioculturally disparate people together, was a certain cause of permanent fissure between Hindus and Muslims. As history shows, it was an error of judgement and the joy of independence was marred by the Partition of India. Sandips of the mainstream nationalism triumphed while those nurturing what Nikhilesh held vis-à-vis humanity remained marginalized, although it is well established that Partition was inevitable then and the mainstream nationalist had no option.[32] Nonetheless, *Ghare Baire* was an articulation of Tagore's distinct approach to humanism. A common thread in Tagore's creative texts was optimism which he nurtured and articulated. The context was not favourably disposed because it was colonial India which was governed with a view to safeguard the interests of the British authority and the loyalists, and it was an India where the well-entrenched sociocultural prejudices were determinants of inter-community relations which allowed the sustenance of exclusion among humans around many axes. Nonetheless, Tagore, through his writings, raised a powerful voice against political domination by a foreign power and a those who protected their interests by defending discriminatory practices. It will not be an exaggeration to suggest that the prevalent socio-economic and political milieu generated impulses which Tagore and some of his compatriots articulated while being deviant from the socially well-established values, and customs. As the available evidence shows—from the early nineteenth century—the oppositional forces against sociocultural biases began to be consolidated and gained momentum during the twentieth century. *Ghare Baire* conveyed the message by focusing on how the three protagonists reacted to the changes in those tumultuous years during and after the 1905–1908 Swadeshi Movement.

Gora was published in 1910 six years before *Ghare Baire* was released in 1916. It was a more complex novel than *Ghare Baire* for multiple reasons because unlike the latter, *Gora* is not just a narrative of transformation of an individual. It also entails a deep analysis of the existent socio-economic and political circumstances in which Gora—the main protagonist in the novel—evolved and questioned the derivative ideas which he nurtured so carefully to support his Hindu identity even to his mother, Anandamoyee. Gender equality is an antidote to social inequality, and eradication of social inequality is a stepping stone to humanizing humanity. *Gora*, the novel, is a testament to this claim. Unlike *Ghare Baire*, the novel portrayed human relations by seeking to explain how well-entrenched prejudices acted decisively in causing and consolidating ruptures amongst human beings. Hence, it was not unusual when Gora witnessed—during his sojourn in a village away from Calcutta—that Hindus treated their Muslim neighbours with disdain; how many remained socially ostracized despite being humans, and patriarchy survived despite stern oppositions by the Brahmos among those who claimed to have been enlightened by being raised in an environment immune from gender bias.

Despite being raised in a family that gradually became self-proclaimed custodians of Hindu orthodoxy with the retirement of the head of the family, Krishnadayal (Gora's father) was convinced that Hindu ethos and cultural values were best in comparison with those of other religious faiths. It was a radical transformation for him since he was critical of obscurantist Hindu practices; it caught his wife, Anandamoyee by surprise; but she remained quiet at this change because she knew that her objection would have no impact. Gora, who lost his parents during the 1857 Mutiny, was raised by his foster parents, Krishnadayal and Anandamoyee. In view of his exposure to English education, he, at the beginning of his adulthood, came close to Brahmo Samaj which was prominent in the campaign challenging Hindu orthodoxy. Being persuaded to believe that Krishnadayal was misled, he rebelled 'at [his] antics [which he also described as] idiocy.'[33]

Due to his belief that his father was inspired by the influences of the so-called holy men who often visited him, he always challenged them to test their knowledge of the *Vedas*. Given their lack of adequate reading of these texts, they invariably lost to Gora in the debates which took place so often in their house. Of the holy men, one of them, Harachandra Vidyabagish earned Gora's respect because he was the most learned of them and was well-equipped to answer his acute questions on *Vedas*. It was Vidyabagish who introduced Gora to the complex world of ancient wisdom which he enjoyed so much that he 'immersed himself completely in discussion on *Vedas*'.[34] With the condemnation of Christian Missionaries of *Vedas* and other Hindu religious tracts in newspapers, Gora crafted another role for himself; instead of attacking Hindu religion and society, he began writing rejoinders to their published texts as nothing but vacuous. Being incensed, he effectively countered them although it stood in contradiction with his habitual responses which he articulated by denouncing 'the *shastras* and popular superstitions at the slightest opportunity'.[35] Despite being opposed to Hindu orthodoxy, Gora was not ready to accept 'a foreigner's contempt for Hindu community [which] seemed to wound him like a goad'.[36] This was the beginning of his transformation which was evident when he declared that

> we shall not feel ashamed in the least, either inwardly or before others, of the rituals, beliefs, scriptures and customs of our birthplace. We shall shield our country and ourselves from humiliation, boldly and proudly accepting all that our nation has to offer.[37]

Here is an example of Gora's commitment to the nation; he was not ready to allow the British to criticize the practices associated with Hinduism. The transformation was visible on two counts; he upheld his commitment as a staunch nationalist who felt dejected when the missionaries condemned Hindus for being encircled in superstitious beliefs, and he reacted violently because his internalized values stood for his identity as an Indian as well. In view of this, Gora can be conceptualized as a Hindu nationalist for he raised his voice against the British with the belief that they should not comment on what was specific to Hinduism and India. He further pressed that 'whether we are good or bad, civilized or barbaric, we refuse to be answerable to anyone about such things! We are what we are. We want to fully experience our own selfhood'.[38] Explicit here is the continuity of the argument he made while challenging the missionaries' efforts. Gora was transformed as a Hindu nationalist who was willing to address the inherent structural characteristics of Hinduism, but was not inclined to allow others to intervene. Historically speaking, there is evidence of Bal Gangadhar Tilak's opposition to Age of

Consent Bill of 1893. One argument Tilak offered resonated with Gora's; namely, the age of consent of girls for marriage was an internal decision and the ruling authority's interference in disturbing Hindu social system was passionately opposed. In conceptual terms, the historian Partha Chatterjee in his work *The Nation and Its Fragments* explained that this was a design which the nationalist evolved to avoid interference in India's 'spiritual' domain. No interference was allowed presumably because if it was permitted, in course of time, the British embarked on changing the core practices of Hinduism.[39] Gora's transformation represented a new conceptual design which gained acceptance among the mainstream nationalists. Tagore by constructing the character Gora in his novel *Gora*, reflected a nationalist trend which helped generate a wave for the need of being together by virtue of being Hindus. It was a new vision which—being rooted in endeavours by Brahmo Samaj—created a space seeking to explore India's lost intellectual traditions.

The Idea of India

Throughout the novel *Gora*, Tagore comprehended the idea of India especially in a context when it was sought to be conceptualized in exclusive terms; many of the nationalists were inclined to 'Hinduize' India which Tagore never liked in view of the multidimensional nature of the country given the existence of communities with various sociocultural identities. It was articulated by Gora at the beginning of the novel while interacting with his friend, Binoy. His idea of India or *Bharatvarsha* was a condemnation of the definition provided by the religious devotees; instead, he upheld India as a tapestry of many identities; it was a space inhabited by people who developed the skill of being together despite different sociocultural footings. To him, '*Bharatvarsha* appears in its entirety, all its features, major and minor, merged into a great unity, a vast harmony; those who are unable to comprehend India in such a fashion see India in fragments and conceive it in terms of what they derive it from foreign discourses'.[40] Hence, he questioned, caste distinction since it was a system of differentiation among humans on criteria which were neither humane nor logical. While countering his friend, Binoy, who appeared to have been inclined to caste distinctions by justifying that it was necessary to avoid social imbalances, Gora further argued that caste was an instrument of oppression by a section. He believed that as long as caste remained, there were serious impediments towards building India as a composite unit. What he carved out was later elaborated in the novel where he put forward a much more convincing definition of India by questioning the tendency to justify spaces around many sociocultural divisions. In order to expose the serious limitations of this argument, he advanced his point by saying that

> if you see the people of *Bharatvarsha* as non-Brahmos, you will distort their image and regard them with contempt, and constantly misunderstand them. You will never get to see them from the perspective that allows one to see them whole. The Lord has made them human; they think in many different ways, act in many different ways, follow many different beliefs and customs, but underlying all this is a basic humanity; within all this is something that belongs to me; to *Bharatvarsha*, something that, when viewed from a true perspective, will pierce its onward shell of pettiness and incompleteness to present before us the vision of a great, noble entity. It is infused with the spirit of long endeavour; in it I can see ancient fire still burning amidst all the ashes, and I have no doubt that this fire will transcend its petty location in place and time to cast up its flame at the centre of this earth.[41]

The above description of India is, at one level, a firm critique of those seeking to conceptualize India in a monochromatic way; at another level, Gora's expression also confirms that India was an entity with a long historical past and not what it evolved in the wake of the British rule. What is most fundamental is Gora's challenge to those seeking to conceive India as a divisive entity since humanity remained indivisible. There are two complementary ideas which he captured when he privileged humanity as an antidote to the divisive designs. First, according to him, sociocultural features were context-driven; so human beings located in specific sociocultural milieu were bound to be different from those raised elsewhere. This is axiomatic to humanity, and hence, it is differently textured which further questions the homogenous formula. In other words, in view of differences in sociocultural texture, it was likely that behavioural traits would also differ. Secondly, as humanity was not static, it invariably changed in response to the newer sociocultural inputs. As Tagore was one of the admirers of British intellectual traditions, he never believed that it was logical to completely discard the derivative Western discourses since they also had a role in shaping the Indian mindset. In view of India's exposure to many sociocultural influences in different phases. What is thus emphasized here is that under no circumstances, *Bharatvarsha* could be conceptualized by essentializing her identity, as could be done for the many Western countries, argued Gora. Given India's unusual historical past, the country has many identities which were an ensemble of unity as well since India was one because—as Gora highlighted—it was a space where humanity flourished. Interestingly, instead of focusing on a particular phase of India's past, Tagore was averse to this idea as he justified the point by comparing humanity with 'a bouquet of flowers'; just like a bouquet weaved around many flowers, humanity, by absorbing many sociocultural inputs, had many shades representing ideas stemming out of differently-textured milieus. So, while seeking to comprehend humanity, one cannot ignore this aspect of unfolding of human civilization. It was reiterated by Gora when he stated that

> The people of this *Bharatvarsha* have been saying many big things for a very a long time; ... even to imagine that all that has become utterly futile is to show disrespect for the truth and that itself is atheism.[42]

Critical here is that *Bharatvarsha* needed to be understood, in terms of a model that drew on the individualities of the Indian sociocultural context and politico-ideological priorities. According to another protagonist, Sucharita, Gora's utterance 'was no mere discourse, it resembled a new creation [which] was so tangible that over time it could dominate one's whole mind and body'.[43] For Sucharita, it was a realization because now she understood what real India was, which was incomprehensible by being confined to British India's capital city, Calcutta.

To further his argument in defence of humanity, Tagore rejected the view that differences around caste and religion were inherent among humans; instead, he believed that the division evolved out of a historical context for the fulfilment of desires by those wielding authority. It was a persuasive statement suggesting that caste discrimination and religious gaps were neither ingrained nor integral to humanity; they were constructed to justify a specific power relationship tuned to the self-fulfilling needs of those with power and authority. Given Gora's insistence that humanity was one, he also apprehended that he was likely to be misunderstood that his was 'a language of Hindu orthodoxy, especially of those who have suddenly assumed a new orthodoxy'.[44] Here one is probably reminded of the activities of the mainstream nationalists during the *swadeshi* campaign and its aftermath when the leading Congressmen appeared indifferent to the existence of Muslims as integral to *Bharatvarsha*; for them, India was a country of Hindus which meant that other religious groups were not taken into account while conceptualizing India. Unable to appreciate the nationalists' effort towards developing a misleading doctrine, Gora, by re-emphasizing that humanity was one, argued that

> I have glimpsed a vast profound unity in the many manifestations and multiple endeavours of *Bharatvarsha*, a unity that drives my wild with joy. Rejoicing at such unity, I have no hesitation in mingling with the most ignorant of *Bharatvarsha's* inhabitants, taking my place beside them in the dust. Some understand this message of *Bharatvarsha*, other don't, but never mind—I am one with everyone in *Bharatvarsha*, —they are all my own people—within all of them, I have no doubt, eternal *Bharatvarsha's* concealed presence is constantly at work.[45]

Intrinsic here is Tagore's expression of the belief that dividing humanity was both motivated and conceptually debilitating because, by virtue of being humans, they remained emotionally connected to one another. This meant that care, concern and empathy for others were built in their mental makeup, and the inchoate connectivity confirmed that despite contrarian tendencies seeking to raise barriers among humans, it acted as a shield, as history proved time and again. Conceptually, the idea was persuasive; but, once Gora went out of Calcutta and reached a village, this led him to realize that the forces striving to separate human beings were not as weak as he assessed. In the city, this was not clearly visible because of the consolidation of a mindset Gora evolved in support of his contention that humanity was one. Once in a village away from Calcutta, what struck him first was that 'our country is like outside the social worlds of the respectable *bhadralok*, the educated, and the Kolkata [Calcutta] dwellers'.[46] It was as much of a shock as a source of complete disenchantment with the vision of India. By being introduced to a world of humanity which was strange to his perception, Gora thus expressed his agony by saying that

> how fragmented, narrow-minded and feeble was this vast, concealed realm of rural *Bharatvarsha*—how utterly unaware of its own power, how completely ignorant and indifferent about its own interests! How extreme were the social differences between places—how many self-created and imaginary obstacles constrained the land from advancing in the world's giant workspace—how much importance it attached to trivialities, how moribund it had grown, clinging to every prejudice and superstition—how somnolent was its mind, how faint its heart, how feeble its efforts![47]

To Gora, it appeared that there were two *Bharatvarsha*—one located in the city of Calcutta, and another which was vast and inhabited by a majority of Indians. The latter was also conceptually different in a radical way because this part of *Bharatvarsha* not only treated humanity with contempt but also created systems of sustaining human distinctions in the mold of hierarchial nexuses which Gora was unable to gauge due to his upbringing in the city. His argument reveals India on two levels; at the level of cognition, he identified the causes of degradation of villages, understood they were organic to their unfolding which meant that reasons were located in how the prevalent social relations were allowed to emerge and survive. At the level of perception, Gora understood that the artificially created schism among human beings within the same village was politically contrived to maintain a power relationship in favour of those who reigned supreme either due to their caste or social privileges; or, in simple terms, they were different because they belonged to a different class by virtue of being wealthy. This *Bharatvarsha* was contrary to how he conceptualized in terms of his understanding of the prevalent socio-economic realities of Calcutta. Indian villagers remained distant in his prism. Given his access to the 'real' *Bharatvarsha*, it can be argued that Gora was reborn—an argument he himself elaborated with reference to an example of breaking of fire and how the villagers reacted to this. Gora was bewildered at the sight of the villagers who were affected by the suddenness of the event, and instead of extinguishing the fire, it was accepted as 'an act of God, or, God's vengeance'.[48] Gora was further surprised that due to the reluctance of the people to work together, when fire engulfed the entire village; this means that during a massive crisis, the villagers remained divided due to their caste and religious identities. It was inhabited mostly by lower castes, many people were indifferent; since the victims were mainly Muslims, Hindus never felt the urgency of dousing fire as they were of a different religious inclination.

A careful reading of the above points supports the contention that Tagore was not romantic in his perception when he dealt with humanizing humanity. His approach was not sermonizing; but was based on his personal experiences of being a zamindar in Shilaidaha in East Bengal. There are similarities between his essays highlighting humanity, the designs for its dehumanization and *Gora*, the novel. His effort was directed to demonstrate that humanizing humanity involved a well-thought-out counter to the processes which were dehumanizing humanity. The villagers' reluctance to come together—even during a life-and-death situation—was not logical, and not persuasive although it was the main factor of divisions being nurtured over generations. It was a well-entrenched conditioning that was a source as well as an endorsement of traditional thinking, as per Tagore, which needed to be combatted by evolving an equally powerful wave of thinking to challenge these foundations. Gora was Tagore's voice which was articulated at two levels; first, he established that the fragmented human existence was an impairment to the rise of humanity, and second he felt that what was required was an evolution of ideas and practices contrary to endeavours which led to even more hierarchies. Although it was not an easy task, Tagore understood that caste discrimination contributed to its sustenance. So, the task involved the removal of justification of exploitation as inevitable because it was divinely ordained, and, inculcation of values and ideas compatible with efforts towards humanizing humanity.

Setting of New Determinants

Humanizing humanity involves setting of new determinants for judging oneself in with respect to others. Tagore explains this point with reference to how Gora felt at the behaviour of the victims of unusual happenings in the village, Ghoshpukur. Tagore referred to an instance of a fire which caused devastations to the village by destroying almost all of the huts and houses. Instead of backing Gora's reasoning that had there been a source of water, the nature of devastations would have been less, they attributed the occurrence to God being unhappy—if not angry—with them. For someone who knew that water was required to douse fire, Gora was amazed at the villagers for having failed to recognize his point. Underlying here is an axiomatic understanding of the situation confronting the rural folk since they 'did not regard these hardships as hardships at all and [because] their life is full of hardships, they hardly get disturbed in case they suffer due hardships of any kind',[49] which meant that hardships were integral to their existence. Gora was tormented, but was aware that there was no way out because he 'realized clearly the terrifying enormity of the burden of such ignorance, stasis and suffering, a burden oppressing the educated and illiterate, rich and poor, allowing nobody to progress'.[50] Tagore was indicative of another bitterness affecting humanity adversely; it was a hostility based on superstitious mindsets and there was a need to undertake continuous campaigns against those nurturing them. So, efforts towards humanizing humanity succeeded with the inculcation of a voice opposed to sociocultural tendencies supportive of superstition and prejudices.

Tagore's apprehension that besides colonialism, Indians also contributed to the forces detrimental to humanism was evident in the novel when the issue relating to Gora's night stay in the village came up. The villagers suggested the name of the local agent of the indigo planters, Madhav Chattujee or Chatterjee, despite being brutalized by him since he acted on behalf of the torturous British indigo planters. Their argument was based on what they inculcated by being bracketed due to their caste identity. As Gora, who was a Brahmin, should not be allowed to sleep in the huts of the Dalits, they suggested that he should spend the night with Madhav Chatterjee, There were two contrary tendencies, the villagers were scared because they were socially molded to believe that Gora should not have been with them under the same roof which was blasphemous to them. The implication could be disastrous because by not making Gora aware of the ritualistic moratorium on him under these circumstances, they would have committed sin for which the providential authority would severely punish them. What followed next was illustrative of how Tagore executed his plan for humanizing humanity. The fact that Gora reacted strongly further revealed that he was one who always believed that humanity was indivisible, and he immediately declined to accept the option and decided to stay with Hindu barber who stayed with the Muslims in that part of the village. There is an issue here that needs to be conclusively addressed. Being a believer in humanism, how did Tagore justify Gora's decision to stay with the Hindu family in preference to Muslim households? If religion was a determinant here, one perhaps would have been inclined to dismiss Tagore's humanizing project as deceptive. But a further clarification depicts how Tagore associated his concern for Hindu-Muslim amity with that of national liberation. Gora was persuaded to stay overnight with the barber's family since the barber and his wife happily gave shelter to Tamiz and his mother who had no one to look after them following the arrest of his father, Pharu Sardar due to his involvement in a fight with the indigo planters. This is the most revealing part of the novel in two complementary ways; not only did Tagore articulate his reservation for Madhav Chatterjee for being unconditionally loyal to the British and for protecting his interests, but he also highlighted the role of the barber and his wife who, by disregarding ritualistic embargo, accepted a Muslim child and his mother as part of their family. His argument for humanizing humanity works at two levels, at the conceptual level, by doing away with the barrier between Hindus and Muslims, Tagore devised a design by questioning how communal schism was constructed to enable the British to further strengthen their strategy of divide and rule; and, at the empirical level, Tagore showed that human willingness was adequate to champion humanity by successfully challenging the forces drawing on divisive mindsets.

The novel stands out because by elaborating the argument supportive of Gora's refusal to accept Madhav Chatterjee's hospitality, Tagore clearly spelt out his understanding of nationalism which was in contrast with the mainstream nationalism. By believing that colonialism and the prevalent sociocultural prejudices were two sides of the same coin, Tagore conceptualized human emancipation in a wider perspective. As history shows, caste and religious prejudices continue to remain a significant determinant in contemporary inter-personal interactive relationships even today. Tagore too had his own existential experiences since he rose to prominence in the public domain. He was aware that Hindu–Muslim discord was one of the worst outcomes of the 1905–1908 Swadeshi Movement, largely due to the failure of the mainstream nationalists to gauge the adverse impact of Muslim alienation on the nationalist template. This was one aspect of how nationalism was reduced to a fight of the Hindus to revoke the first Partition of Bengal. The other aspect relates to the caste gap. It is true that in *Gora*, Tagore did not focus on how caste differences impacted the nationalist campaign adversely. He focused on his famous dance-drama, *Chandalika* (1938) which portrayed how a Dalit girl, Prakriti was socially humiliated; she saw the other side when she met a Buddhist monk who, by accepting water from her, revealed that no one was inferior since humans were created as one, and she therefore had no reasons to readily accept the caste-driven code of conduct prepared by the dominant section of humanity. In the novel *Gora*, the logic of retaining caste purity by being Chatterjee's guest for the night was not only distasteful to Gora but also agonising since he was unable to accept the hospitality of an individual who sacrificed humanity at the slightest provocations. There were many Chatterjees in Bengal who sold themselves to the British for narrow gains and betrayed the core humanistic values. The narrow desire of fulfilling their aims at any cost was ingrained in them which meant that they were ready to resort to any means, even if it cost them, their community or the nation. As a result, not only was Gora internally devastated, he was also aghast when he confronted the villagers who, by nurturing the sociocultural prejudices as socially appropriate, contributed to its continuity. It was, thought Gora,

> a great heresy we are committing in *Bharatvarsha*, making purity a matter of appearances alone! It save my caste purity to dine at the home of a man who torments Muslims by creating all sorts of trouble, but I would lose my caste status in the home of a person who accepts such torments to protect a Muslim boy, and is even ready to suffer social condemnation for it.[51]

By refusing Madhav Chatterjee's hospitality, Gora made a definite choice although he was aware that with the consolidation of the loyalists, it could never be an effective step to force them to let go of their role as British admirers and followers. Even Chatterjee was hardly threatened when the British Superintendent visited the village and Gora confronted him. It was evident in Chatterjee's interaction with the latter in the presence of the police officer. According to him, by informing the police and lodging a complaint against Pharu Sardar he followed his dharma as the agent of the indigo planters. It was not unusual for him because it was an obligation to save the indigo planters as he made his living as their agents. To make his point, he suggested that 'a tiger is a man-eater'[52] did not require an elaboration; similarly, because he was committed to extend his services to the indigo planters, it was expected of him to let them know if they were likely to be harmed by the villagers. Because he knew that it would be difficult to counter Gora, he made the innocent villagers the target of his wrath. Realizing the incapability of Chatterjee, the police officer intervened with a threat to Gora that if he continued to support the villagers and did not 'withdraw voluntarily [he] has to face the consequences'.[53] In his battle against the state power, Gora understood that it was nearly impossible to win because of access to coercive power its ability to evolve a set of loyalists and to draw on their unconditional support to the state in exchange for material gains and social reputation by being associated with the British. The rise of British as India's rulers was also attributed to the failure of *Bharatvarsha* to emerge in unison due to internal division around many sociocultural axes. Being persuaded to believe that 'the degradation of *Bharatvarsha* [was] due to caste discrimination, social evils and the enemies within, Gora was not only intrigued but also realized that it was a herculean task to transform [his] Motherland so easily'.[54] This was a confession which drew out of his frustration that his objective of humanizing humanity was a distant goal. Nonetheless, he never stopped doing what he felt was conducive to the goal. This is reflective of Tagore's own approach to the theme. Despite being riddled with many difficulties, Tagore never gave up what he proposed to undertake in his laboratory, Santiniketan—whether it was a different pedagogy or involving the villagers around his abode in pursuing his desired aims for human development.

Gora's nationalism was humanistic and, at the same time, an acceptance of India's sociocultural practices which made India one of the most humanitarian civilizational spaces. Implied here is a reinforcement of the point that the divisive characteristics which became critical in colonial India were clearly context-driven features. By saying that he 'revere[s] *Vedas*, *Upanishads* and other ancient texts because they are significant in developing civilizational pillars on which *Bharatvarsha* stands and prospers',[55] Gora simply reminded that he inherited India's rich and long intellectual heritage. It had a political purpose since by making people aware of their great intellectual legacies, he fulfilled two objectives at the same time, firstly, by drawing attention to this aspect, he wanted 'to awaken the nation's heart to the greatness of [India's] sacred philosophy, the profundity of [her] devotional tradition [helping] arouse [their] pride in [their] own riches'[56] which would act as a deterrent to their feeling of being traditional intellectually. The inherent tendencies of Hindus 'to insult people, exclude people [which was justified in past] as instructions from *shastras-samhitas*'[57] needed to be rescinded, pressed Gora, to cement a bond among the Hindus and create a bridge with other communities. Disturbed by the fact that it was possible for a Hindu to leave his/her religion; but it was not allowed for others to become a Hindu was a serious structural problem for Hinduism. Unless the Hindus did not 'foster within itself ... the power of conservation rather than the disease of decay, then this unchecked encounter with people from outside will become a lethal blow to its survival'.[58] One is reminded of the adverse impact of conversion by Christian missionaries on Hindus; it was also an apprehension which Tagore articulated although he knew that sociocultural atrocities on the Dalits accounted for this. Gora, by reiterating Tagore's concerns, made this point which immediately attracted attention as he went deep into the problem of social seclusion and its unpropitious effect on his endeavour of bringing people together irrespective of social and cultural differences.

With his intimate and regular interactions with the villagers in Ghoshpukur, Gora saw a *Bharatvarsha* which survived in carefully nurtured social restrictions by the dominant caste Hindus to sustain their hegemony. He was troubled but understood why towns were relatively free from these prejudices—rural areas remained entangled probably because in every household in villages, 'food, sleep, rest, work, everything was conducted, day and night, under the unblinking gaze of society'[59] which left no space for the villagers to be independent. Given their acceptance of social restrictions and prevalent traditions despite being reluctant on occasions, the village elites continued to retain their authority on 'these obedient masses'.[60] They appeared to be happy to remain disempowered which made Gora disappointed which he articulated by saying 'it is doubtful whether such timid, helpless beings, so incapable of judging what was good for them, existed anywhere else in the world'.[61] This was an impediment to the fulfilment of his project of humanizing humanity; equally serious hindrance was their indebtedness to the local money-lenders, which made them compliant to them due to the fact that they remained entrapped in debt. To Gora, it was inconceivable that humans deployed means as 'weapons to suck the blood of other human beings, brutally robbing them of their selfhood'; it was also beyond his comprehension that villagers were ready to follow the rituals even it caused them misery. As an example, he referred to the fact that a poor villager was forced to hold *sradh* [rituals performed after death] even though he did not have money as he spent it all on his ailing father's medication. No one came to his support when he expressed his inability to spend due to his penury, but, 'there was no forgiveness',[62] Gora lamented. It was most unfortunate, he notices that 'this society did not help a man in times of need, nor supported him in times of trouble, it only used [ritualistic] discipline as a threat to subdue him'.[63] He was surprised as well when the Dalits were not ready to violate the customs as it meant the intervention of *bhadraloks* in their spiritual world. Gora was agonized when he placed his proposal of widow remarriage, which was already accepted legally in India; they immediately criticized him for adopting 'the meanest of customs'[64] that were likely to invite God's penance. It was a question of the mindset that was totally immune from the dharma that the ancient sages evolved to give 'everyone strength, energy and wellbeing in the form of service, love, compassion and self-sacrifice'.[65] This was peculiar to the Hindus as Muslims had different customs and beliefs, and, he also witnessed that while 'the Hindus would not close their ranks to stand by each other … the Muslims possessed the unifying element that could draw them together [to support those belonging to their community] … in times of trouble and difficulty'.[66] While probing into this anomaly among the inhabitants of the same village, he was told which he accepted most reluctantly that

> Muslims were united by their dharma or religion [which] … immediately cemented a bond among them [for] they believe that it is a providential instruction to save a Muslim when in danger [and it is thus their religious duty] to stand together and readily surrender their lives … in response to a single call.[67]

Based on his experience, Gora realized that the alienation of Muslims from India weakened the processes leading to the consolidation of a compatible ideational universe for both the communities. He confronted a situation in Ghoshpukur which was an eye-opener and a source of disappointment because he never realized that the roots of communal differences had gone so deep in the minds of the Muslims who constituted a sizeable section of Bengal's demography. According to Gora, the task was difficult, but not undoable. An interjection is required here. Gora spoke in Tagore's language. In his 1926 speech before the annual session of Bengal Provincial Congress, he warned the Congressmen that unless the seeds of communal animosity were completely uprooted, the claim that India was one was just to please oneself as the truth was otherwise. Hence Gora thought that his primary duty was to resolve the sense of estrangement of the Muslims by inculcating nationalist feelings for *Bharatvarsha*. His sense of patriotism prompted him 'to protect his land from humiliation of this detached view by trying day and night to cover his country's entire image with a dazzling emotional aura. [Hence, instead of] … confronting jeering adversaries, [he engaged himself first] for renewing his countrymen's respect for their own land'.[68] What Gora felt was an articulation of Tagore's own assessment of Bengal's political circumstances. By the late 1920s, as historical texts show, communal differences were highly politicized and the Muslims were already persuaded to believe that Bengal Congress was a Hindu organization. The birth of Krishak Praja Party in 1923, preceded by the formation of the Muslim League in 1906, were testimonies of visible psychological changes among the Muslims who now believed that they needed organizations to bolster their politico-ideological demands.[69] Thus, as the novel shows, Gora was Tagore's personification.

When Gora confronted how Hindus and Muslims survived in villages in Bengal—despite being deviant from the well-established canons of Hinduism—he was also a victim of caste prejudices once he started practising the rituals to prove himself as a Brahmin. In this regard, he, to be true to his Brahminical ethos, did not desist himself from undertaking certain steps, to the annoyance to his adopted mother, Anandamoyee. His insistence that his friend, Binoy, should not eat the food offered by his mother because it was cooked by a Christian cook, Lachhmia. He was determined not to allow his friend to eat and argued by referring to the restrictions of eating food prepared only by a Brahmin. Being criticized by Anandamoyee for being a fanatic like his father, she endeavoured hard to convince him that it was not right and contrary to the core values of humanity, which had no impact on Gora. To persuade him again, she stated that Lachhmia 'has always fed you by hand, reared you since you were a child. Until just the other day, you would not relish your food without chutney [prepared] by her. [Furthermore, please do not] forget the way Lachhmia nursed you back to health when you contracted smallpox as a child'.[70] Gora was adamant to not accept any arguments made by his mother which was evident when he asked her to leave her job by 'giving her money for her survival'.[71] Anandamoyee asked if pecuniary support was adequate 'to settle all debts'. She further added that does not it stand in contradiction with your core values of humanism. Instead of responding to the question, Gora simply stated that his friend 'can't dine in your room [because] it is polluted with the touch of a Khristani maid of yours'.[72] Gora's rigidity did not allow him to understand Anandamoyee's argument, which was a reiteration that humanity was indivisible, despite having firmly stated that she was unable 'to appreciate Gora's viewpoints [since] it is violative of what [she] holds throughout her life'.[73] Reference to this debate is useful to comprehend how Gora transformed his ideational preferences once he confronted the reality in Ghoshpukur which led him to believe that religion and humanism were not compatible as long as the former imposed restrictions on inter-personal interactions. In other words, instead of being a cementing force, religion was divisive, as Gora realized, after having experienced the agony of villagers due to their sociocultural differences, despite being inhabitants of the same village. *Bharatvarsha* of his imagination hardly existed in reality; it was divided, mutilated, and humiliated on many levels. Instead of being a unifying force, the notion of India was reduced to being a segmenting energy as the communities at the grassroots hardly remained united when crises hit them.

Gender Disparity as a Barrier to Humanization of Humanity

Rabindranath Tagore stood out as one of the most determined campaigners of gender equality; he owed this concern largely to his family which, by discarding Hinduism and adopting Brahmo ethos, was a pioneer in this respect. His grandfather, Dwarkanath Tagore and his father, Debendranath Tagore, helped inculcate the idea that one of the major impediments towards humanizing humanity was an endorsement of customary practices depriving women of their basic rights as human beings.[74] While Dwarkanath and Debendranath expressed their views by supporting gender equality in their written texts in the important weekly, *Tatvabodhini*, Rabindranath concentrated on this subject in many of his novels, short stories, dance-dramas, plays. It is difficult to focus on each character to demonstrate how he viewed the phenomenon due to paucity of space. However, there is one underlying thread connecting women protagonists in his writings, which means that although they were constructed in tune with the plot of the narratives, they spoke in one language—it was the language of questioning gender disparity by socially nurturing discriminatory practices as integral to human existence. This is the message Tagore conveyed through the characters, by championing gender parity and challenging the prevalent social norms governing gender relationships along with the ritualistic beliefs and practices. Tagore was one of those thinkers who always believed that unless there was gender equality, the claim for humanity being one emotionally and socioculturally deceptive. The message was powerful and articulated in a language which did not impress conventional thinkers. Whether it was Bimala of *Ghare Baire* (1916), Damini in *Chaturanga* (1915), Ela in *Char Adhyay* (1934), Sucharita of *Gora* (1910), Kumudini of *Jogajog* (1929), Binodini of *Choker Bali* (1903), Nandini of *Rakta Karabi* (1925), Prakriti of *Chandalika* (1938), Chitrangada of *Chitrangda* (1892), Mrinal of *Strir Patra* (1914), Sohini of *Laboratory* (1940) or Anila of *Poila Number* (1920), the message was similar. They are the protagonists of Tagore's own viewpoints with respect to gender issues. The chapter analyses two important characters: Sucharita from the novel, *Gora* and Sohini from the short story, *Laboratory,* because they not only articulated a distinct voice in a particular way but also touched upon most of the issues which are pertinent to conceptualize Tagore's approach to gender equality.[75]

Sucharita of *Gora*

Gora epitomizes Tagore's concerns for evolving designs to end gendered exploitation. Set in the prevalent socio-economic tapestry, *Gora*, puts across the points through the main protagonists, Gora and Sucharita. Supporting Tagore's inner conviction for gender-balance in the country in a context of multiple contradictions which grew in importance largely due to socially-entrenched values; it was a persuasive comment on the nature of Indian nationalism that did not become nationalistic because of the failure to create a template of togetherness irrespective of religion and one's socio-economic location. India's record was appalling as far as gender parity was concerned, since there were hardly voices against gender discrimination. It was stated, very unambiguously, by Tagore when Gora mentioned 'we see only half of *Bharatvarsha* [because] we see *Bharatvarsha* only as a land of men; we don't notice women at all'.[76] Appreciating the British for having created a milieu in which women were treated at par with their male counterparts, Gora further added that 'like the English, we would like to see women everywhere, indoors and out, on earth, in water and in space, at meals, feasts and work, everywhere'.[77] The reasons were not difficult to find since

> when members of a household gaze with long familiarity at women performing domestic chores, they don't really see the women at all.

> If we could view our nation's women outside our domestic needs, we would perceive our nation in its beauty and wholeness. We would see an image of the nation easy to die. At least we would never behave mistakenly as if the women of our country are nowhere to be found. ... We need to create a milieu [in which] ... our women can appear in public without loss of dignity [and we must be aware that] ... the seclusion of women has reduced our *swadesh* [country], our own nation, to a half-truth, incapable of infusing our hearts with love and power in their complete forms.[78]

The concern for gender-parity is explicitly stated here: by not recognizing women as integral to human existence, the prevalent views were clearly prejudiced. Women were indispensable in running a home, though their role was hardly acknowledged socially and economically. This conceptualization of women being ignored despite having had a critical role in domestic life is reflective of a part of wider prejudices, which Tagore articulated by underlining that we saw 'the peasant only as farm-labour and the weaver only as fabric producer, we dismiss them as lowly and uncouth, not recognizing them as complete beings, and this rich-poor divide weakens the nation'.[79] Following this argument, Tagore linked gender discrimination with an attitude to belittle women which was articulated when he argued that 'if we imprison the women of our country within their routine of cooking and grinding regarding them reductively as merely the female sex'.[80] This was the root of our deterioration as a nation as one important half of our population was not only ignored but also reduced to social entities without substance. Tagore put forward a persuasive conceptual framework—through Gora's friend, Binoy—to meaningfully generate ideas for common well-being; under no circumstances, women's contribution could be belittled since, as he argued,

> Man and woman represent two aspects of social power; man is power manifest, but the magnitude of his strength does not lie in its visibility; woman's power remains unexpressed, and to try constantly to express this secret power is to propel society towards swift bankruptcy by expending all its stored-up capital. That is why I say, if we perform the holy sacrifice while women take charge of the grain-store, the yagna ritual will be successful, despite the woman's invisibility. Those who try to expend all forms of power for the same purpose, at the same place and in the same way, must be insane.[81]

Tagore lists a fundamental point in defence of gender-equality which was possible to achieve only once women were recognized as an important segment of society. In other words, the aim here was to evolve a supportive environment where gender discrimination disappeared. Nonetheless, the main protagonist of the novel, Gora, now realized that given women's immense important in society, it was not logical to dismiss them just as an appendage. In other words, with Binoy's intervention, Gora imbibed the concern for gender parity given 'women's special presence and influence in society'.[82] Gora appears to have conceptualized his approach to gender issues at two levels. At the level of values, women remained integral to human society was acknowledged; at the level of practice, this was a stepping stone for unifying India as it consolidated the foundation of *Bharatvarsha* drawing on sociocultural diversity which came out very clearly in his statement insisting on

> a vast, profound unity in many manifestations and multiple endeavours of *Bharatvarsha*, a unity that drives [him] wild with joy. Rejoicing at such unity, [he had] no hesitation in mingling with the most ignorant of *Bharatvarsha's* inhabitants, taking [his] place beside them in the dust. Some understand this message of *Bharatvarsha*, others don't, but never mind [he was] with everyone in *Bharatvarsha*—they are all my own people – within all of them [he had] no doubt, eternal *Bharatvarsha's* concealed presence is constantly at work.[83]

What is striking here is Gora's awareness of India or *Bharatvarsha* being one, regardless of sociocultural diversity; he was able to mingle with everyone since he belonged to a nation (sic) that discredited discrimination of any kind as it was a threat to the unity that had evolved over generations. The exhortation—'my own people'—appears to have captured the feelings of Gora. It was clarified by Gora in his interaction with his compatriot, Binoy. According to him, since 'Hindus are a community, … it is impossible to express its essence by confining to any label, … just as the ocean can't be described by its waves, Hindus can't be described as one either'.[84] Being passionately opposed to the design of conceptualizing *Bharatvarsha* as one, he elaborated his stance by adumbrating the view that it would be conceptually wrong to imagine that 'there is no diversity among human beings'.[85] The sociocultural divide was a source of strength because it allowed people to learn to survive and flourish as a community amidst diversity. The forcible unity was harmful to the existence of humans because by silencing diverse sociocultural voices, the endeavour sealed their natural growth. Tagore's Gora thus spoke that

> the brigand races who believe it's best for the world if they vanquish all other races to extend their sole empire, who are too arrogant about their own power to admit that the distinctiveness of other races is of priceless benefit to the world, who spread only slavery across the world —how are you people different from them.[86]

This departure is not futile since it put forward Gora's *Weltanschauung* or world view which was an aid to comprehend his approach to gender equality. It is true that the argument is a little complex because Gora's concerns for gender parity are part of socio-political priorities which stemmed from his own experiences as 'a Hindu', and also out of constant dialogue with the Brahmos, and especially other protagonists in the novel. The role of Sucharita was also not insignificant because her encouragements helped find a course of thought in a persuasive way. A thoughtful woman herself, Sucharita adored Gora for his

> utterance which was no mere discourse, it resembled a new creation. It was so tangible over time that it could dominate one's whole mind and body … and she no longer retained the strength to determine how far her opinions coincided with Gora's.[87]

Gora not only articulated a persuasive message of treating humans as an equal set of multitudes regardless of division, but also endeavoured to develop a design for all on the basis of his firm commitment to humanity. He objected to gender discrimination, and was strongly opposed to socio-economic schisms segmenting one section from the other. His exalted goal was to awaken the nation (sic) as one set of people with multiple sociocultural preferences. He thus declared that

> by professing my respect, I want to awaken the nation's heart to the greatness of our sacred philosophy, the profundity of our devotional tradition. I want to arouse its pride in its own riches. I shall not let the country bow its head in shame, nor make it blind to its own reality by generating self-hatred. That is my vow. … I constantly feel that *Bharatvarsha* cannot be completely represented through masculine perspective alone. It existence will be fully realized only when manifest to the eyes of our women. I have thus no doubt that one a communion between man and woman remains a future, a strong future, for *Bharatvarsha*.[88]

There was no doubt that without gendered partnership, the future of *Bharatvarsha* was bleak. It did not seem to be an easy task, given the well-entrenched sociocultural prejudices. Nonetheless, his earnest call for radical changes in the social, economic, and cultural fields created a template to build a model for furthering Gora's goal. Despite being an orthodox Hindu, Gora's endeavour towards attaining common well-being was the outcome of two major sources; Sucharita's influences supplemented by Paresh Babu's powerful intellectual inputs, and his experience which he gained by extensive travelling in villages. Hence Tagore noted that

> the deeper he penetrated into the world of [the villagers], the more a certain thought began to trouble his mind. He observed that in India's rural areas, social restrictions were far more powerful than in educated, cultured society. In every household, food, sleep, rest, work, everything was conducted, day and night, under the unblinking gaze of society. Each individual had a very simple faith in popular traditions, never questioning such things. Yes, social restrictions and adherence to custom did not empower them at all in their fields of activity. It was doubtful whether such timid, helpless beings, so incapable of judging what was good for themselves, existed anywhere in the world. Beyond adherence to traditions, there was no other good that they wholeheartedly acknowledged, or were willing to understand. It was prohibition, enforced through punishment or partisanship, that they regarded as supreme. The awareness of what must not be done entrapped their nature in a net from head to toe at every step, through various forms of discipline. ... There was no broad unity within them that could draw them all together in good times or bad.[89]

In a longer argument, Tagore referred to the prevalent socio-political and cultural environment to contend that it was an impediment towards fulfilling the objective of common wellbeing; the root cause was the mindset which was opposed to recognize human beings. The well-entrenched caste discrimination and religious chasm between Hindus and Muslims remained a constant source of irritation for those seeking to create an environment for ideologically-justified socio-economic and political equality. In other words, *Bharatvarsha* was divided along gender and caste axes. *Gora* was perhaps the most clearly articulated version of Tagore's oppositional politics seeking to reinforce views for equality of all. Nonetheless, what is little perplexing is the nature of the approach that Tagore upheld to put his ideas in a way so as to generate support for the project that he proposed to carry out. Seeking to identify the roots of our failure to bring about radical socio-economic and cultural changes, Gora was aghast when he noticed that

> humans were using the archaic practices as weapons to suck the blood of other human beings, brutally robbing them of their selfhood. How often he had observed that in performing social rituals, nobody showed the slightest compassion for anybody else! [He was appalled] ... when the father of a poor man was seriously ill, ... the villagers, instead of helping him, [attributed his illness] ... to an unknown sin [forgetting that] the poor man had neither the resources nor any help that was forthcoming.[90]

Here too, Tagore expressed a general concern which was linked with his aims for gender empowerment. It was difficult to achieve the goal because of the widely-held beliefs in favour of ritual-based social behaviour. There was hardly any space for compassion, empathy, and care in society, as he noticed. As a result, the villagers suffer immensely. Gora stated that 'this society did not help a man in times of need, nor supported him in times of trouble; it only used discipline as a threat to subdue him'.[91] The idea here is very explicit: unless a society is compassionate to engender the feeling of togetherness among fellow humans, our existence is neither humane nor worthwhile. A powerful exhortation indeed, it was directed, to create conditions for evolving a level-playing field in which discrimination of any kind was an anathema. Additionally, along with a scathing critique of the prevalent sociocultural practices upholding supremacist mindsets, implicit here was also a call for change by being involved likeminded attitudes and missions.

Unlike Damini in *Chaturanga* and Ela in *Char Adhyay* who were not hesitant in displaying their sexuality, Sucharita in *Gora* is a voice that was tempered, but firm, decisive but polite, and self-generated but contextual. Tagore articulated his views on gender differently, though the foundational concerns remain the same; by characterizing Sucharita as a fearless voice, he raised issues that needed attention. One of the distinct manifestations was the participation of the protagonist, Sucharita, in discussions on socio-political and nationalist issues which, in Calcutta, was exclusively a male domain. By encouraging her to speak out while debating on these concerns, Gora represented a voice complementary to the processes of women empowerment. The Brahmos were pathfinders for many progressive endeavours, like women education, championing views against purdah system, including women in events outside home, among others. Tagore was also a pioneer in many respects, as depicted by his attempts in Santiniketan and Sriniketan.

A careful analysis of Sucharita also reveals that Tagore was not free from paternal biases. While Damini and Ela were primarily guided by their instinctively nurtured desires when justifying their acts, Sucharita was encouraged to speak by Paresh babu, Gora. Additionally, her dislike of Haran Babu, her suiter, created an ambience which enabled her to voice her opinion. It is also true that Damini and Ela, were products of an environment where gender parity was the norm, and, in that sense, their fearlessness was also context-driven. However, in the case of Sucharita, the male protagonists in the novel are seen to have encouraged her to share her views that helped her build an independent personality and also create favourable conditions for her. In other words, by giving her a respectful place in the discussions, Tagore not only created an opportunity for her to express her views but also a means seeking to institutionalize the processes for sustenance for the future. This also means that, for Tagore, it was not a one-time device, but one that was likely to contribute to the development of a mindset supporting gender equality. Gora's rigid approach to moral issues led him to adopt unusual views; his Hindu orthodoxy bloomed alongside his abiding commitment to gender equality. This was one of the main reasons that brought Sucharita out of her shell over the course of various fiery deliberations on socio-political issues that she participated in at home. Sucharita's character arc is therefore, to a significant extent, a product of various paternalistic influences in her life, which was typical of the era and by being sensitive to them in the novel, Tagore, also created a legitimate space for progressive voices.

Sohini of *Laboratory* (1940)

Being fundamentally creative, Tagore always conveyed messages with clear socio-economic and political meaning through his literary works. While *Strir Patra* and *Poila Nombor* were imprints of a system of relationships in which gender issues were debated; the main protagonists raised their voice against discrimination amidst well-entrenched social, economic, and political forces. Tagore's aim was to grow a mindset in favour of gender parity. *Laboratory*, published in 1940, is dissimilar from other creative texts on many counts; first, it is a story in which the main character was a Punjabi woman who represented different intellectual ideas, because she was raised in a milieu which was not similar to that of Bengal. Secondly, Sohini was ready to face any challenge to fight for her justice. In other words, she expressed her commitment to fulfilling her goals. Finally, she hardly wavered in stating 'unpleasant truths', regardless of social consequences, for example she had a baby out of wedlock notwithstanding the fear of being ostracized. In a nutshell, with his focus on an uncommon situation, especially from the point of Bengali psyche, Tagore introduced the readers to themes, relationships, and mindsets that were new and different. Hence, Sohini, treading an unknown path, was an endeavour to capture a reality in which gendered interaction was conceptualized differently. However, there was a common thread of thinking that characterized women in general; Sohini—despite being a Punjabi—wanted to carry forward the tradition that her Bengali husband bequeathed, because that was the only way she could express her unconditional love to him who treated her like a companion to fulfil the nationalist mission.

The story line is unconventional. Tagore dealt with the zeal for self-independence and was also keen to show that women were competent to be able partners if they were convinced of their role in fulfilling the nationalist mission. Sohini met Nandakishore, her future husband, when he went to Punjab due to professional needs. The marriage between Sohini and Nandakishore, though unusual in the conventional sense, was based on the common desire to do something good for society. Nandakishore had the intellectual prowess and Sohini had complemented him when he began his laboratory as a business venture. Drawn by his desire to be self-dependent, Sohini's husband nurtured his wish of making India scientifically independent and he was confident that it was not difficult since 'Indians have the brain though they lacked the initiatives [presumably because] of the alien regime that, by being severely restrictive, inhibits Indians' natural desires'.[92] Furthermore, his intelligence allowed him to not be misled or cheated. This impressed Sohini when she observed how 'the well-established businessmen of Punjab failed to deceive which they usually do with a non-Punjabi'.[93] This was one of the reasons that endeared Sohini to Nandakishore and it finally led to their marriage. In other words, being swayed by Nandakishore's intelligent ways of handling those who were cunning and deceitful, Sohini admitted to him being the right person for her. Tagore's wider concerns are highlighted here, first, Laboratory is a story where the urge to become economically self-independent is explicit. This was a concern Tagore clearly articulated in the 1904 text, *Swadeshi Samaj*. Nikhilesh of *Ghare Baire* epitomized the concern—which was contrary to the nationalist design—of the application of force in case the nationalist dictates for discarding foreign clothes and burning them in bonfire were violated. As shown, it had bounced back during the 1905–1908 anti-partition campaign in Bengal. With the purpose of creating indigenous facilities to develop scientific knowledge, Nandakishore represented a desire that Tagore had epitomized as different from his nationalist colleagues for self-independence. Second, this is a story which also drew on the poet's concern for gender equality. By being candid, even while expressing her choice of Nandakishore as her husband, Sohini presented herself as an independent agency who did not seem bothered by what others would say about her decision to marry a person from a different sociocultural milieu. Sohini was different from Anila of *Poila Nombor* and Mrinal of *Strir Patra* in the sense that unlike them, she was engaged in an endeavour which was complementary to the mission that her husband had. The story line is explicit, Sohini was involved in the work because she wanted to, which displayed recognition of Sohini, a woman, as an independent agency in socio-economic circumstances that were not favourably disposed towards gender parity. The role of Nandakishore was significant here since he devoted his energy to prepare the ground for Sohini to be independent and capable of thinking on her own. In his words,

> incompatibility is likely to arise if an engineer husband keep his wife confined to the kitchen which is normally the case in most of the households; the implication is disastrous because unless both husband and wife are united with the desire to realize identical objectives, the married life will be everything by self-fulfilling; so, what is required to done is to create a milieu in which husband and wife meets each other as compatriots which will make wife responsible to her husband and vice versa.[94]

Here Tagore not only elaborates but also defends the argument supporting why interdependent gendered relationships were critical for social well-being. As long as inter-personal relationship is clouded by gender equations, bonds are likely to be fragile; but if it is based on recognizing each other as integral to the relationship, it is immune from becoming an adversity. Tagore felt respect for each other is important for any relationship as hierarchy is anything but conducive to a healthy understanding between individuals. This should be followed even more in marriages as women join the family by completely relocating from the environment in they were born and raised. Here, Nandakishore talks in Tagore's language, and supports that no conjugal bond survives, let alone flourishes, unless it is cemented by respect. So, Sohini was not an exception as she corresponded with the characters created by Tagore to pursue his concern for gender equity.

Nandakishore's sudden death came as a shock. Many sought to take advantage of Sohini's widowhood by attempting to coerce her into selling the laboratory. However, this is where Sohini came into her own, and fiercely refused such manipulative proposals. Her fight to save the laboratory led her to a young scientist, Rebati Bhattacharya, who Sohini thought could be of assistance. This decision was governed by Sohini's firm belief to ensure the continued existence of the laboratory, which was the result of her late husband's hard work, and also express her love and gratitude for him. She owed her transformation to her dead husband was a constant refrain which also reminds us of Bimala of *Ghare Baire*. Bimala, who became what she became largely due to Nikhilesh's initiatives, similarly Sohini kept remembering that it was possible she would have turned out to be a different person had Nandakishore not encouraged her to study texts for scientific knowledge with him. She was always protective of the laboratory, so much so that she refused to hand it over to anyone, including her daughter who had—she was persuaded to believe—no emotional attachment with its continuity and even if the laboratory was folded-up, it would have hardly had any impact on her. So firm was Sohini's belief that she even disclosed that her daughter was born out of wedlock,[95] which completely ruled out her claim of being a legal heir to Nandakishore. This is also illustrative of how protective Sohini was of the laboratory which evolved out of the hard work that she and her husband put for a cause. Besides her unconditional love for her deceased husband, another incident that showed her as a compassionate human was when she was found to be extra-caring towards 'a stray dog which was almost dying due to malnourishment', 'that symbolizes her idea of devotion to god', as the author stated, 'in contrast to the ritualistic Hindu tradition of sacrificing animals at the altar for providential blessings'.[96] Here, Tagore through Sohini's voice, was questioning the established rituals which were deceptive since they bred superstitious beliefs and prohibitive ideas instead of being socially-conducive.

Sohini is an articulation of Tagore's concern for self-reliance, women empowerment, and universal humanism. There is a historical continuity as far as self-reliance is concerned since what he argued in the 1904 text, *Swadeshi Samaj*, and articulated in *Ghare Baire* was also manifested in Sohini. In other words, it was a reiteration of the concern that Tagore held so dear throughout his life. Regarding universal humanism, Sohini represents a new woman who was so devoted to her husband because of his contribution to make her capable and free from prejudices present in social hierarchy. Linked with this was also Tagore's firm belief that unless women were adequately empowered to fight their own battles, this remained vacuous. Tagore's paternalistic attitude towards women needs to be highlighted here because this was the tradition handed to him since the days of Rammohun Roy. Hence it was not surprising that Sohini, who was grateful to her husband for being so confident in her, declared that

> in relation to the qualities that he [her husband, Nandakishore] found in me, he regarded my shortcomings as insignificant. He reposed his complete trust in a non-descript woman like me, as I have never betrayed his trust. My being incapable did not stand between him and me [because] ... my smallness he always ignored, but gave me unstinted support where he found that I was worthy. Who knows to what level I would have sunk, had he not valued my good qualities which remained hidden when he met me for the first time.[97]

This was an unqualified confession that Sohini made to express her gratitude to Nandakishore. What Tagore conveyed here was his belief in humanity which was a casualty presumably because humans privileged material gain over these human values. In that respect, the message that Sohini delivered was a reinforcement of what Tagore strongly felt. Another aspect which appears to be revolutionary in that time's context was the open declaration of being involved in physical intimacy leading to the birth of a baby. This was admitted by Sohini when she said

> I feel ashamed to confess that I had been involved in relationships which were socially-unjustified. The very thought that I have been close to a number of men still ruffles me. ... Our temptations lied hidden under our flesh and bones, but flares up at the slightest provocation. It does not inhibit me to [disclose] that very early in my life I went to the bed with many men. We, women are not chaste all our life though we pretend to be so. ... Let me tell ... that I had not clear perception of what was right and what was wrong [and] there was nobody to guide me. So, I plunged into evil ways (sic) as I have been able to come out of it. Yes, my body was tainted, but not my soul.[98]

Here, Tagore treaded into an unconventional terrain since Sohini's forthright disclosure of infidelity was unthinkable in a context where the Victorian morality was always privileged. For him, this was clearly an endeavour to not only challenge but also boldly state that a woman's body was her domain. In a sense, Tagore speaks directly to the conceptualization of the idea that Carol Hanisch developed in her path-breaking essay 'The Personal Is Political', published in 1969.[99] Hanisch argues about women being independent agencies for doing what they deem appropriate. Challenging the claim that women needed to be guided, she further maintains that men through their revolutionary struggles brought about radical changes in the plight that women were subject to due to the well-entrenched socio-economic prejudices was far from being true. What is striking in Tagore's Sohini was the bold confession of being involved in 'an illicit relationship' and having a baby which was unimaginable. There are two aspects that need attention here, one, Tagore was forthright in stating about a socially unrecognized relationship and outcome which was, in his opinion, perfectly possible, and second, that, by accepting Sohini's baby as his, her husband, Nandakishore, also demonstrated that he was not guided by the Victorian morality championing Catholic predispositions. So, *Laboratory*, the short story, is both a pathfinder and a harbinger of a new era of conceptualizing gender relations.

Concluding Observations

Tagore is a voice of human emancipation at a particular juncture in India's journey as a civilizational entity. Being raised in a cosmopolitan family which, according to him, evolved a distinct ideational vision out of 'a confluence of three cultures: the Hindu, the Mohammedan and the British'.[100] Tagore was indebted to his grandfather, Dwarkanath Tagore, and his father, Debendranath Tagore for his politico-ideological priorities which were based on a creative blending of both derivative Western and indigenous discourses. Being a follower of the first Renaissance thinker, Rammohun Roy, he never discarded Western ideas as many of his contemporaries did, nor did he follow rituals handed down to him from many orthodox Hindu thinkers. Given his family's massive contribution in the development of his unique ideational vision, he reminded his son, Rathindranath Tagore, of his responsibility to maintain the tradition of their family. In a letter to him, Tagore warned Rathindranath of the devilish influences which were deterrent to the consolidation of a culturally conscious collective. Hence he should build strong character, complemented by hard work, patience, and the zeal to sacrifice for the country. In order to strengthen his point, Tagore further added that due to his association with a great family, and a great country with a very rich intellectual tradition, he should work had to be worthy of being a representative of *Bharatvarsha*.

As stated above, Tagore was free from prejudices which the loyalists always nurtured. Instead, he was proud of the rich Indian legacy and his family. It was a family that had played a critical role in creating a milieu of radical transformation in the prevalent power relationships. Both his grandfather and father fought for the cause of humanity which he pursued with utmost seriousness when he rose to prominence as one of the leading public intellectuals in British India. In view of his popularity as a critical thinker, he had many readers who helped spread his ideas for humanizing humanity.

There are many creative texts establishing Tagore as someone who led an intellectual revolution by questioning age old customary practices segmenting sections of people. Three important social impediments confronted by him were caste prejudices, communal animosity, and gender disparity. *Ghare Baire* is one of the powerful statements Tagore articulated to challenge Bengal's existing sociocultural set-up of divisions among humans based on religious registers. They were primarily designed to retain power relationships and to safeguard the interests of the dominant section. The novel, while commenting on the nature of the campaign for revocation of the first Partition of Bengal in 1908, also delved with the processes leading to visible changes in the prevalent sociocultural conditions. *Ghare Baire* can also be said to have forewarned the nationalists of the serious consequences of the separation of Muslims from the mainstream nationalist template.

Gora is perhaps one of the most complex novels Tagore ever wrote. Not only is it the lengthiest text, but it also stands out as a novel for its complexities. A careful reading of the text suggests that besides dwelling on the main theme, the novel contains many sub themes which Tagore connected to persuasively argue the point that humanism was prior to anything else. By finely weaving strands of relations between genders, between oppressor and oppressed, between morally corrupt individuals and their adversaries, between humanists and those clinging to contrarian tendencies, among other things, the novel, *Gora*, is a trailblazer since it was perhaps one of the first instances of an intensive dialogical interaction between the protagonists championing why Brahmos were far more humanistic than Hindus for the latter remained orthodox, obscurantists and rigid in their beliefs. The debate between Sucharita and Gora is illustrative here. Although Gora liked Sucharita, he was not persuaded to accept her characterization of Hinduism as an instrument for dehumanizing humanity. As soon as Gora had an opportunity to witness life at the grassroots, he was not only convinced but also appreciated her for having introduced him to this mode of conceptualizing humanity. Out of the experiences he gained by being in Ghoshpukur, he realized what he felt about Hinduism was far from how it was interpreted by those in power and authority.

The chapter, by looking at Tagore's approach to gender disparity, also introduced a less discussed aspect in creative writings. *Gora* is a perfect example because it was a female protagonist, Sucharita who elaborated

Tagore's assessment of gender issues and they were articulated differently by different sections of society. Despite the fact that Sucharita's views were exclusive, given her upbringing in Calcutta, she, nonetheless, highlighted the dialectical interconnection between gender parity and the prevalent sociocultural milieu. This is rather inexplicable since Tagore took Gora out of Calcutta to express his views on how rural folks in Bengal were tortured not merely by the British indigo planters, but also by those helping sustain the hegemony of the dominant caste Hindus. There were many Madhav Chatterjee's who represented the same mindset for the protection of their exclusive socio-economic goals. *Gora* also firmly establishes the argument that Hindu–Muslim amity was not an exception, but a familiar expression of rural life in Bengal. Hence, taking care of a Muslim child by a Hindu barber was not a social aberration, but was a manifestation of how humanism prevailed over divided mindsets. While Sucharita was a voice of educated urban middle classes, Sohini represented some of the qualities of her Bengali counterpart. The difference was perhaps because being a Punjabi girl, Sohini imbibed context-driven ethos which Bengali women did not have access to. For instance, raising a child who was born out of wedlock was inconceivable in Bengal because it was socially unacceptable. Perhaps Tagore constructed Sohini to show that gender was a context-driven conceptualization and needed to be understood contextually.

True to the main theme of the book, the chapter provides significant inputs to understand how Tagore pursued his goal of humanizing humanity by attacking the prevalent sociocultural prejudices nurtured over generations. Tagore was also a voice seeking to challenge the status-quo as he felt that communal distance between Hindus and Muslims, and gender and caste discrimination were detrimental to the progress of humanity as a collective. As long as divisions around these axes were allowed to continue, humanity would remain fragmented and Tagore's goal of humanizing humanity would remain elusive.

2

Essays Reverberating Concerns for Humanity

Known for being a powerful exponent of universal humanism, Rabindranath Tagore never compromised with his commitment. Opposed to colonialism, he also criticized the British hegemony in India for it was detrimental to the progress of humanity as one collective. Being raised in colonial India, he saw the colonial power as a subject that helped him understand colonial brutality over the governed. Indians lost their identity as human beings and were tortured to the hilt by the colonizers. Before Tagore emerged on India's sociocultural scene, his grandfather and father were not as staunch opponents of British rulers as he became because they felt that the foreign ruler was complementary to their attack on many sociocultural prejudices. Thus, their approach was reconciliatory and they joined hands with the British philanthropists to radically alter India's sociocultural tapestry that was anything but progressive. The overall situation in India was most appalling because Indians became victims of colonial exploitation and they were also discriminated socioculturally due to many superstitious beliefs and practices. In other words, there were two types of exploitations the colonized were subject to: colonial exploitation, and sociocultural discrimination. While the first gained roots with the conquering of India by the British in 1757 and the formal establishment of monarchical rule with the 1858 Queen's Proclamation, the latter was an age-old problem which was never mitigated effectively despite many attempts by social reformers. Out of the battle against colonialism for political emancipation emerged many groups with different politico-ideological priorities. As history shows, the formation of the Indian National Congress in 1885 heralded a new era in India's freedom struggle with the emergence of this political outfit as the main organization against the colonial domination; the scene had undergone a sea-change once the new/democratic nationalists rose to prominence by articulating a new voice that was opposed to reconciliatory modes of challenging the foreign authority. Led by Lal-Bal-Bal (Lala Lajpat Rai, Bal Gangadhar Tilak and Bipin Chandra Pal) and their colleague

Aurobindo Ghose, Indian freedom struggle witnessed a new phase when the nationalist activists were ready to hit the representative of British power, if necessary, by deploying coercive methods. This phase led to the ascendancy of Gandhi, who radically altered the texture of Indian nationalism by leading the activists in nonviolent resistance that he evolved by creatively blending Western and indigenous discourses. This brief account of how Indian freedom struggle unfolded provides the context in which Rabindranath Tagore raised cudgels against colonizers and those who helped to continue the archaic customary practices separating one section of humanity from another. Tagore's condemnation of colonialism was complemented by his equally scathing attack on the prevalent sociocultural milieu, which identified one section as untouchables to sustain these imbalances.

Tagore's battle was far more difficult than many of his nationalist compatriots because, at one level, he opposed the alien power for being totally indifferent to the ruled, and at another, he raised his voice against those who thrived by exploiting the majority simply because of their identity as untouchables. His was a socio-political struggle to transform mindsets encouraging exploitation of one segment by another. This was also deftly captured in Chapter 1. In order to pursue his primary goal, he utilized whatever means he had at his disposal till he reached his purpose, but it was cut short by his death in 1941. Nonetheless, what is required to be emphasized here is the fact that Tagore was one of those powerful voices that was never vitiated by the prevalent power relationships. He fought relentlessly and paid the price which hardly deterred him from pursuing his goals.

Tagore was a rebellious voice, not in the conventional sense, but in the form of literary creations which helped evolve not only a tradition, but also nurture it by being relevant to those espousing the same goal across spataillly and temporally. He was inspirational to people belonging to different strata's which confirms the argument that Tagore's creative writings were transcendental. This argument is a reinforcement of the claim that the language for human emancipation is globally intelligible because it is meant to empower those who are victims of exploitation due to well-entrenched sociocultural prejudices. Despite being contextual, his voice is universally valid as it instrumentalizes the efforts of those seeking to break the chain of enslavement by drawing sustenance from those interested in fulfilling their partisan goals. As mentioned above, he was not a nationalist in the sense Gandhi was, because he did not directly participate in the anti-British campaign although, by supporting the nationalist endeavour through his writings, he ignited and helped sustain the nationalist zeal in adverse circumstances. One needs to be careful while bracketing Tagore as a nationalist in the conventional sense of the term. In fact, it will not be an exaggeration to suggest that Gandhi and his nationalist colleagues may not be as relevant as Tagore in today's context because their task was complete once India became decolonized in 1947, and their design might not be relevant in India's changed socio-economic and political environment. For Tagore, none of the assumptions are valid since his creative texts continue to inspire people across space and culture long after his death, and his innovative tracts defining unique designs of struggle for humanizing humanity serve as inspiration to his successors who hold the same politico-ideological objectives. So, Tagore was a nationalist in international mould since he was firm believer of universal humanism which prompted him to sharpen his attack on those evil forces thriving due to encouragement by those who were guided by their biased motives.

By analyzing Tagore's essays, the chapter argues that the goals he pursued in his literary texts were similarly pursued in this format as well. In other words, like his novels, short stories and plays, his critical essays also represent an endeavour to bring about radical sociocultural and politico-economic changes in favour of humanity. To do that, the chapter, by focusing on a set of selective essays which were based on his understanding of humanity as one collective, also seeks to justify that they were as nationalistic as the efforts undertaken by the nationalists in the conventional sense of the term. Given the paucity of space, it is difficult to deal with innumerable essay he wrote during his presence in the public domain. Hence, the chapter is based on a careful dissection of three major essays as they are articulations of how Tagore conceptualized his design of humanizing humanity with his conceptualization efforts.

The chapter seeks to pursue two major arguments supplemented by a peripheral argument, first, being a vociferous supporter of universal humanism, Tagore's primary concern was the development of designs for humanizing humanity which were often brutalized by multiple forces working in tandem to fulfil their narrow interests; the second argument revolves around Tagore's stern counter to the efforts undertaken by those determined to undermine humanity. The purpose here is to understand how Tagore combatted the designs which were purposely constructed to muzzle voices for humanizing humanity. The peripheral argument focuses on Tagore's contextual reading of processes responsible for dehumanizing humanity in colonial India. To address these concerns, the chapter undertakes a thorough study of three critical essays representing Tagore's distinct approach to the phenomenon: these three essays are *Lectures on Nationalism* (1916), *The Religion of Man* (1930) and *The Crisis in Civilization* (1941). The purpose of selecting these three essays is to understand how Tagore addressed his concern for humanity by dwelling on how mankind needed to be conceptualized; how the expansionist nationalism contributed to the consolidation of human desires for dehumanizing humanity, and how it resulted in a major crisis in human civilization. One should also remember that Tagore always condemned those sociocultural prejudices which were upheld to justify segmentation of human around multiple social axes.

Unlike Gandhi, who, in his *Hind Swaraj* (1909) condemned industrial or Western civilization as responsible for human decay, Tagore found the answer by critically analysing the internal processes helping to raise a caucus which reaped the benefit of civilizational growth for a microscopic minority instead of allowing human beings to enjoy the fruits.

Nationalism (1916)

Tagore's approach to nationalism was not exactly an attempt at theorizing nationalism, but a critique which led to its conceptualization in a unique fashion. It was an articulation of his experience of nations behaving in the context of the First World War which was contrary to how he conceptualized humanism. Nationalism was a rat race for establishing the hegemony of the victorious at the cost of the vanquished; it was an index of demonstrating one's physical might and strategic superiority. Aghast at the rise of the tendency of exploitation of the less powerful by the more powerful nations, Tagore not only condemned the attitude of those nurturing such narrow designs, but also raised his voice against them. He believed that instead of contributing to the well-being of human collective, it would surely destroy human civilization in the near future. Nationalism was a menace to humanity, felt Tagore, since it was a design of one section of humanity to hegemonize the other section by means of coercion and practices, which laid the foundation of a destructive mindset. It was a mindset that needed to be attacked by all for sustaining human beings as a well-knit collective regardless of different sociocultural and religious identities.

Rabindranath and Nationalism

Opposed to the idea that nationalism was just a politico-ideological tool of homogenizing socioculturally disparate human beings, Tagore's conceptualization focuses on the view that it was a strategy to politically liberate an enslaved nation. *Ghare Baire* and *Gora* epitomize his mode of articulating nation, nationalism, and national identity. In these two novels, Tagore insisted that India as a sociocultural compact comprised many nationalities with identifiable sociocultural characteristics. Under these circumstances, it was difficult to conceive of India as a mono-cultural society. Illustrative here are the dialogues between Sandip and Nikhilesh (the protagonists) in *Ghare Baire. Gora* was a reinforcement of the idea in the sense that once Gora was in Chor-Ghoshpukur he also realized that Hindu–Muslim amity was critical to the nationalists' mission for liberating India politically. Nikhilesh upheld views which Sandip always challenged because he believed that Muslims' insistence on retaining their distinct sociocultural identity as Muslims was a deterrent to the realization of the goal of making India as one political entity which Nikhilesh espoused. These two novels made one fundamental point that, according to Tagore, nationalism in its very sense was antithetical to humanism. It was divisive. A careful reading of these two literary texts confirms the claim that Tagore was not persuaded by the Western belief that a nation emerged out of 'a critical combination of three factors—power, education and shared culture'.[1] Based on J.S. Mill's explanation of how human beings could form a well-knit formation, the idea gained momentum that a nation was meant to unify people who were educated enough to understand that being together was useful among those with shared culture. In order to sustain this unity, there should be an authority which would act in cementing the bond in case there was a threat to its continuity or it was likely to be fragmented due to internal or external factors. The idea has become more nuanced in contemporary researches. Nonetheless, when Tagore was writing in opposition, he always insisted that it was not applicable in India. It was exemplified in *Ghare Baire* when Nikhilesh condemned Sandip for neglecting Muslims altogether as he believed that they were neither integral to the nation nor were willing to cooperate with the mainstream nationalist endeavour; they were separatist, claimed Sandip, and he was not ready to understand why they behaved the way they behaved vis-à-vis the Swadeshi Movement. It was reiterated by Tagore in *Char Adhyay*, which also elaborated his condemnation of violence and the belief that Muslims' alienation was natural since they had no emotional tie with India as a country. The assumption was an articulation of well-entrenched prejudices against the Muslims in Bengal because they had different religious practices and a distinct class status.

There should be a cautionary note here; Tagore did not write on nationalism per se. He dealt with the phenomenon while dwelling on issues of sociocultural fragmentation, both at the national and global levels. At the national level, he believed that love for one's country; which Indian nationalist forces exemplified in their efforts; was not nationalist in the Western minds. His idea was contextual because of his experiences as a landlord in the Muslim preponderant East Bengal where Muslims were discriminated against. So, his idea of nationalism was a boundary-less phenomenon; it should be a design to bring people together regardless of sociocultural gaps which was not possible because of the well-entrenched discrimination between these two demographically preponderant communities. With his foresight, Tagore realized that the lack of sociocultural cohesion was likely to be detrimental to communal harmony. He read the human pulse long before any of his nationalist colleague. With the formation of the Muslim League in 1906, it was evident that Muslims had no faith in the National Congress and hence they had their independent political platform to champion their cause. It gradually became an instrument to mobilize the Muslims in the context of colonial rule which also succeeded by applying the Divide and Rule policy.

Tagore argued that nationalism was a tool of seclusion because he was a witness to the unfolding of processes leading to the consolidation of Muslims as a well-knit community capable of fighting their own battle for securing their legitimate demands. Indian nationalism was not one; it was differently textured for two major communities: Hindus failed to assuage the Muslims' feelings of being undermined from the beginning of the nationalist onslaught because of a complex set of reasons.[2] So, it can be argued that the idea of partition had its root in the failure to gauge the impact of Muslim alienation on the campaign for liberating India politically by the nationalists. As nationalism was based on exclusivity, it could never be a design cementing a bond among disparate sociocultural communities. Given the fact that India was a conglomeration of communities or a 'nation' of nations, it was not the right conceptual parameter to understand the nature and texture of the collective, which comprised of many communities with distinct sociocultural identities.

Hence, nationalism was divisive and incapable of holding together a society of many socioculturally separate communities. It was a tool of division which was contrary to what Tagore adopted throughout his public career. Being contextually-governed, nationalism was thus harmful for India as a nation which flourished over centuries by being accommodative of many races with different religious denominations. Tagore's upbringing laid the foundation of his acceptance of multiple traditions which was an enriching source of his experiences since it helped build a design by drawing on different sociocultural impulses. The strategy that it helped build was hardly monochromatic, but multidimensional.

Tagore was most unhappy by an endorsement of the nationalists' political steps directed to separate Muslims in particular, despite having admitted that they constituted a significant section of Bengal's demography. As nationalism was fractionalized, Tagore criticized the phenomenon for being divisive. It was an instrument justifying the undermining of humanity on the basis of separate religious identities. Nationalism is also oppressive, as it was a theoretical design to forcibly submerge multiple sociocultural identity within the dominant one. This was manifested historically, especially with the rise of colonialism which Edward Said captured and meaningfully explained in his book *Orientalism* (1978). By forcing the native population to accept the derivative sociocultural traits, the colonizers developed a narrative that was a source of constant frustration of the colonized. In some countries, the colonizers succeeded in completely snapping the sociocultural roots of the vanquished and established their way of life as the only acceptable mode for survival. Many African countries are an example here. Being distinctive and also with deep-rooted civilizational ethos, supported by both rich intellectual and sociocultural traditions, it did not happen in India although the colonizers' endeavour succeeded in separating a section of the elites who hesitatingly supported the British rule for their partisan benefits. One is led to argue that India is probably one of those rare countries which sustained a creative blending of both derivative and indigenous sociocultural practices.

The above argument is meant to defend a wider discourse which Tagore offered to validate his claim that nationalism was a device of dehumanizing humanity. There are two complementary parts of this argument; first, this is an unambivalent articulation of the view that by defending exclusivity, nationalism was hardly a design to do away with the barriers among human beings which developed in the wake of colonialism and internalized prejudices. During colonialism, several of the sociocultural practices were done away with due to the consolidation of a belief by the native intellectuals. Prominent among them was the abolition of *sati* custom in the early nineteenth century with the intervention of Rammohun Roy. There were many Indian nationalists who worked hard to restrain the British authority from entering India's private domain since they believed that it was an unwarranted interference by the British power. For instance, Tilak opposed the 1891

Age of Consent Bill which legalized enhancement of marriageable age for girls; by implying that it was an exclusively Hindu spiritual domain, and so, the foreign authority was to be severely challenged.[3] Although the instance may not be directly linked with the point Tagore offered; the aim here is also to show that British nationalism also acted to the advantage of the Indian nationalist trying to do away with restrictive sociocultural practices. With this in mind, it can be argued that Tagore's approach to nationalism was clearly political, for he was opposed to the aim of nationalism of totalizing human identity which never seemed proper as human beings were inherently multi-dimensional.

Tagore was a victim at two levels, at the national level, he stuck to his belief that indigenous discourses were as useful as the derivative Western discourse to comprehend Indian identity which was a creative mix of the two. The arrival of the British and the introduction of British philosophical visions crated space for these ideas to take roots in the Indian soil. At the global level—after having confronted the devastating impact of nationalist upsurges leading to near decimation of humanity—Tagore believed that nationalism was anything but conducive to human civilization; it was, at best, a well-argued design to deliberately crumble humanity to prove that one nation or a set of nations was superior to the rest. A humanist to the core, Tagore raised his voice with reference to the Enlightenment philosophy based on care, concern, compassion, and empathy for humanity. It hardly received attention from nationalist powers who, by participating in the race to prove their invincible capacity, did not seem bothered that their ego meant devastation of humanity.

Tagore's three lectures are advices to a humanity that was on the brink of severe devastation, if not collapsible, which were based on his own concern for humanity that he derived from both Western and indigenous discourses. As mentioned, his approach to the phenomenon was clearly political since he saw the change of power relations in the globe after the war was going to be further divided because the victorious nations' justification for dominating the vanquished nations did not appear to be unusual. Nationalism led to extremities which is one factor seeking to demean humanity as nations were powerful enough to combat resistance. So, nationalism placed one nation or a group of nations as inferior to those who were well-equipped to pursue their goals. In a divided world, the concern for humanity had low priority which Tagore was unable to accept given his steadfast commitment to universal humanism. His writings are representations here. Besides novels, short stories, and other literary texts, he raised his cudgels against the global powers for being engaged in many nefarious activities, including war, leading to the devastation of humanity. What is striking is that Tagore wrote his most cutting critique of nationalism during the First World War. This is also to clear the misconception that Tagore was just a littérateur who contributed to Bengali literature; he was also a great social reformer who had specific approaches to humanizing humanity. The idea gained momentum and he was awarded the Nobel Prize in Literature in 1913. This is partly true because, besides taking Bengali literature forward, Tagore was perhaps the most sensitive individual who created a new mode of thinking by questioning the anti-human nature of governance that flourished under the British stewardship, and the customary practices subjecting human beings to torture in the name of 'traditions'. Here, we must add a clarification that Tagore was hardly a silent spectator when humanity was brutalized in India and in the world. Hence, he was involved in a struggle, the nature of which was different, for instance, in India, besides challenging the forcible implementation of policies at the cost of the common men, he was equally harsh to those nurturing views and practices seeking to torture those who were socio-economically non-dominant. Hence, a fair assessment of Tagore's ideas involves a thorough analytical dissection of his critical essays which highlights his role as a social reformer in India's colonial context.

Critique of Nationalism

Delivered as speeches first in 1916 in Japan and USA, during the middle of the First World War, and later converted into a booklet entitled *Nationalism Ki* (What is Nationalism), was an expression of Tagore's disillusionment with how the rise of nation states became a source of dehumanizing humanity. His ideas were based on his dialectical interaction with the colonial context in India, and his understanding of the global arena where the nation states were involved in eliminating human beings in the name of proving their superiority in the war. A humanist to the core, Tagore was disenchanted with nationalism as a phenomenon because it meant to mercilessly carry forward the whimsical designs of those who pursued their partisan goals, ignoring how their endeavour led to miseries, agony and helplessness for others.

A few notes need to be made before an analysis of the essay: first, the three essays dealing with the phenomenon are based on Tagore's understanding of the role of nation-states involved in the First World War to demonstrate their skills to adversely affect humanity. It does not require any further explanation that the war resulted in the killing of human beings and destruction of property: both public and private. Second, with this set of essays, Tagore embarked on intellectual activities challenging the nationalist project to be harmful to humanity in general. A war established the superiority of a nation, or a set of nations, but the cost was too high to enjoy the fruit of victory. Instead of spending resources for well-being, a war was an effective means to divert them for the gains of the powerful nations. There were many who waited for war since it created crisis of food, among others. The hoarders take full advantage of this situation and sell the food items with high premium which contributed to their coffees at the cost of the hapless individuals. So, central to Tagore's effort was to address a serious issue which was one of the major sources of human decadence throughout human civilization.

As an optimist to the core, Tagore began his essay by claiming that the difficulties human beings were forced to encounter were temporary. It was expressed when he mentioned that 'man's history is being shaped according to the difficulties it encounters'[4] which means that difficulties, instead of being debilitating, allowed human beings to prepare a new roadmap for their existence. Tagore was aware that the nature of difficulties varied from socio-economic and cultural contexts he thus warned that hegemonization would not work. What was required was to assess the prevalent circumstances to devise an appropriate plan for human betterment in unfavourable circumstances. Tagore, while expressing his agony, expressed that though 'God made mad to be human; but the modern product has such marvelous square-cut finish, savouring of gigantic manufacture, that the Creator will find it difficult to recognize it as a thing of spirit and a creature made in His own divine image'.[5] Explicit here was Tagore's condemnation of industrial civilization which transformed human beings from being compassionate to one another into mechanical beings solely interested in expanding their wealth at the cost of others. Interesting here was his argument which linked nationalism with industrialization, which was similar to that of Gandhi, who in his *Hind Swaraj* pursued the same point by saying that industrialization changed the world into a market and the industrially developed nation states undertook coercive means to fulfil their personalized goals. The result was the acceptance of nation-states as capable of safeguarding the interests of a few which was contrary to the core objectives for which many intellectuals fought so far. Industrialism replaced humanity by the individual desires of augmenting wealth, and nation-states were considered the best mechanism in this regard. Tagore pointed that 'this time it was nations of the West driving its tentacles of machinery deep down into the soil'.[6] The consequences were disastrous because Tagore machine-driven civilization

> goads all its neighbouring societies with greed of material prosperity, and consequent mutual jealousy, and by the fear of each other's growth into powerlessness. The time comes when it can stop no longer, for the competition grows keener, organization grows vaster and selfishness attains supremacy.[7]

Here, Tagore further linked the contemporary episodes of debasement of humanity with the consolidation of industrial civilization. Here too, Tagore and Gandhi held similar views. Gandhi also attributed the decline of compassion to competition since it generated rivalry among human beings. Human beings no longer remained as they were before industrial society became hegemonic and unfolded viciously, cutting across spatial boundaries. The world had become one, but was divided with the establishment of colonies by the powerful Western powers. So, not only was humanity divided between colonizers and colonized, but it also justified the application of force as a means to retain and also expand the territorial control by those victorious nations. The only goal of nation-states was to make wealth regardless of the consequences. The uncontrolled rise of industrialism was responsible for a situation in which human values were sacrificed since they were detrimental to the transformation of the world into a global market. For Tagore, the desire for increasing wealth also led to a situation where women were left alone due to gender biases. It meant that industrialism also contributed to the prevalent power relations between man and woman; since the latter was seen to be of no help to this human feat, they no longer remained critical to the growth of a new civilization in which machine and the urge to make wealth remained hegemonic. So, humanity was divided both horizontally and vertically as global population was fractioned between conqueror and vanquished and even among the conquerors, women were left behind. Tagore built his argument by not only critiquing nation states that were guided by partisan aims, but also by identifying the rise of nation-states as responsible for human decay. This was noted when he mentioned that 'when this organization of politics and commerce, whose other name is nation, becomes all-powerful at the cost of the harmony of the higher social life, then it is the evil day for humanity'.[8] Essential here was the view that industrialization, instead of contributing to the common betterment, was actually a source of danger to humanity as a whole. While making this point in this context, Tagore qualified his statement by demonstrating that industrialization, despite being harmful, allowed Indians to be acquainted with the Western discourses. Therefore, he argued that

> if it is true that the spirit of the West has come upon our fields in the guise of storm it is nevertheless scattering living seeds that are immortal. And when in India we become able to assimilate in our life what is permanent in Western civilization we shall be in the position to bring about a reconciliation of these two great worlds. … This is not a new phenomenon [because] India does not belong to one race, but to a process of creation to which various races of the world contributed—the Dravidians, and the Aryans, the ancient Greeks of the Persians, the Mohammedans of the West, and those of central Asia. Now, at last, has the turn of the English come to become true to this history and bring to it the tribute of their life.[9]

Ideationally, the above argument is relevant to Tagore's balanced assessment of cross-cultural transaction as beneficial for human progress through the emergence of new ideas. With the arrival of many races in India, it became a repository of multiple cultural resources. Further to this assertion, he mentioned that he was impressed by the British as a race because it had 'produced great-hearted men, thinkers of great thought, doers of great deeds. It has given rise to a great literature. [And, they are the ones who] love justice, freedom and hate lies'.[10] This was one part of the argument; the other part highlighted what he felt when Britain imbibed the spirit of nationalism which allowed the nationalists to prefer 'a stifling design of harming humanity'.[11] Tagore was caught in a dilemma because he did not expect the West to be so vicious when it was the product of the thoughts of core thinkers of strengthening human bond regardless of class, race and creed, and secondly, he was saw a contradiction between 'the spirit of the West and the Nation of the West'[12] with the unfolding of the rulers torturous self in India. He believed that the former was dwarfed by the latter and hence the benefits of Western civilization were 'doled out in miserly measure by the Nation, which tries to regulate the degree of nutrition as near the zero-point of vitality as possible'.[13] Furthermore, with the uncontrolled marches of the Western nations, human freedom was compromised if not completely denied which was a paradox of Western civilization because it stood out for its battle for human freedom and the same civilization denied freedom to the vanquished. The paradox was that 'while the spirit of the West marches under its banner of freedom, the nation of the West forges its chains of organization which are most relentless and unbreakable that have ever been manufactured in the whole history of man'.[14] Under no circumstances could nations be a source of human freedom despite the fact that the Western nations drew its sustenance from great thoughts. Tagore clearly brought this out in his statement emphasizing that those 'who live under the delusion that [they] are free, are every day sacrificing [their] freedom and humanity to this fetish of nationalism living in the dense poisonous atmosphere of world-wide suspicion and greed and panic'.[15] So, nationalism was a misleading force befooling human beings, especially those who are associated with the nationalist project and victims of the nationalist march for 'the wisdom of the nation is not in its faith in humanity but in its complete distrust'.[16] Tagore was convinced that instead of humanizing humanity, the idea of nation was 'one of the most powerful anesthetics that man has invented [and] … under the influence of its fumes the whole people carry out its systematic programme of the most virulent self-seeking without being in the last aware of its moral perversion'.[17] The obvious outcome was gradual loss of importance of human values and the ascendancy of those tendencies undermining them. Given the devastating impact of the rise of the nation, Tagore had no doubt to suggest that

> the nation has thriven long upon mutilated humanity. Men, the fairest creations of God, came out of National manufactory in huge number as war-making and money-making puppets, ludicrously vain of their pitiful perfection of mechanism. Human society grew more and more into a marionette show of politicians, manufacturers, and bureaucrats, pulled by wire arrangements of wonderful efficiency.[18]

Central here was Tagore's stern critique of the rise of nation and nationalism since they were means to carry forward the designs of a select group of human beings. Finer sentiments of humanity were replaced by the selfish desires of those who privileged personal interests over those of humanity. As a result, those who held views pertaining to humanity became marginalized and were required to deploy force against them in case they deviated from what they dictated. The world had become a place for nurturing narrow interests by sacrificing the wider goal of humanity.

So far, Rabindranath Tagore focused on the changes in the West following the hegemony of nations. To defend the idea that self-existence of a nation did not always follow the pattern one witnessed in the West, Tagore justified it with reference to how Japan constructed its identity as a nation; by not emulating the Western mode but by charting out a new narrative of its rise as a nation-state. Instead of imitating the West because imitation was

> a source of weakness and it is like dressing [one's] skeleton with another's skin, giving rise to eternal feuds between the skin and the bones at every movement, … Japan imported her food from the West, but not her vital nature. [which made Tagore to further argue that she] cannot altogether lose and merge herself in the scientific paraphernalia she has acquired from the West and be turned into a mere borrowed machine. She has retained her soul, which must assert itself over all her requirements.[19]

Here lay the hope for humanity, according to Tagore, since a soulless nation was likely to phase out of existence as history demonstrated. In an era of disillusionment, Japan had shown the road for humanity, believed the poet by

> infusing hope in the heart of Asia; this is a hope which provides the hidden fire which is needed for all works of creations. … She must infuse the sap of a fuller humanity into the heart of modern civilization. She must never allow it to get choked with the noxious undergrowth, but lead it up towards light and freedom, towards the pure air and broad space, where it can receive, in the dawn of its day and darkness of its night, heaven's inspiration.[20]

According to Tagore, Japan was equipped to show to the rest of the world a roadmap for humanity to flourish in a situation which appeared to have caused a loss of faith in humanity by being true to its sociocultural resources. Here, a brief comparison with what Aurobindo wrote in his famous text *Bourgeois and Samurai*, published in *Bande Mataram*[21] seems pertinent. Aurobindo viewed Japan's rise by reverberating the ideas of Tagore. By creatively blending what they derived from the West with their indigenous socio-psychological resources, Japan rose as a powerful nation in the comity of nations, whereas India failed because it ignored the rich past and surrendered to the derivative discourses for success. One of the reasons for Japan's rise as a tough competitor to the belligerent Western nations was

> the ideal of *maitri* [amity]—*maitri* with men and *maitri* with nature. And the true expression of this love is in the language of beauty, which is so abundantly universal in this land. This is the reason why a stranger, like myself … feels a readiness to participate in the joy and glory of such [revelation] of the human heart.[22]

With the rise of nations, human beings appeared to have forgotten the means of coming together which Tagore identified as *maitri*. Japan, by being appreciative of this quality, reignited Tagore's zeal and he felt that they were the only hope in an otherwise hopeless situation. Japan could bring back those values which helped humanity flourish despite adversaries. Japan effectively countered that display of 'abnormal vanity of [one's] superiority … by moral callousness and ill-be-gotten wealth [and of] arrogance by defeating nations by indulging in activities contrary to humanity'.[23] Japan represented a new force which was capable of showing human beings the values contributing to humanity, not only to remain as privileged over other undermining tendencies but also to act as a reinvigorating force for combatting those who were determined to sabotage. So, Tagore said that 'the sunrise of the East … is destined once again to illuminate the whole world'.[24] A visit to Japan kindled a great hope in Tagore for revitalizing humanity as a force for the survival of mankind because nationalism was 'a great menace'[25] which was responsible for India's decadence and for the loss of its rich intellectual and sociocultural identity. So far, Tagore has focused on nationalism as a political design and he dealt with the phenomenon accordingly. The Indian situation was different because besides the colonial chain, Indians were also subject to socially-supported practices of division between human beings. So, the battle had to be waged at two levels, at the political level, one was required to fight against colonial hegemony; at the sociocultural level, Tagore highlighted that,

> we are to remove those social customs and ideals which have generated a want of self-respect and a complete dependence on those above us—a state of affairs which has been brought about entirely by the domination in India of the caste system, and the blind and lazy habit of relying upon the authority of traditions that are incongruous anachronism in the present age.[26]

Tagore referred to the debilitating caste system as detrimental to the development of *maitri* among people in India. In other words, as long as caste discrimination remained, Indians were unable to develop amity amongst themselves. This was the also point highlighted by B.R. Ambedkar when he presented the final version of the 1949 Constitution of India to the Constituent Assembly by saying that sociocultural prejudices articulated by caste division were responsible for India to rise as a compact of collectivity.[27] While fiercely critiquing caste system, Tagore also criticized the loyalists who were servile to the colonial rulers; they were misguided by their perception that servility would give them what they desired. They assumed that by being forgetful of their self-esteem, they would gain certain benefits, which was wrong as it had been historically demonstrated that controllers continued to be good as long as the controlled were of help to the former. In his way, Tagore explained that

> the passions which are unbridled in them are creating huge organizations of slavery in the guise of freedom [and, he further added that] those who have made the gain of money their highest end are unconsciously selling their life and soul to rich persons or to the combinations that represent money. Those who are enamoured of their political power and gloat over their extension of domination over foreign races gradually surrender their own freedom and humanity to the organizations necessary for holding other peoples in slavery.[28]

Reiterated here is the idea of being misled by the clever application of the British model of oppression in India. Many Indians were inducted in government to show that they were integral to the administration. This was an attempt to inculcate a powerful sense of being among the loyalists, this was a ploy of the colonizers to deceive the colonized of being ruled. Those who were associated with the government had no freedom except to run the administration according to the British rules. They were living, claims Tagore, under a delusion. It was further reaffirmed when he stated that

> those of us who have come under the delusion that mere political freedom will make us free have accepted their lesson from the West as the gospel truth and lost their faith in humanity [because] we must remember whatever weakness we cherish in our society will become the source of danger in politics.[29]

He believed that if being servile became part of Indian psyche, it was going to remain even after political emancipation. Once those in governance were persuaded that submission to the authority was a good instrument for effective administration, the habit would continue; such a system inhibited progress because change was a serious threat to those wielding power. This is one aspect of how Tagore viewed servility as a trepidation; the other was his deep critique of commercialism which he articulated by saying,

> the commercialism with its barbarity of ugly decoration is a terrible menace to all humanity, because it is setting up the ideal of power over perfection. It is making the cult of self-seeking exult in its naked shamelessness. … [Therefore] when the callous rudeness of power runs amuck in the broad-day of humanity it scares away by its grossness of the ideals which we have cherished with the martyrdom of centuries.[30]

Humanity was being halted because of the unbridled growth of commercialism in the wake of the search by the victorious Western nation-states, the failure of the vanquished to stand strongly against the colonizers, and the surrender of Indians for exclusive benefits. The analysis of why India continued to remain under shackles appears to be convincing. A born optimist, Tagore ended his lecture on nationalism by exhorting that the days were not far away when the situation would change radically. It was possible once *maitri* was internalized by those ready to sacrifice for humanity. Tagore underlined that 'let our civilization take its firm stand upon its basis of social cooperation and not upon economic exploitation and conflict'.[31] Tagore was opposed to tendencies challenging human cooperation was too obvious to deserve elaboration; and given his absolute commitment to universal humanism—as he witnessed how the victims of nationalism were brutalized in the colonial world—his idea that nation states were instruments of oppression gained global recognition.

As shown, Tagore's approach to nationalism was a critique of the phenomenon in a context when European nation-states established their hegemony in colonies. In India, the colonizers faced less difficulty because many leading intellectuals in India welcomed the British as it was considered better than the prevalent system of governance. At the outset, Tagore was also supportive of colonialism because he thought that it would be effective enough to successfully combat the well-entrenched superstitious practices. As time passed, the nation-state brought out its claws and adopted steps to homogenize India, contrary to its civilizational ethos. In his lectures, by identifying serious limitations of nationalism, Tagore devised a new theoretical paradigm to explain nationalism as an ideological commitment to a nation which could be socioculturally diverse but remained one because of the underlying civilizational bond bringing diverse people together. Tagore sought to capture a nationalism that was a context-driven device for cementing a bond for winning a battle for all those seeking liberation from an exploitative and brutish state power. In his perception, nationalism was just a personification of a combination of socioculturally distinct people who joined hands to pursue a collective goal successfully. It was a design that emerged out of his fierce critique of nationalism that was characteristically narrow and culture-specific. With the nearly phasing out nation-states in view of cross-continental movements of human beings, the erstwhile conceptualization of nationalism is no longer tenable; and, with his foresight, Tagore, by exposing the obvious limitations of nationalism as a theoretical yardstick to persuasively explain the phenomenon, provided a creative conceptual template to understand complex human identities in a non-national language. Perhaps due to his acceptance of the *Upanishadic* dictum which states that human beings, by being part of this world, are members of the same family, Tagore internalized the idea and questioned attempts to mutilate humanity in terms of race, class, and/or ethnicity. His idea of nationalism needs to be understood differently because it had elements of universalism which was immediately rejected as it hardly corresponded with the Western values of nationalism. Tagore's critique was conceptually refreshing, especially at a point of history when nationalism triumphed with the unstoppable march of European nation-states in conquering one state after another. With his insightful understanding of how the phenomenon unfolded Tagore argued that the hegemony of nation-states was as ephemeral as the expansive Empire-states in the past for conceptualizing human unity in contemporary global context.

The Crisis in Civilization (1941)

Tagore's essay, *Nationalism Ki* lays the foundation of his critique against dehumanizing humanity, *The Crisis in Civilization* is a reinforcement and expansion of the same contention, that forces were strong enough to relegate the poor sections of humanity to insignificance. Last essay of his life, this text is also an attempt to evolve strong argument to condemn the powerful elements seeking to delegitimize the rights of the deprivileged since they also belong to humanity. The war was an extreme example of how a section of humanity pursued its aims by sacrificing the core values of humanity; humans became fodder for the rich and privileged. Tagore was intrigued because it was not only contrary to his basic faith in humanity, but he was also unable to halt the march of these forces espousing devilish goals. The essay was an articulation of his frustration at one level, and, at another, the indifference of the rest of the humanity because of reasons which he failed to fathom. Despite being a very brief text, this essay remains perhaps one of the most clearly written tracts where he expressed himself candidly.

It was a text which, as mentioned, was a manifestation of Tagore being both; an optimist and a pessimist: pessimist because the faith in humanity that was championed over centuries was being sacrificed by those who appeared absolutely indifferent to the cause since it was not supportive of their designs; and an optimist since he felt that it was a temporary phase in human history and humanity would rise sooner or later. Tagore's pessimism did not appear to be unfounded because he witnessed the First World War and the beginning of the Second World War which led to massive killings, and the victorious nations did not seem to have any restrains. A perennial optimist, he felt that ideas and values in support of his life-long belief in universal humanism would emerge out of the destruction caused by the wars. The humanistic ideas did not exclusively belong to the colonized East; the Western Enlightenment philosophy endorsed the same and yet the European nation-states plunged into activities leading to the decline of humanity all over the world.

By drawing on global intellectual traditions, Tagore argued that even in the West, there were many thinkers and ideologues who were devoted to the humanistic causes. He was however intrigued that those who were baptized in the Enlightenment traditions undertook missions for enslaving humanity in the East. The purpose was to undermine them as it was contrary to the aim of enriching a section of humanity. As the powerful nations were involved in destructive activities, the non-dominant sections were at their mercy which was a design of discrimination.

Tagore was bewildered at the decadence of those holding the legacy of Enlightenment. He remained confused as to how the British became so ruthless in India when they established their politico-ideological hegemony. By deploying coercive means, the rulers laid and consolidated the foundation of political domination; and by creating a large contingent of Indians as loyalists, they sustained their ideological hegemony. Tagore was hardly surprised at the fact that Indians also supported the arrival of British rulers in India. In fact, beginning with his intellectual mentors; Rammohun Roy and his grandfather, Dwarkanath Tagore, along with their compatriots welcomed the British since they felt that with their presence, India would become a socioculturally progressive society. Tagore followed this legacy. In fact, he was one of the vocal supporters of the Raj, just like Gandhi, at the outset of his involvement in the nationalist struggle. It appears that they had a conceptual misreading of colonialism. By nature, colonialism was exploitative; which was marked by the fact that the colonizers deployed whatever means they found appropriate for fulfilling their goal regardless of its moral aptness. From the very beginning, colonial authority indulged in practices guided primarily by their desires. Being exposed to world history and the treatment of the conquerors vis-à-vis the vanquished, it does not seem that Tagore, Gandhi and those admirers of colonialism failed to read the nature and texture of colonial rule. It was true that they were swayed by the Western Enlightenment ideas of Hobbes, Locke, Rousseau among others; but they appeared to have misunderstood that for Enlightenment philosophy to strike roots, the contextual impulses were equally significant. As history shows, ideational vision was organically enmeshed with the prevalent socio-economic and politico-cultural milieu. Thus, the Enlightenment ideas were likely to be of use provided the contextual ideas remained congruent with different socio-economic and politico-cultural milieus. Primary here is the point that there were no logical reasons to accept the Western philosophical views as axiomatic; there were no reasons to believe that they were futile. Therefore, what is suggested here is to creatively blend them in a way to make them relevant to the colonized. Tagore and Gandhi, by being uncritical supporters of Western Enlightenment once they appeared on public domain presumably because they felt that it was strong enough to control the colonizers and to tune governance to the needs of the people at large.

In the essay, Tagore spoke about his fascination for British literature and his inspiration from it. The reasons were simple—first, it was based on his assessment of literature which helped him learn the art of placing a theme artistically, second, it was easier for him to read and understand texts written in English given the fact that English literature was easily available in India and by acquiring the skill of understanding the texts in English which was the result of the 1835 British policy decisions, pushed by TB Macaulay. Furthermore, the lack of availability of other famous texts written in a language other than English was another reason for Tagore's attraction to English literature.

The title of the essay, *The Crisis in Civilization*, needs probing here. Instead of 'crisis of civilization', Tagore preferred 'crisis in civilization' for specific reasons. English poet and philosopher Edward Carpenter wrote a famous text, entitled *Crisis of Civilization* (1883) to denote crisis of a civilization that emerged in the West following the Industrial Revolution. Industrialism led to a civilizational crisis which did not bother the people before it struck its roots in human civilization; which means that had human civilization been free from industrialism, the crisis of civilization would not have affected humanity adversely. It was an argument seeking to reverse the cycle of history, which was neither logical nor possible. Industrialism was a product of human endeavour to ease human life; hence, it was welcomed by ignoring its debilitating impact on humanity. Tagore's approach was a little different. Instead of rejecting industrial civilization altogether, he believed that it was useful to humanity since it had eased human task to a considerable extent on many occasions. The reluctance of the Western countries to share the benefit of industrialism bothered him. Industrialism could have served as a means for human betterment; but it was resorted to for establishment of hegemony of one section of humanity at the cost of the other as he saw during both the wars.

The crises were thus created by human beings to harm humanity which also means that human beings were also causes of human discomfort. To be more precise, this was a comment by Tagore on the unfolding of industrial civilization in a fashion that hardly took into account what was most useful for humanity as a whole; instead, it was a design developed out of the supervision of a few who wielded power and authority. Humanity was being slaughtered for reasons which were neither conducive nor laid out a template for conceptualizing humanity as one compact. There were forces which were supportive; there were forces which were indifferent; and there were forces opposed to dehumanize humanity. By being a devout humanist, Tagore always raised his voice against human tendencies seeking to undermine humanity by ensuring material gains for the empowered sections of humanity. Tagore was however not alone; his compatriots also held identical views as far as humanity was concerned. Nonetheless, the crises in civilization were hardly addressed effectively, which led to a rise of ulterior motives which went unchallenged.

Tagore's *The Crisis in Civilization* was a reminder to those engaged in relentless battle against a civilizational trend justifying torture of human beings by those who were powerful and well-equipped to harm humanity. Hence, he argued that 'while ... other countries were marching ahead, India, smothered under the dead weight of British administration, lay static in her utter helplessness [For this decadence of] a great and ancient civilization, the British cannot disclaim responsibility'.[32] Tagore addressed the issue at two levels. At the ideational level, being tuned to the universal faith in humanity, he challenged what crippled human existence. As he believed, it was an exclusive ideational design which survived and flourished in the wake of the consolidation of forces creating a space in which ideas and practices supportive of immorality thrived. At the practical level, 'crisis' appeared unmanageable as human tendencies leading to crisis were too strong to be contained effectively in circumstances which were not tilted in favour of those who remained undaunted champions of humanity. This was the reason he cited to explain why he lost faith 'in the claims of the European nations to civilization'.[33] According to him, India, by being governed by the British, failed to get 'the minimum necessities of life as adequate provision for food, clothing, educational and medical facilities for the people'.[34] The British rule was a continuity of cruelty under the garb of rule of law which he reinforced by saying that 'so long as no personal injury is inflicted upon any member of the ruling race, this barbarism seems to be assured of perpetuity, making us ashamed to live under such an administration'.[35] However, Tagore never lost hope and believed that the time was not too far when humanism would triumph with the liquidation of forces responsible for harming human beings adversely. To exemplify his comment, he referred to the noble contribution of his British colleagues, the English reformer C.F. Andrews, the British philanthropist L.K. Elmhirst, among others, who left an impact on Tagore's approach to humanizing humanity. He admitted that their characters were 'without parallel—in no country or community he [had] come across such greatness of soul'.[36] Thus, Tagore explained a model which was based on his experiences; at one level, he drew on individual experiences; at another, he drew his conclusions which were applicable globally. To further illustrate the point, he expressed his disillusionment at the rise of

> the demon of barbarity [that] has given up all pretence and has emerged with unconcealed fangs, ready to tear up humanity in orgy of devastation. From one end of the world to the other the poisonous fumes of hatred have darkened the atmosphere. The spirit which perhaps lay dormant in the psychology of the West, has at least roused itself and desecrates the spirit of Man.[37]

Explicit here was his critique of Western civilization which was directly linked to his experiences of how European nations indulged in activities (and their own interests) leading to the devastation of humanity. This is a significant part of his assessment of how the Western civilization undertook a mission to mutilate humanity. However, he emphasized that,

> the crumbling ruins of a proud civilization strewn like a vast heap of futility, [he was not one those who] shall not commit the grievous sin of losing faith in Man; [rather] ... he would look forward to the opening of a new chapter in human history after the cataclysm is over and the atmosphere rendered clean with the spirit of service and sacrifice. ... A day will [therefore] come ... when the vanquished Man will retrace his path of conquest, despite all barriers, to win back his lost human heritage.[38]

Notwithstanding his disenchantment with the rise of violence leading to the crash of humanity, Tagore was not in agreement with the claim that human civilization was on the verge of collapse even though the nature of violence and the application of lethal weapons to destroy the enemies in the Second World War made many believe that it was the end of human civilization. Tagore had the foresight to argue that man would reclaim his space by privileging humanity over anything else. In other words, despite devastation, Tagore's confidence prevailed and many forces congregated to protect humanity, which reaffirmed that humanity reigned supreme even in adverse situations.

Although in his lecture, Tagore focused on the decadence of humanity at the global level, he also made passing references to the sociocultural prejudices happily nurtured by caste Hindus in India. As long as this permanent division was allowed to survive, humanity would remain closeted and compartmentalized between superior and inferior segments in society. In this manner, apart from highlighting how the globally powerful nations continued to assert their authorities over the weak, he also condemned the indigenous modes permanently partitioning humanity on the basis of accident of birth. His writing was therefore illustrative of humanistic concerns. Two points need reiteration to show that Tagore's dilemma over the assessment of the role of Western civilization was based on his actual reading of how it evolved at the cost of humanity, and how humankind reclaimed its legitimate space from those who fulfilled their exclusive interests. Being an innovative thinker, Tagore happily changed his ideational appreciation of the Western civilization as soon as it ceased to be humanistic; it only shows that his conceptualization of humanizing humanity was not based on derivative conceptual parameters, but was an offshoot of his dialectical interaction with the context which shaped his mode of thinking decisively.

The Religion of Man (1930)

First delivered as the Hibbert Lecture at Oxford in 1930, Tagore later developed this in the form of long essay focusing on what should be the religion of man. Although he articulated his view in *The Crisis in Civilization*, it was in the Hibbert Lecture that he developed the foundational concepts of thinking vis-à-vis humanity. Instead of comprehending the phenomenon in its conventional sense, he referred to those values, and ideational visions which helped man understand the organic link with humanity. There are two distinct components in this essay: one, he questioned how religiosity did not mean compliance with well-defined instructions by human beings, and two, he emphasized that religion denoted observance of concerns which were useful to uphold humanity regardless of sociocultural differences. His idea was of appreciation for a human collective that remained indivisible. Tagore questioned the institutionalized religion which, by championing exclusivity, created a fissure between human beings in terms of sociocultural and spatial distance. Based on this assumption, he also made a point about *Vedas* and *Upanishads*. According to him,

> *Upanishads* contained messages … which still illuminate humanity [because] … they are not associated with any religion, but they have the breadth of a universal soil that can supply with living sap all religions which have any spiritual ideal hidden at their core. … *Upanishads* are based not upon theological reasoning, but on experience of spiritual life. … Moreover, the *Upanishads* do not represent the spiritual experience of any one great individual, but of a great age of enlightenment which has a complex and collective manifestation, like that of the starry world. As a result, different creeds may find their sustenance from them, but never can set sectarian boundaries round them.[39]

The above is Tagore's critique to those who associated *Upanishads* with Hinduism which Tagore found ridiculous since a careful dissection of these texts reveals that they neither corresponded with Old and New Testaments nor with the Quran for two fundamental reasons; first, the Christian and Islamic religious texts were about a single individual and his contributions to these particular religions and were also about a particular phase of human history. So, they were individual centric and space driven texts. Contrarily, neither the *Vedas* nor the *Upanishads* were about an individual or a particular phase of human history. As Tagore rightly claimed, they were historical documentaries of human civilization codified by many people in different phases. civilization. Second, as these texts documented human history, they were to be treated at par with Old and New Testaments or Quran or, any religious texts. Hence, the argument that none of them could be linked with an individual or with a specific phase of history does not seem to be exaggerated. In other words, the argument offered by Tagore was to challenge the Christian claim that Christianity was humane and non-segregationist which were highlighted time and again by the Christian missionaries once they were deployed to expand the religion of the ruling classes. As evident in history, the British colonizers expanded their sphere of influence by force and by conversion of Hindus into Christians. Many lower caste Hindus accepted Christianity to avoid atrocities from the colonizers and to accrue benefits by being religiously congruent with those in power.

Tagore's argument has substance. At one level, he defended the claim that the *Vedas* and the *Upanishads* were not religious texts like the Bible or the Quran, but, historical documents which people in various phases of human development articulated. The idea gained prominence because as a Brahmo he read these ancient texts in a different light completely. Opposed to customary practices, the Brahmos were inclined towards

Christian deism since the Brahmo Samaj was founded by Rammohun Roy in 1928. Tagore's father and grandfather carried forward the Brahmo tradition long after the death of Rammohun Roy. At another level, Tagore, after having read the texts in Sanskrit, realized that what he internalized as a Brahmo, was true in spirit which convinced him further that without comprehending them, the idea of India remained incomplete presumably because, as he argued, without accepting that *Vedas* and *Upanishads* were continuity of human history, the study of the unfolding of humanity remained incomplete.

Tagore accepted humanistic ideational visions but never rejected the ideas he inherited by being a colonized subject. As mentioned, being receptive to the Western discourses for some of the fundamental principles of humanism, he accorded equal importance by highlighting their role in advancing humanity. The argument was however qualified the same discourse endorsed human atrocities in the colonial world, which confirms that it was limited in its appeal for there no was scope for universal humanism. The essay, *The Religion of Man* was a campaign Tagore undertook to champion universal humanism, and challenge the global forces seeking to permanently segment humanity.

Tagore was surprised by the endorsement of human atrocities by the same Western discourses which also championed humanity. The essay was also an optimistic statement as it was a temporary phase because humanism, with its inherent strength, always had the potential to rise again. Ideationally, the essay did not seem to be novel for it was a reinforcement of the vision that he championed in his literary and creative texts. As emphasized, Tagore was guided by his unconditional faith in universal humanism unlike Gandhi, who nurtured views contrary to what he upheld because he was a political leader. For example, Gandhi who was a priest of nonviolence asked his followers to adopt any means they preferred for fulfilling their politico-ideological objective, as the 1942 Quit India epitomized. Tagore however never fumbled or deviated from his ideational goal of universal humanism regardless of the consequences.

Tagore's conceptualization of *The Religion of Man* was a critique of the reconceptualization of humanity at the behest of the strongest. With his unconditional faith in humanity, Tagore believed that this phase was ephemeral as history was witness. Furthermore, it was reinforced by his visit to many countries in Asia, Europe, and America. Once Visva-Bharati was founded in 1921 as a centre of learning and an alternative to English education, he was convinced that he was correct in upholding the view that humanity was indivisible. He received support from his

British friends in building and strengthening Visva-Bharati, and there were many well-wishers in various parts of the world who came forward to help him in his venture. Visva-Bharati became a global institution of ideas which Tagore evolved by highlighting how he viewed humanity. The religion of man and the growth of humanity were dialectically linked because the former was dependent on the appreciation of the latter. Tagore's optimism was not groundless because the cyclical movement of human history. This was articulated by the British writer P.B. Shelley by emphasizing that 'if winter comes can spring be far behind'.

Dissection of the Essay, *The Religion of Man*

In a preliminary reading, one may misconstrue the essay to be about religion and its evolution in different phases of human civilization. A deeper reading reveals that it was Tagore's conceptualization of civilization and its unfolding and evolution in conjunction with the battle for setting out processes for humanizing humanity. Tagore argued that,

> our civilization, in the constant struggle for a great Further, runs through abrupt chapters of spasmodic divergencies. It nearly begins its new ventures with a cataclysm; for its changes are not mere seasonal changes of ideas gliding through varied periods of flowers and fruit. They are surprises lying in ambuscade provoking revolutionary adjustments. ... Also, however violent may the revolutions happening in whatever time or country, they never completely detach themselves from a common cause. They find their places in a history which is one.[40]

There are three core ideas which Tagore articulated in his essay. First, this essay is not only an attempt to understand how humanity evolved, but also a comment on the processes leading to a specific way in which human civilization changed throughout history. Tagore believed that humanity was hardly static and it had characteristics which needed to be understood contextually. Secondly, transformation in human civilization did not follow a pattern since changes were an outcome of revolutionary intervention by human beings, meaning those who were status-quoist were replaced by transformations. The reason was obvious; human civilization was always receptive to revolutionary metamorphosis of the prevalent human relationships in order accommodate new sociocultural and politico-ideological forces. Finally, Tagore held the view that human civilization reformed due to sudden and abrupt changes which were disruptive, but brought about changes for humanity. This was inconceivable because human cycle kept on moving for 'a great Further', as per him. So, in his perception, *The Religion of Man* was a constantly evolving mode to conceptualize changes in humanity.

How was it possible for Tagore to evolve such a conceptually provocative formulation? He responded by saying that he was born in a family that never imposed any ideational values by forces. His father introduced him to India's ancient texts, *Vedas* and *Upanishads*, but never insisted on accepting them, and he 'refused to accept any religious teaching merely because people in [his] surroundings believed it to be true [since he] could not persuade [himself] to imagine that [he] had a religion [as] everybody whom [he] might trust believed in its value'.[41] Given the fact that he was nurtured in an atmosphere of freedom when faith was concerned, he argued that in his upbringing, he was unrestricted from 'the dominance of any creed that had its sanction in the definite authority of some scripture, or in the teaching of some organized body of worshippers'.[42] Tagore deftly bought India's situation to the centre, an India Tagore in India which was famous for being 'orthodox and sectarian'. A Renaissance man, Tagore questioned clinging to the tradition as a surrender to beliefs which were neither meaningful in the changed sociocultural milieu nor persuasive. He was fiercely critical of them because, 'the mechanical spirit of tradition is essentially materialistic',[43] and he further added that 'it is blindly pious but not spiritual, obsessed by phantoms of unreason that haunt feeble minds in the ghastly disguise of religion. For our soul is shrunken when allow foolish days to weave repeated patterns of unmeaning meshes round all departments of life'.[44] As evident here, he attributed his development as an independent thinker to the environment in which he was raised which helped him build a critical mindset to reject prejudiced traditions. He also championed the view that in order to get out of the web of unreason, one was required to be critical of impacted growth of human civilization.

Thus, man's religion could never be static because it was the beginning of human decay, and it needed to be combatted for strengthening values contributing to humanity. To demonstrate his point, Tagore referred to an *Upanishadic* parable highlighting two birds sitting on the same branch, one had food and the other looked at him. As per the *Upanishads*, the enjoyments of the bird with the food and the other one enjoying since the former was satisfied, were different. Human beings housed both these birds: the bird who derived pleasure by eating was equal to those who satisfied themselves by fulfilling their goal while the bird who was happy by watching the happiness of the other had 'expressed disinterested vision of joy'.[45] On this basis, Tagore clarified that as long as human beings remained committed to the fulfilment of their exclusive goal, they could hardly be useful for taking humanity further because they were unable to think beyond certain boundaries. The *mantra* for human beings to flourish allowed them to be sensitive to others, despite not being related, but in the sense that they all belonged to humanity. What should have been critical was to adapt to human life. As per Tagore, unlike the bees who enjoy being together in a hive, human beings prefer to live in opposition to others as soon as their interests were adversely affected. Here, Tagore referred to the impact of colonialism on humanity. As history depicts, European colonization was governed by forcibly capturing countries, and by completely ignoring the devastating outcome of their intervention on humanity. Condemning 'the recklessly anti-human colonial design',[46] he identified one of the major reasons for his powerful critique of the sustenance of colonial rule in India by being brutal and harsh on many occasions.

Tagore's essay, *The Religion of Man* provides a discourse on freedom which was not freedom in his sense because the conceptual parameter, independence, did not entail harmony of relationship. Tagore argued 'we realize not through out response to it in knowing, but in being'.[47] So long as human communion was not attained, we would 'remain away from freedom [which] … awaits us there where we reach truth, not through feeling it by our senses or knowing it by our reason, but through the union of perfect sympathy'.[48] There are two major arguments here, he made it clear that freedom was not the true path for universal humanism; because human beings nurtured a narrow vision of humanity till they realized the importance of taking care of other fellow beings. This was articulated with the rise of colonial powers and decline of the core values of how conceptualize humanity. To Tagore emphasized that humanity was not just a collective of human beings, but it also represented those exalted objectives contributing to the rise of humanity as one. *The Religion of Man* was a clear call for humanity to rise and prosper in an unfavourable national and global milieu. A born crusader against the tendencies belittling humanity Tagore held the view that regardless of relentless attacks on humanity, it would rise from the ashes. This is also expressed by him as

> age follows age in human history, and man continues in his ceaseless search, not for the satisfaction of his material needs, but in order to strive with all his might for the revelation of the Universal Man in the world of men, to rescue his own inmost truth from the crude obstacles set up by himself. … The strain of his sorrow and suffering has been infinite, but they mark his strong perseverance to shatter the bonds of his imprisoned ideals.[49]

A careful reading of the above discussion helps to understand how Tagore conceptualized his ideational vision for humanizing humanity. In view of his firm belief that humanity was indivisible he voiced his displeasure against the British colonialism, or, for that matter, any of the institutional arrangements partitioning humanity. This argument had wider implications because he attacked colonizers from both outside and inside who tended to devise a social system with carefully nurtured sociocultural prejudices against a section of humanity. There were many instances of human setbacks; but history was also full of examples demonstrating that human ability knew no bounds. It meant that dehumanizing humanity was an aberration of history since forces for humanizing humanity always prevailed by defeating those holding contrarian politico-ideological priorities.

Concluding Observations

Rabindranath Tagore was a thinker who expressed his distinct politico-ideological priorities in different intellectual formats: creative literary writings and innovative essays with clearly-defined objectives. By concentrating on his critical essays, the chapter shows that he never lost sight of his main concern in a world that was divided due to the desire of a section of humanity to enslave the rest. Like his novels that were vehicles of his ideational vision, his essays represent a new way of reaching out to readers to spread the view that he held so dear to him throughout his public career. Hence, it is wrong to reduce Tagore to just a littérateur in view of the socio-political messages which he articulated very clearly in all his intellectual creations. His versatility was evident. It was easier for him to convey what he felt when he witnessed the rise of nationalism guided by selfish desires of those who were unfamiliar with his idea of universal humanism.

An analytical scan of Tagore's creative essays reveals that Tagore was one of those patriots who, despite not having taken part in the nationalist struggle, always championed their cause as it was supportive of how he conceptualized humanity. Each of his essays was an effort towards building and substantiating the core argument of his creative works. His impact was immense worldwide; in fact, it will not be an exaggeration to suggest that he swayed public opinion in the world against the torturous British rule, and against those aggressive nations that always privileged the deployment of coercive means to forcefully execute plans to fulfil their self-governed motives. In view of his critiques Tagore successfully created an acceptable space in various Western countries which gradually became a platform for organizing campaigns to contain forces contrary to human well-being.

The three essays in this chapter stand out because they voiced Tagore's relentless opposition to tendencies thriving at the cost of humanity. The 1916 essays on Nationalism were a challenge to states that preferred war because it was a means to successfully pursue their objectives. It was also a powerful critique of those Indians who, by being servile to the alien politico-ideological inclinations, struck at the foundation of the patriotic initiatives of those championing India's political emancipation. Additionally, it was a well-argued conceptual piece exposing the limitations of the concept of nation as an inspiring parameter. The second essay, *The Crisis in Civilization*, focused on how Tagore transformed from being an admirer of British civilization to a critic of the Empire because he was disappointed at how the rulers executed policies in their colonies. colonized. By focusing on the crises in contemporary civilization, he felt that industrialization became a menace to human civilization since it was seized by those who cared only for their benefits and gains. The essay, entitled *The Religion of Man* was written in a wider canvas. As discussed at length, this essay unequivocally put how the deviation of humankind from the core values of humanity led to insurmountable problems, and the solution of which required collective intervention; which seemed impossible so long as human beings remained divided horizontally and vertically. The essay had tremendous impact on the global opinion since it was first delivered as a lecture at Oxford University in 1930 which spread his arguments in the world almost instantaneously. Tagore put in clear terms his spiritual priorities by suggesting that he derived his foundational ideas about humanity from Indian ancient texts of *Upanishads*. His explanation for his uncritical acceptance of these texts which were wrongly associated with Hinduism shows that for him they were historical documentaries of past human civilization; they neither drew on the heroic struggle of an individual or a description of a great age when a particular religion struck organic roots. Instead, they were written by many in a differently-textured phase of human civilization. This was perhaps one of the most creatively-articulated argument challenging the conventional assessment of these historical documentaries which provoked many to view them differently. Hence, *The Religion of Man* can be said to have laid the foundation for universal humanism. We must add a caveat here. With his recognition in the West once he was awarded the Nobel Prize, he gained a global audience that helped him assess the Indian question in terms of his own ideational vision.

There is no denying that these essays stand out as they were tuned to Tagore's definitive politico-ideological preferences. Under no circumstances did he deviate from this fundamental goal since he felt that there was no adequate critique of the rising cruelty at the behest of the industrially-advanced countries. Many Western thinkers pointed out industrialism debased humanity; Tagore, by joining hands with them, became the Eastern voice which gradually spread to the rest of the world. Thus, he Tagore played a critical role in developing a humanistic language which was hardly known to the rest of the world. It was not language of nationalism, but one of accepting humanity as one regardless of class, race and ethnicity. The divisive designs which Tagore characterised as an aberration of history, needed to be combatted effectively to prevent the recalcitrant nations from undertaking feats contrary to humanity. His views were based on goals for safeguarding humanity and for spreading the message of 'living together separately.' Tagore represented a global voice in favour of universal humanism which was flattened by a section of humanity by undertaking exercises seeking to demean his life-long mission. Nonetheless, by being committed to universal humanism, he was not only a source of encouragement as long as he was active but even after his demise, his endeavour at championing universal humanism continues to remain as inspiration as it was in the past.

Part B

M.K. Gandhi (1869–1948)

Mohandas Karamchand Gandhi (1869–1948), also known as the Mahatma, charted a new course for human salvation by introducing nonviolent resistance against the brutal forces seeking to dehumanize humanity. He realized that since violence produced violence, it was required to be completely avoided to safeguard humanity. This was one of the reasons for accepting nonviolence as a creed of his struggle against the imposed alien authority. It was a unique method of combatting the mightiest colonial power of the twentieth century. To his credit, he not only mobilized a large section of Indians for the battle, he also persuaded many world leaders to adopt nonviolent resistance against the enemy. During his sojourn of twenty-one years in South Africa he challenged the racist South African government for being discriminatory against the local Zulus and the migrant Indians. Despite being ruthless in combatting those who challenged the political authority, he never allowed his followers to become violent. In fact, he first experimented with nonviolent resistance in South Africa which later became famous globally as *Satyagraha*. The expression was an outcome of an essay competition which the weekly *Indian Opinion* conducted in South Africa and out of the essays, the idea of *Satyagraha* emerged which immediately received Gandhi's approbation.

Gandhi's South African experience helped him develop a conceptual framework for helping humanity. Like Tagore, he also believed in universal humanism with one major difference since he was keen to hit the British adversely. Being involved in sustained struggle on many occasions, Gandhi never appreciated violence while challenging the authorities because it was contrary to the core values of his politico-ideological priorities. His primary objective was to eliminate personal and communal animosity because he, like Tagore, believed that humanity was indivisible. So, no adverse attack was permissible so long as he led the anti-British campaign.

Gandhi was ideologically indebted to thinkers like the Russian pacifist Leo Tolstoy, the British socialist John D. Ruskin and the American exponent of nonviolence H.D. Thoreau. Except Thoreau, none of them were activists in the actual sense of the term. Thoreau was the only person who opposed the aggressive US government when a part of Mexico—which later became the US province Arizona—was annexed. Not only did he stop paying taxes, he also launched a nonviolent campaign against the government which undertook activities that resulted in the killing of human beings to satisfy the desires of those wielding power and authority. Despite being arrested, he never deviated from his espoused mode of combatting the deviant government. Gandhi in the twentieth century India employed nonviolent opposition to the British authority despite continuous provocation by the agents of the British government.

A study of his campaign in South Africa and later in India reveals that, to him, the commitment to nonviolence was prior to human emancipation. As he believed means to be primary and ends secondary, he went to the extent of withdrawing a successful campaign during the 1920–1922 Non-cooperation phase since the volunteers or the *Satyagrahees* turned violent which he defined later as a Himalayan blunder. Nonetheless, there is no denying that the Mahatma was a strong believer in nonviolence and he remained so till he died in 1948.

One fundamental point that needs attention was his argument that nonviolence could never succeed unless one nurtured nonviolence internally. This is a fundamental precept of Gandhi's model of humanizing humanity. He believed, as long as human beings were not completely free from violent mindsets, it was difficult to make them nonviolent. In other words, one needed to be nonviolent by internalizing values to its support; unless this was done, imposition of nonviolence from above would not yield results. So, Gandhi approached nonviolence at two levels, at the micro level, he strongly felt that violence needed to be abjured completely and the sentiments in its favour were required to be completely done away with. At the macro level, especially when the volunteers took part in the nonviolent struggle, they should never indulge in attacking the perpetrators violently. A *Satyagrahee* needed to be taught how to inflict pain on themselves and yet, never take out their anger on those who were responsible for wrecking violence on those involved in nonviolent struggle.

One must not however draw a conclusion that the Gandhi-led nonviolent struggle was the only resistance the British rule confronted. It has already been shown in contemporary research on the nature of Indian nationalism that Gandhi's intervention had had its wider ramification and many other campaigns even without being nonviolent also acted positively in India's nationalist onslaught against the alien authority. There is an argument that the Gandhian nationalism provided too wide a template to accommodate many diverse streams of thoughts questioning British colonialism. As contemporary evidence demonstrates, Gandhi reigned supreme since he took over the leadership of the campaign under the Indian National Congress. With his rise on the Indian scene he gathered many Indians which made it possible for him to organize a gigantic struggle against the conquerors.

Gandhi owed his success to the formulation of an agenda that immediately attracted many Indians to join him. For instance, the 1930–1932 Civil Disobedience Movement gained momentum partly because of the success of the Congress activists in raising a corps of volunteers for the cause, and partly due to the selection of the violation of the Salt Act, which prohibited Indians to prepare salt without paying a tax. It was an attempt by the government to take away the rights of the people to prepare salt out of sea water with no tax to the government. For the people, especially in the coastal areas, it was an attack on their daily existence and an unwarranted intervention which, as the *Satyagrahees* felt, needed to be resisted.

There are two chapters in this part that dwell on how Gandhi conceptualized and executed his design of humanizing humanity by undertaking steps to challenge efforts towards dehumanizing humanity. As mentioned above, Gandhi was an activist-theoretician, which means that he theorized his ideas on the basis of his dialectical interaction with the prevalent socio-economic realities and politico-ideological priorities. The first chapter in this part, by dealing with the campaigns he led since he rose to prominence in Indian political scene, argues that Gandhi, by being involved in anti-British campaign, articulated a new mode of challenging the perpetrators of violence. Interestingly, Gandhi was aware of sociocultural prejudices of many Hindus against Muslims and vice versa; but his opposition to internal social division impaired his attempt at developing India as a collective, did not appear to be as fierce as was expected. This was perhaps because it was likely to weaken the nationalist platform which was dominated by caste Hindus. The second chapter is meant to show how he conceptualized humanity as a whole on the basis of his stern critique of industrialization and Western civilization because he believed that the brutal character was largely due to the deliberate desire for expansion of market. The aim here is to demonstrate that Gandhi was a product of both theory and practice. Being influenced by Tolstoy, Ruskin, and Thoreau, he adopted nonviolence which was complemented by being grounded in principles championed by Hinduism, Buddhism, and Jainism. One is convinced to argue that Gandhi's approach to humanizing humanity was based on multiple philosophical sources, both Western and indigenous. One is required to go deep into the philosophical discourses which materialized in *Satyagraha* or nonviolent resistance.

3

Campaigns for Humanizing Humanity

Gandhi was a political activist who believed that it was possible to drive the British out of the country only by launching a fierce political campaign. His mode of nonviolent resistance was derived from internalization of ideas of Leo Tolstoy, John D. Ruskin, H.D. Thoreau, among others, as well as from indigenous intellectual discourses, including those stemming out of the texts critical to Hinduism, Buddhism and Jainism. In a world where violence was predominant, Gandhi championed nonviolent ethics which, he was persuaded to believe, was a necessity to sustain humanity from being harmed. Gandhi's model was unlike that of his predecessors, who evolved a model of freedom struggle drawn on means which did not completely preclude the utilization of violence, if necessary. For them, means did not appear as critical as it was to Gandhi. In his perception, struggle against the enemy should never be violent and it was possible once the participants learnt how-to take-out anger from within oneself. In other words, one needed to have a violence-free mindset and only then was one equipped to take part in the struggle that Gandhi spearheaded, first in South Africa and then in India.

A perusal of Gandhi's campaign against brutalized political authority reveals that he never deviated from nonviolence while challenging a well-equipped public authority. There were many reasons for his conviction. The most prominent one was his steadfast commitment to nonviolence as a creed. For him, to be a *Satyagrahee* in its undiluted connotation, was to be in complete compliance with the basic creed of nonviolence. This was the only criterion for being a participant in the Gandhi-led struggle. As means were prior to the ends, Gandhi was never persuaded to give up his faith in nonviolence. A committed priest of nonviolence, the Mahatma was even ready to halt a campaign, as it happened with the 1920–1922 Non-cooperation Movement, since the volunteers resorted to violence which ran counter to Mahatma's belief.

Based on his assessment that the foreign rulers would remain brutal and torturous so long as no resistance was mounted, he launched *Satyagraha* in South Africa during his sojourn of nearly twenty-one years (1893–1914) which helped the migrant Indians fulfil many of their long-standing socio-political demands, as will be shown below. This was the first phase of his nonviolent campaign which unfolded in a foreign soil. With the inauguration of a nonviolent campaign against the racist South African government, Gandhi ushered in a new chapter in human history. He demonstrated that against the effort at dehumanizing humanity, there were means to humanize humanity. It signified that the former was an exception to the rule as human history confirmed that whenever there were attempts at ruining humanity, forces for its sustenance emerged and succeeded in defeating the contrarian tendencies at jeopardizing humanity. With this faith in his mind, Gandhi was hardly scared of the well-equipped South African government and those with racist prejudices against the migrant Indians and the local Zulus.

Was the battle against the forces that continued the debasement of humanity evenly poised? A surface reading of how those championing humanity suffered may lead one to answer in affirmative although a detailed elaboration of the combat between good and evil reveals that it was not so. That is to say, those with ill motives against humanity succeeded temporarily, but, ultimately, a sustained struggle against these forces resulted in pushing out the evil successfully. A detailed analysis reveals that a battle which was fought to establish immorality was likely to be defeated regardless of the circumstances. The global history is a testimony of the claim. For instance, the 1779 American Revolution and the 1789 French Revolution brought about radical changes since people *en masse* participated in the battle against injustice; a long-drawn struggle against slavery in the US culminated in the adoption of the 1893 Emancipation Act which legally banished slavery from the US. These are examples to demonstrate that individuals with ulterior motives were certain to disappear as history demonstrated although in each of these revolutions, violence played a critical part. Gandhi was the first person who made the world realize that nonviolence could also be as effective as violent onslaught on the evil doers. This was preferred to violent campaign, argued Gandhi because human cost was negligible if not nothing which meant that in a violent struggle, both the fronts suffered due to heavy causalities while this was not the case vis-à-vis nonviolent movements. By countering the well-equipped state machineries in South Africa and India with nonviolence, Gandhi proved that it was not just a religious dictum with no substance; it could easily be a device to liberate the hapless human beings provided they also imbibed nonviolence both as a spirit and an effective design for fighting their battle.

A scan of the movements that unfolded with Gandhi at the helm of affairs underlines that he was actively involved in campaigns in South

Africa in the late nineteenth and early twentieth centuries. On his return to India in 1914, he was involved in the struggle against British colonialism where he again experimented with nonviolence while seeking to win political freedom from the British yoke. There was, of course, a major difference since in South Africa, he fought for the rights of the migrant Indians and he was concerned about the local Zulus who were equally subjected to inhuman torture by the racist South African government. In India, he launched a fierce nonviolent campaign which drew a majority of the Indians, barring, of course, the Muslims who had a separate agenda during the freedom struggle which they articulated in their claim for a sovereign Muslim state or Pakistan. Despite the differences in the nature of the struggles that evolved at the behest of Gandhi, there was, of course, a striking similarity: in both South Africa and India, he deployed nonviolent means to fulfil his ideational vision. It was a vision championing specific politico-ideological priorities drawing on nonviolence. Under no circumstances, was he ready to sacrifice his commitment to nonviolence even though many of his compatriots did not always agree with him; but his capacity to remain as a leader of the masses defused the challenges to his unquestionable authority over his colleagues in mainstream nationalism.

As the chapter is about the means which helped Gandhi achieve his objective for emancipating the enslaved section of humanity, it is divided into two complementary components. Given the fact that he laid the foundation of nonviolent struggle in South Africa, the first part of this chapter is a detailed analysis of how he charted out a new narrative for humanity based on his belief in nonviolent resistance. In other words, it was a resistance he organized, the basis of which was nonviolence. His success in wresting demands from the racist South African government caught the entire world by surprise. The second part begins with Gandhi's arrival in India in 1914 which heralded another chapter in India's freedom struggle. As shown in the available printed monographs, with the foundation of the Indian National Congress, India's campaign for political freedom was institutionalized: the first phase was dominated by the Moderates who believed in liberal-constitutional means and that India's liberation was possible only with the support of British colonizers. In contrast to the Moderates, the New Nationalists, led by Lala Lajpat Rai, Bal Gangadhar Tilak and Bipin Chandra Pal accepted passive resistance as a means to gain *swaraj*; they were different from the erstwhile Moderates since they were also ready to apply violence in case it was necessary to attain the goal. With Gandhi on India's political horizon, the entire scene underwent a sea change. The country was baptized in nonviolence with Gandhi being the principal priest. The second part thus dwells on those regional and pan-Indian campaigns that evolved under Gandhi's stewardship since 1919 Champaran *Satyagraha*.

Besides seeking to show how nonviolence became an effective means, the aim of the chapter is also to demonstrate the nature of Gandhian leadership. Gandhi remained supreme; but there were many Gandhians across India who led the campaign in accordance with what they learnt from the Mahatma. The chapter thus provides an argument that even in the absence of Gandhi in many areas of India, he acted as a source of inspiration to those fighting for the goal which the Mahatma so assiduously championed regardless of the consequences. The chapter also admits that there were many political outfits that held different ideational perspectives, and yet, it was the Gandhi-led mainstream nationalism which was always predominant in India's struggle for freedom.

Emergence of a Nonviolent Crusader

Before we embark on an analysis of how Gandhi fought the battle in South Africa for humanizing humanity, let us focus on an incident which radically altered his future from being a lawyer to a relentless crusader. The Maritzburg incident which was a manifestation of how Gandhi suffered due to the colour prejudices of the train conductor when he was on his way to Pretoria from Durban in a winter month. He was thrown out of a first-class compartment despite having bought a ticket for the same to accommodate a white passenger. For the first time, he saw how racism worked in a racially segregated country. While describing the incident and how he felt, he thus mentioned that he had two options: one was to go back to Bombay after finishing the legal battle and led a happy life or to stay back to fight against racism. According to him, this incident created an aspiration to fight back the racist regime; he explained this by remarking that his return to Bombay was nothing but cowardice because,

> the hardship to which [he] was subjected was superficial—only a symptom of the deep disease of colour prejudice. [hence, he] should try, if possible, to root out the disease and suffer hardship in the process. Redress for wrongs I should seek only to the extent that would be necessary for the removal of colour prejudice.[1]

It was clearly stated that Gandhi prepared himself for the ensuing battle against the racist regime because that was his choice regardless of the consequences. He also realized that it was not possible for him and his Indian colleagues to try options other than nonviolence because the state was powerful enough to muzzle their voice as soon as it was raised. Hence, he resorted to nonviolence because the state had never experienced nonviolent resistance and those managing the state were equally bewildered to contain the nonviolent resistors. So, in so far as strategy was concerned, Gandhi succeeded at the outset since the state was clueless on how to combat the opponent who remained nonviolent. To his followers, he appeared to have won in securing their support. Long after his South African sojourn, he stated how he felt when began nonviolent struggle in South Africa, to a group of students in a province in the southern tip of India, Madras. In his account, the author, R.K. Narayan reminisced that to convince his followers in South Africa, he exhorted that before you aspire to root out racial prejudices,

> you must drive every vestige of violence from your system [because] … it was not going to be a fight with sticks and knives or guns but with love. Until you are sure you have an overpowering love at heart for your enemy, don't come forward. You must gradually forget the term 'enemy'. You must think of him as a friend who must be loved. You must train yourself to become a hundred per cent *ahimsa* soldier. You must become so sensitive that it is not possible for you to wear sandals made of the hide of slaughtered animals; you should prefer to go barefoot rather than wear the hide of an animal killed for your sake, that is if you are unable to secure the skin of an animal that has died a natural death.[2]

Intrinsic here is perhaps the most well-articulated description of Gandhi's nonviolent resistance. There are three important features of how the Mahatma viewed his mode of opposition: first, under no circumstances, a *Satyagrahee* never nurtures enmity for his/her opponent which connotes that political enmity does not entail animosity between two individuals. By implication, Gandhi wanted to inculcate a sense of bonhomie despite being politically opposed to one another. Secondly, while identifying the means, the Mahatma privileged love, care, compassion, and empathy. Here one is reminded of Tolstoy's conceptualization of enemy being treated as friends; only then, human society would be immune from hatred and hostility. Finally, to illustrate his point, he also drew attention to an example. By asking *Satyagrahees* not to contribute to cow slaughter for preparing their sandals, he made a general point by requesting his followers to practice nonviolence in their day-to-day lives as well. Because if it was not followed in life, mere verbal commitment was futile and the purpose of nonviolent resistance was certain to be defeated.

Unfolding of the Campaign in South Africa

Once in South Africa, Gandhi began confronting the racist government. Within a week of his arrival in May 1893, while he was travelling from Durban to Pretoria, he was thrown out of a first-class railway compartment despite having a genuine ticket. It was very cold night and he suffered terribly in the waiting room at Maritzburg station. In his words, 'doubt took possession of my mind. Late at night, I came to the conclusion that to run back to India would be cowardly. I must accomplish what I had undertaken'.[3] He was bewildered at the outset, but was determined to fight. His experience at Charlestown, a rail terminus was not very different either. He took a stagecoach to reach Standerton. Here too, the white officials forced him to sit on the floor, and not on the seat for which he paid. His refusal to move out of his seat evoked anger and resulted in a physical assault on Gandhi. He had borne the beating but did not concede the demand. On arrival in Standerton, he narrated his experience to his Indian friends but was disappointed by their responses. According to them what had happened to him was not very unusual for the Indians in the Transvaal. He reported the incident to an agent of the coach company knowing fully well that no action was to be taken against the assailants. He continued his journey to Pretoria. He was denied a first-class ticket by the station master of Johannesburg who allowed him to buy it only after Gandhi defended his case by referring to railway rules and regulations. An argumentative Gandhi won the battle and began his journey for Pretoria. Here too, he was confronted with racist white South Africans and was about to be pushed out the compartment, but for the intercession of a European fellow passenger. This lone incident of kindness was significant in Gandhi's conceptualization of racism. It would be wrong to dismiss the entire white population as racist, he thus felt. The need of the hour was to put moral pressure on the white leadership to recognize the legitimate needs and demands of the coloured population.

The five days journey from Durban to Pretoria seemed to Gandhi to be one of the most creative experiences of his life. He saw racism in action. He was appalled by the fate of the Indian merchants who had learnt to swallow humiliation without protest. He pondered over and decided not to accept injustice as part of the natural or unnatural order of South Africa. He would challenge the atrocious policies of the government simply because they did not fit into the 'graceful' British empire. Racism had no legitimate place in the British Empire. Racism was a policy perfected by the rulers by taking full advantage of the ignorant

Indians who were not aware of their rights and duties under the empire. So, Gandhi realized that Indian settlers suffered largely since they were illiterate. Hence, he felt the need to have basic English education among the Indians. Moreover, Indians lost on several counts also because they were not organized and thus failed to fight the government as a group. He translated his ideas into practice once in Pretoria. He organized a meeting for Indians 'to present to them a picture of their conditions in Transvaal.' It was a grand success. He broached the idea of an organization and volunteered to teach English to the Indian merchants.

Gandhi was preparing Indians for a showdown with the government. The scene was not however favourable for two reasons: Transvaal, ruled by the Dutch, was a Boer state and hence was outside the orbit of the British Empire; and the Boer government had already chased a large contingent of Indian settlers out of the Orange Free State. Gandhi supported the British during the Boer war because this gesture, as he thought, would strengthen the case of the Indians in South Africa when they demanded fair deal in return. Hence despite his strong feeling against the racist South African government, Gandhi articulated his bitterness during the 1890s in a very mild language which upset his colleague. He defended his stance as a loyal subject of the British Empire by saying that

> [I]f an unflinching devotion to duty and extreme eagerness to serve our sovereign can make us of any use in the field of battle, we trust, we would not fail. The motive underlying this humble offer is to endeavour to prove that, in common with other subjects of the Queen Empress in South Africa, the Indians too, are ready to do duty for their Sovereign on the battlefield. The offer is meant to be an earnest of the Indian loyalty.[4]

'... the English-speaking Indians came to the conclusion that they would offer their services unconditionally and absolutely without payment ... in order to show the colonists that they were worthy subjects of the Queen.'[5]

Evident here is that Gandhi, who grew up in the tradition of loyalist discourse, justified his argument by reference to the duty of the subject race to the empire in crisis. Even as a subordinated nation, Gandhi demanded rights of South African Indians because as British subjects, Indians were entitled to rights. This is probably a watershed moment in Gandhi's political thinking, because he was no longer prepared to be unconditionally loyal to the British paramountcy. What can be argued here is that the South African experience appeared significant in identifying the limitations of a racist administration vis-à-vis the subject race. Here began the transformation of Gandhi from a loyalist to a most effective political leader, challenging the continuity of the Raj in the subcontinent of India by organizing a nonviolent mass campaign in opposition to the mighty imperial power, He did so by asserting, though within the constraints of bargaining and pressure politics, the subjects' right to rebel.

His first major encounter with colonial government came a year after his arrival in Durban in 1894. Gandhi found out that the Natal government was pushing a legislation to deprive Indians of the right to vote on grounds of race. He prepared his brief by reference to well-established British conventions and others canons of British jurisprudence. Conceding that 'disenfranchisement' was possible on property qualifications, Gandhi defended his argument as a loyal subject of the Empire by saying that as citizens of the Empire, discrimination against the Indians in South Africa was illegal and thus indefensible. He even suggested that the government might consider the scheme adopted in Cape Colony where voting rights were granted to those possessing property worth of 75 pounds and an annual income of 50 pounds. Despite the strength of the argument, Gandhi failed to persuade the government that adopted the Bill by simple majority in the Natal legislature. He did not concede defeat. Gandhi decided to send a petition to the colonial secretary in London. The petition had 10,000 signatures covering almost the entire population. Several copies of the petition were sent to prominent British politicians. Gandhi brought the event before the media in both Britain and Natal. The bill was finally blocked at Westminster and the Queen declined to give her consent, achieving the goal for which Gandhi fought. Two unique developments took place simultaneously. First, as mentioned earlier, Gandhi felt that the lack of an organization for the Indians in South Africa was one of the major weaknesses in their struggle. So, he launched the Natal Indian Congress in 1894. Despite having political goals, this was an organization which was devoted to the moral and social upliftment of its members. Gradually the Natal Congress became a lively forum for the Indian settlers and Gandhi was undoubtedly its galvanizing force. In fact, the reduction of the annual poll tax imposed on indentured Indian labourers from 25 pounds to 3 pounds was the first successful political agenda of the Natal Congress. The amount was enormous as it was not consummate with the average income of the labourers, as Gandhi argued. The second development was indicative of Gandhi's rise as a strategist. Gandhi was not allowed to practice in the Supreme Court because the Bar Society of Natal was opposed to his inclusion. Since Gandhi proved that the denial was reflective of racist bias against the Indians, the Chief Justice of the Supreme Court admitted him but in keeping with the etiquette of practicing barristers, ordered him to discard his turban in the court room. A change in Gandhi's attitude was noticeable. He had preferred to walk out of the court room a year ago when he was subjected to the same condition, but now, he conceded the restriction. Justifying his action as the most appropriate, Gandhi thus argued,

> I saw my limitations. The turban that I had insisted on wearing in the District Magistrate's Court I took off in obedience to the order of the Supreme Court. Not that if I had resisted the order the resistance could not have been justified. But I wanted to reserve my strength for fighting bigger battles.[6]

On his return to Durban in December, 1896 after a brief visit to India, Gandhi experienced another racist attack against him and those with him in the ship that was to anchor in Durban. A crowd of more than 3,000 had congregated to prevent him and fellow Indian passengers from landing in the port. The crowd resolved to 'burn Gandhi [since] he has vilified [white South Africans] in South Africa and wants to flood Natal with Indians'.[7] Gandhi was saved by the wife of Mr. RC Alexander, the old and 'popular' superintendent of Police of Durban. The scene was so inflammatory that Gandhi had 'almost given up the hope of reaching home alive'.[8] Finally with the support of Mrs. Alexander, he escaped in the disguise of a constable.

The more the racist attacks on Gandhi, the stronger he became in his determination and will. When in 1906, the colonial government sought to impose the Transvaal Asiatic Law Amendment Ordinance which required all Indians to register again, Gandhi immediately resorted to action. This Ordinance was a continuity of the 1885 Boer legislation that set up a register of Asiatics. According to this legislation, Indians were legally bound to give their 'thumbprint' to obtain the right of residence. The same restriction was sought to be reimposed. This Ordinance was also more draconian than its earlier counterpart in the sense that it insisted on finger-printing of all ten fingers. In addition, failure to register would immediately lead to fines, jail or deportation. Not only was the proposed step most humiliating to the Indians, but it also disillusioned Gandhi, who thought that his support to the British in the Boer War would at least change the governmental attitude toward Indians. To register their protest, Indians in Johannesburg gathered at the English Theatre on 11 September 1906. It was resolved that nobody would submit to this legislation. Gandhi was inspired and found resources for his monograph entitled *Satyagraha* in South Africa. Interestingly, Gandhi still did not lose faith in the British jurisprudence, as he challenged the legislation on grounds of fair play to the subjects of the crown. His statements in the meeting however also revealed that Gandhi was also being graduated as a rebel against colonial rule. It was evident when Gandhi welcomed imprisonment for his protest against the Immigration Restriction Act of 1907. Once it was made a law—which came to be known as the Black Act—he launched a protest movement by refusing to register. After he was released, he went to London to persuade the government to allow at least the educated Indians to enter Transvaal. But the racist South African government would not relent. Gandhi was disillusioned for the empire was now seen as offering slavery, not partnership.

The opposition to the Black Act contributed to Gandhi's conceptualization of the *Satyagraha*. During the Transvaal civil rights campaign (1907–1913), he had an opportunity to test and refine his unique protest movement, known as *Satyagraha* that had already gained momentum. Two issues figured prominently during this phase of *Satyagraha*: abolition of the Black Act and removal of restrictions on the entry of Indians into Transvaal. The colonial government reacted immediately by verbally assuring to review the Black Act, provided Indians registered voluntarily. Trusting the government, Gandhi thus urged fellow Indians by saying that 'we must register voluntarily to show that we do not intend to bring a single Indian into the Transvaal scrumptiously or by fraud.[9] Gandhi was befooled. Indians registered but the Black Law was hardly outlawed. Gandhi's response to the government betrayal was the famous incident on 16 August 1908 when, outside the Hamidia Mosque in Johannesburg, thousands of the registration certificates, old as well as new, were burned.

A controversy arose over a judgment of the Cape Supreme Court that derecognized Indian marriages since they were not registered as they were in South Africa. There was no law for the registration of ordinary marriages in India and validity of these marriages was never questioned earlier. With Searle judgment, these marriages were made null and void since they were beyond the pale of legal marriages in South Africa. The consequence of this judgment was disastrous because it 'nullified in South Africa,' argued Gandhi, 'all marriages celebrated according to the Hindu, *Mussalman* and Zoroastrian rites.'[10] The many married Indian women thus 'ceased to rank as wives of their husbands and were degraded to the rank of concubines while their progeny were deprived of their right to inherit the parents' property'. Such an insinuating judgment was bound to provoke moral outrage. The lawyer Gandhi petitioned to the government for reconsideration of this judgment. No respite was forthcoming. The rebel Gandhi preferred *Satyagraha* against 'this unspeakable insult.'[11] Women voluntarily joined the movement against the judgment. New Castle miners, especially indentured Indian labourers, went on a strike. Gandhi's *Satyagraha* had a new constituency. On 6 November 1913, more than two thousand began their journey from Charlestown and crossed the frontier into the Transvaal to reach Tolstoy farm that housed the civil resisters arrested for defying the Black Act and the immigration ban. They were arrested in Transvaal and brought back to Durban for imprisonment. This was a grand success for Gandhi's *Satyagraha* in which women took the leadership. This was a revelation to Gandhi and his approach to gender question underwent radical changes. By agreeing to involve the women in political movements as equal partners, the 'orthodox' Gandhi seemed to have appreciated their contribution in the wider struggle against the racist government. The transformation in his views is probably due to the influence of Western feminism given the fact that gender equality was not adequately addressed in the Indian tradition as strongly as in the West.

Gandhian *Satyagraha* gave a jolt to the racist South African government. The Indian Relief Act of 1914 abolished the requirement for the Indians to register and carry passes. The tax of 3 pounds was shelved. The system of indenture was discontinued and Indian marriages were recognized. Despite having conceded some of the principal demands of the *Satyagrahees*, the racist government still stuck to the policies of immigration—both between states and into South Africa. So South African experiments catapulted a brief less barrister, as Gandhi was, when he reached Durban, to the centre stage of political movements involving those who were muted before for historical reasons.

The Outcome of the South African Experiment

Gandhi was forced to leave India for South Africa to earn his livelihood since he hardly had any work in Bombay. So, when the Indian businessman, Dada Abdullah Jhaveri requested him to fight a legal battle for him in South Africa which was governed by British jurisprudence, he immediately agreed to accept the brief. It was a godsend opportunity to him especially when he was in quest of jobs in Bombay. Little did he know that his trip to South Africa charted a new course to his life as history progressed. A lawyer became a crusader against racism which unfolded in South Africa in its most virulent form. The local Zulus and the migrant Indians were involved in trade and commerce and other menial jobs for mere survival, As he confronted racism himself, he understood that there should be a strong opposition to save humanity from being brutalized by one of the most heinous crimes against humanity being perpetrated by the racist government in South Africa. Indians settled there were also victims, but they hardly had the courage to mobilize themselves to combat racism as a collective. This indicated that they were unable to rise presumably because they did not have a leader to lead them. Gandhi was still not in the scene except for his introduction by Dada Abdullah to the local Indians in Durban, the place where he landed first in South Africa.

The 1893 Maritzburg incident (when he was removed from a first-class compartment despite having the required railway ticket) was a turning point in his career. He now realized that racism was a deliberately-contrived design to divide humanity for securing benefits for the whites; it was a crime to humanity because racism was, in other words, an endeavour for dehumanizing humanity. It was justified given the rise of the whites as governing races almost all over the world. Not only did they colonize the Asian nations, but Africa was also not spared. So, racism was not independent of colonialism as it was rooted in the latter with the sole purpose of devising machineries for exploiting the weak and deprivileged.

Gandhi's South African experience of more than two decades made him confident and prepared him for a protracted struggle against the British rule in India. He might not have achieved what he strove for, but he returned home with a new method of action and a long-mediated programme for India's regeneration. *Satyagraha* was a new mode of protest that Gandhi crafted and tested in his struggle against racism in South Africa. The strength of *Satyagraha* lay in human suffering which *Satyagrahees* knew even before they got involved in *Satyagraha*. Since the spirit of revenge was alien to *Satyagraha*, none of the *Satyagrahees* nurtured enmity with the perpetrators when they encountered extraordinary difficulties.

The role of Gandhi in South Africa can be viewed in two prisms: on the one hand, he fought for humanizing humanity which he articulated by successfully mobilizing the migrant Indians against the restrictive laws and practices championing racial discrimination. On the other hand, it was ironical that the same Gandhi undertook steps to differentiate the so-called educated and behaviourally 'civilized' Indians from the local Zulus who lacked all these qualities. So, at one level, Gandhi was a priest of humanitarianism; and, at another level, he stood in contradiction to what he held so dear to him. The conundrum needs to be understood with reference to Gandhi's firm faith in the constitutional liberalism of the

British variety. Perhaps, unknowingly, or inadvertently, Gandhi became a victim of Western liberal dispensation which did not seem unlikely given the continuity of British rule in India. He was opposed to the whites and criticized them for nurturing racial discrimination; regarding the local Zulus, he was disinclined to join hands with them as he felt that they were inferior to the enlightened Indians. His reasoning was due to the fact that they were trained to be British with the intervention of the British rulers whereas their Zulu counterparts remained backward which probably explained why Gandhi endeavoured to retain the Indians identity as different from the indigenous South Africans. Barring this exception, Gandhi's involvement in the struggle against South African racist regime represented a communitarian design which was manifested, for instance, in the Indian Ambulance Corps that he formed during the 1899 Boer War. It was a Corps of volunteers that was 'a microcosm of all classes and creeds … [comprising] Hindus, Muslims, Christians, and Sikhs, Madrasis and UP countrymen (sic), free Indians as well indentured labourers'.[12] This tradition was firmly established in the Phoenix Farm in Natal and later the Tolstoy Farm in Johannesburg although Gandhi's focus on the Indian cause prevented him from involving the non-Indian Africans as potential political allies. In defence, one can argue that Gandhi was concerned with the Indians who were subject to racist discrimination and hence he concentrated on them. Moreover, because he attributed racism to mere colour prejudice, he believed that this was something 'quite contrary to the British tradition and only temporary and local'.[13] He perhaps missed out the serious structural implications of racism for South African society.

The South African experience also helped Gandhi conceptualize the nature of Western racism in its most brutal form. By avoiding cross-cultural communications, the South African whites sought to articulate their racist aim of preservation of the distinct nature of their civilization. Gandhi challenged the major arguments defending racist exploitation by the South African government. In his opinion, no civilization would ever lose its dynamics simply because of contact with others; in fact, cross-cultural borrowing would enrich its contents. He was critical of the idea that 'nations which do not increase their material wants are doomed to destruction'.[14] This remained at the root of the western nations' expansionist strategy. It was in pursuance of this strategy that 'Western nations have settled in South Africa and subdued the numerically overwhelmingly superior races of South Africa.'[15] The opposition of the Indian indentured labourers caused consternation among the white settlers who felt threatened economically by the growing importance of the Indian businessmen in trade and commerce. There was no doubt that trade by Indians hit the British traders hard which meant a decline in their income. The consequences did not appear to be unusual which was manifested in the dislike of the Europeans for the brown Indians. Moreover, South Africa offered a unique ambience in which Gandhi made several social and political experiments for inculcating a sense of camaraderie among the Ashram dwellers despite being different socioculturally which he probably could not have managed in India. For instance, the Phoenix Farm that was established in Natal in 1904 translated Gandhi's vision of a society that was free from caste, clan, and ethnic prejudices. This is where Indian women were free from the patriarchal bondage; they were relatively 'free' than their counterparts in India. Phoenix thus became 'a nursery for producing the right men [and women] and right Indians.'[16] To enforce his belief, he thus further stated that 'whereas in India there may be undesirable restraints, there are no such undesirable restraints in Phoenix. For instance, Indian ladies would never have come out so boldly as they are doing at Phoenix'.[17] Tolstoy Farm that came into being in 1910 continued with the same tradition. These farms were testing grounds for Gandhi of his ideas. So dear was the idea of a farm that he founded Sabarmati Ashram (near Ahmedabad) after his return to India in 1914. The purpose was to create an ambience in which differences based on artificial modes of segregation were an anathema to human existence. The idea of Ashram was introduced in India just to continue with the traditions Gandhi established while combatting a brutal racist South African government. With the co-existence of people with socioculturally differentiated characteristics in Ashrams, not only did the inhabitants evolve a habit of accepting each other without prejudices, they also spread the message of bonhomie to the rest of society. Ashrams, in other words, were grounds for generating those qualities championing togetherness and collective amity regardless of one's sociocultural identity. They thus contributed to the processes for humanizing humanity which hardly thrived fully till the processes of dehumanizing humanity were completely defused.

Gandhi in India

Similar to his role in South Africa, Gandhi, on his return to India, was involved in struggles challenging efforts at dehumanizing India by those who undermined humanity for fulfilling their partisan aims. The battle against the racist South African government was determined by his concern for the migrant Indians who were denied many opportunities because of the racist prejudices of the ruling authority. Once in India, he mobilized supporters for two types of battles: on the one hand, he raised his voice against the exploiters of those who remained socially peripheral and politico-ideologically left out. On the other hand, he, by attacking the British government, also challenged colonialism which, he rightly thought, was responsible for the emergence of an uneven society. Core to the argument is the view that Gandhi, by conceptualizing colonialism as responsible for dehumanizing humanity in India, created a new mode of thinking by linking it with his opposition to the British rule. In other words, implicit in the view was his concern for humanity which was a casualty following the onset and consolidation of colonialism in India.

One needs to understand his role in various local and pan-Indian campaigns as his efforts towards re-establishing the claim that humanity was prior to anything else and once it was brutally attacked as was the case in India, one was required to combat since it was an impediment to the unfolding of humanity without shackles.

As historical evidence suggests, Gandhi devised his pan-Indian strategy after he tested the effectiveness of *Satyagraha* at the local levels: he began his journey as a political leader at Champaran in Bihar and Kheda in Gujarat in 1917 and 1918, respectively. Here he launched *Satyagraha* for the redressal of peasant grievances. The 1917 Champaran *Satyagraha* was not actually a head-on collision with the district authority; here, Gandhi asked those who were aggrieved against the imposition of the *tinkathia system* of cultivation by the European Indigo planters to write petitions to the local judge who was asked to arbitrate between the peasants and the Indigo planters to establish the rule of law. The *tinkathia system* was the Indigo planters' forcible introduction of cultivation of Indigo in two-third of the land owned by local cultivators which meant that they were left with less amount of land to grow paddy and other items which were required for their survival. A unique political action, the 1917 Champaran *Satyagraha* under Gandhi's stewardship ushered in a new era in India's struggle for establishing humanity which was muzzled in the wake of colonialism. His act of civil disobedience, and determination to endure prison convinced the peasants that the Mahatma was their saviour. His extreme simplicity had brought him closer to them than all the erstwhile leaders, which caught his compatriots by surprize as Rajendra Prasad, who accompanied him during the Champaran campaign, expressed that 'it is a matter of mystery to me how these people seemed to develop the confidence that their deliverer had come'.[18] Not only his co-workers, even the British sub-divisional officer was intrigued by the excitement of those who came to welcome him in the Bettiah railway station which he reported by saying that

> We may look on Mr. Gandhi as an idealist, a fanatic or a revolutionary according to our particular opinions. But to the raiyats, he is their liberator, and they credit him with extraordinary powers. He moves about in the villages, asking them to lay their grievance before him, and he is daily transfiguring the imagination of masses of ignorant men with visions of an early millennium.[19]

The Champaran Satyagraha forced the government to adopt the 1918 Champaran Agricultural Act whereby those compelled to let their land for indigo cultivation were given some relief. What Gandhi left was carried forward by local peasants and Champaran became a strong base for nonviolent political mobilization though the Congress leadership never allowed them to organize protests against the indigenous landlords. The oppressed fulfilled their cause by adopting a position of superior morality, that of nonviolence, in circumstances when the deployment of physical forces by the rich and privileged was conveniently overlooked by the colonial authority. Furthermore, Gandhi charted a new course of action for the disempowered by following the British system of jurisprudence. Hence it was argued that Gandhi 'held the British to their own laws [which] demonstrated how effective the Gandhian method was in pursuing human causes.'[20] Despite the failure of the peasants to lead movements against the vested interests, the Champaran *Satyagraha* articulated a voice of protest against those who were involved in activities demeaning humanity. Gandhi emerged as the supreme leader and nonviolence thus gained salience. This was not a subaltern protest, but one in which the subalterns were inducted into the process of political mobilization which led one analyst to suggest that the Champaran *Satyagraha* represented 'a battle in which many different levels of consciousness coexisted [presumably because of] the complex perspective of the participants'.[21] Following this argument, one is thus persuaded to view the Champaran *Satyagraha* as a successful beginning of a kind of battle which was strong enough to contain those forces supportive of undermining humanity.

Similar to the Champaran experiment, the 1918 Kheda *Satyagraha* was a Gandhi-led no-revenue campaign. Hard-hit by economic hardships due to the destruction of crops by rains, rise in agricultural wages, high rate of inflation and the outbreak of bubonic plague, the Patidar peasants organized a movement against the government's decision not to waive land revenue. Launched by Mohanlal Pandya and Shankarlal Parikh of the small town of Kathlal in the district of Kheda of Gujarat, the movement gained momentum as Gujarat Sabha, under the stewardship of the

National Congress was involved to lead the campaign. Once approached by the Gujarat Sabha, Gandhi arrived in Kheda in March 1918 to launch a *Satyagraha* campaign against the government decision to confiscate the properties of the defaulters. The campaign lasted for four months and in June the government of Bombay decided not to implement the order and peasants who failed to pay the revenue were spared. Like the Champaran *Satyagraha*, the movement, spearheaded by the local Congress activists, continued with local support. Gandhi's presence was more symbolical than anything else. Even his lieutenants, Vallabhbhai and Vithalbhai Patel remained insignificant throughout the movement because the local grassroots leaders reigned supreme. As a cementing factor, Gandhi brought the *Satyagrahees* together for the movement that had an agenda, set by the local leaders on their own terms. In other words, the role of Gandhi did not seem to be as significant as is generally publicised. Illustrative here was the refusal of the local peasants to join the British army during the First World War. The peasants were heard shouting at Gandhi, reported one of the local administrators by saying that 'we made you so great! We helped you make *Satyagraha* work—and see what you ask of us now'.[22] Nonetheless, what stood out was the fact that Gandhi participated in the struggle though at an advanced stage since he was persuaded to believe that the government policy was harmful to people at Kheda. His primary concern was for humanity that was being brutalized deliberately by the rulers' representatives for their personal gain at the cost of the deprivileged peasants. Despite having felt bitterly down, Gandhi never lost sight of this aspect of the Kheda *Satyagraha* which was, to him, a watershed in the sense that the forces seeking to undermine humanism could hardly be decisive in the unfolding of universal humanism.

During the Kheda *Satyagraha*, Gandhi also participated in Ahmedabad textile mill strike of February–March 1918 which was called by the workers because they faced a substantial reduction in their monthly income once the plague-bonus was withdrawn suddenly. This was a different kind of experiment in which Gandhi fought for the workers' legitimate claims. It was decided by the striking workers to invite Gandhi to lead them because, following his success in Champaran, he was believed to be a leader capable of guiding them in attaining their goal. When the workers in Ahmedabad became restive, Gandhi was invited by Anasuya Sarabhai (1875–1972), a social worker who happened to be the sister of Ambalal Sarabhai (1890–1967), the president of the Ahmedabad Mill Owner's Association, to intervene and resolve the crisis. What triggered the strike was the withdrawal of the 'plague-bonus' to the workers, equivalent in some cases to 80 per cent of the wages that was paid to dissuade the workers from fleeing the plague-ravaged towns. Once the epidemic was over, the mill owners decided to discontinue the practice. This decision hit the workers adversely because of the hike in the prices for essential commodities due to the outbreak of the War.

Drawn on his belief that there was no major contradiction between capital and labour, Gandhi sought to defuse the crisis through dialogues with the mill owners. The mill owners appeared to be adamant and characterized Gandhi's intervention as unwarranted. On 22 February 1918, the mill owners locked out the weavers despite Gandhi's repeated requests. With the closure, Gandhi decided to champion the workers' demand though he asked them to tone down their earlier demand of 50 per cent wage increase to 35 per cent hikes. Although the workers agreed to Gandhi's suggestion, the mill owners did not relent. The workers were equally adamant because their demand was not unjust in view of the difficulties they confronted for even making the two ends meet. At this juncture, Gandhi began the 'first' of his seventeen 'fasts unto death' on 15 March 1918. This fast that lasted for three days appeared to have forced the mill owners who deeply respected Gandhi because of his insistence on an amicable settlement, to resolve the issue through a dialogue between the strikers and their employer. The agreement that finally ended the strike appeased the workers because their demand was partially fulfilled as they got a 27.5 per cent wage hike instead of their original demand for 35 per cent increase. So, the compromise formula looked like a face-saving formula and a tactical defeat for Gandhi though he forced the mill owners to accept the principle of arbitration in which workers' representatives and their employers had a say. Hence, *The Times* criticized Gandhi for 'blackmailing' the workers by endorsing the agreement prepared by the mill owners although his intervention was also hailed as 'an effective device' to break the *impasse* between the workers and industrialists.[23]

The 1918 agreement represented a significant character of Gandhi's design of serving humanity. It is without doubt that the Mahatma was heavily tilted for the deprivileged although it did not mean that he was against the owners of capital for he believed that they were also human beings and thus needed to be treated accordingly. By evolving his model of trusteeship, he clarified that the industrialists were also providentially ordained to discharge a particular role; so, no society remained complete without their support.[24] With his belief that humanity was indivisible and those who were relatively rich were required to be guided in the principle of trusteeship, he sought to inculcate responsibility in the rich and affluent as trustees for the poor.

Fundamental here was his idea that for humanity to develop as one collective, it was most important to create a space for human values to grow roots and prosper in society by nurturing them meaningfully. Gandhi was a saviour for the poor and tortured, but not at the cost of those who held opinion and adopted policies contrary to the former, because he felt that human prosperity was possible only by being appreciative of one another. Gandhi's approach to humanism was unlike Tagore's, since he felt that for India's economic development, the support of the entrepreneurs was as important as that of the workers. Hence, he did not completely dismiss the ideas of the employers at the Ahmedabad Textile Mills, because it would imply a face-to-face opposition to those who were believed to be of great use for India's developmental activities following decolonization. There were thus two complementary aspects in Gandhi's perception of humanism: on the one hand, he was completely for those who remained brutalized by those who had access to instruments for brutalization of the less privileged; on the other hand, given his strategic calculation, he also upheld the rights of the well-privileged sections of society since, as human beings, and by extension as God's children, they also deserved care and attention in case their existence was at stake. These three movements projected Gandhi as an emerging leader with different kinds of mobilizing tactics. He is said to have

> forged a new language of protest for India by both building on older forms of resistance while at the same time accepting the colonial censure of all forms of violent protest. … Part of their efficacy lay in the strong moral base that [the Mahatma] gave to this mode of protest through his doctrine of nonviolence and compassion for humanity.[25]

Critical here are two significant ideas which form the core of Gandhi's approach to nationalism: as repeated above, for him, nationalism was just a temporary phase of human civilization which was characterized by deliberately contrived schism among humanity. As it was a passing phase of human history, Gandhi seemed to have accepted many ideas which may appear to be contradictory to his fundamental faith in universal humanism. The three *Satyagrahas*, he led in Champaran, Kheda and Ahmedabad, are illustrative here. Gandhi did not lose sight of the forest for the sake of the trees as, for him, both were important constituents because one was incomplete without the other. Similarly, his approach to humanism was not Marxist which involved the liquidation of the haves, since they were responsible for keeping the have nots deprived since time immemorial which was justified by theorizing the idea that society was always class-divided. In contrast, Gandhi perceived human existence with reference to how humanity developed over the ages. In colonial India, he was there to organize battles to combat not just the foreign authority, but also many of the evil forces constricting humanity to develop naturally. So, his battle was waged on many fronts. As he believed that for socio-economic development of a society, the help from various segments was required, he devised politico-ideological designs to take care of the interests of those who were otherwise despised as exploiters. Unlike many of his compatriots in mainstream nationalism, he never allowed himself to be swayed by divisive approaches to humanity since it did not appear to him as appropriate at that juncture of human history, especially as it unfolded at the aegis of colonialism and other socioculturally entrenched forces. He wanted to retain the multicultural politico-ideological platform fighting the nationalist battle in collaboration with many other forces upholding India's political emancipation as the primary goal. In this context, given his role as a politician, it was most appropriate then, that his idea of humanism was more comprehensive than that of his counterparts.

Through his involvement with these movements at a stage when they struck roots in the concerned localities, Gandhi projected a specific kind of leadership: he was not a primary but a secondary organizer. There is no doubt that the movements gained different heights with his intervention. As evident in Champaran and Kheda, the Gandhian intervention in elite-nationalist politics, established for the first time that an authentic nationalist movement could be built upon the organized support of the peasantry, though its political object was not what Gandhi endorsed. The peasants were meant to become willing participants in a struggle wholly conceived and directed by others. Gandhi provided a national framework of politics in which peasants were mobilized but did not participate in its formulation. This was also true of the Ahmedabad strike where Gandhi accommodated the interests of the mill owners even at the cost of the workers since their demand was partially conceded. Based on his belief that capital and labour were not contradictory to each other, Gandhi agreed to the negotiated settlements as probably the best solution under the circumstances. Workers failed to get what they had asked for. Yet, Gandhi's role was most significant in articulating a form of political mobilization in which the workers were also decisive.

With his involvement in mass movements in Champaran, Kheda and Ahmedabad, Gandhi emerged as a mass leader who felt the pulse of the people perhaps most accurately than anybody else during the freedom struggle. And the consequence was obvious because it was Gandhi who transformed the struggle for freedom to a wider nationalist campaign involving various categories of people including those who remained detached. As Jawaharlal Nehru most eloquently put,

> [Gandhiji] attracted people. They did not agree with his philosophy of life, or even with many of his ideals. Often, they did not understand him, But the action that he proposed was something tangible which could be understood and appreciated intellectually. Any action would have been welcome after the long tradition of inaction which our spineless politics had nurtured; brave and effective action with an ethical halo about it had an irresistible appeal, both to the intellect and emotions. Step by step he convinced us of the rightness of the action, and we went with him, although we did not accept his philosophy. … Gandhiji, being essentially a man of action and very sensitive to changing conditions … the road he was following was the right one thus far, and if the future meant a parting it would be folly to anticipate it. All this shows that we were by no means clear or certain in our minds. Always we had the feeling that while we might be more logical, Gandhiji knew India far better than we did, and a man who could command such tremendous devotion and loyalty must have something in him that corresponded to the needs and aspirations of the masses.[26]

Jawaharlal Nehru's assessment is the reinforcement of the argument that Gandhi needs to be assessed at two different levels; hence, his approach to humanism cannot be evaluated monochromatically. At the level of nationalism, he was a rebel who was determined to wrest political freedom from the colonial rulers by deploying the method of nonviolence. He was also adamant in his belief in nonviolence as the withdrawal of the 1920–1922 Non-cooperation Movement following the outbreak of violence leading to the death of many constables of British police in the famous 1922 Chauri Chaura incident suggest. A priest and a staunch devotee of nonviolence, Gandhi was willing to sacrifice the end if the means became violent. At the level of humanism, he appeared to be discriminatory because, in his perception, the rich had also the right to survive; they should not be victimized for being rich. His notion of trusteeship was a perfect response when his critics questioned his double standard while discharging his responsibility for the well-off sections of society. His distinctive approach to humanizing humanity was qualitatively different from many of his colleagues and critics, including Rabindranath Tagore who was not persuaded by the Mahatma that humanity could be assessed by applying different conceptual yardsticks. Nehru's assessment was however different; by arguing that Gandhi understood India well, he applauded the Mahatma's unique capability of creatively blending his nationalistic role with that of a humanist. As a nationalist, because his aim was to defeat the brutalized British government; hence, his primary function was to build and sustain a common nationalistic platform for all, regardless of sociocultural and economic differences; it was a platform for Hindus, Muslims and others with different religious identity, for the poor and the rich, for those from towns and villages. This was reflected in his effort towards mobilizing masses for the fulfilment of a cause. As he was governed by this well thought-out strategic calculation, he was restrained in expressing his opinion vis-à-vis the exploiters from within, since his views on colonialism were articulated unambiguously in his decisions to launch campaigns against the British authority. At the level of his cognitive understanding of humanism, one is intrigued that as a nationalist what he held ran counter to what he felt for humanity as a whole. Perturbed by malicious tendencies, both nationally and globally, towards dividing humanity, he, it appears would not spare an opportunity to express unequivocally his tilt for the poor as they were victims of exploitation by the rich. This was expected of him as he was also committed to universal humanism. The reality was however otherwise; not only did he support the claim of the rich against the poor, he also persuaded them to remain cooperative with the former. It does not seem strange if one judges the Mahatma also as a political leader who engaged in a relentless struggle for India's political emancipation for which the role of the rich was as critical as that of the poor. His belief was that it was a temporary phase of humanity when the rich and the poor needed to come together against an infiltrator, the British colonizers. Furthermore, his notion of trusteeship also suggests that he also devised a perfect design to inculcate a sense of responsibility towards the poor among those with wealth. Based on these inputs, it is fair to argue that Gandhi's approach to humanizing humanity needed to be conceptualized with reference to the prevalent context in which the forces for dehumanizing humanity were strong enough to weaken his endeavour for meaningfully addressing the chasm between rich and poor. One is reminded of Rousseau's concern that 'man is born free, but everywhere he is in chains'. Similarly, through his insistence on substantive human equality, he reverberated Rousseau's anxiety that despite being born free, in the prevalent sociocultural milieu and the governing politico-ideological vision, human beings ceased to be so. What was thus required was to address the decadence of humanity in a strategically-devised piecemeal manner by first creating a sociocultural milieu and a complementary ideational vision supportive of universal humanism. By accepting the rich, despite being exploitative, as partners in fulfilling his humanistic goal, Gandhi charted a unique course of action by articulating a voice of protest which catapulted him to the centre-stage of Indian nationalism. The reasons are not difficult to understand: by accommodating those who could have been dismayed by his insistence on dividing the rich from the poor, Gandhi succeeded in articulating universal humanism in a fashion that was pragmatic and historically-governed.

Gandhi on the All-India Scene

The Rowlatt *Satyagraha* translated the Gandhian deeds into action at the pan-Indian level. Drawing on his faith on the spontaneous resistance of the masses to injustice, Gandhi was confident of the success of the campaign against the Rowlatt Act. Designed to crush the revolutionary movements in Bengal, Maharashtra, and Punjab, the 1919 Rowlatt Act authorised the British government to act sternly against those, identified as terrorist groups. The Act recommended the amendment of the Indian Penal Code in a manner that enabled the government to 'check activities prejudicial to the security of the state' and also invest the ruler with the authority to short-circuit 'the processes of law in dealing with revolutionary crime'. Despite opposition by the Indian members in legislative council, the Bill was adopted on 18 March 1919. Gandhi was upset with the enactment of such a draconian law and decided to challenge the government on this count. In his letter to V.S. Srinivasa Sastri, he wrote,

> I consider the Bills to be an open challenge to us. If we succumb we are done for. If we prove our word that the government will see and agitation that they have never witnessed before, we shall have proved our capacity for resistance to arbitrary or tyrannical rule ... for myself if the Bills were to be proceeded with, I feel that I can no longer render peaceful obedience to the laws of a power that is capable of such a devilish legislation as these two bills, and I would not hesitate to incite those who think with me to join me in the struggle.[27]

How did Gandhi begin the movement that transformed him as a pan-Indian leader? As a constitutionalist, he first wrote a pledge for refusal to the legislation that allowed the government to act arbitrarily. He then sent a telegram to the Viceroy, Lord Chelmsford explaining the reasons for his decision to launch a *Satyagraha* against the Rowlatt Act which he published in the media to put his demands in the public domain.

The movement was launched on 6 April 1919. The 1919 *Satyagraha* was an important moment in Gandhi's political ideas in two specific ways; first, Gandhi now realized the potential of the growing mass discontent in the anti-British struggle; and secondly, this *Satyagraha* was also a litmus test for the Mahatma who was now confident of *Satyagraha* as a technique for political mobilization. For Gandhi, '[t]his retention of Rowlatt legislation in the teeth of universal opposition is an affront to the nation. Its repeal is necessary to appease national honour'.[28] Hence he urged,

> whether you are *satyagrahees* or not, so long as you disapprove of the Rowlatt legislation, all can join and [he was confident] that there will be such a response throughout the length and breadth of India as would convince the Government that we are alive to what is going on in our midst.[29]

The Rowlatt *Satyagraha* was the first country-wide agitation against the British and it not only 'transformed nationalism in India from a movement representing the classes to a movement of the masses,'[30] but it also paved the way for Gandhi's emergence as a dominant figure in Indian politics. The movement officially began with the nation-wide *hartal* on 6 April, 1919. It was a peaceful *hartal* and no untoward incidents were reported. The movement however lapsed into violence once Gandhi was arrested on 9 April. The arrest of Gandhi was a pre-emptive measure which provoked unprecedented mass violence during the movement. For the government, it was a testing time for it had never confronted a movement of this nature before. To contain the agitation, it therefore unleashed a reign of terror. The worst incident was the massacre of innocent people on 13 April in Jallianwala Bagh in Amritsar. Terrorize Martial Law was imposed in towns in Punjab to terrorize the people participating in the movement. On this fateful day, a peaceful unarmed crowd, mainly villagers who came for a fair and had not been told of the ban on meetings, were brutally gunned down by the British police officer in charge of the district, Michael O'Dyer. The killings provoked mass disquiet. But Dyer's only regret before the Hunter Commission was that he ran out of bullets and the narrow lanes prevented him from bringing an armoured car for 'it was no longer a question of merely dispersing the crowd, but one of producing a moral effect not only on those present but more specifically throughout the Punjab'.[31] The unprecedented scale of the British repression quelled the situation and the movement had shown signs of dissipation. Yet, the nationalist campaign caused concern to the British authority for two reasons, first, it put the British authority, for the first time, on the defensive. Secondly, the movement did not seem to have run out of steam even after the arrest of Gandhi. Defending the spontaneous outburst against the brutal authority as natural, a pamphlet was being circulated especially in the cities in which people were exhorted to participate in the movement against the Black Bill. Urging the people not to sit 'idle' because

> the Black Bill has been set in motion [and] the leader of the *Satyagraha* and a great man of action—Mahatma Gandhi—has been arrested. ... Now is the time to show how much inherent power the Indian possess. When man has got power to avert his own calamity, then what difficulty can there be in abrogating the Black Bill. ... [S]o long as the Rowlatt Bill is not repealed, every Indians should take the vow of *Satyagraha* ... and be ready to sacrifice for the cause.[32]

Mahatma's appeal acted magically because most of the Indians were fuming at the atrocious British design of terrorizing the people of India by resorting to indiscriminate firing at the disarmed crowd. For Gandhi, it was not just an attack on a section of British subject; it was also an unpardonable act of brutality on humanity by those who were fortunate enough to have had access to lethal weapons of destruction. Under no circumstances, it was justified because after baptized in the Enlightenment values of care, concern, compassion, and empathy, it was a crime, even for the rulers who allowed the decision of O'Dyer to be executed at the cost of innocent human life. Not only was this design a crime to humanity, Gandhi also charged the colonizers with 'the motive of decimating humanity for partisan goals'.[33] It had an electrifying effect on those involved in *Satyagraha* at a time when Indians took onto themselves the responsibility of hitting the rulers back by following the Gandhian mode of protest.

How did Gandhi mobilize people? It is true that Gandhi gave the Indian masses a new *mantra*—the *mantra* of *Satyagraha*. While challenging the British during the Rowlatt *Satyagraha*, he was supported by the Home Rule League, built by Annie Besant and Bal Gangadhar Tilak and their followers. He also drew upon the support extended by his Muslim friends. Nevertheless, before embarking on action, Gandhi had set up his own organization. *Satyagraha* Sabha was constituted with its head office in Bombay. The Sabha was vested with the responsibility of conducting the campaign against the Black Bill. Yet, the success of the Rowlatt *Satyagraha* in those selective areas was largely attributed to the enthusiastic participation of the local leaders. In Bihar, Bengal and Delhi, prominent local leaders were involved from the very beginning.

Without Hasan Imam's participation in Bihar, the movement would not have gained momentum; similarly, the role of C.R. Das and Byomkes Chakrabarti in Bengal was most significant in sustaining the momentum of the *Satyagraha*. In Delhi, Swami Shraddhanand played a crucial role in political mobilization during the campaign. Apart from these lieutenants who had organic links with the localities, Gandhi's success was attributed to an indigenous model of political action, namely *Satyagraha* that mobilized common people in a manner that had never happened earlier. It is true that one of the reasons for Gandhi's success in galvanizing the masses for action despite adverse consequences was his skilful exploitation of popular religious symbols. But this will not conclusively explain the growing popularity of Gandhi for even before him Tilak in Maharashtra and Aurobindo in Bengal resorted to religious symbols for political mileage, but with limited success. What was distinctive about Gandhi was his intelligent application of symbols, religious and otherwise, which were meaningful to a cross-section of the Indian population, located at various levels of social hierarchy. Instead of endorsing the much hyped 'composite culture', Gandhi always believed that Muslims were distinct social community. Since religion was the dominant loyalty among the Indians, he believed that it would be politically inappropriate to dismiss religion as 'divisive'. This is what explains the increasing participation of the Muslim leaders and their followers in the Rowlatt *Satyagraha* and other Gandhi-led pan-Indian movements that followed soon. Muslims joined the movements spontaneously in Bengal, Bihar and Punjab largely because the local Muslim leaders urged them to do so. As evident, Gandhi emerged as an effective strategist and the Rowlatt *Satyagraha* was a defining moment in Indian nationalism in more than one sense. Not only did the campaign spread the nationalist message across the country, it was also illustrative of Gandhi's capacity to draw masses irrespective of caste, community, and religion.

Emergence of Gandhi as a Pan-Indian Leader

An assessment of Gandhi's role as a politician during the nationalist phase reveals that what he proposed to undertake by vehemently opposing the British, was governed by his heart-felt desire to liberate humanity from shackles. His endeavours in opposing the ruthless British rule was representative of other global thinkers who were involved in practices which, they felt, were complementary to salvation of humanity. Gandhi was a rare individual who lodged a political campaign against an authority that appeared to have struck at the foundation of his life-long goal. This was the transformation of human existence from being enslaved to one that was immune to tendencies which undermined core human values for gains. Central here is the argument that as a nationalist activist, Gandhi had an immediate purpose and an ultimate goal: the immediate purpose was to bring the alien rule to a halt; the ultimate objective was to contribute to humanity which was brutally sacrificed by a section for safeguarding the interests of a minority. The politico-ideological campaign he had launched needs to be conceptualized in this prism. As shown above, the three regional movements in 1918 and 1919 had one primary goal of standing in support of those who fought against the means of oppressing the indigenous population, by the whimsical representative of the rulers, to pursue a goal by challenging the core values of humanism.

The Non-Cooperation (1920–1922) and the 1930–1932 Civil Disobedience Movements

Gandhi inaugurated a new era in India's freedom struggle involving various social strata. He was also instrumental in transforming the Indian National Congress from an urban-based loose organization dominated by lawyers mainly from the metropolitan cities of Calcutta and Bombay into a political party with its organizational network even in villages. The structural core of Gandhi's democratization of the Congress lay 'in the proliferation of units capable of attracting and channelling a mass membership base.'[34] The Congress that was just a platform for ventilation of grievances became a mass organization to challenge the British government. There is no doubt that it was only at the aegis of Gandhi that the Congress metamorphosed into a giant organization with its tentacles all over the country. As Jawaharlal Nehru most eloquently put,

> [t]he whole look of the Congress changed; European clothes vanished and soon only *khadi* was to be seen; a new class of delegate, chiefly drawn from the lower middle classes became the type of Congressmen; the language used became increasingly Hindustan, or sometimes the language of the province where the session was held, as many of the delegates did not understand English, and there was also a growing prejudice against using a foreign language in national work; and a new life and enthusiasm and earnestness became evident in Congress gatherings.[35]

The freedom struggle thus acquired a mass base in an unprecedented way. Furthermore, despite internal ideological divisions within the Congress, its nationalist goal was never compromised. Gandhi became the supreme leader and *Satyagraha* had emerged as an effective mode of nationalist protest.

The Non-Cooperation Movement (1920–1922)

Mass arousal during the Rowlatt *Satyagraha* was unprecedented and convinced Gandhi of the growing popular discontent against the British rule. It was not therefore surprising that he launched another anti-government campaign in 1920 which lasted for two years. Known as the Non-cooperation Movement, it was inspired by a brilliantly simple but politically dangerous idea that, since the colonial state in India owed its sustenance to the cooperation of Indians, it would disintegrate if they withdrew it and set up alternative institutions to replace the existing-ones. Following his usual style, Gandhi began the Non-cooperation Movement by a notice in advance to the Viceroy. The Movement drew on non-cooperation with the government. It had several stages. Beginning with resignation from government services, non-cooperation was also articulated as refusal to use the institutions of government and schools and at a later stage, to pay taxes and serve the armed forces, and the burning of foreign clothes. Gandhi was forced to adopt such stern measures as a last resort. 'I can retain', argued Gandhi, 'neither respect nor affection for a Government which has been moving from wrong to wrong to defend its immorality'.[36] Gandhi's campaign was against the government which had become inhuman in its ruling, although he justified his stance by saying that it was his last option which was evident when he mentioned that 'I … have offered my closest cooperation to this Government for a number of years and, at the end of its all, I had some bitter experiences. It is owing to them that I have undertaken this terrible, bit noble and glorious fight'.[37] His aim was not to disturb normal life in India, but to send a message that if human beings were tortured for peace, he would not remain quiet. The Non-cooperation Resolution was directed neither for 'wreckage … [nor] for harming humanity, [but] to reestablish those values of humanism for which mankind struggled for generations'.[38] He was firmly of the opinion that Europe, by being deviant from the core values of universal humanism,

> represents the spirit of Satan [and] the Satan's successes are the greatest when he appears with the name of God on his lips. [Instead of

> worshiping the almighty] Europe is worshipping mammon [because] the urge of material possessions at the cost of humanity ... [appears to have] coiled them as a poisonous snake does before squeezing its prey to death.[39]

Thousands of people, whether formally associated with the Congress or not, plunged into action against 'the satanic' government. By way of condemning the Raj and its minions who upheld the governance from the point of Christianity, the religion of human salvation, Gandhi codified his argument to defend that religiousness was not tantamount to service to humanity. According to him,

> religion needs to be purged of its distortion [which the Europeans are adept to do], ... and hence, ... it is necessary to expose the hollowness of moral pretensions on the part of those who prefer material wealth to moral gain; it is easier to wean an ignorant fanatic from his error than a confirmed scoundrel from his scoundrelism.[40]

Explicit here was his firm belief that under no circumstances, human moral values could be sacrificed since human beings remained different from other living beings because they governed their life in accordance with age-old commitment to 'live and let live'. The Non-cooperation Movement was a warning to the colonizers and the loyalists that as colonialism was a mechanism to debase humanity given its instinctive nature, it was to be pushed out of India. So the Congress Movement which Gandhi led was not just for political emancipation but meant to re-establish morality as it was a critical ingredient to humanism.

Gandhi was hailed as 'a saviour' even by Rabindranath Tagore, despite his criticism of Gandhi's strategy of Non-cooperation, including boycott of foreign clothes and English education. While the former was not possible given the high price of *khadi* clothes, the latter was criticized because it would neither be useful for the young minds for inculcating 'patriotism in them [nor] it would acquaint them with the moral objectives of the movement the Mahatma has launched'.[41] In his detailed response to why he insisted that the learners should not be asked to leave their schools and colleges, he further suggested that

> the reason of refusal to advise the those students [who came to him for advice at the height of the Non-Cooperation Movement] to leave their schools was because the anarchy of mere emptiness never tempts me, even when it is resorted to as a temporary measure. I am frightened at

> the abstraction which is ready to ignore living reality. These students were no mere phantoms to me. Their life was a great fact to them and to the All. I could not lightly take upon myself tremendous responsibility of a mere negative programme for them which would uproot their life from its soil, however thin and poor that soil might be.[42]

Tagore hardly differed from Gandhi when he gave a clarion call for the campaign against a brutal system of governance that evolved at the aegis of the British, except that the latter was not persuaded to accept that mere boycott was adequate to inculcate humanism in its real connotation. For Tagore, human development was possible only through a meaningful design that contributes to the development and consolidation of core human values, for which the clamour for non-cooperation was vacuous. Despite being critical of Gandhi's strategy, Tagore was also confident that 'the movement headed by a man like Gandhi whose saintly life made him adored all over India would bring … the ship at the port of destination.'[43] The interaction between Tagore and Gandhi, in spite of being a display of differences between these two great minds was also an aid to understand how they conceptualized the aims of the movement which was also directed to ensure human well-being. There were areas of chasm since they differed in their ideational priorities: while Gandhi felt that the campaign was useful to advance the cause of humanity by resorting to the means he devised, Tagore thought otherwise, presumably not to undermine the Mahatma's endeavour, but to set things right in accordance with what he deemed appropriate for securing his ultimate objective of universal humanism.

It was based on the idea that since the continuity of the British government depended on the cooperation of the Indian subjects it would collapse once the Indians withdrew. The programmes involved resignation from the government jobs, refusal to participate in the government institutions and schools and later to pay taxes and burning of foreign cloths.[44] His idea of burning foreign cloths provoked much unease with Tagore who wondered if Gandhi was not encouraging the flames of narrow nationalism and xenophobia. As he argued,

> the clothes to be burnt are not mine, but belong to those who most sorely need them. If those who are going naked should have given us the mandate to burn, it would, at least, have been a case of self-immolation and the crime of incendiarism would not lie at our door. But how can we expiate the sin of the forcible destruction of clothes which might have gone to women whose nakedness is actually keeping them prisoners unable to stir out of the privacy of their homes?[45]

Similarly, withdrawal from the schools and colleges never appeared to be a wise call. Tagore refused to endorse the campaign because 'the great injury and injustice which had been done to those boys who were tempted away from their career before any real provision was made, could never be made good to them'. He was not persuaded to believe that Western education 'injured' the young minds and be altogether rejected. The root of the misconception lies elsewhere. As Tagore pointed out, 'what has caused the mischief is the fact that for a long time we been out of touch with our own culture and therefore the Western culture has not found its prospective in our life very often found a wrong prospective giving our mental eye a squint'.[46]

While Tagore was convinced, like M.N. Roy, that this programme would alienate the masses since mill products were cheaper and hence affordable, Gandhi defended the agenda by saying that it would not only harm the British commercial interests but also foster the cultural self-confidence of the masses. In his words,

> Non-Cooperation is the nation's notice that it is no longer satisfied to be in tutelage. The nation had taken to the harmless, natural and religious doctrine of Non-Cooperation in the place of the unnatural and irreligious doctrine of violence. ... Non-Cooperation is intended to give the very meaning that the Poet is yarning after. An India prostrate at the feet of Europe can give no hope to humanity. An India awakened and free has a message of peace and goodwill to a groaning world. Non-Cooperation is designed to supply her with a platform from which she will preach the message.[47]

On another occasion, he further added,

> Our Non-Cooperation is neither with the English nor with the West. Our Non-Cooperation is with the system the English have established, with the material civilization and its attendant greed and exploitation of the weak. Our Non-Cooperation is a retirement within ourselves. Our Non-Cooperation is a refusal to cooperate with the English administrators in their own terms.[48]

Similarly, Gandhi did not endorse Tagore's criticism of boycott of English education. While appreciating English learning, the Mahatma was critical of the pernicious effect of English education on the Indian minds. According to him,

> English is being studied because of its commercial and political value. ... English is being made mother tongue in families. Hundreds

> of youth believe that without a knowledge of English freedom of India is practically impossible. … The only meaning of Education is a knowledge of English. … All these are for me signs of our slavery and degradation. It is unbearable to me that the vernaculars should be crushed and starved as they been.[49]

As shown above, Tagore's critique of the aim of the Non-cooperation Movement drew on his own perception of the 'constructive work' that he experimented during the 1905–1908 Swadeshi Movement in Bengal.[50] He was opposed to coercion because his experience of the *swadeshi* mobilization had shown its adverse consequences. When the movement was at its zenith, Tagore denounced its reliance on coercion and the alienating impact it had on the masses it claimed to enthuse and activate. His critique of the Non-cooperation techniques followed the same logic. The pervasive use of social boycott and other forms of coercion was therefore 'regarded by him as evidence of the *swadeshi* activist's failure to persuade people to their cause'.[51] He thus argued that 'we have not been patient enough to work our way gradually towards winning popular consent'.[52] That was at the root of the nationalist failure to unite all Indians in 'a grand patriotic mobilization'. The debate between Gandhi and Tagore brought out the contrasting perspectives on this subject that had, as shown, its root in the Swadeshi Movement as well. While Gandhi was confident that the Non-cooperation agenda was the most appropriate socio-politically, Tagore expressed his doubts on the ground that the 'narrow political aim' of the Movement was likely to jeopardize its wider goal and objectives. The debate remained inconclusive, but raised certain major questions on Gandhi's social and political ideas that appeared to have decisively influenced Indian minds.[53]

Just like the debate over the strategy of Non-cooperation, the exchange of views between Gandhi and the poet on *charkha* and *khaddar* was reminiscent of different perspectives in which they were conceptualized. Tagore was not persuaded, let alone impressed, by the campaign for *charkha*. As he admitted,

> the depths of my mind have not been moved by the *charkha* agitation … for its inherent weaknesses [and he therefore apprehended] that all intense pressure of persuasion brought upon the crowd psychology is unhealthy for it [because] it will create blind faith on a very large scale in the *charkha* … which is liable to succumb to the lure of short cuts when pointed out by a personality about whose moral earnestness they can have no doubt.[54]

In two articles, published in the *Modern Review*, Tagore summarized his arguments to question the applicability of *charkha* in the context of the colonial India. First, he was confident that *charkha* was not a competitive substitute for machine and given the complex problems that masses confronted both due to colonialism and other obvious social and political constraints. For Tagore, 'no wealth is greater than lightening man's material burdens'. Stating in a figurative way, he further argued that 'wheel in the shape of the spinning wheel, or the potter's wheel or the wheel of a vehicle, the wheel has rescued innumerable men from [poverty] and [reduced] their burden'. Symbolizing wheel as the growth of science, Tagore underlined the importance of the wheel in augmenting resources for human civilization. As he articulated, 'man gradually realized that his wealth has gone on compounding itself in the ever-increasing rotation, refusing to be confined to the limited advantage of the original *charkha*'.[55] As an archaic, but useful invention at a particular historical juncture, *charkha* appeared to have exhausted its potential to contain poverty effectively. His second argument against *charkha* was built on this. He was unambiguous in stating that 'the *charkha* is not competent to bring us the *swaraj*, or remove the whole of our poverty because it is based on the false expectation that people will automatically be drawn to spinning'. Seeking to delink *swaraj* from *charkha*, Tagore further argued that

> to give the *charkha* the first place in our striving for the country's welfare is only a way to make our insulted intelligence recoil in despairing inaction. A great and vivid picture of the country's well-being in its universal aspect, held before our eyes, can alone enable our countrymen to apply the best of head and heart to carve out the best way along which their varied activities may progress towards their end.[56]

Swaraj was the self-fulfilment of people's concern regardless of differences in ethno-religious terms. It was not simply an act of 'spinning thread, weaving *khaddar*, or holding discourses'; it was a plan of action involving the masses with a vision of society, free from exploitation of all kinds. So, Tagore, not convinced by the narrow conceptualization of *swaraj* merely in terms of *charkha*, highlighted both the depth of *swaraj* as a socio-economic blueprint for future India and also its significance in inculcating mass interest in certain specific meaningful programmes relevant to the people of British India. The third argument that Tagore made in opposition to *charkha* relates to the realistic feasibility of this device when imposed on the people without their consent. Gandhi felt that the success of *charkha* lay in utilizing the surplus time of the cultivator; the more the cultivators involved themselves the more effective the *charkha* would become. Tagore was not in agreement because the basic assumption behind the argument concerning the profitable employment of the surplus time of the cultivator was flawed unless the cultivators themselves spontaneously accepted *charkha* which was most unlikely, as Tagore believed that it was improbable for two reasons: first, the cultivator acquired a special skill with his hands, and special bent of mind by dint of consistent application to his particular work. Hence 'to ask the cultivator to spin is to derail his mind; he may drag on with it for a while, but at the cost of disproportionate effort and therefore waste of energy'.[57] Second, if *charkha* was imposed on the cultivators who might not have the inclination it would lose its significance and effectiveness. In other words, the acceptance of *charkha* was not spontaneous and hence the consequence could be devastating because as Tagore most eloquently put that

> it would be wrong to make the cultivator either happier or richer by thrusting aside, all of a sudden, the habits of body and mind which have grown upon him through his life. … To tell the cultivator turn the *charkha* instead of trying to get him to employ his whole energy in his own line of work is only a sign of weakness (sic). We cast the blame for being lazy on the cultivator, but the advice we give him amounts rather to a confession of the laziness of our mind.[58]

According to Tagore, spinning was not creative for 'by turning its wheel man merely becomes an appendage of the *charkha*; that is to say, be but does himself what a machine might have done; he converts his living energy into a dead turning movement. [In the process] he becomes a machine, isolated, companionless'.[59] Critical of this mechanical involvement in spinning that was of no consequence for *swaraj,* Tagore suggested concrete steps which were organically linked with our life. For instance, as he perceived, the village that was self-sustained economically and supported each of its inhabitants in distress could lay the foundation of *swaraj* in the true sense of the term. As he most unambiguously put, 'the village of which people come together to earn for themselves their food, their health, their education, to gain themselves the joy of so doing, shall have lighted a lamp on the way to *swaraj*'.[60]

Gandhi responded to the poet's critique in his rejoinders in the *Young India.* Instead of countering the arguments, made by Tagore, the Mahatma, in a very cryptic way, stated his view points in defending *charkha* as indispensable for India's economic well-being. In response to the charge that he insisted on spinning to the exclusion of all other activities, Gandhi argued that this was far from the truth because he never wanted 'the Poet to forsake his muse, the farmer his plough, the lawyer his brief and the doctor his lancet. [Instead], he asked the famishing to spin for a living and the half-starved farmer to spin during his leisure hours to supplement his slender resources'.[61] The idea based on sound logic articulated a device for supplementary incomes for the starving peasants and their families. Juxtaposed with this idea was his unequivocal condemnation for machine. He was not opposed to machine per se; what he apprehended was the consequence of machine civilization that would make human labour redundant, a consequence most devastating where human labour was in abundance. As Gandhi argued,

> machine must not be allowed to displace the necessary human labour. An improved plough is a good thing. But if by some chance one man could plough up by some mechanical invention of his the whole of the land of India and control all the agricultural produce and the millions had no other occupation, they would starve, and being idle, they would become dunces, as many have already become … [i]t is therefore criminal to displace hand labour by the introduction of power-driven spindles unless one is at the same time ready to give millions of farmers some other occupation in their homes.[62]

The other part of the argument is equally significant where *charkha* was a symbol of involvement with the day-to-day life of the poor and thus was a powerful device to conceptualize the reality. As he suggested to the poet that 'if [he] spun half an hour daily his poetry would gain in richness [for] it would then represent the poor man's wants and woes in a more forcible manner than now'.[63] Furthermore, Gandhi replied to the charge that the *charkha* was calculated to bring about a deathlike sameness in the nation. To Gandhi *charkha* was a powerful symbol to unite the disparate Indian masses. Hence *charkha* to him was 'intended to realize the essential and living oneness of interest among India's myriads'.[64] *Charkha* was not simply an economic activity. Instead, it brought people together by involving them in an activity that was a source of supplementary income, and a device to link them automatically with the rest of India politically.[65] In other words, although articulated as an economic activity it was an organizing device with a clear political message to those involved in the Gandhian *Satyagraha*.[66] Spinning for Gandhi was therefore a symbolic form of identification with the masses while Tagore was suspicious of any such appeal that tended to gloss over the inherent diversity among the Indian people.

Gandhi promised *swaraj* within a year if Non-cooperation was total and widespread. Gandhi was charged by many as being unrealistic in making such a promise. It was a hollow statement if we interpret literally because to expect independence within a year of Non-cooperation was utopian as the British state was firm and strong in every respect as the preparedness of the government had shown during the agitation against the Black Act. What was the message then? With this slogan, Gandhi sought to articulate his dream of a strong India that was capable of winning independence. For him Non-cooperation was not only a way of demonstrating the hollowness of the colonial state without the cooperation of the average Indians, but also to show that Indians were capable of managing their business with ease and comfort. There was another dimension as well. His assurance for *swaraj* within a year also inspired the masses to involve in the anti-British movement despite the adverse consequences. He injected 'freedom from fear' into the crowds. A new zeal of the masses was evident. Not cowed-down by the brutalities of the British government, the masses ventured into the world of imagined communities for an aspired goal of independence. 'The essence of his teaching was', thus argued Jawaharlal Nehru,

> fearlessness and truth, and action allied to these, always keeping the welfare of the masses in view. … It was a psychological change, almost as if some expert in psycho-analytical methods had probed deep into the patient's past, found out the origins of his complexes, exposed them to his view, and thus rid him of that burden.[67]

The campaign began in June 1920. What was unique about the campaign was that, for the first time and perhaps the last time, Hindus and Muslims fought together against the British with, of course, different aims to fulfil. The Non-cooperation–Khilafat merger was testimony to Gandhi's ability to temper rivalries and to secure cooperation among the Hindu–Muslim political leadership. As a true liberal, he expressed his unflinching faith in the British constitution and peaceful methods of *Satyagraha*. He also realized that Hindu–Muslim unity was a pre-requisite for India's future as a nation. Muslims joined hand with Gandhi to gain political mileages. Once they were recognized as a critical minority in India, neither the British nor the Congress could afford to ignore them in any negotiation for future India. Realizing the politics of 'presence', Muslims also agreed to extend support to the Congress agenda that included *Satyagraha* against the British government for the Punjab 'wrongs.' So, for both Gandhi and Ali brothers, the brain behind the merger, the Non-cooperation Movement was a master strategy in uniting Hindus and Muslims for a nationalist cause. The unity was however short-lived because the nucleus of politics shifted with the growing mass participation in movements against the British.

While association with the Khilafat movement was also strategic Gandhi's arguments against the Punjab 'wrongs' were emotionally-charged. He minced no words while condemning the ruling authority that belittled basic human values. Defending his decision to go ahead with the Non-cooperation agenda even without the support of his colleagues, he thus argued,

> Government be an insufferable wrong, if the report of Lord Hunter's Committee and the two dispatches be a greater wrong by reason of their grievous [condoning] of these acts, it is clear that we must refuse to submit to this official violence. Appeal to the Parliament by all means if necessary, but if the Parliament fails us and if we are worthy to call ourselves a nation, we must refuse to uphold the Government by withdrawing cooperation from it.[68]

On another occasion, he expressed his disillusionment with the government that lost the moral authority to rule due to the Punjab 'wrongs'. He explicitly condemned the British government when he stated,

> [b]ut to my amazement and dismay, I have discovered that the present representatives of the Empire have become dishonest and unscrupulous. They have no real regard for the wishes of the people of India and they count Indian honour as of little consequence. I can [thus] no longer retain affection for a government so evilly manned as it is now-a-days.[69]

Gandhi believed that the British government in India was brutal and had 'no intention of enacting the ideals of [the British] constitution'.[70] He was constitutionalist only in a limited sense: he made a representation to the government before he embarked on the campaign. In this sense, there was continuity with his style, adopted in South Africa and its aftermath in India in the context of the Rowlatt *Satyagraha*. The comparison ends there, because the aim of the Movement was to harm the British socially, economically, and politically. Gandhi had reasons to be confident because of the following factors: first, Indian masses had supported him in his campaign against the Black Act. Despite his failure to repeal the Act, Gandhi emerged as an undisputed leader who involved the masses in the movement against the ruler. What separated Gandhi from his erstwhile nationalist colleagues was his success in setting a common political agenda for the people at large and thus expanding the constituencies of nationalist politics. Second, although it was a strange coincidence, Gandhi drew political capital out of the Muslim grievances against the British for demeaning the Caliph. By appreciating the Khilafat cause, the Mahatma created conditions for Hindu–Muslim amity at least for a political goal. There is no doubt that the Khilafat campaign gained significance presumably because of its merger with the Non-cooperation Movement and also by Gandhian endorsement of the Khilafat cause. Thirdly, by the time, the Non-cooperation Movement was to be launched, Gandhi had already become a nationalist leader with considerable followings across the country. It was possible presumably because of the wide publicity that he got after successful *Satyagrahas* in Champaran, Kheda and Ahmedabad. These experiments also drew to Gandhi a group of local leaders who were inspired by and committed to Gandhi's political ideology. Not only did they provide Gandhi with adequate organizational support, they also created conditions for Gandhian values to grow roots even in areas where Gandhi had hardly visited. Fourthly, by revitalizing the Congress, he also prepared a strong organizational network to pursue the nationalist goal. From a mere political platform, active only on the occasion of the annual sessions, the Congress became a movement organized around well-defined principles and strategies. It would not be wrong to suggest that by the time the Non-cooperation Movement was launched, the Congress became Gandhian in the sense that other competitive ideologies were either peripheral or extinct for all practical purposes. It is true that the Congress translated the nationalist vision into practice by undertaking various programmes in which the role of the masses was significant; but Gandhi always remained its steward.

The Non-cooperation Movement also brought different strata of society, including the peasants to the forefront of the nationalist politics. Illustrative here was an example from Gorakhpur. As Shahid Amin has shown, the local peasants took part in the campaign as it was providentially ordained on them because, to them, Gandhi was an incarnation of providential authority. As a result, they believed that 'the bullets fired by the British police turned into water by the grace of Gandhi [which] … was', as the author felt, 'the construction put by the crowd on the failure of the police's symbolic firing',[71] although the situation took a different turn when police killed three of the *Satyagrahees* by indiscriminate firing on the crowd. Gandhi was readily accepted by the participants especially in the villages presumably because he accorded top priority to village reconstruction through self-help, Gandhi articulated his plan for an economic revival 'through spinning wheel and hand-woven cloth (*charkha* and *khadi*), panchayats or arbitration courts, national schools and campaign for Hindu–Muslim unity and against the evils of liquor and untouchability'. Although these programmes may not have been uniformly effective as strategies for political mobilization, they nonetheless unfolded a new process by involving the hitherto neglected section of society in a struggle which despite its pronounced political content, was equally a battle against the well-entrenched vested interests in the localities. It was not therefore surprising that peasants of Kanika in Orissa challenged the local zamindars for having demanded an extra rent. Drawing upon Gandhi, the militant section of the Orissa Congress leaders organized the peasants for the establishment of Gandhi-raj when no one would have to pay rent; so convinced were the peasants that they boycotted and intimidated, on occasions, those who were inclined to pay rents to the zamindars. The movement though led by the Orissa Congress, did not receive Gandhi's approval, and was later unconditionally revoked. Gandhi was however inclined to encourage a no revenue campaign in a *rayatwari* settlement area, like Bardoli (in Gujarat) and not in any zamindari region where it would inevitably involve 'no rent'. By trying to contain 'no rent' campaigns, Gandhi projected a specific type of leadership which mobilized peasants exclusively on his terms and conditions. Peasants were organized and mobilized on unifying issues which transcended even the well-defined boundaries among the antagonistic classes. So, it was logical when Gandhi deprecated all attempts to create a discord between landlords and tenants and advised the tenants to suffer rather than fight for they had to join all forces for fighting the most powerful zamindar, namely the Government.

The Civil Disobedience Movement, 1930–1932

Gandhi launched the civil disobedience in 1930 to challenge both the British rule which appeared to him 'a perfect personification of violence and also the growing hatred towards the agents of this rule which took the form of causal assassination'. 'The call of 1920', he further wrote, 'was a call for preparation. The call in 1930 is for engaging in the final conflict'.[72] Gandhi's eleven point[73] ultimatum to the Viceroy however disappointed many leading Congressmen including Nehru since it contained no demand for any change in the political structure, not even the dominion status. 'Bewildered' at Gandhi's charter of demands which ultimately boiled down to a campaign for salt preparation, Nehru thought that it was a sad climb down from the *Purna Swaraj* resolution. As Nehru argued, '[s]alt suddenly became a mysterious word, a word of power. The Salt Tax was to be attacked; the salt laws were to be broken. We were bewildered and could not quite fit in a national struggle'.[74] Irwin, the viceroy was not perturbed at all: in a letter to the secretary of state, Wedgewood Benn, he thus wrote, 'at present the prospect of a salt campaign does not keep me awake at night'.[75]

Gandhi's eleven points incorporated demands of almost every section of Indian society. By choosing salt as the central issue, he strove to organize an anti-British campaign in which the participation of a majority of the people was ensured since salt was essential for everyday survival. The boycott of foreign cloth was also included as a strategy because of its effectiveness in the earlier Congress campaigns. Hence the Civil Disobedience Movement revolved primarily around attacks on the government salt monopoly and the boycott of foreign cloth. Although the 1930 Civil Disobedience Movement began with the breach of salt laws, civil resistance spread to other fields. Simultaneously with Mahatma's march in villages, an intense propaganda was carried on by those involved in the campaign asking the people to give up service under the British government and to prepare for non-payment of tax as well. It was not therefore surprising that the violation of the Salt Act soon became just one activity and resistance to the government took various forms. Jawaharlal Nehru attributed this to

> the promulgation of various ordinances by the Viceroy prohibiting a number of activities. As these ordinances and prohibitions grew, the opportunities for breaking them also grew and civil resistance took the form of doing the very thing that the ordinance was intended to stop.[76]

At every village where Gandhi stopped, he spoke briefly. On one occasion, while reiterating the famous eleven points, he attacked the Salt Act by saying that

> Who can help liking this poor man's battle? The cruel tax is not respecter of persons. It is therefore as much the interest of the *Musslamans* as of the Hindu to secure its abolition. This is a fight undertaken in the name of God and for the sake of millions of paupers of this country.[77]

Besides highlighting the inhuman nature of the British government Gandhi in his speeches always couched his argument with issues relevant to the village life, on *khadi,* cow-protection, hygiene and untouchability. He also appealed to those serving the government. By the time the Dandi March came to an end, about one-third of seven hundred and sixty village headmen resigned. This might not have seriously affected the alien administration though it was symbolically significant when the governmental authority did not seem to be weak. Gandhi thus had no hesitation in describing the Movement as one of success which he voiced by saying that

> in the present struggle, which we have started to establish *Ramarajya*, both the poor and the rich are ready to give me monetary help, but I look up to the people for strengthening me. You will have redoubled my strength when, following me, you come forward to manufacture Salt. By leading you along my path, I wish to bring glory to one and all among us [and], … for the present, I am asking for soldiers for this fight. Civil disobedience of the Salt Law is within the power of all—men and women, young and old.[78]

As a strategist, Gandhi succeeded in infusing popular misery with a political content by attributing it to the oppressive nature of the British rulers. Being aware that the rulers would deploy many measures to destroy and demoralize the *Satyagrahees*, he also encouraged them to face the consequences because they were serving the country and humanity. One of the immediate measures which the political authority adopted was to arrest the civil resisters to quell the campaign and Gandhi knew that this was inevitable. Hence, in order to raise the morale of those participating in a campaign for redressing human grievances, he urged them that

> our civil disobedience is fulfilled when we seek imprisonment. Disobedience would cease to be civil if we defied legitimate jail discipline. We may therefore shout or create a row in the jails. We should not refuse to work when it is demanded of us according to rules. We should rather be anxious to do as much awork as we can and that too as efficiently as we are capable of. It would be nice if even 'simple prisoners' volunteered to do some useful work not necessarily with a view to getting any remission.[79]

The campaign became an all-India phenomenon. No part of India remained aloof from Gandhi's clarion call. One of the reasons was certainly Gandhi's magnetic personality, and the Congress volunteers' hard work which was evident in with the development of its organization even in remote hamlets in India. One should also appreciate Gandhi's strategic sense of picking up the preparation of salt as the main agenda of the Movement; it became popular because salt was an unavoidable ingredient of daily food of people cutting across social strata. Astonished by the immense popularity of the civil disobedience campaign, the moderate Tej Bahadur Sapru (1875–1949) thus candidly admitted,

> The Congress has undoubtedly acquired a great hold on popular imaginations. On the roadside stations where until a few months ago, I could hardly have suspected that people had any politics. I have seen with my eyes demonstrations and heard with my ears the usual Congress slogans. The popular feeling is one of excitement. It is fed from day to day by continuous and persistent propaganda on the part of the Congressmen—by lectures, delivered by their volunteers in running trains and similar activities . . . there is no doubt whatever in my mind that *there is the most intense distrust of the Government and its professions.* Indeed I have little doubt in my mind that racial feeling has been fanned to a very dangerous extent . . . it seems to me that the Congress is really fighting for its own supremacy in the country.[80]

With a gradual expansion of its organizational network, the Congress became stronger than before. For Gandhi, the violation of salt law was the last throw of 'a gambler [insisting that] even the risk of violence was worth it'.[81] The movement appeared inevitable given the government intransigence to concede the most humane demand, which was unfortunate, as Gandhi himself opined, because 'on bended knees I asked for bread and received stones instead'.[82] Hence, he repudiated the salt law and regarded it as his 'sacred duty to break the [salt law] which aims at subjecting the poor to terrible suffering'.[83] The violation of Salt Law reignited the nationalist spirit which was missing, as per Gandhi and his colleagues in mainstream nationalism. It was a glorious moment for the Congress for its success in galvanizing the masses for the cause and, as the archival sources suggest, the 1930–1932 civil disobedience was a source of consternation to the Empire.

The campaign was political in character. Nonetheless, it was organized around the deprivation of Indians of having the right to prepare salt without paying tax since there was no moratorium on this by any rulers because salt prepared by drying sea water was god's gift to humanity. As soon as the British government adopted Salt Law, it was not only an attack on the natural right of the ruled, but also was an attempt to take away a gift of the nature which they inherited from their forefathers. Two ideas appeared to worked in Gandhi's favour: on the one hand, by choosing the infringement of Salt Law, the Mahatma instantaneously created a space for people to come together since salt was indispensable for human survival. So, the agenda was couched in a humanistic mould which immediately cemented a bond among those who were disgruntled by such a heinous design to harm them and jeopardize their existence. On the other hand, unlike the earlier Non-cooperation campaign, which was an act of withdrawal, civil disobedience was a verbalization of a voice of protest which included a series of activities seeking to undermine the British authority. In order to execute their plans, *Satyagrahees* were asked by the Mahatma to accept prison sentences happily since it also meant not only a service to the nation but also a meaningful step to ensure human well-being. Civil disobedience was thus not merely a politico-ideological design, it was, at the same time, a humanizing device by challenging the dehumanizing tendencies of those wielding authority.

Do or Die: Gandhi's Articulation of Freedom

As it has been consistently argued so far that Gandhi participated in regional and pan-Indian campaigns against the political oppressors to develop a language of protest for humanity. Although his political activities were confined first to South Africa and later India, his politico-ideological vision had a global ramification simply because he represented a powerful voice of the deprivileged against those being involved in exploiting the rest for fulfilling their narrow and personal gains. It is now well-known that Gandhi, despite being a loyalist at the beginning of his public career, became disenchanted with the rulers in South Africa for being racist, and in India, for being exploitative and supportive of policy priorities for sustaining India's servility to the colonizers. As shown above, both the Non-cooperation and Civil Disobedience Movements were directed at the rulers and their cronies since what they did was contrary to humanity. By questioning the forcible imposition of rules and regulations enforced by coercion and other brutal means, Gandhi contributed to the articulation of the voice for humanity which was being silenced by the colonizers for safeguarding their exclusive benefits. There were two important conceptual points here: on the one hand, it is wrong to reduce Gandhi's planned opposition to the British rule as just a political effort because underlying in these campaigns was a wider objective, namely service to the humanity. It was not surprising that Gandhi's model inspired the Afro-Americans who continued to remain victims notwithstanding the adoption of the 1893 Emancipation Act by the US President, Abraham Lincoln which outlawed slavery. As the available archival resources show, African-Americans like Howard Thurman, Walter Rauschenbusch, Reinhold Niebuhr, and W.E.B. Du Bois, among others, were in touch with Gandhi since the early 1920s because they believed that the model of nonviolent resistance was likely to help them successfully combat the brutalized US government; it worked since after a protracted battle for their civil rights in the US, African Americans were guaranteed the right to vote in 1965.[84]

The Quit India Movement was not merely another instance of the civil disobedience campaign, it was also 'an open rebellion'. All the past *Satyagraha* movements, writes the *Harijan* were protests against 'the unwanted or unapproved acts' of the Raj,[85] the authority of which was however conceded. Hence, the Congress

> registered protests by breaking the salt laws, forest regulations, the enforcement of section 144 Indian Penal Code, curfew orders, executive bans on meetings etc. and [we] bowed our heads to lathis of the police who represented the collective self of the people—the government, or underwent sentences of imprisonment as model prisoners etc.[86]

The situation however changed soon as

> even the tacit recognition of the government by the people is consciously withdrawn, a government ceases to have any sanction and persons who attempt to exercise governmental authority are usurpers and no obedience is due to them and any punishment meted out having no sanction became the acts of ruffian.[87]

The AICC resolution of 8 August demanding that the British authority should end completely, irrespective of the wishes or demands of various parties was a significant departure from the earlier practices, when the authority of the government had political sanctions to carry out the laws such as they are, and hence was legitimate. With the onset of the Quit India movement, the political equation between the Government and Congress had undergone a radical change in the context of the British being identified as 'a usurper of authority and power'.[88] The final countdown began when the Congress leadership, including Gandhi, appealed to the provincial Congress committees to remain united in the context of the last battle for freedom. Nehru, after his trip to the United Provinces was convinced that the forthcoming campaign was likely to attain the goal in view of the emotional attachment of the people with the cause of 'independence' and the role of Gandhi in galvanizing the masses into action. In his words,

> the mood of the country had changed, and from a sullen passivity it rose to a pitch of excitement and expectation. Events were not waiting for a Congress decision or resolution; they had been pushed forward by Gandhiji's utterances and now they were moving onwards with their momentum. It was clear that, whether Gandhiji was right or wrong, he had crystallized the prevailing mood of the people. There was a

> desperateness in it, and emotional urge which gave second place to logic and reason and a calm consideration of the consequences of action.[89]

For the Congress, India's independence was contingent on the British withdrawal and hence the resolution was passed accordingly. What however was different was the Congress instruction to the effect of asking the participants to act independently in the forthcoming struggle in case of the arrests of the leaders. The AICC thus encouraged,

> A time may come when it may not be possible to issue instructions or for instructions to reach our people and when no Congress committees can function. When this happens, every man and woman who is participating in this movement must function for himself or herself within the four corners of the general instructions issued. Every Indian who desires freedom and strives for it must be his guide urging him on along the hard road where there is no resting place and which leads ultimately to the independence and deliverance of India.[90]

The message, the resolution conveyed, was categorical in the sense that the AICC urged the people to take part in what was identified as 'the last battle for freedom.' For Gandhi, 'this [was] the last struggle of [his] life' and he did not want to wait any longer because 'delay is injurious and waiting any further would be humiliation for us.'[91] He thus appealed to the people to follow the *mantra,* Do or Die:

> we shall either free India or die in the attempt; we shall not live to see the perpetuation of our slavery. Every true Congressmen or [Congress] women will join the struggle with an inflexible determination not to remain alive to see the country in bondage and slavery.[92]

In a message to the nation just before his arrest, Gandhi spelt the task more precisely. Reiterating his faith in nonviolence, he thus elaborated,

> everyone is free to go the fullest length under *ahimsa*; complete deadlock by strikes and other non-violent means; *Satyagrahees* must go out to die not to live; they must seek and face death; it is only. when individuals go out to die that the nation will survive. *Karenge Ya Marenge* [We will do or die].[93]

Neither the AICC resolution nor Gandhi's last message was allowed to be reported in the press. So, there was less commotion especially immediately after the incarceration of the entire Congress leadership including Gandhi. The government strategy seemed to have worked in snatching the wind away from the Congress sail, as Tottenham misconstrued by preventing the Congress message getting across to the people. Although there were protest marches in Bombay, Gujrat and Bengal following the adoption of the resolution, they did not pose a serious threat to the British administration. In other words, the decision to gag the press paid-off, at least initially, and a confident Viceroy sought the Secretary of State's permission to deport Gandhi in particular, to save India from further crisis. When Linlithgow put it before the Executive Council for discussion they unanimously and vigorously opposed the deportation which would cause immediate reactions in India and would result in Gandhi staging a fast abroad, with a consequent crop of speculation and rumours about his ill-treatment, among others. Convinced in view of the strong opposition of the majority of the Executive Council members, L.S. Amery, the Secretary of State did not press the issue. There were also differences of opinion at the highest level of British administration as to whether Gandhi should be released if he undertook a fast unto death. The Viceroy held the view that Gandhi should not be set free 'even if he fasted to death.' All the Governors except that of Sind opposed the Viceroy vehemently. R. Lumley, the Bombay Governor, for instance, was 'certain that it would be gravest political blunder to allow him to die in detention.'[94] The Governor of the Central Provinces was 'emphatically of the opinion that local reactions would be most unfavourable. We would be left with no friends in India and even some of the Indian members of the Superior Services will turn against us.'[95] And hence, he urged the Viceroy 'that Gandhi should be released and restricted to Sevagram if he embarks on a fast.'[96] Apprehending the disastrous consequences of Gandhi's death during the imprisonment, Churchill's war cabinet appeared inclined to shift Gandhi to his Ashram in case of fast provided he could still be isolated from the outside world at Sevagram. As there was no categorical support for his view at the highest level of the Raj, Linlithgow had no alternative but to accept that

> we must be prepared in the event of a fast to set Gandhi at liberty (leaving it to himself to decide where he wants to go or whether he prefers to remain in Aga Khan's house at Poona) once fast begins to endanger his life and I feel, in the circumstances, this is the best alternative,[97]

one could think.

The August Revolution: A Radical Movement

The August movement was probably the most radical, both in its attitude towards the British and in terms of methods employed. Gandhi's 'Do or Die' slogan was an ultimatum to the British, leaving no space for negotiation at all. Such an attitude was not there in either the Non-cooperation or Civil Disobedience Movement when the Congress leadership was always keen to settle the disputes through some kind of compromise. Gandhi too agreed to accept this even at the cost of undermining the cause he fought for; its consequences were far-reaching: On the one hand, masses who took part in the anti-British campaign felt betrayed—which was likely to affect the future Congress mobilization adversely. Just as Gandhi opposed radical social movements which tended to disrupt social equilibrium, he was identified as a conservative political activist who declined to disturb the alien rule. On the other hand, the failure of the past Congress movements, led by Gandhi or his success in containing them at his will, strengthened the Raj in two ways, one, in its drive to challenge effectively the Congress campaign, the British had in Gandhi a friend who, due to his commitment to nonviolence, steered the political agitation in such a way as not to cause severe disruption in the British rule; and second, once the major organized political force was thus neutralized, the British administration could concentrate on controlling other radical socio-political movements challenging its continuity. So, despite the apparent threat to the Raj, both the Non-cooperation and the Civil Disobedience Movements let lose a political process, conducive to the prevalent rule which shaped, to a large extent the anti-imperial movement before the onset of the open rebellion.

Whatever the implications of the past Congress-launched political movements, their significance cannot be denied especially in gradually radicalizing the Congress which loomed large in the August revolution. The Congress had anticipated that the nature of the movement would be different and hence, it was not surprising that the instructions to the Congress workers were tuned to capture the heightened mass radicalism in the wake of the open rebellion; which was radical for the Congress volunteers who resorted to open violence in a number of cases. It is debatable whether Gandhi would have allowed such movement to continue in view of his strong antipathy to violence. The movement became violent gradually and British provocation had played a significant role. In fact, this also introduces another dimension to the structure of politics during the open rebellion. The movement's deviation from a true Gandhian path shows the autonomy of the unorganized level where political articulation and mobilization were begin carried out through different idioms which were meaningful only in the context of a completely different ideological perception. This supports the argument highlighting the autonomy of unorganized politics following a unique pattern and demonstrating new dimensions of the structure of grassroots politics.

The argument seems convincing in the light of the August 8 resolution and the transformation of the movement after the incarceration of the top Congress leadership.

Concluding Observations

Gandhi represented a new wave in the Indian nationalist struggle. At one level, he was a political activist and thus he adopted policies and designs to pursue his political goal, viz., India's salvation from colonialism; at another level, he was a humanist and had expressed his vision which, he felt, was complementary to his activities for liberating India from the British shackles by resorting to nonviolent resistance. As mentioned above, he presented a definite ideational vision by creatively amalgamating his political goal with that of his urge for humanizing humanity. In the recent past, while questioning the US state for refusing to constitutionally guarantee voting rights to the African Americans despite the promulgation of the 1893 Emancipation Act legally abolishing slavery, Martin Luther King Jr., always upheld 'universal brotherhood' and thus King never endorsed sanctions against the individuals who happened to be misguided and misled and were thus 'taught' wrong despite their role in misdeeds.[98] His challenge was thus directed against the forces of evil rather than against those responsible for evil deeds.[99] What was to be done was 'to get rid of the system and thereby create a moral balance within society'.[100] Following his success in the 1955 Montgomery bus strike, which began after an African American woman, Rosa Parks was asked to leave a seat in the bus to accommodate a white passenger, King thus suggested that

> [w]e must act in such a way as to make possible a coming together of white people and coloured people on the basis of real harmony of interests and understanding. We seek an integration based on mutual respect. ... We must now move from protest to reconciliation.[101]

Gandhi had a similar perception: he was opposed to the English rule in India because it was unfair and based on misconception about human beings; his campaign was thus directed against the unjust system and not against individual English man. 'I have no hate in me for a single Englishman', argued Gandhi.[102] 'My enmity is not' he further stated, 'against the Englishmen, it is against their rule'. It was a historical duty that he was born to perform in the most nonviolent way; hence 'if a hair of an Englishman was touched, he [would] feel the same grief as he [would] over such a mishap to [his] brother'.[103] A humanist to the core, the Mahatma never deviated from this vow. The same was true of his attitude towards the Muslims. He never expressed his anguish if his 'Mohammedan brothers sacrifice cows willingly for satisfying their dietary requirements [because by opposing them] he would lose them as brothers'.[104] Under these circumstances, the best option for him was 'to approach [his] Mohammedan brother and urge him for the sake of the country to join [him] in protecting her [cow]'.[105] His concern for the Muslims, which shaped his politico-ideological preferences was always privileged because he felt that if he applied force, it would cause unnecessary skirmishes and also animosity between the Hindus and Muslims which were neither desirable for the country and also an anathema to his belief in universal humanism. Hence, the option that he was left with in view of undiluted faith in universal humanism was 'to let the cow go for the simple reason that the matter is beyond [his] ability [and, as he further added that] if [he] were overfull of pity for the cow [he] should sacrifice [his] life to save [cows] but not to take [his] brother's'.[106] Highlighted here was Gandhi's concern for humanity which he would uphold even it meant an endorsement of cow sacrifice since it was integral to Muslims' dietary needs.

As discussed above, Gandhi's primary goal was to transform India from being a colony to an independent country which means that so long as India remained colonized, the prevalent circumstances were detrimental to the rise of humanism in the real sense of the term. His assessment was not merely limited to colonial India. In fact, as human history demonstrates, human beings are naturally inclined to oppressed those who were socio-economically weak and backward. A careful reading of human history since the rise of private property and family, would show that these tendencies evolved organically with humanity. Explanatory here was the history of serfdom and slavery. The rivalry between the dominating and dominated was as old as human civilization. Colonialism was just a phase when humanism was debunked of its spirit for which many thinkers and activists sacrificed their lives for the cause. Gandhi, of course, stands out, not only because he fought relentlessly against racism, which was an artificial design developed by a section of humanity to deprive the rest of their legitimate rights and claims as human beings. He was unique in another respect. As the campaign which he spearheaded in adverse circumstances underline, he provided humanity with a new device for combatting those seeking to gain by being partisan. In other words, Gandhi's nonviolent resistance was a conceptually innovative design based on experiences of many ideologues who helped him devise this specific mode of opposition to those subjecting human beings to inhuman torture. Since 1898, he was involved in the struggle for humanizing humanity and in doing so, he also realized that one of the reasons for dehumanizing humanity was the acceptance of humiliation, exploitation and torture as fated. Rabindranath Tagore also acquiesced with him in this regard because he also confronted situations in rural Bengal when people hardly endeavoured to extinguish the fire because they considered it to be god's caprice or they were destined to suffer such a calamity. Tagore addressed this social anomie in his specific ways while Gandhi preferred to mobilize people for redressal of their grievances due to either the lackadaisical attitude of the rulers or their motivated designs for securing benefits for them. So, Gandhi fought a politico-ideological battle when the alien authority ruled India and the indigenous masses were at the receiving ends.

Historically, Gandhi had to redesign the nationalist voice which was represented in the Western discourses especially when the nationalist opposition was first institutionally articulated with the foundation of the Indian National Congress in 1885. The politico-ideological scene underwent a sea change in the course of time and Gandhi emerged on India's political horizon when Indian masses did not seem to be as defensive as they were before because they now realized that colonialism was anything but humanistic. That Gandhi privileged humanity was proved when he withdrew the 1920–1922 Non-cooperation Movement since the nationalists deviated from the principle of nonviolence when the *Satyagrahees* threw the British constables in fire in Chauri Chaura in United Provinces. His approach to Hindu-Muslim question was also governed by the same consideration which, however, ran counter to some of the leading nationalists who felt that Gandhi was too soft to the Muslims for no reason. Nonetheless, Gandhi remained unfazed and he always nurtured the view that he publicly held vis-à-vis communal issues.

Even from the point of the politico-ideological agenda of the campaigns he led, one also discerns elements of humanism as critical to his ideational vision. From the 1918 Champaran *Satyagraha* till the 1942 Quit India Movement, he always perceived his role as a nationalist as complementary to his ultimate goal of universal humanism. In his ideational priority, colonialism and dehumanization went in tandem. Hence one fed the other which meant that if one was removed from human civilization, the globe would be free from reasons of being debased and decentred. What was however primary was the development of a mindset in support of the core values of universal humanism; the task did not seem to be so easy, but was not insurmountable. An analytical dissection of the campaigns under his stewardship reveals that they were another well-organized ideologically-governed human effort to seek to halt dehumanizing humanity which itself was an inspiring step for endeavour towards humanizing humanity.

The above campaigns were instances of how the concern for humanizing humanity attract many to participate in struggle when humanity was sought to be dehumanized. Many of Gandhi's predecessors fought the battle as it was religiously ordained to treat humanity as indivisible; but, for Gandhi, colonialism emerged out of selfish concerns of the European nations to feed industrialization that would not have succeeded without the contribution of many Afro-Asian countries which were forcefully colonized by them. India had hardly had a different trajectory. Although there were many internal factors which helped the British to conquer India, it was primarily due to the hunger for territorial hegemony of the industrialized Europe that led to the formation of colonies in Afro-Asian countries as they were too weak to effectively halt their march in the territory at their disposal. So, opposition to colonialism entailed, at one level, political emancipation from British rule; at another level, it had wider ramifications since the doing away with the imposed governance was also complementary to humanizing humanity. Colonialism was not just a political affront, but also an attack on the core values of humanism which were sacrosanct as well. Gandhi's campaigns thus served two purposes at the same time: combatting an alien authority was tantamount to service to humanity because colonizers were hardly restrained even their policy decisions adversely affected humanism. What is accordingly upheld is the view that the Gandhi-spearheaded anti-British onslaughts were endeavours both at removing the British rule and at combatting forces seeking to dehumanize humanity which consequently meant that his politico-ideological designs were favourably disposed towards humanizing humanity.

4

Conceptualizing Humanizing Humanity

India's struggle for freedom was multidimensional in the sense that there were many politico-ideological forces that acted decisively in wrestling freedom from colonialism. Gandhi's designs of nationalist campaigns were prominent among them. It is accepted now that contrary politico-ideological narratives also played critical roles in the battle for India's independence. What is striking however is also the fact that despite differences, these narratives generally acted under the Congress which was an umbrella organization providing space to organizations notwithstanding visible politico-ideological priorities. It was an arrangement that allowed an organization with less supporters to remain in the foreground—and for the Congress, it helped them emerge as an acceptable political design cutting across ideological variations. Especially during the period when the Mahatma reigned supreme, the role of many of the Congress-dependent organizations appeared to have eclipsed which demonstrates that his popularity among the masses.

What is now critical is to address how Gandhi became what he finally became in India's freedom struggle. Many explanations are available. He emerged as one of those people in the grassroots by adapting himself to their lifestyle. It does not therefore seem strange that a typical Indian barrister, who accepted the British dress code and the language while fighting legal battle in South Africa between 1893 and 1914, transformed himself into a typical Indian—not only in dress but also in the language which made him easily acceptable to the Indian masses after he took on the responsibility of leading India's freedom struggle. His successful launch of both regional and pan-Indian anti-British campaign was dealt with in detail in Chapter 3. Here, the purpose is to understand his ideational universe that helped him carve out a new narrative for reawakening freedom hopes in Indians to fight against the well-entrenched British suzerainty.

Gandhi was not just a historical personality in the sense that he continued to inspire even in the twenty-first century rebels fighting for their legitimate space in a world that is not immune from weapons and forces trying to harm humanity. In other words, Gandhi was a voice for those who always stood against the forces seeking to dehumanize humanity; he was also an equally powerful mode of action for humanizing humanity. As history shows, Gandhi was a continuity of the ideational priorities suggestive of designs for contributing to the consolidation of values, mores and practices in support of humanity in adverse circumstances. Gandhi was an intervention—perhaps one of the most meaningful ones—in a world of thinkers who also carried the cross for humanity, especially when it fell victim to torturous governance and inhumane sociocultural practices justified for the maintenance of social tranquillity. So, the battle had to be waged at two levels: at the macro level, Gandhi and his predecessors fought relentlessly for the marginalized sections of humanity and also continued the battle, at the micro level, for rescinding those archaic and derivational customary practices being nurtured by self-proclaimed custodians of sociocultural equilibrium. Especially in a country like India, modernized in the wake of British rule, which did not appear to have been totally immune from primordial sociocultural prejudices of the upper caste Hindus against the Dalits. Being a political leader who spearheaded a campaign against the British authority, Gandhi also raised his voice against internal colonization of Indian minds, especially the caste prejudices and discrimination against the Dalits.

As mentioned above, Gandhi nurtured ideational visions which had already gained momentum in the past. As a crusader, he carried forth the traditions amidst complex socio-economic and politico-cultural circumstances. Unlike many of his predecessors, who privileged universal humanism, Gandhi was simultaneously involved in pursuing two goals: one, an exclusive political goal of liberating India from the British yoke, and, and the other was directed towards human salvation by removing age-old prejudices justified by the intrinsically conditioned caste system. He was not alone for the first task as he was supported by his colleagues in the National Congress and those associated with the organization in various parts of India. The second task however, put him under dire stress since many his colleagues, even in the organization that he led, did not appear to be happy with him as it meant destabilizing the prevalent sociocultural balances. It is similar to the dilemma faced by Thomas Jefferson who retained Africans as slaves for managing his lifestyle as a landlord; but in the 1787 Philadelphia Convention, he argued that all men are created equal—while defending the federal constitution. Gandhi however tactfully managed the task since he prioritized his aim for India's political liberation over anything else.

Gandhi owed to those who influenced him creatively and intellectually to construct his model of nonviolent resistance. Furthermore, contact with many of his mentors also helped him evolve his unique approach to humanity. Being a religious man, he picked up many of ideas from the scriptural sources as long as they contributed to the development and sharpening of views vis-à-vis humanism. What stands out in his philosophical priorities was his unflinching commitment to humanism being one indivisible compact. His opposition to the rulers was primarily due to their attempts at separating humanity into superior and inferior; against those nurturing caste prejudices because they accepted a caste-based division of society.

The journey that Gandhi began by successfully leading *Satyagraha* in Champaran, Kheda and Ahmedabad during 1918–1919, culminated in the transfer of power from the British to India in 1947. The aim of this chapter is to highlight the fundamental pillars of his conceptual parameters that helped him develop nonviolent resistance, a move that continues to be relevant long after his death in 1948. There are two major arguments in the chapter: the first argument revolves around the conceptual inputs that Gandhi privileged while developing his own ideas; and the second argument is an attempt to show how the changing socio-economic milieu and politico-ideological compulsion of running an organization assisted him in the articulation of an ideational priority. The task is challenging, but worth-pursuing since it unfolds a new mirror to assess Gandhi's role as a crusader who waged war against activities that led to dehumanizing humanity.

Unfolding of an Ideational Vision

Gandhi stands out because of his nonviolent methods to achieve his politico-ideological ends as was evident when he withdrew the 1920–1922 Non-cooperation Movement because the volunteers deviated from being nonviolent in their opposition to the representatives of the rulers. Although, in the case of the 1942 Quit India Movement, he did not seem to be as committed to nonviolence as he was in the past; he explained this by countering that an exploitative system needed to be opposed as strongly as possible to defend humanity. In other words, as appalled as he was by many of the government feats for undermining humanity, he did not rule out the deployment of violence if necessary to remove a torturous ruling authority.[1] Nonviolence appeared to have received less attention as it could have been ineffective. Gandhi's suggestion was a strategic one which could be justified if the situation demanded to attain the goal of, humanizing humanity. He illustrated his point by stating that,

> I do believe where is only a choice between cowardice and violence, I would advise violence. Thus, when my eldest son asked me what he should have done, had he been present when I was almost fatally assaulted in 1908, whether he should have run away and seen me killed or whether he should have used his physical force which he could and wanted to use and defended me, I told him that it was his duty to defend me even by using violence.[2]

It was made clear by the Mahatma that the deployment of force was contingent on the situation; in grave circumstances, the volunteers could resort to violence if no option was left to pursue. Gandhi, by referring to what his son was allowed to do in 1908 to save him from being fatally wounded, also left no doubt about the use of violence in certain situations. What disturbed him, however, was the application of violence even in places that did not require violent resistance. Hence, he argued that, over time, this principle had been 'perverted and it had been followed formulaically, and often hypocritically'.[3] By clarifying why he supported violence in specific circumstances, he 'sought to restore to it its true sense'.[4] Hence he argued that

> the religion of nonviolence is not meant for the *rishis* and saints. It is meant for the common people as well. Nonviolence is the law of our species as violence is the law of the brute. The spirit lies dormant in the brute and he knows no law but that of physical might. The dignity of man requires obedience to a higher law—the strength of the spirit.[5]

Implicit here are two important claims critical to Gandhi's faith in nonviolence: on the one hand, he justified that nonviolence was an obvious strategy for protecting humanity; it was a strategy of the common people for defending themselves against attacks; on the other hand, he also upheld the view that mental strength to stand face-to-face against those who tended to deploy means to hurt their opponents was required to practice nonviolence. He further elaborated the theme in a text, entitled 'the doctrine of the sword', which he published in *Young India*, by saying that

> I have therefore ventured to place before India the ancient law of self-sacrifice. For *Satyagraha* and its off-shoots, non-cooperation and civil resistance, are nothing but new names for the law of suffering. The *rishis*, who discovered the law of nonviolence in the midst of

> violence, were greater geniuses than Newton. They were themselves greater warriors than Wellington. Having themselves known the use of arms, they realized their uselessness and taught a weary world that its salvation lay not through violence but through nonviolence.[6]

Here, he was emphasizing the consequences one was likely to face while challenging the opponents. The point that a nonviolent resister willingly inflicted pain and injury onto themselves underlined that one needed to be courageous to accept this. As nonviolent struggle was also a test of patience, Gandhi insisted that nonviolence was a strategy which needed time to unfold. So, those who participated were required to have boundless patience and the capability to withstand physical injury and pain. This was very difficult, although Gandhi, by being an effective mass leader, inculcated the spirit of sacrifice for a greater cause which he articulated as opposition to those dehumanizing humanity and, involvement in the campaign for humanizing humanity. To work for this cause, Gandhi argued for the consolidation of a mindset set to a complete withdrawal of violence despite provocations. At another level, he insisted on the nurturing of a mindset that left no room for violence; it was most important for nonviolence to strike roots in one's behavioural traits. It was clearly stated when he mentioned that

> *Ahimsa* [nonviolence] is not the crude thing it has been made to appear. Not to hurt any living thing is doubt a part of *ahimsa*. But it is its least expression. The principle of *ahimsa* is hurt by every evil thought, by undue haste, by lying, by hatred, by wishing ill to anybody.[7]

By stating the core values of *ahimsa*, Gandhi elaborated its features by iterating that faith in nonviolence was critical to the success of nonviolent resistance. As he outlined,

> *Ahimsa*, truly understood, is, in my humble opinion, a panacea for all evils mundane and extra-mundane. We can never overdo it. Just at present, we are not doing it at all. *Ahimsa* does not displace the practice of other virtues, but renders their practice imperatively necessary before it can be practised even in its rudiments. … Mahavira and Buddha were soldiers, and so was Tolstoy. Only they saw deeper and truer in their profession, and found the secret of a true, happy, honourable and godly life. Let us be joint sharers with these teachers and this land of ours will once more be the abode of gods.[8]

On another occasion, he advanced his arguments in favour of nonviolence by identifying integral features when he stated that

> Non-violence in its dynamic condition means conscious suffering. It does not mean meek submission to the will of the evildoer, but it means the putting of one's soul against the will of the tyrant. Working under this law of our being, it is possible for a single individual to defy the whole might of an unjust empire to save his honour, his religion, his soul and lay the foundation for that empire's fall or its regeneration.[9]

This confirmed his undiluted faith in nonviolence, which he internalized as one of the most effective means of combatting evils seeking to dehumanize humanity. To reignite the zeal of the volunteers participating in nonviolent resistance to colonizers, he further noted that

> 'your duty is not to run away from an enemy. it will be a grave lapse if you do, saying in excuse *ahimsa paramo dharmah* [nonviolence is as good as religious faith which cannot be abdicated]'. You wish destruction of your enemy some way or other. Because you cherish belief in non-violence, it does not mean that you are effectively observing the rule, for in that rule there is no place for running away in fear. It is your duty to defend those among the Indian people who want themselves, their women, their moral standards, and their wealth to be defended. How to do this? Those who have no faith in the principle which is dear to me and which I embrace may certainly take up arms. It is for this reason that I welcome the right of enlisting as volunteers which has been granted to us. I shall advise the people in this hall to join up. If anyone asks me whether he would be offered a commission or not, I would tell him to reserve such grumbling for the future, and not be too particular for the present and so miss the opportunity offered. Let us tell the Government that we are ready. That will be worthy of us.[10]

The above statements are probably the most crisp remarks made by the Mahatma on the nature of nonviolence resistance. Explicit here are three critical characteristics of a campaign rejecting violence- one, fear needed to be won, which meant that those who participated in the struggle should never feel scared of the counter-attack by the opponents; it further underlined that the volunteers were endowed with tremendous mental strength to sustain their commitment to carry forward, two, the battle for attaining the goal had to be completely nonviolent; which implied that those nurturing means other than *ahimsa* were to discouraged to take part since it was contrary to the core beliefs of Gandhian struggle, and third, as soon as the volunteers joined their colleagues, they were instantaneously involved in the struggle against perpetrators of violence and activities contrary to humanism.

Evolution of an Ideational Vision

As already established, Gandhi was baptize politically baptized in a context that witnessed various organized attacks on humanity in South Africa and India. *Satyagraha* or nonviolent struggle against efforts towards dehumanizing humanity struck roots while challenging the racist government in South Africa. As shown in chapter 3, Gandhi succeeded in forcing the political authority to accept the demands he thought were necessary for people. His dialectical interaction with the Indian socio-economic realities was certainly a significant input; besides this, he also acknowledged the invaluable contribution of 'three moderns [who] have left a deep impress on [his] life and captivated [him]: Raychandbhai by his living contact, [Leo] Tolstoy by his book, *The Kingdom of God is Within You* and [John D] Ruskin by his *Unto This Last*'.[11] Additionally, the Bombay based Raychandbhai, became an intellectual mentor to Gandhi. He was impressed by his 'wide knowledge of the scriptures, his spotless character and his burning passion for self-realization'.[12] Gandhi appeared to be swayed by him and he was confident that 'his intellect … [and] his moral earnestness … evolved the conviction in him that he would never willingly lead me astray … [and] in my moments of spiritual crisis, he was my refuge'.[13] The interaction continued even after he left the country for South Africa; Gandhi after his return to Bombay in 1914. Why was Raychandbhai so critical in the evolution of Gandhi's core values? As he wrote in his autobiography, Gandhi found many of the answers he was searching for to understand humanity and the claim that it was a compact collective. The Mahatma mentioned that he greatly owed to Raychandbhai for one, having kindled his interests in the Hindu texts of *Vedas* and *Upanishads* since they were aids to comprehend how India evolved as a community of communities; secondly, for having instilled in him the idea that without a mentor, it was difficult to grasp the complex themes mentioned in the scriptural texts, and finally, because he was in favour of celibacy even within marriage which was a definite step towards *ahimsa*.[14]

For Gandhi thought had no meaning unless it was lived-out. A new idea incited interest in him only if it was worthwhile. Once a book gripped his imagination, he always pondered over its message and put it into action to uncover the truth. His reading interest was varied, though he preferred to read religious and moral literature. He not only read Plato's *Apology* and William Salter's *Ethical Religion* (1889), but also translated them in his mother tongue, Gujarati. Three books that influenced Gandhi when he was in South Africa were Henry David

Thoreau's essay on *Civil Disobedience* (1849) which was, according to him, 'a masterly treatise'; Leo Tolstoy's *The Kingdom of God is Within You* (1893) which not only 'overwhelmed' him but also 'left an abiding impression on him' and in which he claimed to have first discovered the doctrine of non-violence and love;[15] John Ruskin's *Unto This Last* (1862) 'brought about instantaneous and practical transformation in [his] life' and he 'determined to change [his] life in accordance with the ideals of the book'.[16]

Gandhi's devotion to nonviolence was based on internalizing the ideas of Leo Tolstoy, Henry David Thoreau, Edward Carpenter, and John Ruskin, besides drawing from major religions of India, including Hinduism. In his own confession, besides his mother who instilled in him 'saintliness'[17] '[t]hree moderns have left a deep impress on my life and captivated me: Raychandbhai by his living contact; Tolstoy by his book, *The Kingdom of God is Within You*; and Ruskin by his *Unto This Last*'.[18] Gandhi was drawn to Raychandbhai, the saintly Jain jeweller who he met in Bombay before his departure for England because of 'his deep intellect, … moral earnestness, and … a conviction that he would never willingly lead [Gandhi] astray … [and] put him in the right spiritual path'.[19] On another occasion, he admired Raychandbhai because he 'was the one who had gone beyond all limitations and had succeeded himself in completely identifying with every living creature. … He was free from contradiction between speech and behaviour'.[20] Not only was he introduced to the complexities of life, Raychandbhai also helped Gandhi understand the core principles of Jainism which 'taught [him] to judge a *Mussalman* from his standpoint and a Christian from his. [He was thus] gifted with the eye to see [himself] as others see [him] and *vice versa*'.[21] After a careful reading of how the Mahatma assessed Raychandbhai, it can be fairly argued that he was one of the initial mentors who guided him to appreciate the core values of humanity. As he proceeded with life despite odds, he always attributed Raychandbhai's valuable inputs to his capacity to reconceptualize humanism in a different fashion.

Similarly, as stated earlier, he was clearly inspired by Leo Tolstoy's *The Kingdom of God is Within You*. In two significant ways, Gandhi was influenced by Tolstoy—first, Gandhi was drawn to the Sermon on the Mount that figured prominently in *The Kingdom of God is Within You*. He learnt five cardinal principles of human existence reflecting qualities like compassion, humility, self-criticism, forgiveness, and renunciation of material gain—which, in other words, is articulated in what is known as 'the turn of the other cheek' philosophy. The second important idea that Gandhi drew from Tolstoy was love. In his letter to Gandhi, Tolstoy elaborated that love was the only way to rescue humanity from all troubles, and that was the only method of saving people from exploitation. In very ancient times, he argued, love was proclaimed with special strength and clearness among many people to be the religious basis of human life. Love, and forcible resistance to exploitation, involved a mutual contradiction as to destroy utterly the whole sense and meaning of the conception of love.[22] Hence, he concluded that the sole meaning of life was to serve humanity by contributing to the establishment of the kingdom of God which could only be done by the recognition and profession of truth by every man.

The other thinker who had a strong bearing on Gandhi's thought was John Ruskin, especially his text—*Unto This Last and Other Essays*. According to Gandhi, 'the book was impossible to lay aside once I had begun. I determined to change my life in accordance with the ideas of the book'.[23] He believed that he discovered 'some of his deepest conviction of life [that] made [him] transform his life'.[24] Two significant ideas of Ruskin that seemed to have critically influenced Gandhi were dignity of labour and concerns for the poor. Drawing from this, Gandhi argued that 'the good of the individual is contained in the good of all', and God was the owner of the universe and human beings were mere 'trustees'—resonating Thomas Aquinas—'God alone has the absolute dominion over material nature'. According to Gandhi, Ruskin redefined wealth in a different perspective were it was articulated in terms of 'happiness' that it brought to human life in 'a righteous' manner. The third major figure that significantly influenced Gandhi was Henry David Thoreau, especially his famous text—*Civil Disobedience and Other Essays* (1849). Gandhi was persuaded to believe in civil disobedience which meant 'disobedience to the state' within the accepted social forms. Like Thoreau, he also felt that 'there will never be a really free and enlightened State until the State comes to recognize the individual as a higher and independent power, from which all its own power and authority are derived, and treats him accordingly'.[25] Edward Carpenter, the famous English socialist poet, also cast a significant influence on Gandhi. Being critical of Western modern civilization, Carpenter proposed, in his *Civilization: Its Cause and Cure and Other Essays*, that civilization was 'a form of disease that human societies pass through'.[26] Drawing on an analogy of 'diseased human body', Carpenter further clarified the point by saying that

> just as … in human body, when the inner and positive force of Health has departed from it, that it falls prey to parasites which overspread and devour it; so when the central inspiration departs out of social life does it writhe with mere maggots of individual greed, and at length fall under the domination of the most monstrous egoist who had been bred from corruption.[27]

Gandhi elaborated this point in a more poignant way in his *Hind Swaraj* (1909) by comparing modern civilization with a crippling 'snake coil' that harmed human civilization in more ways than one. Similar to Thoreau, who justified civil disobedience against a brutal state, Carpenter defended protest as inevitable because

> the protest is not merely or chiefly against specific forms of injustice; it is rather to all intent and purposes, a protest against our present social system itself as intrinsically undemocratic, and as necessarily contributing to poverty and dependence on the one hand and excessive wealth and injustice on the other.[28]

Identically, Gandhi justified protest against colonialism as perhaps the only way to save humanity. Despite being a loyal subject of the British Empire, he challenged the authority since it deviated from the well-established norms of governance and basic democratic values and principles.

Gandhi learnt about nonviolence presumably because of his grounding in India's socio-economic circumstances. As he narrated in his autobiography, his faith in non-violence was rooted in his appreciation of religion driven critique of violence. Despite being born in a typical Hindu family, he was drawn to other religious traditions. Because his father was keen to learn about other religious texts from Islam, Jainism and Christianity, he always encouraged in discussions at home which inculcated in him 'toleration for all faiths'.[29] Although he appreciated the Sermon on the Mount,[30] he disliked Christianity because of the alleged role of the Christian missionaries in 'forcible conversion [and] also pouring abuse on Hindus and their gods'.[31] In conceptualizing his argument for non-violence, Gandhi was thus indebted to several intellectual sources, including major religions. His ideas were thus an outcome of his constant engagement with those appropriate texts that clearly charted a nonviolent course of action. It may have been a strategy that became effective presumably because of the context in which nonviolence was appreciated in preference to other contending ideological alternatives. He opted for nonviolence because he was persuaded to believe that in those circumstances, nonviolence was likely the most effective design to gather supporters for his cause. Being a strategist who also evolved his politico-ideological priorities based on inputs from pacifists, Gandhi was probably a pioneer in organizing a nonviolent campaign against forces seeking to debilitate humanity. According to him, colonialism, besides being a design of economic exploitation, was also geared to debase the core values of universal humanism. Nonetheless, at a particular juncture of human history, these evil forces rose to attempt to dehumanize humanity. This was not an exception; it was a permanent feature of the unfolding of human history, as codified by many in different phases of human civilization. Gandhi's endeavour was complementary to the efforts undertaken by many who held ideational preferences. Fundamental here is the point that Gandhi's commitment to nonviolence was a continuity of a trend that unfolded in various phases in the progress of humanity. He was emphatic in his belief that nonviolence had a long history in human civilization and it became an important tool to combat forces determined to dehumanize humanity. This was not a weapon of the weak, but of the strong, because nonviolence emerged as a powerful tool for humanizing humanity out of a creative blending of ideas and designs derivative of many intellectual and sociocultural traditions. By drawing on the historical roots of nonviolence, Gandhi was now able to clearly explain how he evolved his idea of nonviolence by saying that,

> [i]t was the *New Testament* which really awakened me to the rightness and value of Passive Resistance. When I read in the *Sermon on the Mount* such passages as 'resist not him that is evil, but whosoever smiteth thee on thy right cheek turn to him the others also', and love your enemies and pray for them that persecute you, that ye may ne sons of your Father which is in heaven, I was simply overjoyed, and found my opinion confirmed where I least expected it. *The Bhagavad Gita* deepened the impression, and Tolstoy's *The Kingdom of God is Within You* gave it a permanent form.[32]

Nationalism and Humanizing Humanity

As a devout believer in universal humanism, Gandhi never appreciated the idea of nationalism as it was inherently divided in its criteria. For him, this was a ploy by those who failed to understand humanism in the real sense of the term. Long before he appeared on India's political scene, he championed the idea of living together separately. He illustrated his point by emphasizing that what was critical was to develop a mindset drawing on 'fellow-feelings for one another'.[33] Gandhi focused on this aspect because Muslims were reported to have been swayed by the fact that they were insecure in Hindu-dominated India. His argument was straight: a belief in *ahimsa* did not allow anyone to force others who had no faith in it. By contrasting the acceptance of *ahimsa* by the Hindus and Muslims' reluctance, he argued that it was perfectly possible to remain together despite having contrarian approaches to nonviolence. Being opposed to violence, Gandhi insisted that the sole duty of a practitioner of nonviolence was to plead to his opponent that the idea of killing ultimately harmed humanity as a whole; so, it needed to be stopped for humanity's sake. With his new vision, not only did he challenge the stereotypical version that Hindus were different from Muslim socioculturally, and thus could never remain together, but he also generated new insights questioning the nationalistic approach to inter-communal relations. This was clearly argued when he pressed that 'it is … preposterous to suggest that Hindus and Muslims cannot live together amicably because the Hindus believe in *ahimsa* and the *Mohammedans* do not'.[34] This was perhaps one of the first attempts by the Mahatma to expose the inherent inadequacies of the idea of a nation based on exclusive markers. That it was fundamentally ill-conceived was persuasively argued by defending that separate religious identity was hardly an effective device for cementing a bond among the people especially when they related to others belonging to different religious groups. This was obvious since by being together in specific locations, drawing on one another was not an exception but instinctive.

Gandhi's assessment of the issue was based on his existential experiences of being an Indian in a context when the foreign rulers, by deploying divide and rule strategy, endeavoured to reap the benefit of division between the two demographically preponderant communities. This argument was echoed by Rabindranath Tagore, who while corroborating what the Mahatma suggested, emphatically argued that identity in the subcontinent was not uni-dimensional. Challenging the concept of 'nation' as it undermines the multi-layered Indian identity, Tagore reminds us of the combined role of the 'little' and 'great' traditions in shaping what he loosely defined as the Indian nation.[35] India's diversity, felt Tagore, was its 'nature [and] you can never coerce nature into your narrow limits of convenience without paying one day very dearly for it'.[36] Not only 'have religious beliefs cut up society into warring sections . . . social antagonisms [between the Hindus and Muslims] have set up impassable barriers every miles—barriers which are guarded night and day by forces wearing the badge of religion'.[37] For Tagore, the gulf between the communities was largely due to the 'cultural forces', released by British colonialism that 'fractured the personality of every sensitive exposed Indian and set up the West as a crucial vector within the Indian self'.[38] As India's social system got distorted, '[l]ife departed', agued Tagore, 'from her social system and in its place she is worshipping with all ceremony the magnificent cage of countless compartments that she has manufactured'.[39] Interrogating the 'totalizing' dimension of the nationalist project—where a single entity, called nation, always prevails over other forms of identity—Tagore sought to provide an alternative to an 'essentialistic' invocation of identity in the shape of a nation. According to him, while articulating the civilizational identity of India, the importance of underlying cognitive and ethical claims, which are invariably lodged in and originate from contradictory social locations, could never be undermined. So, the European modular form of nation was conceptually futile and politically inapplicable because India's civilizational identity was multiple and thus difficult to capture on a single axis.

Gandhi held identical views. Like Tagore, he rarely used the term, nation, in the sense Jinnah referred to it. Yet, Gandhi failed to halt the historical processes whereby the Indian Muslims bargained for a separate Muslim state successfully. Jinnah's role was equally significant. In the penultimate year of the transfer of power, the Jinnah-led Muslim League secured parity with the Congress and in the 1946 Shimla conference, the League and Congress representation was equated.[40] What came in the form of the 1940 Lahore resolution became feasible. Jinnah's appeal to 'unsettle the settled notions . . . of Muslims being a minority [that] had been around for so long'[41] was finally becoming a reality. So, not only did the *Quaid-i-Azam* succeed in dramatically altering the role of the Muslims in the over-all constitutional settlement on the eve of the Great Divide, but he also transformed the Muslim community into a nation by ascertaining 'territorial sovereignty to a heterogeneous community turned homogeneous nation'.[42] The Muslim community, for Jinnah was, therefore not 'an abstract historical-political entity . . . but a separate nation with distinct interests [which] could not be treated only as a minority'.[43] This was categorically stated by the founder of Pakistan, MA Jinnah who defended division of India as the only option to fulfil the demand of the Indian Muslims. According to him,

> there are two major nations in India. This is the root cause and essence of our troubles. When there are two major nations how can you talk of democracy which means that one nation majority will decide everything for the other nation although it may unanimous in its opposition ... these two nations cannot be judged by Western democracy. But they should be treated as equals and attempts should be made to solve the difficulties by acknowledging this fact.[44]

Jinnah was categorical that under no circumstances, would India remain one; dismemberment of India was the only option and he justified this with reference to the well-entrenched sociocultural differences between Hindus and Muslims. Gandhi however was not persuaded; he offered two core arguments to counter Jinnah—first, he put forward a contextual argument by highlighting that the logic of creating religion-based nation state was faulty since religion could neither be a stabilizing nor a unifying factor in humanity. So, by seeking to gloss over the obvious diversities among the Indian Muslims for a sovereign state, Jinnah ignored the long-drawn historical processes in the community formation of a community. Secondly, for Gandhi, nation was hardly a criterion to conceptualize the complex and deeply heterogeneous communities in the subcontinent regardless of religion. Couched in a humanitarian fashion, the second argument dwells on the devastating consequences of conceptualizing Hindus and Muslims as separate nations. Holding politics responsible for the Hindu–Muslim schism, Gandhi pledged to

> rescue people from this quagmire and make them work on solid ground where people are people. [Therefore his] appeal [was] not to the Muslims as Muslims nor to the Hindus as Hindus, but to ordinary human beings who [had] to keep their villages clean, build schools for their children and take many other steps so that they [could] make life better.[45]

To Gandhi, nation, as a categorizing device was perhaps the narrowest in its manifestation ignoring the inherent diversities of the communities. Conceptually non-viable and practically inappropriate, the application of nation as a category weakened the anti-British struggle, he argued, because of the clash of interests between the Hindus and Muslims once they were characterized as separate nations. The idea of nation was not only nonviable, but also highly misleading because it was an attempt to divide humanity around those axes which were, instead of bringing people together, inherently separating them. With their own experiences in Britain, colonizers appeared to have played with sociocultural differences among the colonized to perhaps gauge if the nationalistic design was effective enough to raise barriers separating one section from another. They succeeded since the divide and rule strategy worked favourably in a milieu when the confluence of many factors led to the 1947 Partition of India based on religion.

The Idea of *Swaraj*[*]

Although the idea was articulated differently by Bal Gangadhar Tilak when he declared that '*swaraj* is my birthright', his predecessors—the Moderate thinkers—also talked about the phenomenon though in a limited sense. As an idea and a strategy, *swaraj* gained remarkably in

* The argument in this section appeared in a rudimentary form in my earlier works on Indian nationalist thought.

the context of the nationalist articulation of the freedom struggle and the growing democratization of the political processes that already brought in hitherto socio-politically marginal sections of society. So, *swaraj* was a great leveller in the sense that it helped mobilize people despite obvious socio-economic and cultural differences. Underlining its role in a highly divided society like India, *swaraj* was defined[46] in the following ways: national independence, political freedom of the individual, economic freedom of the individual, and spiritual freedom of the individual or self-rule. Although these four definitions are about four different characteristics of *swaraj,* they are nonetheless complementary to each other. Of these, the first three are negative in character while the fourth one is positive in its connotation. *Swaraj* as 'national independence', individual 'political' and 'economic' freedom involves discontinuity of British rule, absence of exploitation by individuals and poverty, respectively. Spiritual freedom is positive in character in the sense that it is a state of being where everyone aspires to actualize once the first three conditions are met. In other words, there is an implicit assumption that self-rule is conditional on the absence of the clearly-defined negative factors that stood in the way of realizing *swaraj* in its undiluted moral sense. While elaborating *swaraj*, the Mahatma linked it with *swadeshi* in which his theory was articulated. In other words, if *swaraj* was a foundational theory of Gandhi's social and political thought, *swadeshi* was the empirical demonstration of those relevant social, economic, and political steps for a society. Dwelling on the nature of *swadeshi*, Gandhi thus argued,

> *swadeshi* is that spirit in us which restricts us to the use and service of our immediate surroundings to the exclusion of the more remote. If we follow the *swadeshi* doctrine, it would be your duty and mine to find out neighbours who can supply our wants and to teach them to supply them where they do not know how to proceed, assuming that there are neighbours who are in want of healthy occupation. Then every village of India will almost be a self-supporting and self-contained unit, exchanging only such necessary commodities with other village where they are not locally producible. This may all sound nonsensical. Well, India is a country of nonsense. It is nonsensical to parch one's throat with thirst when a kindly Mohammedan is ready to offer pure water to drink. And, yet thousands of Hindus would rather die of thirst than drink water from a Mohammedan household.[47]

Swaraj was not merely political liberation; it broadly meant human emancipation as well. Although the Moderates were pioneers in conceptualizing the idea in its most restricted sense, *swaraj* was most creatively devised by the Mahatma who never restricted its meaning to mere political freedom from British rule. In his words, 'mere withdrawal of the English is not independence. It means the consciousness in the average villager that he is the maker of his own destiny, [that] he is his own legislator through his own representatives'.[48]

Political freedom is an important characteristic of *swaraj*. For the Moderates, political freedom meant autonomy within the over-all control of the British administration. Even the most militant of the Moderates like Surendranath Banerjee, always supported constitutional means to secure political rights for the Indians within the constitutional framework of British India. Unlike the Moderates, the Extremists did not care much about the methods and insisted on complete independence, which meant a complete withdrawal of the British government from India. Although both these positions were qualitatively different, *swaraj* was identified by its narrow connotation of political freedom glossing over its wider dimension that Gandhi highlighted. For the pre-Gandhian nationalists, the idea of freedom was articulated in a negative way, à la absence of colonial rule—for Gandhi, freedom was the right of the citizens. For Mahatma, *Satyagraha* was a device to acquire rights instead of 'receiving rights'. He had no rights in South Africa because he was an Indian. He argued in an imperial context, rights remained linked with the interest of the ruler . In other words, the claim that rights and freedom went together was relative to the circumstances in which they were politically fashioned. Furthermore, his articulation of *Satyagraha* was one of the most creative conceptualizations on how to secure rights and freedom. According to him, 'passive resistance [*Satyagraha*] is a method of securing rights by personal suffering. It is the reverse of resistance by arms'.[49] This is how Gandhi distanced himself from his predecessors by highlighting the wider connotations of *swaraj*, and insisting that *swaraj* was a means to secure rights for the denied.

Economic freedom of the individual is the third dimension of *swaraj*. Given the inherent exploitative nature of colonialism, poverty of the colonized is inevitable. For the Moderates, including Gokhale and Naoroji, the guarantee of constitutional autonomy to India, was likely to result in the reduction of poverty. This was because Britain, as the emerging industrial power, was expected to develop India's productive forces through modern science and technology and capitalist economic organization. They were soon disillusioned as India's economic development did not match with what they had expected from the British rule. Instead, Indians were languishing in poverty despite 'a free flow of foreign capital' to India. Thus, according to the Moderate leaders, the essence of nineteenth century colonialism 'lay in the transformation of India into a supplier of food stuff and raw materials to the metropolis, a market for the metropolitan manufacturers and a field for the investment of British capital'.[50] Underlining the most obvious contradiction between foreign and indigenous capital, Naoroji characterized the latter as an instrument of 'exploitation of Indian resources' and unskilled Indian workers in the foreign-owned plantations and coal mines.[51] These workers, in the words of Naoroji, 'acted as mere slaves, to slave upon their own land and their own resources in to give away the products to the British capitalists'.[52] This argument was reiterated by the Extremist in their economic critique of colonialism. On this basic assumption, Bipin Chandra Pal of the Lal-Bal-Pal trio from the Extremist wing of the Congress, put forward a devastating critique of the colonialism by saying that

> the introduction of foreign, mostly British, capital for working out the natural resources of the country, instead being a help, is, in fact, the greatest hindrances to all real improvements in the economic condition of the people. It is as much a political, as it is an economic danger. And the future of New India absolutely depends upon an early and radical remedy of this two-edged evil.[53]

Perhaps the most original contribution to the conceptualization of economic freedom was 'the drain theory'. It was therefore argued by the nationalists that

> a large part of India's capital and wealth was being transferred or 'drained' to Britain in the form of salaries and pensions of British civil and military officials working in India, interest on loans, taken by the Indian government, profits of British capitalism in India and Home Charges or expenses of the Indian Government in Britain.[54]

As a result, India continued to be poor while Britain flourished economically. So, economic freedom that constituted an important dimension of *swaraj* involved a complete liquidation of the ruling power in India. The idea reflected in Gandhi's conceptualization of economic freedom. For him, economic freedom meant 'freedom from poverty'. There are, according to the Mahatma, three criteria of judging whether a society suffered from poverty. These include the availability of the necessities of life (decent food, clothing and dwelling), the ability to enjoy the fruits of one's toils, and the opportunity for growth of an individual. Articulating his argument in a liberal fashion, Gandhi was qualitatively different from his predecessors in the sense that unlike the Moderate–Extremist critique of colonialism where individual is submerged in the collectivity, his was a serious and perhaps the most well-argued theoretical position vis-à-vis individuals as a collective. So, *swaraj* operated on two levels: on the one hand, it was a protecting device where individuals were the focal point; it also operated, on the other hand, at the collective level where individuals participated as a nation in several political experiments that Gandhi conducted underlying the possibilities of a merger of individual identity with that of the collective.[55]

Self-rule is probably a unique dimension of *swaraj* indicating its qualitative difference with political freedom. As a concept, it denotes the process of removing the internal obstacles to freedom. Conceptualize self-rule as an important ingredient clearly indicates the importance of moral values which are relative to society. One may argue that the removal of colonial rule would automatically guarantee economic and political freedom. This is hardly applicable to self-rule presumably because it is 'a self-achieved state of affairs' rather than something 'granted' by others.

Swaraj as self-rule was conceptualized in two contrasting ways. The Moderates viewed *swaraj* purely in its narrow political meaning, namely, limited political freedom within the British Empire.[56] So, it was not out of place for Dadabhai Naoroji to insist on 'self-government and treatment of India like other British colonies'.[57] In other words, what Naoroji had insisted was British rule on British principles. The Moderate opinion revolved 'a tone of sweet reasonableness'.[58] For them, self-rule involved 'modification' of the British administrative system, not its removal. The articulation of self-rule was historically conditioned since the primary goal of the Moderates was to keep a low profile so as to not provoke a repression which would nip the nationalist effort it the bud. So, for historical reasons, the Moderates were not able to transcend the limitations of their time and their aim was defined as the promotion of 'the interests and well-being of the people for the Indian Empire'. Accordingly, they also expected those who participated in the nationalist campaign to behave as 'responsible members' of the Empire. Dadabhai Naoroji had therefore no hesitation in stating that

> if we honestly expect that English nation will do its duty towards us, we must prove worthy by showing that we are never unreasonable, never violent, never uncharitable. We must show that we are earnest, but temperate, cognizant of our rights, but respectful of those of others;

> expecting the fairest construction of our own acts and conceding these to those of others.[59]

Swaraj was narrowly conceptualized by the Moderate wing of the early Congress was possibly due to the constraint and the circumstances of an expanding imperial power though it was attributed to 'the fear of ruling bureaucracy'.[60] But their compromising stance vis-à-vis the Empire provoked those who later became the Extremists in radically altering the concept of *swaraj*. *Swaraj,* in its early Extremist conceptualization, refers to a particular system of governance that

> lay down a minimum standard of life, with a minimum wage rate and the taxes should be regulated by capacity to pay [because] it is extremely unjust that a man possessing one acre of land should pay the same rate as a man possessing 500 or 50,000 acres. The higher the income the higher [should] be the tax.[61]

So, *swaraj* is therefore political self-rule with specific prescriptions seeking to protect economic interests of both the rich and poor. So, for Bipin Pal, one of the foremost Revolutionary Nationalist ideologues, *swaraj* was 'autonomy absolutely free of British control' and it was for all Indians. He visualized India to be 'democratic and federal [comprising] republican states (British Indian provinces) and constitutional monarchies (native states)'.[62] In contrast, Aurobindo equated *swaraj* with absolute political independence—'a free national government unhampered even in the least degree by control'. In his conceptualization, *swaraj* was not

> a mere economic movement, though it openly strives for economic resurrection of the country … not a mere political movement though [it involves] political independence. [It was] an intensely spiritual movement having for its object not simply the development of economic life or attainment of political freedom, but really the emancipation, in every sense of the term of Indian nationhood and womanhood.[63]

While Aurobindo focused on the overall nature of *swaraj*, Pal sought to identify its structural contour within the British rule.

Drawing on both descriptions, Bal Gangadhar Tilak, perhaps the most important leader of the Revolutionary Nationalist movement, elaborated the conceptualization of *swaraj*. Unlike the Moderates who argued for gradual introduction of democratic institutions in India, Tilak insisted on immediate *swaraj* or self-rule. His concept of *swaraj* was not complete independence but a government of Indian themselves that 'rules according to the wishes of the people or their representatives. Similar to the British executive that 'decides on policies, impose and remove taxes and determine the allocation of public expenditure', Indians should have the right 'to run their own government, to make laws, to appoint the administrators as well as to spend the tax revenue'. This is one dimension of his thought; the second dimension relates to the notion of *prajadroha* or the right of the people to resist an authority that loses legitimacy. In Tilak's conceptualization, if the government fails to fulfil their obligation to the ruled and becomes tyrannical, it lacks legitimacy to rule. What is interesting to note is that Tilak's *prajadroha* also justifies the enactment of laws to prevent unlawful activities of the people. If contextualized, this idea makes sense because he was aware that a total rejection of the government would invite atrocities upon the nationalists who neither had the organizational backing nor a strong support base among the people. So, his support for governmental preventive mechanisms was strategically conditioned and textured.

Tilak also added a new dimension to *swaraj* that not only had a political connotation (self-rule) but also a moral [and] spiritual connotation (self-control and inner freedom). Keeping this in view, Tilak thus defined *swaraj* as

> a life centered in self and dependent upon self. There is *swarajya* in this world as well as in the world hereafter. The *rishis* who laid down the law of duty betook themselves to forests, because the people were already enjoying *swarajya* or people's domination which was administered and defended in the first instance by the *Kshtriya* kings. It is my conviction, it is my thesis, that *swarajya* in the life to come cannot be the reward of a people who have not enjoyed it in the world.[64]

Tilak played a historical role in the construction of a new language of politics by being critical of 'the denationalized and Westernized' Moderate leaders who blindly clung to Western liberal values, disregarding their indigenous ideals while articulating their opposition to the British rule. Tilak's political views are, therefore an amalgam, argues N.R. Inamdar, 'of the Vedanta ideal of the spiritual unity of mankind and the Western notions of nationalism as propounded by Mazzini, [Edmund] Burke, [JS] Mill'.[65] It is possible to argue that Tilak had a wider appeal; for his campaign was couched in a language that drew upon values rooted in Indian culture and civilization in contrast to the Moderates. So, Tilak was not merely a nationalist leader with tremendous political acumen he represented a new wave of nationalist movement that created an automatic space by providing the most powerful and persuasive critique of Moderate philosophy, and articulating his nationalist ideology in a language that was meaningful to those it was addressed to. This is how Tilak is transcendental and his ideas of *swaraj*, boycott and strike had a significant sway on Gandhi, who refined and tuned some of the typical Extremist methods in a completely different socio-economic and political context—when the nationalist struggle had its tentacles not only in the district towns but also in the villages that remained peripheral in the pre-Gandhian days of freedom struggle.

In tune with Tilak's conceptualization, Gandhi also underlined the fact that *swaraj* is also 'a self-transformative' activity. In other words, *swaraj* was about 'the constantly confirmed consciousness of being in charge of one's destiny, not just about liberty, but about power'.[66] Swaraj, in Gandhian formulation, entails 'a disciplined rule from within'.[67] Defining *swaraj* as 'self-conversion' and 'mental revolution' to experience 'inner freedom', he argued that '*swaraj* is a state of mind to be experienced by us [and it] consists in our efforts to win it'.[68] This is what runs through in Gandhi's following statement,

> it is *swaraj* when we learn to rule ourselves. It is, therefore, in the palm of our hands. Do no consider this *swaraj* like a dream. Here there is no idea of sitting still. The *swaraj* that I wish to picture before you and me is such that, after we have once realized it, we will endeavour to the end of our lifetime to persuade others to do likewise. But *swaraj* has to be experienced by each one for himself (sic). One drowning man will never save another. Slaves ourselves, it would be a mere pretension to think of freeing others.[69]

The Gandhian idea of *swaraj* as self-rule seems to be based on the philosophical notion of *advaita,* which is 'etymologically the kingdom or order or dispensation of "*sva*, self, myself" [or] the truth that you and I are not other than one another'.[70] So, the Gandhian struggle for *swaraj* and by extension, the Indian struggle for *swaraj* under the leadership of thinkers and revolutionaries such as Tilak and Aurobindo was 'always implicitly an *advaitin* struggle, a struggle for the kingdom of self or autonomy and identity as opposed to the delusion and chaos and dishonour, heteronomy and divisiveness'.[71] The British rule was simply unacceptable because it was a symbol of power of illusion of not-self, otherness, to be precise, *Maya* hindering the effort 'to see God face to face in the truth of self-realization'.[72]

Characterizing *swaraj* in its widest possible connotations and not merely as self-determination in politics, Gandhi sought to articulate *swaraj* in ideas. Political domination over man is felt in the most tangible form in the political sphere and can be replaced easily. Political subjection primarily means restraint on the outer life of people, but the subtler domination exercised in the sphere of ideas by one culture on another continues to remain relevant even after the overthrow of a political regime. So, to attaining self-rule in its purest sense involves a challenge to cultural subjection, perpetrated by those who are colonized, as well. Gandhi's definition of *swaraj* as a self-transformative device is an attempt to thwart the well-designed colonial endeavour of cultural subjection that was likely to survive even after the British rule probably due to the uncritical acceptance of colonial modernity. Cultural subjection is different from assimilation in the sense that it leads to, according to Bhattacharya, 'a creative process of intercommunication between separate cultures without blindly superseding one's traditional cast of ideas and sentiments'.[73] While explaining this implication, Bhattacharya further argues that

> we are beginning to realize that we have for long wrongly counted on principles that have application only to countries that are already free and already established and have not had sufficient perception of the dark thing they call 'power' which is more real than any logic of political scholarship. In the field of social reform, we have never cared to understand the inwardness of our traditional social structure and to examine how far the social principles of the West are universal in their application.[74]

So, *swaraj,* if understood in its narrow conceptualization, is reduced to a mere political programme ignoring its wider implications where the very foundation of cultural subjection is challenged. Gandhi was also aware that inner freedom remained unattainable without a conducive socio-political environment. Hence, there was need for removal of the British rule to ensure both political and economic freedom. In other words, while a conducive environment was essential for freedom, it needed to be created and maintained by appropriate political and economic activities. The ability to act well in the socio-economic political arena is 'the test of the new meaning of self-rule [that] prepares one to lead the life of an active citizen. That is why, in [Gandhi's] view spiritual freedom cannot remain an asocial [neither] an apolitical nor an atemporal condition'.[75] *Swaraj,* in Gandhian conceptualization, translates into, argues Fred Dallmayr, 'the self-rule of a larger community, that is, into a synonym for national democratic self-government or home rule'.[76] As an empirical construct relevant to a political community, *swaraj* is closely linked to the idea of *swadeshi* and the cultivation of indigenous (material and spiritual) resources of development. The *swaraj*-based polity comprised small, cultured, well-organized, thoroughly regenerated, and self-governing village communities. They would administer justice, maintain order and take important decisions, and would not merely be administrative but powerful economic and political units. In view of its given texture, they would have, argues Bhikhu Parekh, 'a strong sense of solidarity, provide a sense of community, and act as nurseries of civil virtue'.[77]

Religion and Nationalism

As argued above, Gandhi was not a political activist by definition, he was involved in a gigantic political struggle for India's emancipation from the British hegemony. It was evident time and again, especially when he linked the nationalist campaign with the salvation of humanity. For him, his participation was an aid to the human emancipation or a concerted attempt to liberate humanity from day-to-day difficulties and other impediments damaging humanity due to the pursuit of selfish activities. One should add a caveat here. His notion of religion was hardly ritualistic; it was a design to contribute to humanizing humanity which implied endeavour towards restraining those who were involved in belittling, if not undermining humanity at the slightest pretext. While identifying the aim of the nationalist struggle, he categorically stated that as long as British rule was allowed to continue, humanity was certain to be brutalized. Hence, he was determined to remove the foreign rulers. This was one aspect of his ideological goal which would be achieved with India's decolonization. Parallel to this was his fundamental aim which was 'to realize God, and all his (sic) activities, social, political, religious, have to be guided by the ultimate aim of the vision of the Almighty'.[78] This sentence needs to be read with the following sentences to clarify that he was not a religious guru but a social reformer who evolved sociocultural and politico-ideological designs to contribute to humanity. As he further stated,

> the immediate service of all human beings becomes a necessary part of the endeavour, simply because the only way to find God is to see Him in His creation and be one with it. This can be done by service of all. I am a part and parcel of the whole, and I cannot find Him apart from the rest of humanity.[79]

One was mentally equipped to realize God, by serving humanity, argued Gandhi. Although it had not been stated categorically, he also underlined that he always envisioned humanity to be compact; so, the division among human beings in terms of caste, class and ethnic identities was clearly an anathema in his ideational universe. It was highlighted when he emphasized that

> I subscribe to the belief or philosophy that all life in its essence is one, and that the humans are working consciously or unconsciously towards the realization of that identity. The belief requires a living faith in a living God who is the ultimate arbiter of our fate.[80]

Reinforced here is the claim that humanity is one and the goal of humanism would be realized once it was upheld by all. Being aware that the reality was not so favourably disposed because for many believers, their religious identities were a constraint as they were taught to follow one path to reach God, dismissing others beliefs as irrelevant in the process. Being opposed to this endeavour at dividing humanity, Gandhi warned that 'religion is after all a matter … of the heart [and which] … gives one the greatest solace in the midst of severest fire is God'.[81] According to him, religion was not a set of dos and don'ts, it was a mode of realizing the core values of spiritualism in accordance with the set of beliefs one preferred to nurture. Unless one was equipped to accept others as one of them, one was unable to be religious in the actual sense of the term. Gandhi further argued that 'religion declares that so long as man harbours evil he is impure and unfit to stand before God. So, the first duty of any of you who has such thoughts is to confess about it and thus purge yourselves of the evil'.[82] Here was the view that Gandhi's faith in Hinduism did not mean that he was free to exploit those with different religious predilections. Furthermore, as humanity was one, the question of division and differences did not arise. What stood out in Gandhi's views on religion was religious schism was created and was an impediment for human progress, and being baptized in a particular religious faith never meant that those other different religious inclinations were adversaries. There are two major implications of such an argument, first, Gandhi was a nationalist activist responsible for spearheading a campaign which was no longer united with the view of the consolidation of Muslim separatism; secondly, despite the rise of divisive politics at the behest of the Muslim League the Mahatma upheld that only by being true to this well-nurtured faith, it was possible to realize his ultimate goal of humanizing humanity.

What Gandhi meant by religion was neither scriptural texts, nor dogmas undermining one faith for another. Religion, to him was a device to bring about transformations in human existence which were unavoidable as far as humanization of humanity was concerned. While elaborating the theme further, Margaret Chatterjee, one of the dozens of scholars of Gandhian ideational vision, argued that 'what Gandhi's religious thought offers [was] … a challenge to think through and live through the breadth and depth of opportunities for sharing, whether worldly goods or those deepest intimations which are warp and woof of the inner life'.[83] Religion was a tool to ensure humanization of humanity, and it was possible because it taught humans to sacrifice for others. By seeking to inculcate feelings, religion was not, at all, merely ritualistic, but a design to transform humanity from being confined to a narrow boundary to one being integrated with other beings. Hence, she argued that 'religion', according to Gandhi,

> envisaged as a way of life of the caring individual who participates in a multi-faith community, striving nonviolently to establish a just society, would close to the conception of the founder figures, saints and seers of the different traditions [which was a realistic aim provided] our hearts are large enough to draw on the heritage of the entire human family and to live accordingly.[84]

Clearly articulated, the above argument by Chatterjee, is helpful in comprehending the dialectical interconnections between Gandhi's perceptive thoughts and his existential experiences—both as an individual and a political leader who had an opportunity to interact with people from different identities. As a devout Hindu, religion was indispensable to the Mahatma but it did not prevent him from learning from the core precepts of other religions. As he mentioned in his autobiography, he 'got an early grounding in toleration from all branches of Hinduism and other sister religion, including Jainism and Buddhism'.[85] With a kind of upbringing in a family that was receptive to multiple religious faith, Gandhi developed a mindset which was neither narrow nor obsessed with any one philosophical dispensation. His exposure to Raychandbhai and writings of Leo Tolstoy at a young age helped him consolidate what he learnt at the beginning of his adult life in India and England. One must not ignore that being religious was not a guarantee for the believers to be committed to humanity. Had it been so, the Christian Missionaries in India would have charted out a different course of action; had the Hindus nurtured the same view, Hindu–Muslim division would never have reached such a devastating proportion. So, religion, by itself, was not a device to spread views about human solidarity cutting across socio-economic and politico-cultural barriers. What Gandhi endeavoured was to build and strengthen a mindset to rise above religious pettiness and accept humanity as one indivisible unit. Ideationally, the objective was not only defensible but also worth-pursuing although there were practical difficulties in imbibing the values complementary to the realization of the goal. Nationalism of the Western variety was a constraint since its aim was to homogenize human identities which might be an option for the socioculturally homogenous societies of the West; but, contrary to the African-Asian countries. India was not an exception, despite the fact that Hinduism remained a dominant religion, although its diverse articulations and manifestations in human behaviour in various parts of the country challenged the conventional understanding of religion. Two important claims can be made here- on the one hand, it is not logically persuasive to define religion monochromatically because its nature is also context-specific; since barring the core principles, the behavioural traits of those subscribing to one religious faith differed from one part of India to another. Gandhi was against unionization of religious faith perhaps due to his belief in a family appreciative of the view that Hinduism was less an ecumenical religion and more a way of life. On the other hand, Gandhi felt that Christianity was a divisive religion because by proselytizing Hindus, Christian Missionaries were involved in dividing Hindus. Hence, Gandhi never conceived religion to be integral to the process of humanizing humanity. Hence, he urged that his struggle against colonialism was neither against the Christian missionaries nor against the English nor the Europeans; but, 'it is a struggle between religion and irreligion, powers of light and powers of darkness'.[86] By condemning the Christian missionaries as they were involved in seemingly spreading God's message to humanity with 'a Satanic motive of undermining the religious faith of those forcibly converted',[87] Gandhi highlighted how the moral custodians of Christian values helped develop tendencies towards dehumanizing humanity. He felt, 'every canon of public morality has been broken by the victors in the name of virtue'[88] which was not only debilitating for humanity but also detrimental to the selfless sacrifice of many genuine Christians who were silently working for humanizing humanity in collaboration with those with different religious priorities located in various part of the globe.

Summarizing the Argument

Gandhi was a political leader who rose to prominence because he fought the British nonviolently. Besides being a leader with a definite political agenda, he was an ideologue of a struggle with a completely nonconventional mode of opposition. He was a political voice couched in a religious language to accord its salience among the majority of the Indians who were religious-minded. With a short-term goal of national independence and long-term goal of humanizing humanity, Gandhi was perhaps one of the rare global leaders who successfully blended two objectives most creatively. *Swaraj* was the ultimate goal because India's freedom meant attainment of self-rule which was complementary to his ultimate objective of realizing humanization of humanity.

Swaraj is a conceptual riddle with multiple philosophical dimensions, articulated empirically in different ways. Notwithstanding its clear political overtone, the idea is multidimensional is evident from the fact that it was sought to be conceptualized in multiple intellectual discourses during the freedom struggle. For instance, M.N. Roy conceptualized *swaraj* in a completely different way. Critical of the Gandhi's notion of *swaraj*, Roy argued that

> neither self-government realized progressively by constitutional means, nor '*swaraj*' conquered by Non-Cooperation will change the economic condition of the [masses]. Even full Dominion Status, conceded overnight, would not give political rights to the workers and peasants. A Dominion Parliament controlling the entire policy of the government would not protect the toiling masses from the exploitation of the capitalist and land-owning classes. Such a parliament would defend the interests of the property-owners and act at the beck and call of the Money-bag. The national would still remain in the bonds of slavery. Therefore, the interests of the majority demand complete separation from all imperial connection and the establishment of a Republican State based on the democratic principles of Universal suffrage.[89]

Given his ideological affinity with Marxism, it was expected of Roy to suggest that *swaraj* in the right sense of the term was possible, only by liquidating the imperial governance. Despite being theoretically correct, Roy appeared to have ignored the fact that for this type of struggle to succeed, what was required was the creation and consolidation of a different kind of mindset, which was sadly lacking in India. Here was the fundamental difference between Roy and Gandhi, who understood the Indians better than any of his compatriots and devised sets of strategies to galvanize the masses into action despite adverse consequences. So, instead of combatting the adversaries, Gandhi wanted to win them over by suffering because it

> is the law of human beings; war is the law of the jungle. [Hence,] suffering is infinitely more powerful than the law of the jungle for converting the opponent and opening his ears, which are otherwise shut, to the voice of

> reason. … The appeal of reason is more to the head but the penetration of the heart comes from suffering. It opens up the inner understanding in man. Suffering is the badge of human race, not the sword.[90]

Gandhi conceptualized the nationalist battle in a different perspective which did not correspond with Roy's who judged the struggle within the theoretical inclinations of Marxism. Hence, it was expected that Roy's views were at variance with those of Gandhi. Nonetheless, the debate between them reveals that not only did Gandhi stick to his point of view, but he also proved himself to be theoretically consistent which further underlined that his commitment to nonviolence and universal humanism were never diluted, even in the face of fierce critiques by those who mattered in the nationalist struggle.

Historically textured, the idea of *swaraj*, though emerged at the dawn of the Indian nationalist movement, had undergone radical changes in response to the shifting nature of the anti-British campaign. At the outset, the Moderate nationalists defined it in a very limited manner, underling the evident political tone of *swaraj* without seeking to explore its multifaceted nature that unfolded gradually. Nonetheless, the Moderates were pioneers in conceptualizing the nationalist movement that was incipient in terms of an indigenous vocabulary. Here lies the unique contribution of those who always articulated their anti-British protest in a constitutional way. Although it was politically restraining in the period that followed, *swaraj* as home rule gained salience when the nationalist movement revolved around elites with a very narrow social basis.

In its second phase, the nationalist articulation was far more complex, both ideologically and in terms of the participants, the nature of which had undergone a metamorphosis due to the expansion of the social base of the anti-British campaign. Reflective of the ideological mood of the period, *swaraj* was redefined and reinterpreted considering the ideas and discourses that governed the nationalist intervention. It's limited meaning of political freedom did not remain as decisive as before in circumstances when the peripheral segments of society began to get involved in the central domains of the elites. In the Extremist phase, *swaraj* was associated with 'inner freedom' of the individuals and was translated in indigenous practices, because of its easy acceptance by the Indian masses. Two factors seem to have worked, first, given its Indian roots, *swaraj* had an advantage as a political force, and secondly, *swaraj* as self-government had also provided a blueprint for future governance. So, it was not surprising when Tilak included Home Rule with self-control and inner freedom of the individuals in his definition of *swaraj*. As a result, not only did he accord a new salience to the nationalist campaign, but he also paved the way for the Mahatma to construct *swaraj* in a way that ideologically motivated the masses even in the face of a massive retaliation by the British government.

The Gandhian intervention in *swaraj* is unique in two specific ways, first, it is neither a doctrine of governance nor a device to ensure political freedom. Hence *swaraj* in its limited sense was what Gandhi neither aspired, nor stood for. Secondly, by defining *swaraj* as self-rule, the Mahatma sought to capture its metaphysical basis, which if explained in a mundane political form, would remain unrealized. Hence the departure of the British was only one of the conditions of *swaraj*. It is true that '*swaraj* does consist', as Gandhi argued, and 'in the change of government and its real control by the people, but that would be merely the form. The substance that I am hankering after is a definite acceptance of the masses and therefore a real change of heart on the part of the people'.[91] This is where Gandhi and Nehru ideologically, they were both convinced that *swaraj* 'must mean more than political independence, and must be seen to bring real change in the lives of the ordinary people, particularly the most disadvantaged'.[92] Gandhi, as argues by the Brown, a historian

> came to this conclusion as a result of his religious conviction that for the individual, service to the poorest was the way to discover the divine and that true self-rule depended on a new sense of moral community rather than on political arrangements.[93]

Contrarily, Nehru maintained that the well-entrenched indifference of the people to the poor was not easy as Gandhi conceived. He argued that freedom would only be genuine if people were released from the bondage of poverty and ascribed social status, and given new life chances and choices. He also recognised that the nation had to go on being forged; that is, created in the lived experience of Indian people, particularly those who had had little part in the initial processes of nation-building, or who felt threatened and excluded. He thus 'recognized that forging the nation was a long-term process of moulding attitudes also of giving many disparate and previously disadvantaged groups to stake in the nation'.[94] So, this is a state of mind that needed to be experienced internally. Without such an experience, argues the historian Parel while interpreting Gandhi's definition, '*Swaraj* would remain a mere theory or doctrine; it would never become an internal principle of action in the external political sphere'.[95] In other words, *swaraj* is an interconnected theoretical terrain with a specific form and principles. This conceptualization is unique in more ways than one . And, its significance lies in the complex unfolding of the concept that evolved in a particular historical context with roots in the philosophical trends of what is generally conceptualized as Indian reality. In this sense, *swaraj*, both as a theory and practice, is an innovative intervention that remained meaningful in the different phases of the nationalist movement that underwent ideological changes. Although *swaraj* was made popular by Bal Gangadhar Tilak while combatting the British authority, it was Gandhi who infused a new meaning to the phenomenon which was effective enough to draw masses to him.

Concluding Observations

Gandhi was not a theoretician, but a political leader who, while charting out a new means for humanizing humanity, evolved unique conceptual parameters to understand the reality and suggest what was required to be done to halt human decadence. As shown above, there were many theoretically innovative inputs which informed Gandhi when he was building a mass campaign based on the spiritual idea of *ahimsa*, which was upheld by their approach to worldly existence. By accepting nonviolence as a weapon to organize a pan-Indian campaign against the mightiest Empire of the twentieth century, the Mahatma rekindled interests in India's rich philosophical and intellectual traditions. As soon as *ahimsa* was accepted as a politico-ideological tool, Gandhi also integrated it with 'tolerance' and 'service' to humanity. His aim was thus not nationalistic, but a global well-being of humanity. Or, in other words, as he was appalled by the rise of tendencies debilitating humanity, he strongly felt that India's freedom and tendencies towards dehumanizing humanity needed to be fought together. While evolving his unique approach to humanity, he paid as much attention to the Western discourses as he did to indigenous intellectual tradition. Hence he was credited with 'reinventing Indian tradition, … like Vivekananda [who] by drawing on the exhortations of the sixteenth century social reformer, Chaitanya, attributed India's social reawakening to the ideals of charity (*seva*) and tolerance (*sahanshilata*)'.[96] What he had in mind was elaborated in his advice to his fellow colleague, Akhandananda when he stated that 'you must give your body, mind and speech to the welfare of the world. [Instead of surrendering to the deities in the temples], surrender yourself to the service of the poor, the illiterate, the ignorant, the afflicted [and] help them by your selfless *seva*'.[97] His instructions were later translated as 'practical *Vedanta*'.[98] On the basis of similarities of ideas between Vivekananda and Gandhi, especially in regard to their efforts towards humanizing humanity, the former was reported to have anticipated Gandhi with, of courses differences on some issues presumably because they had different socio-economic and politico-cultural contexts in which they rose to prominence. Being unanimous in their views that selfless *seva* to the disprivileged was akin to service to the providential authority, they deplored Western civilization, and emphasized that ethical and spiritual freedom were dialectically interconnected with political freedom; both championed 'forms of physical courage and moral fearlessness'; both wanted to retain caste in a revised form and a readily accepted measure of inequality. They, of course, differed presumably because of the differences in the context in which their ideas evolved. For instance, while Vivekananda's 'universalism prioritized *Advaitic*—and hence Hind—religious concepts as the prerequisites for tolerance and religious diversity, Gandhi tirelessly promoted neighbourliness to counter tensions among communities, especially with Muslims'.[99] This brief interjection is made to argue that Gandhi's politico-ideological priorities also had Indian roots. Before Gandhi, many thinkers endeavoured to execute their ideas to chart out different roadmaps for India's salvation by attacking foreign domination and sociocultural prejudices; they were also engaged in developing a mindset opposed to humanizing humanity. Like Vivekananda, the Mahatma also realized that much of the distresses for Indians were largely due to execution of policies directed for the well-being of the British. Instead of accepting them as inevitable—given the capability of the colonizers in harming them—the *Satyagrahees* fought them back nonviolently. While carving out a conceptually-creative narrative for India, Gandhi set his tasks on the basis of his ideational vision which was based on both derivative Western intellectual inputs and indigenous discourses. One of the persuasive texts where Gandhi formulated his ideas is *Hind Swaraj*, published in 1909, for defending his point of view by developing a fierce critique of Western civilization because it was one of most significant steps towards dehumanizing humanity.

The aim of *Hind Swaraj* was 'to confront the anarchist and violence-prone Indian nationalists with an alternative to violence, derived from Gandhi's earliest experiments with *Satyagraha*'.[100] As Gandhi wrote, '*Hind Swaraj* [was] written in order to show that [his countrymen] are following a suicidal policy [of violence], and that, if they but revert to their own glorious civilization, either the English would adopt the latter and become Indianized or find their occupation in India gone'.[101] Even the title of the book was most significant; he included his version of *swaraj* which was relevant to India. This was the first and perhaps the most elaborate discussion of *swaraj* from Gandhi's perspective. For Gandhi, the aim of his project was therefore to recover 'the self under colonialism'.[102] Attributing colonialism in India to 'our weaknesses', Gandhi thus argued,

> The English have not taken India; we have given to them. They are not in India because of their strength, but because we keep them. … Recall the Company Bahadur. Who made it Bahadur? They had not the slightest intention at the time of establishing a kingdom. Who assisted the Company's officers? Who was tempted at the sight of their silver? Who bought their goods? History testifies that we did all this. … When our Princes fought among themselves, they sought the assistance of Company Bahadur. That corporation was versed alike in commerce and war. It was unhampered by questions of morality. … Is it not then useless to blame the English for what we did at the time? … it is truer to say that we gave India to the English than that India was lost.[103]

Many Indians became blind supporters of British rule because they—by being morally decadent—felt Gandhi, were unable to appreciate the importance of freedom in the growth of humanity. There is another side to the argument. Gandhi was contemptuous of Western civilization which, under the garb of civilizing the colonial 'subjects' pursued its 'selfish interests'. Based on 'brute force', the Western civilization was both 'narrow' and 'perverted'. So, in Gandhi's perception, by providing legitimacy to colonialism, the modern civilization subverted 'the natural evolution' of societies clinging to the traditional ways of life. Drawing from the civilizational resources of a traditional society like India, Gandhi produced 'the most effective trans-cultural protest against the hyper-masculine world view of colonialism'.[104]

Hind Swaraj was the most creative response to the perversion of industrial capitalism. For Gandhi, industrialization remained the driving force behind Western civilization. 'Machinery is' he characterized, 'the chief symbol of modern civilization; it represents sin'. [Hence] if the machine craze grows in our country, it will become an unhappy land'.[105] Condemning the role of machine in 'de-humanizing' the workers toiling in the factories for 'profit' in which they had no share, the Mahatma argued that 'it is necessary to realize that machinery is bad. We shall then be able to do away with it. … If, instead of welcoming machinery as a boom', he further mentioned, 'we would look upon it as an evil, it would ultimately go'.[106] According to Gandhi, 'a snake-bite is a lesser poison' than 'the mill industry' because while the former merely harmed the body, the latter 'destroys body, mind and soul'.[107] Gandhi's critique of machine civilization was a creative response. While the earlier nationalists attributed the Western conquest of India to 'a superior military strength', Gandhi probed into the processes that led to such a drastic rise of the Western powers. Unlike his colleagues, Gandhi had no doubt that 'the source of modern imperialism lies specifically in the system of social production which the countries of the Western world have adopted'. It is the limitless desire for 'ever-increased production and ever-greater consumption and the spirit of ruthless competitiveness' that not only sustained the system but also impelled these countries to establish colonies that could be exploited for economic gains.[108] Industrialism was evil because the purpose of production was not to create an egalitarian, but to create a capitalist society. For industrialism to survive and thrive, Western industrial nations needed colonies to market their goods. Since colonialism and industrialism were complementary to each other, industrial capitalism was, as Gandhi saw, inherently harmful to human civilization.

Hind Swaraj was a long statement of Gandhi's introspection that acted in shaping his politico-ideological preferences that unfolded during India's freedom struggle. Fundamental here are a few points which are critical to comprehend Gandhi's approach to humanizing humanity. One, the Mahatma raised a strong voice against colonialism since it evolved with the sole purpose of protecting the material interests of a section of humanity. It was a design to separate humanity as superior and inferior: the superior had taken onto itself the responsibility of designing the steps to chart out a blueprint for humanization of humanity which was clearly prejudiced and sectarian. So, colonialism was a tool of dehumanizing humanity. Secondly, in this socio-economic and politico-ideological context, forces within India also contributed to the process of undermining the core values of humanity with support from the colonizers, and the prejudice ploys at play. India became a space where processes at dehumanizing humanity struck organic roots. On the whole, Gandhi's endeavour was not just exclusively political because he articulated a powerful voice against forces seeking to undermine humanity in a context which was tilted in their favour. Although, as Gandhi believed, that this was a temporary phase in human history, his involvement in India's freedom struggle also shows that humanization of humanity required effective challenges on the part of those willing to devote themselves to efforts seeking to nip the processes supportive of dehumanizing humanity in the bud.

Part C

B.R. Ambedkar (1891–1956)

Tagore and Gandhi approached humanization of humanity within liberal-constitutional framework that were in tandem with indigenous discourses. They charted out a new course for humanity which was toughened in India, both due to imposed colonial rule and the established sociocultural prejudices. For them, caste, class and religious differences were an anathema to a civilized society. Hence, in their writings and activities, they addressed the sociocultural and politico-ideological issues responsible for human decadence. Rammohun Roy's acceptance of British liberalism at the dawn of colonial rule in India loomed large as days passed on. The Brahmo Samaj, inaugurated in 1828, was also a forerunner of social transformation following liberal mode of thinking, although the members of the Samaj were equally inspired by India's lost intellectual resources. So, with the arrival of the British, many efforts were made to chart out a new narrative for India based on derivative inputs. Hence, it is argued that British colonialism brought about radical changes in the prevalent ideational visions which appeared to have adapted to the metamorphosed circumstances and politico-ideological priorities that were predominant before the advent of British rule.

While Western liberalism created a legitimate space for India's social reformers, it also led to the generation of ideas questioning the sociocultural template which was discriminatory against those who were called untouchables due to their birth. Gandhi and Tagore did not support discrimination due to individuals' ascribed identity; but, they did not pay adequate attention to the eradication of division based on caste identities. They had their own arguments although they were unable to make the kind of difference, they had expected because the social environment was not as favourably disposed as was necessary to radically alter the fate of those who remained peripheral due to customary practices.

One of the prominent names in the campaign for wresting a legitimate and respectable space in society for the Dalits was Jyotirao Govindrao Phule (1827–1890) who, despite being a Dalit, raised cudgels against caste atrocities in the name of social balance which meant protection of those who survived by exploiting the socioculturally peripheral sections of society. Opposed to the hegemony of the upper castes because it was contrary to humanity, Phule appeared to have been heavily influenced by liberalism of the West. Unfamiliar of the fact that the Western countries were equally divisive, Phule wrongly believed that as the Europeans were free from sociocultural prejudices, it was easier for them to understand how Indians were being tortured with the consolidation of caste system. There is however a misconception that Indian liberals who drew on Enlightenment principles were indifferent to the caste differences because this is not true. They did not pay adequate attention to this aspect of Indian society because they privileged some of the issues which were directly linked with the achievement of their politico-ideological goals. As history shows, both Gandhi and Tagore commented extensively on the adverse impacts of caste difference although they did not translate their opposition into effective campaigns because of their distinct politico-ideological priorities. Despite their failure to undertake activities for eradicating caste prejudices, their campaign for education irrespective of caste, played a critical role in making the people belonging to lower castes aware of the prevalent prejudices. So, Indian liberals, beginning with Rammohun and his colleagues in Brahmo Samaj, in particular, also had a dominant role in evolving a mindset opposed to caste hierarchy and efforts towards degrading a section of humanity with specific caste identities.

While assessing the contribution of Indian liberals, we must add a warning. Their ideas were governed by the prevalent context and issues which required immediate attention. For instance, the Hindu–Muslim animosity attracted Tagore's attention as this issue was predominant in Bengal—where he was born and raised—in the reckoning of the nationalists and also those who were involved in socially-relevant activities. Gandhi had a different socio-economic and politico-ideological context in which he was nurtured; it was a context where caste was critical to the shaping of human mindset; being aware of the importance of *varnashrama,* he never supported division of human around any axis since it was contrary to his conceptualization of humanizing humanity.

Indian liberals were also divided on the issue whether to focus on political emancipation from British shackles or human emancipation from the age-old sociocultural prejudices. For most of them, the battle for India's political independence was far more important than getting involved in campaigns for sociocultural changes. Hence, caste-prejudices were allowed to remain given the lackadaisical attitude of those who presided over India's struggle for political freedom from British hegemony. It had two diametrically opposite consequences, first, the liberals were blamed for being soft on their colleagues who continued to nurture caste prejudices because it was supportive of benefits they accrued due to the continuity of division of humanity according to caste. The other consequence was a split within the nationalist camp because there were many who strongly felt that Gandhi and his compatriots were reluctant to pursue the campaign against caste system. For the nationalist campaign, it created a fissure since those who did not support the campaign for rescinding caste system decided to be with the British because they believed that with the support of the state, they would succeed in claiming what they had been demanding. This was a matter of alarm among the nationalists, especially after the alienation of the dominant section of Muslims from the mainstream nationalist platform. For their indifference to the caste question, the nationalists had to pay a high price as we will see with the rise of B.R. Ambedkar (1891–1956) as the spokesperson for the untouchables or Dalits. It deserves a mention here that Ambedkar defended the rights of the marginal castes based on the canonical liberal ideas by upholding that division of humanity stood in contradiction with the core values of humanity.

The sections in Chapters 5 and 6 revolve round the ideational vision of Ambedkar which not only mobilized the Dalits but also helped them to establish themselves as citizens of independent India. As history shows, his efforts paid well and Dalits, at least in the public domain, were no longer considered peripheral. They became an integral part of India's social awakening and transformation, as well as equal stakeholders in society.

5

Reconceptualization of Humanizing Humanity

Born in 1891 to Dalit parents, Bhimrao Ramji Ambedkar introduced new concerns to the nationalist ideational vision. Since the inauguration of liberal constitutionalism in India in 1885 following the foundation of the Indian National Congress, the nationalist politico-ideological priorities did not offer adequate space to those socioculturally recognized as 'inferior', compared to the upper castes among the Hindus. Despite being aware of this aspect, nationalists hardly addressed caste imbalances as meaningfully as they deserved; instead, they appeared to have ignored the Dalit grievances because they were believed that they would be better equipped to deal with them following India's independence. The fact that the mainstream nationalists were not forthcoming in addressing these genuine issues does not mean that they put them under the carpet permanently; they opted to do so because they did not want to divert attention away from the campaign for political emancipation. Gandhi, who reigned supreme in India's political struggle against colonialism and among the nationalists, felt that with the establishment of village *swaraj*, caste segregation was likely to disappear because it was a system of governance based on an ideational vision of recognizing everybody at par with one another. So, Gandhi was confident that the indigenous model of village *swaraj* was well-equipped to effectively combat sociocultural segregation rooted in human practices for ages. The Mahatma's argument was without substance, argued his *bête noire*, B.R. Ambedkar who rightly mentioned that an age-old system of segregation accruing benefits to those at the higher echelon of society could never be ready to give up what they were accustomed to receive by dint of being born in upper caste families. The debate was non-conclusive since in the nationalist context, Ambedkar did not have the aura and political strength which his opponent had and he thus forced to take his point to its logical conclusion. Despite his strong reservation of the views Gandhi offered, he most reluctantly swallowed them; but it created a ripple which grew in importance in the nationalist priorities as India's freedom struggle drew to a close.

The story of Ambedkar's rise on India's political horizon as a counter-voice is also a story of the unfolding of liberalism in its most complex form. Being baptized politico-ideologically by his academic mentor, John Dewey at Columbia University, and by being exposed to the liberal ambience of the West, Ambedkar realized that the Indian social system was terribly brutal, if not inhuman, towards those who were born as Dalits. In other words, notwithstanding the nationalist commitment of humanizing humanity in opposition to the colonizers, it was so often diluted, if not bypassed, when the question of the caste-driven atrocities came to the fore. Indian nationalism was, according to Ambedkar, a design for pampering the caste Hindus at the cost of the millions of deprivileged sections of humanity, just for the accident of birth. For Indian liberals, liberalism became a ploy to sustain the exclusive rights of those who were not only privileged but also, by being dominant in the political dispensation, were well-equipped to gear the system in accordance with their preferences.

Ambedkar was a voice of regeneration and hope for those who remained deliberately left out by those with caste and class privileges. It was a great challenge for him amidst adversaries who were hardly sympathetic to his cause for selfish reasons. Just like Gandhi who won many battles against the rulers by charging them for deviating from the core tenets of liberalism, Ambedkar utilized the same tool against his colleagues in the nationalist campaign. Their concern for liberal values, argued Ambedkar, was considerably diluted once they were asked to address caste-related discrimination. It did not seem like a paradox because the Congress nationalists defended caste since it was necessary for them to sustain their constituencies of support among the caste Hindus. So, the political design which developed at the behest of the Congress was bound to be segregationist, because it was to be of help for the maintenance of their hegemony over a large section of humanity.

In view of the apparently deliberate near avoidance of steps to mobilize opinion against caste segregation by the Congress, one may question that its effort towards humanizing humanity appeared to be vacuous or at least without much substance. This implied that that their attack on the forces engaged in dehumanization of humanity could never be as effective as was made to believe. This is both an important conceptual and strategic question from the view of Dalit empowerment which Ambedkar held so dear to him. Conceptually humanization and dehumanization are dialectically interlinked; so, humanization remains a mere slogan unless the processes towards dehumanization are not allowed to strike roots. As Ambedkar showed, neither Congress nor any of the leading political parties associated with the nationalist campaign did not seem to have seriously dealt with the Dalit issue which was manifested in the uproar that he confronted as soon as he put in the public domain, his concern for his brethren. As the caste Hindus were mentally conditioned to their privileges, it did not appear to him, to be unusual, rather an obvious reaction that they felt threatened of losing their benefits; benefits they gained by being exploitative of those hapless individuals. Ambedkar was aware that the battle he lodged was not an easy one, not merely because the opposition was strong but also because of the hegemonic presence of a mindset supportive of caste system even by the victims of the system. It is similar to the situation in which Rammohun raised a strong campaign against the brutal custom of Sati when many orthodox Hindus opposed him as vehemently as possible; the fate of Vidyasagar was not dissimilar as he was also castigated by his brethren when he supported the Widow Remarriage Act in 1856. Ambedkar had also faced similar constraints when many of his colleagues did not extend the support, he expected, presumably because of the social hatred by the dominant section of caste Hindus one was likely to be confronted with. Nonetheless, Ambedkar rewrote the history of oppression in circumstances which were not tilted in his favour and stood out as a messiah in human history who, by carving out a new narrative for humanizing humanity, changed the course of human civilization from being sectarian to being universal in its texture and outlook.

The core points of this chapter have been laid down to form an argument demonstrating how Ambedkar accomplished his mission in an adverse milieu. The chapter pursues this argument in two parts: in the first part, the chapter reviews some of the initiatives which are drawn from his assessment of liberal constitutionalism of the Western variety and his firm critique of the indigenous discourses supportive of caste discrimination; the second part focuses on his written texts where he substantiated his argument in support of his contention. In other words, the chapter is both an elaboration of Ambedkar's own point of view and the context in which he fought against odds.

Unfolding of a Voice

Ambedkar was a voice for humanizing humanity; it was a voice that drew its inspiration also from a mindset challenging the defiance of core liberal norms. Based on his thorough understanding of core philosophical beliefs of liberalism, he argued that caste-system was anything but liberal as it was based on rejecting the fundamental liberal principle of treating human beings as equal. Besides his internalization of the basic liberal ideational vision, his existential experience as an untouchable helped him understand the difficulties of being born so. Ambedkar's ideational priority was a protest and, at the same time, an attempt to evolve a conceptually-persuasive model of analysis to understand the situation in which segregation was acknowledged as a socially acceptable norm instead of unconditional equality.

The argument in favour of unconditional equality is made within the theoretical format of 'the politics of difference' drawing sustenance from well-nurtured/and age-old 'prejudices' based on a constructed notion of superiority-inferiority paradigm. Prejudice is usually accompanied by the pronouncement/and the defence of 'difference,' as a marker of natural, obvious talents and hierarchy with its articulation in the difference between men and women, black and white, Hindus and Muslims, modern and primitive, civilized and barbarians, Christians, and Jews and so on. The construction and proclamation of difference form 'the core of the majority of judgments on the question of enfranchisement and disenfranchisement, the privilege of unmarked citizenship on the one hand, and the handicap and marginality, on the other'.[1] Denial of basic human dignity to a group of people is always justified as proper and appropriate by the dominant political discourse, endorsing the continued economic and cultural power of the traditionally dominant classes, and also the perpetual support to the means of violence (psychological, physical, legal and illegal) to sustain an inegalitarian system. It is not easy to overturn 'the long habits of stigmatization, degradation and denial in the minds of the oppressors, nor the fear that accompanies them in the minds of oppressed'.[2] The prevalence of well-nurtured differences is an outcome of socio-economic and political processes that shaped sociocultural discrimination in India. Such a divisive mindset stands in contradiction to the liberal philosophy that simply questions discrimination of any type. In other words, it was obvious that sustained sociocultural prejudices against a large section of Indian demography was allowed to survive also due to sectarian desires of fulfilling partisan interests. The discriminatory sociocultural template based on an uncritical acceptance of the politics of prejudice justified discrimination because of 'sociocultural differences' among human beings. Caste prejudices are also an articulation of the politics of 'positional differences' which also determines the processes of 'inclusion' and 'exclusion' in a social collective. Such an approach enables one to persuasively explain a distinct manifestation of structural inequality which is also context-specific because sociocultural prejudices do not always appear in the same form across areas of human settlement. This is also an indication that the voice of protest acted decisively in undermining those enjoying the fruits of caste segregation. Nonetheless, there is no denying that well-entrenched structural inequality, based on prejudice-driven differences, remain an important feature of human civilization once hierarchy is accepted as a determinant of one's social existence.

Ambedkar's Priority

Ambedkar's intellectual interests covered a wide range of issues pertaining to religion, philosophy, political theory, evolution of humanity and tendencies towards dehumanizing humanity, among others. As our concern is to comprehend how he conceptualized his design for humanizing humanity, the focus is on this aspect of his thought and activities. It does not require a detailed analysis to recognize that his struggle against untouchability was one of the major themes in his approach to the phenomenon, since he believed that as long as artificial segmentation of humanity was allowed to survive, no effort, however serious it was, was adequate to realize humanization of humanity. So, untouchability was, for him, a conceptual tool to elaborate how he saw structural inequality in India, in addition to being his lived reality. Hindu society was partitioned both horizontally and vertically and caste remained critical to the vertical division based on the accident of birth. Thus, he argued that untouchability was 'a product of the uniquely Hindu form of inequality as embodied in the caste system'.[3] Caste segregation was ingrained in Hindus from their birth. Occasionally, there were voices questioning the continuity of such an obnoxious system of division, but they did not have enough steam to strike at its root. Presumably because the social norms of segregation were so deeply rooted, it was not possible to even unsettle the circumstances in which the segregationist mindset thrived.

Inequality and human society are dialectically entwined. Human society is plagued by various forms of inequality around class, religion, and ethnic axes. Caste was peculiar to India and has a long history. Although it was identified as having been devised to be a mode of division of labour, in the course of time, it became a source of power and authority against those who were categorized untouchables. With untouchability as a dominant social feature, it became determinant of one's existence in the social hierarchy which justified whether one was polluted or not due to their birth in a particular community. What was also significant, as Ambedkar underlined, was that once one was born with a specific caste identity, one remained the same till one's death. These established norms and order are

> hereditary both in status as well as its function [because] … once an untouchable always an untouchable. Once a Brahman, always a Brahman. Once a sweeper, always a sweeper. Under it, those who are born high, remain high; those who are born low, remain low. … The established order is based on inexorable law of karma or destiny which is fixed once for all and can never be changed. Their destiny has no relations to the merits of the individuals living under it. An Untouchable however superior he may be mentally and morally, is a below a Touchable in rank no matter how inferior he may be mentally or morally. A Touchable however poor he may be, must always take rank above an Untouchable, however rich he may be.[4]

Explicit here are the major arguments in favour of his contention that untouchability by being hereditary remained an integral part of Hindu society; it was inflexible since one's birth remained the only decisive factor in placing an individual in the established social hierarchy. While elaborating the plight of the untouchables, Ambedkar argued that Hindu society created a system of permanently dividing one section as unfit to be part of the society and hence, ruled by the touchables. In Ambedkar's formulation, it was 'a republic of the Touchables, by the Touchables and for the Touchables. The republic is an Empire of the Hindus over the Untouchables [who] have no rights because they are outside the village republic and because they are the so-called republic, they are outside the Hindu fold'.[5] Despite being forced to stay outside the fold, caste Hindus, challenged Ambedkar, were unable to survive without their service. It was a socially given condition of the untouchables' existence in society because 'the Hindus treat the Untouchables as being born to serve them [and] … they cannot refuse … whenever the latter call upon to do so [which is based on the belief that Hindus] can commander the labour of the Untouchables'.[6] Hence, Hindus benefitted with the continuity of caste segregation; it was good fortune for them because the continuity of untouchability 'gives [Hindus] a system in which nobody will be anybody. They also do not want a system in which they will be somebodies and others will nobodies. … The system of untouchability sustains the natural pride of the Hindus and make them feel as well as look big'.[7] By challenging the deep-rooted division in Hindu society around caste identities, Ambedkar hit at the foundational principles of Hinduism which also endorsed a system of dehumanizing humanity on the basis of a whimsically carried system of exclusion among human beings. His voice was against the discriminatory practices which were impediments towards humanizing humanity, because according to Ambedkar, once the barrier was done away with, it would adversely affect caste Hindus' superiority vis-à-vis untouchables, which was a cardinal principle of Hindu social order. The claim of the untouchables for equality was always resisted because it was not considered as 'a menace to the Hindus [but also] … was a threat to the Hindu domination [since] the rise of the Untouchables was sure to displace many caste Hindus from their position of power and authority'.[8] So, there was an economic angle to caste segregation as it evident from the forceful service rendered from untouchables to the caste Hindus without remuneration. Ambedkar reinforced the point that Hindus had a natural inclination to sustain such a dehumanizing endeavour by shedding light on the economic dimension. To justify and maintain discriminatory practices, it was expected of the caste Hindus to evolve institutionalized mechanisms There were challenges in the past and yet, the fact that they were allowed to continue suggests that the opposition was feeble in comparison with those claiming to be the self-proclaimed custodians of the system of dehumanizing humanity.

The claim that a mere touch of an untouchable caused pollution was symptomatic of a serious social ailment which remained effectively unaddressed because of the development of sociocultural designs that were in its favour. The emotional segregation between touchables and untouchables began with one's birth; it was sustained by what Ambedkar described as 'territorial segregation' by which, he meant that untouchables were never allowed to live in the areas earmarked for Hindus because of the intentional social distance. It was intentionally constructed to avoid being polluted by the presence of the untouchables in the vicinity of where Hindus lived. This was therefore not just 'a case of social separation, a mere stoppage of social intercourse for a temporary period; it is a case of territorial segregation and of a *cordon sanitaire* putting the impure people inside a barbed wire into a sort of cage'.[9] As a result, Ambedkar argued further, 'every Hindu village has a ghetto; the Hindus live in the village and the Untouchables in the ghetto'.[10] With this context, he made another observation which complemented his argument for defending the view that caste was tantamount to dehumanizing humanity. Just like racism in the US which created a permanent fissure between the whites and their Afro-American counterparts, caste system devised and justified a mechanism of declaring a class of humanity as 'impure' and as sources of pollution. The US system of social distance which emerged with the introduction of slavery which sustained the division between the 'Negroes' and the Whites was responsible for delaying the adoption of the Fourteenth Amendment of 1866 which lifted the embargo on accepting even the slaves as equal citizens although they remained disenfranchised till 1965 following the adoption of the Voting Rights Act. A brief reference to the processes leading to the revocation of the policy of segregation in the US was used for highlighting that there was an end, at least in principle, of the system of division in the US, which followed a protracted war against racial discrimination. The situation in Hindu society was diametrically opposite, insisted Ambedkar, by remarking that although the

> impurity was of short duration and was done away with following the promulgation of appropriate legislations in the US, the Hindus' belief in permanent impurity [is] ... based on the rule 'once impure always impure' ... cut off the [untouchables] permanently from social intercourse with their caste Hindu counterparts. ... There has never been a case of people treating a section of their own people as permanently and hereditarily impure.[11]

Analogous here is the view that Ambedkar held the bull by its horns in the sense that not only did he question the age-old system of discrimination which was clearly at variance with humanizing humanity, but also challenged the efforts by the Hindu zealots for sustaining such a system that permanently divided humanity while offering protection to the exclusive rights upper caste Hindus.

While summarizing his arguments in favour of his model which he built for humanizing humanity, Ambedkar highlighted that untouchability was unlikely to disappear given the strong opposition of caste Hindus, since it meant rescinding of their inherited advantages from birth. Untouchability was an aid to the age-old system of accruing benefits by the caste Hindus by utilizing the untouchables to their advantage. It was categorically stated he mentioned that

> the system of untouchability is a gold mine to the Hindus. In it the 240 million of Hindus have 60 million of Untouchables to serve as their retinue to enable the Hindus to maintain pomp and ceremony and to cultivate a feeling of pride and dignity befitting a master class, which cannot be fostered and sustained unless there is beneath it a servile class to look down upon. In it the 240 million of Hindus have 60 million of Untouchables to be used as forced labourers; ... in it the 240 million of Hindus have 60 million of Untouchables to do the dirty work of scavengers and sweepers which the Hindu is debarred by his

> religion to do and which must be done by non-Hindus who could be no other than Untouchables. In it the 240 million of Hindus have 60 million of Untouchables who can be kept to lower jobs. … In it the 240 million of Hindus have the 60 million of Untouchables who can be used as shock-absorbers in slumps and dead-weights in booms, for in slumps, it is the Untouchables who is fired first and the Hindu is fired last and in booms the Hindu is employed first and the Untouchables is employed last. [So, untouchability is not a religious] but an economic system which is worse than slavery.[12]

Explicit here is the argument offered by Ambedkar to defend the contention that untouchability was socially useful for the caste Hindus because of the benefits which were integrally connected with the sustenance of such segregation. By comparing the plight of an untouchable with that of a slave, he further suggested that it was worse because in case of the latter, there was an end to the torture, as the US Civil Rights Act of 1964 upheld, but in regard to the former, it was not going to end ever; so, the untouchables had no respite till death because whatever one underwent by being an untouchable remained an important feature of untouchable's existence in a society that deemed it as a nameless being. Ambedkar's own feeling when he lamented, in his response to a letter from Gandhi that he, by being an untouchable, did not have a home of his own, is in the same vein. It was a critical comment, made when the Mahatma asked him to be respectful of his homeland by avoiding ruthless attacks on it, when he devoted wholeheartedly to the cause of a country which was his home land as well. In reply, Ambedkar made perhaps the most perceptive point by linking the particular lived reality with general nationalist vision in this regard. He thus stated his argument by emphasizing that

> you say that I have got a homeland, but still I repeat that I am without it. How can I call this land my homeland and this religion my own wherein we are treated worse than cats and dogs, wherein we cannot get water to drink? No self-respecting Untouchable worth the name will be proud of this land. The injustice and sufferings inflicted upon us by this land are so enormous that if knowingly or unknowingly we fall prey to disloyalty to this country, the responsibility for that act would be solely hers. I do not feel sorry for being branded as a traitor; for the responsibility of our action lie with the land that dubs me a traitor. If, at all, I have rendered any national service, … it is due to my unsullied conscience and not due to any patriotic feelings in me. If in my endeavour to secure human rights for my people, who have been trampled upon in this country for ages, I do any disservice to

> this country, it would not be a sin; and, if any harm foes not come to this country through my action, it may be due to my conscience. Owing to the promptings of my conscience I have been striving to win human rights for my people without meaning or doing any harm to this country.[13]

The rather long quote given above is illustrative of Ambedkar's anguish and a heart-felt desire to fight for a cause even if that led to Gandhi's displeasure. He was not prepared to give up his battle for human rights for all. There is a powerful conceptual point here: by insisting that equality and untouchability stood in contradiction with each other he insisted that untouchability had no conceptual validity. In other words, by arguing against discrimination that was contrary to the notion of equality, he developed a conceptual yardstick wherein equality was understood in its undiluted sense. Implicit here is also the idea that equality, as a concept, cannot be relative, which means that for equality to be established in inter-personal relationships, it must be absolute in character and sense. By endorsing a familiar liberal conceptual claim, Ambedkar appears to have echoed the concern that his academic mentor, John Dewey, raised in the context of the African-American being racially discriminated; which, to him, not only defied the Jeffersonian dictum, 'all men are equal' but also distorted the concept for partisan aims. 'Untouchables are', Ambedkar argued,

> owned by the Hindus for purposes which further their interests and are disowned by them when owning them places them under burden. The Untouchables can claim none of the advantages of an unfree social order and are left to bear al the disadvantages of a free social order.[14]

There could not be a more explicit statement than this, which clearly brings out the social locations of untouchables in the Hindu social order. For the caste Hindus, untouchability was, as Ambedkar had shown, an instrument for personal aggrandizement, of course, at the cost of other fellow human beings. This was worse than slavery which saw its eclipse following the massive ideological campaign opposed to its sustenance, while untouchability remained, almost intact, presumably because of the carefully devised and well-nurtured social sanctions for taking care of caste Hindus' partisan interests. Core to Ambedkar's argument was the contention that untouchability was an artificially designed social arrangement which needed to be done away with for building a democratic society drawing on liberty, equality, and fraternity.

As per Ambedkar, inequality was ingrained in Hindu society which led him to exhort that 'Hindu, thy name is inequality'.[15] This statement had political ramifications because, according to this assumption, Ambedkar believed that mere political freedom from British rule was not a panacea for the untouchables as long as caste system was allowed to survive. In response to a question by Gandhi who remained perplexed as to why Ambedkar and his followers stayed away from the freedom struggle, Ambedkar most curtly replied that

> Untouchables have not joined the 'Fight for Freedom' … not because they are the tools of the British Imperialism but because they fear that freedom of India will establish Hindu domination which is sure to close them and for ever all prospect of life, liberty and pursuit of happiness and that they will be made the hewers of wood and drawers of water.[16]

Further to his argument he also added that their absence from the 'Fight for Freedom' was articulated well in the slogans which they always gave to justify why they did what they did. One of the slogans of the untouchables was that they did not want to replace a foreign domination by 'Hindu Raj in which the governing class would be *Bania* and the Brahmin with low class Hindus chosen for menial jobs'.[17] While defending his refusal to be part of the freedom struggle, Ambedkar attributed the casteist mindset of the Hindus to the reluctance of the untouchables in participating in the battle against the imposed foreign authority. According to him,

> Untouchables refuse to be content with mere freedom from British Imperialism. [In so saying, they articulated the view that] mere political freedom is not enough. Free India should be made safe for democracy. Starting with this aim, they say that on account of the peculiar social formation in India, there are minority communities pitted against a Hindu Communal Majority, that if no provisions are made in the constitution to cut the fangs of the Hindu Communal Majority, India will not be safe for democracy. The Untouchables therefore insist on devising a constitution which will take note of the special circumstances of India contain safeguards which will prevent this Hindu Communal Majority in Indian society from, getting possession of political power to suppress and oppress Untouchables and will directly invest the Untouchables with at least a modicum of political power to prevent their suppression and exploitation, and to enable them at least to hold their own, in their struggle for existence against the Communal Majority.[18]

Political freedom was, for Ambedkar, not a guarantee for the establishment of substantive equality; in fact, it would ensure the hegemony of caste Hindus at the cost of the deprivileged. This argument was a rebuttal of the charge made by many of the mainstream Congress nationalists for his refusal to be part of the Gandhi-led freedom struggle. By being part of the British administration, they argued, he had clearly spelt out his allegiance to the rulers even that meant opposition to the Congress campaign for decolonization. Ambedkar referred to the communal situation because as India drew to freedom, the communal schism became critical to the transfer of power. It was a *fait accompli* that India's independence meant dismemberment of the country based on Mohammad Ali Jinnah's two nation theory. So, what Ambedkar apprehended was likely to be true soon, namely the change of authority was complete with the rise of the Hindu Communal majority at the saddles of power. Ambedkar's apprehension was not unfounded because when the untouchables were given separate electorate in the 1935 Government of India Act, just like the Muslims whose electoral prospect was protected by the 1932 Communal Award, it was Gandhi who resorted to fast unto death to restrain Ambedkar and his colleagues from insisting on getting separate electorate for the untouchables. It was the moral blackmailing by the Mahatma that forced Ambedkar to finally withdraw from his demand for separate electorate because it was perhaps beyond his capacity to withstand the adverse impact had Mahatma died due to the fast on this occasion. In 1933, a pact, known as the Poona Pact, was executed between the Congress and Ambedkar to permanently commit that untouchables would remain with Congress in so far as electoral arrangements, following the adoption of the 1935 Government of India Act, were concerned.

Ambedkar's decision to accept Gandhi's suggestion of not insisting for separate electorate for the untouchables put him in a serious dilemma. It was 'a baffling situation' for him because there was before him

> the duty, which [he] owed as a part of common humanity, to save Gandhi from sure death; there was before [him] the problem of saving for the Untouchables the political rights which they acquired. [He] responded to the call of humanity and saved the life of Gandhi by agreeing to the call of humanity and saved the life Gandhi to alter the Communal Award in a manner satisfactory to Gandhi.[19]

The Poona Pact was a watershed moment in India's nationalist history because it brought, for the first time, Ambedkar face-to-face with the Mahatma; perhaps, due to strategic calculations, Ambedkar accepted the conditionalities which he was asked to accept, Ambedkar perhaps also realized that the fulfilment of the sectarian objective was not complementary to the goal he was aspiring to achieve; in a context when the struggle for India's independence gathered masses around Gandhi, it would have been suicidal for him as Congress support was required to attain his goal of eradicating caste prejudices. In other words, as an activist, he was persuaded to believe that Congress opposition to his campaign for humanizing humanity was likely to lose its appeal since it also meant derecognition of the untouchables as equal to all other human beings. There could have been another reason for Ambedkar to go along with Gandhi in so far as the Communal Award was concerned. Despite not having campaigned for the abolition of untouchability completely, Gandhi believed that it was divisive and also inhuman and thus contrary to how he conceptualized humanity. In view od Ambedkar's fierce critique of Gandhi being 'a paradox of history', he expressed his doubt whether mere political freedom—which was Mahatma's objective—was of any help in human salvation. Ambedkar defended his argument by highlighting that notwithstanding Gandhi's sustained campaign for political independence, the fact that he strongly argued for keeping 'intact a social structure which, permits the domination of one class by another on a hereditary basis which means a perpetual domination of one class by another'.[20] Ambedkar did not seem persuaded by the argument that, for Gandhi, it was a strategic decision to not disturb the prevalent social balance, because he believed that if a person of the stature of Gandhi supported human existence in a social structure which was divisive, it was likely to sway many of his supporters. The strategic argument thus lost its viability and the orthodox Hindus were thus encouraged to be extremely happy given Gandhi's uncritical support to the available power-relationships governing inter-personal interactions based on birth.

That the Poona Pact was also an outcome of Ambedkar's astute decision to ascertain Congress support was evident further when he assessed the role of Gandhi vis-à-vis the untouchables. He admitted that bereft of Congress assistance, the untouchables were not

> in a position to sustain itself in the struggle for existence [because] the religion to which they are tied, instead of providing for them an honourable place, brands them as lepers, not fit for ordinary intercourse. [Furthermore], economically [they are] ... entirely dependent upon the high caste Hindus for earning its daily bread with no independent way of living open to [them]. Nor are all ways closed by reason of the social prejudices of the Hindus but there is a definite attempt all throughout the Hindu society to bolt every

> possible door so as not to all [the untouchables] any opportunity to rise in the scale of life.[21]

Through a surface reading of the argument, one may argue that it is a critique of Hindu society which spread its tentacles in such a way as to not develop the untouchables in a natural fashion. This appears to be a little over-stretched, given the fact that majority of the untouchables, especially in rural India, were largely paupers and survived as agricultural labourers. Unless there was a symbiotic relationship with those capable of providing the untouchables with sources of earning livelihood, their survival was sure to be at stake; similarly, if the untouchables decided to not work for those having means to provide them jobs, they would also suffer. Hence, being aware of the realities in villages where the caste Hindus contributed to the sustenance of most of the untouchables who lived from hand to mouth, Ambedkar appeared to have couched his argument accordingly which allowed him to make his point without infuriating the caste Hindu supporters of the Congress in rural areas, ensuring a sustained source of livelihood for the untouchables. In order to defuse consternation among his supporters which did not seem incomprehensible, Ambedkar also expressed that Gandhi would not push me to the wall by forcing him to make 'a choice between his life and the rights of [his] people [for he] … can never consent to deliver [his] people bound-hand and foot to the caste Hindus for generations to come'.[22] Reverberated here is also a strategy to sustain Ambedkar's support base because he knew that his relatively soft attitude to Gandhi who was always characterized by him as a villain in so far as untouchables were concerned, might alienate some people. The interpretation appears to be persuasive in view of the political compulsion confronting both Gandhi and Ambedkar. Gandhi was cornered by many of his colleagues following the justified claim of the Muslim League, for being the mouthpiece of Indian Muslims. With the conclusion of the Round Table Conferences (1930–1932) in London which held a series of discussion before the adoption of the 1935 Government of India Act, it was clear that Muslims were no longer part of the mainstream nationalism, not only because they had Jinnah to strongly argue their claim, but they also had strong regional leaders like Fazlul Haq in Bengal, and Sikander Hayat Khan in Punjab to defend their rights as a socioculturally different collective. Under these circumstances, Gandhi's fast was perhaps the only option left for the Congress to stop further division within the Congress which was on the table especially after the British guarantee of separate electorate for the untouchables. So, Gandhi and Ambedkar were locked in a no-win situation because Congress would further be weakened if the untouchables left and formed a separate collective, and untouchables were also not well-equipped socio-economically without Congress standing behind them. The Muslim League did not support the untouchables as they thought they were unreliable political partners in its campaign for Pakistan.

The argument that he offered while justifying separate electorate for untouchables underlined that, for him, it was not just a social problem, as is often conceptualized. Unlike the issues of dowry, remarriage, or age of consent, which were mostly social problems and needed to be tackled accordingly, untouchability was not so for a substantial reason, Ambedkar insinuated. As he felt, untouchability

> is a problem of quite different nature in as much as it is a problem of securing to a minority liberty and equality of opportunity at the hands of a hostile majority which believes in the denial of liberty and equal opportunity to the minority and conspires to enforce its policy on the minority. [So,], Untouchability is fundamentally a political problem.[23]

This is one of the most perceptive comments made by Ambedkar to defend that the recognition of the untouchables as integral to socio-political processes was a political design, since it was complementary to radical changes in the power-relationships in which caste Hindus and untouchables were placed. In other words, once they were recognized at par with the caste Hindus, their participation in the political processes would allow them to be equal partners with the latter. A new social set-up was likely to emerge when untouchables would no longer be as despised as before and by working hand-in-hand, they could lead the processes of social endosmosis to develop and flourish automatically. Hence, Ambedkar was unsure of what to make of Gandhi's fast unto death except that it was an attempt to pursue his sectarian objectives by permanently putting the untouchables in isolation which he explained by saying that

> it is difficult to understand why political recognition of and political safeguards for the security of the Untouchables should retard their social unification with the Hindus if there is a genuine desire to set in motion processes which will bring about such a result. The Congressmen don't seem to have clear ideas of the inter-relation between political and social factors [which] … is well-illustrated by [their] opposition to separate electorate and [their] preference to joint electorates.[24]

He reiterated the point that unless the untouchables were recognized as integral to society, the discussion of eradicating of sociocultural prejudices against them was futile. Gandhi's insistence on joint electorate to avoid further division in India especially in the context where Muslims were being projected as a separate nation, was probably a political design although it was not persuasive enough to Ambedkar. He was convinced that the Mahatma was politically governed for safeguarding the Hindu Communal Majority given his reluctance to accept separate electorate for the untouchables and by resorting to fast unto death, he further confirmed his role as a representative of the caste Hindus. Ambedkar believed that not only Mahatma, but his entire troop in the nationalist campaign were not ready to endorse the change in the prevalent power relationship which was tilted heavily in favour of the Hindu majority. Disappointed at his failure to convince the Mahatma to go along with him vis-à-vis separate electorate for the untouchables, he lamented that

> it is … puerile to say that the political recognition of the Untouchables as a separate element and granting them constitutional safeguards will perpetuate separation between them and the Hindus if the Hindus desire to put an end to it.[25]

Ambedkar's insisted on separate electorate as he thought that it was a source of empowerment for the untouchables, because by choosing candidates from among themselves, they would now be well-equipped to express their views in the public domain themselves; they did not need representation from those who could have been sympathetic towards them, but were unable to feel what they felt. Hence, he demanded separate electorate for the untouchables. According to Ambedkar, the argument did not translate well for Gandhi and his other colleagues in the Congress, because they thought that 'separate electorate means the fragmentation of the nation'.[26] While being critical of this assessment, he further argued that the representation by the untouchables was the best means to present their own views in the elected platforms. He defended this position emphasizing that 'separate electorate is the only mechanism whereby real representation can be guaranteed to the Untouchables'.[27] To bolster his argument in defence of separate electorate, he linked his view with the idea of denial of the legitimate due to the untouchables due to the selfish desires of the caste Hindus. Hence, he expressed that

> the Hindu in opposing the so-called Communal Scheme of the Untouchables with his so-called National Scheme is not fighting for a principle not is he fighting for the nation; he is simply fighting for

> his own interests. He is fighting to have in his hands the undivided control over political power. His line of defence is [thus] not to allow any shares to be drawn so that like the Manager of the Hindu joint family he can use the whole for his exclusive benefits.[28]

The interesting point that Ambedkar made here is the comparison with the instinctual desire to control in Hindus, as was evident in the joint family system. It was a common feature that the head of the Hindu joint family tended to retain his control over the family as his fiefdom and whenever attempt was made to defy the head of the family, the repercussions were usually disastrous. The breakdown of Hindu joint family was facilitated due to the emergence of changing mindsets and behaviours that were reluctant to share the authority of controlling the property belonging to a joint family. This became a natural instinct for the caste Hindus, insisted Ambedkar. What appeared to be surprising was not so, as according to Ambedkar, it was a translation of how caste Hindus were influenced politico-ideologically since the beginning of their socialization within a family. So, by challenging separate electorate, the caste Hindus, instead of appreciating one of the fundamental tenets of democracy, stood in contradiction to how they appeared in the public domain—which was clearly at odds with what they actually felt, argued Ambedkar.

As the campaign for separate electorate fizzled out, as shown above, with the intervention of the Mahatma, Ambedkar was forced to entomb what he so far stuck to. There was, however, a positive outcome of the struggle for separate electorate which was known as 'the New Life Movement' among the untouchables. The objective of this movement was to set the untouchables free from 'the thraldom of the Hindus' which was an outcome of the deliberate creation of a domain for the untouchables by the caste Hindus. Ambedkar identified that untouchables living in areas earmarked for them allowed the Hindus to divide them territorially; their location in specific areas put them in a ghetto which was not integrated with areas where Hindus lived. So, it was easier to recognize them as untouchables by providing a separate territory for them; it was a territorial partition between caste Hindus and untouchables. Towns were not, of course, as territorially divided as Indian villages, where untouchables were marked by being located in the delineated areas in the villages. Hence, the untouchable had 'no escape from untouchability' in villages which perpetuated such a divisive mode of human existence.[29] This mindset needed to be done away with; the task was easier said than done, Ambedkar rightly apprehended. As a way out of such a humiliating social existence, 'the New Life Movement' demanded that

> the hegemonic control of the caste Hindus should be broken and the Untouchables who are as a matter of fact socially separate should be made separate geographically and territorially also, and be grouped into separate villages exclusively of Untouchable in which the distinction of the high and the low and of Touchable and Untouchable will find no place.[30]

When Ambedkar was blackmailed by the Mahatma, he felt that no other option was more effective in pursuing the demand for separate electorate than with the help of an organization with an exclusive aim, namely providing the untouchables their legitimate sociocultural and politico-ideological dues. According to him, his main battle against the Hindus was not for exclusive political rights but to ascertain the recognition of the untouchables as human beings with dignity and fairness. The New Life Movement was instrumental in spreading the message across India, claimed Ambedkar presumably because it was a demand which was justifiably made in a context when the untouchables were openly discriminated against because of their social identity In a very categorical manner, Ambedkar thus mentioned that

> the Untouchables all over India are fighting against the indignities and injustices which the Hindus in the name of their religion have heaped upon them. … The silent struggle [is a manifestation of] challenges of the Untouchables for setting up a new sociocultural ambience in which the distinction between caste Hindus and Untouchables will completely disappear [although] it is a very difficult struggle because … it is a contest between the economically and socially strong Hindus and an economically poor and socially small group of Untouchables.[31]

True to his commitment to humanizing humanity, Ambedkar linked 'Hindu tyranny'[32] with the debasement of those socially identified as untouchables. To reinforce his argument that a campaign for a definite cause was of great value in humanizing humanity, he referred to the 1893 Emancipation Proclamation, adopted in the US by President Abraham Lincoln. Despite being aware that even after the declaration, the Afro-Americans remained at the mercy of their white employers and did not become as free as they expected, Ambedkar still hailed the declaration because it was a strong message to the countrymen that

> it is by no means small comfort to know that that conscience of the country is not altogether dead and frame of righteous indignation may one day burst forth. [Contrarily], the Hindu conscience is neither sensitive enough to even suggest that. … Untouchability is a sin nor is

of help to support the campaign for securing for the Untouchables a legitimate space in society.[33]

With his thorough probing of the Hindu demand for political freedom, Ambedkar also found that what Hindus were doing stood in contradiction to how they behaved vis-à-vis the untouchables. Unlike the Americans who admitted that racial segregation was a slur on the American conscience which made them assure the 'Negroes' of good days ahead, the caste Hindus remained indifferent to the demand of the untouchables for being treated at par with them. So, for him, it was ironical that 'they clamour for freedom—the pity is that they get support [and what is unfortunate is that] they never feel Untouchability is a moral sin and a civil wrong.'[34] What stands out here was Ambedkar's critique of India's freedom struggle which was an attempt to wrest freedom from colonialism. On a surface reading, it was a fair demand. But; in light of internal colonization of the caste Hindus over the untouchables, it appeared to be misguided since freedom was conceptualized in its narrow sense; it was meant to free the privileged section of the society at the cost the hapless untouchables who remained in chains for ages simply because they were identified so by the well-entrenched sociocultural prejudices of one section of humanity against another for reasons connected with the protection for partisan interests.

Gandhi and Ambedkar

The purpose here is not to focus on the debate between Gandhi and Ambedkar, but to highlight some of the fundamental points which put them in completely different categories in terms of their varied perspectives in conceptualizing humanity and humanism. Broadly speaking, both of them fought for freedom: the former for the country and latter for a section of Hindus, untouchables, who remained perennially peripheral both socio-economically and politico-ideologically. What is also striking to remember is that both of them felt that mere political freedom was not adequate; the most important aspect of freedom was human emancipation from shackles of various kinds. Nonetheless, they differed radically from each other because their conceptualization of freedom in relation to humanity was diametrically opposite. There should be a caveat here: Gandhi acquiesced with Ambedkar that doing away with untouchability was complementary to the realization of freedom in its true sense; he, however qualified his assessment by saying that political freedom from colonialism was the first precondition for freedom in its absolute sense. So, the argument that Gandhi completely abdicated Ambedkar's demand does not appear to be as correct as is made out. In contrast, Ambedkar did not believe that political freedom was necessary to undertake other measures for eradicating socioculturally debilitating features, and hence, he always insisted that social freedom or rescinding of the segregationist caste system had to be done before India's political liberation. It was perhaps because of this belief that he also sided with the British government on many occasions as he thought that only by meaningful state intervention, his objective of creating a level playing field for all was likely to be attained.

The battle-line was drawn: Gandhi was a villain since he obstructed the adoption of separate electorate for the untouchables; by placing political emancipation as the first nationalist priority, he also suggested that at the juncture of India's progress as a 'nation', one could easily afford to relegate the caste question to one of the priorities which were not as important as the removal of the British. In other words, Ambedkar's notion of humanizing humanity diverged with that of the Mahatma in two significant ways: on the one hand, Gandhi strongly felt that humanization remained constrained so long as India was colonized; so, for fulfilling his goal of universal humanism, it was necessary to create an independent India by making her politically free. His strategy of freedom struggle failed to sustain the political unanimity between Hindus and Muslims because the latter, with M.A. Jinnah as their leader, were already separated from the national mainstream both due to the prejudices of caste Hindus against them and the effective deployment of the British policy of *divide-et-impera*. Hence, he was logically justified in strongly opposing Ambedkar's insistence on separate electorate for the untouchables. On the other hand, Ambedkar was determined not to dilute his struggle for humanizing humanity and, in his perception, till caste-segregation was completely weeded out, humanity in India was certain to remain divided vertically. His aim was to create circumstances to gradually remove sociocultural prejudices of the caste Hindus against the untouchables because instantaneous eradication was neither possible due to severe sociocultural opposition by the beneficiaries nor practical as a strategy when the differences between caste Hindus and untouchables were far deeper, as they were nurtured for centuries. Hence, he immediately accepted separate electorate for the untouchables which meant that he believed it was an effective device for empowerment, and his demand for untouchables being treated as equal was to be fulfilled with its introduction. Although Ambedkar received enormous public attention, his insistence on separate electorate for the untouchables did not sit well with the Congress leadership, especially its supremo, Gandhi. So, the battle was unevenly poised and the outcome was predicted well in advance. Ambedkar succumbed to the pressure made by Gandhi and the entire country which forced him to abdicate his decision to go for separate electorate for the untouchables.

Perhaps, Ambedkar was aware that Gandhi would not have accepted separate electorate because he was 'neither a revolutionary not a democrat'. His main objective, he further argued, was to make India 'safe for Hindus and Hinduism [and, to avoid] … untouchability being a source of disruption of caste system'.[35] Hence, it was understandable why he crafted a design to keep untouchables as what they were. Ambedkar also defined Gandhi concern for the untouchables was nothing but 'shedding crocodile tears [because] by pretending to be kind to them, he wants to destroy the New Life Movement [which was] … an endeavour [of the untouchables] for separation and independence from Hindus'.[36] It did not catch Ambedkar by surprise because, according to him, it was expected of since Gandhi 'is a Tory [Conservative] by birth as well as faith'. This description of Gandhi being a conservative explained how Ambedkar conceptualized the Gandhian politico-ideological design. What was predominant was, according to Gandhi his determination to wrest political freedom first, which he strongly felt was an aid to humanizing humanity or eradication of constraints impairing the rise of humanity as one compact.

Contrary to Gandhi, Ambedkar was clearer in his perception regarding humanizing humanity. Like someone who was strongly opposed to processes leading to dehumanization, he privileged the adoption of politico-ideological designs for, firstly, eradicating elements of dehumanization and secondly for unfolding ideas in favour of humanizing humanity. Untouchability was an ingrained source of discrimination that caste Hindus internalized by being as they were. In other words, they were born with a mindset supportive of discrimination against those who were untouchables; discriminatory customary practices where this in-born prejudices gained credence through socialization was present during the upbringing of children in families with these ingrained sociocultural biases. So, Ambedkar was convinced that so long as caste prejudices were allowed to survive, freedom in its real connotation remained elusive. Hence, he argued that

> not to make a distinction between the freedom of the country and the freedom of the people in the country is to allow oneself to be milled,

> if not deceived [because] ... nation, [despite being] philosophically being one, [but] ... sociologically it cannot but be regarded as one [and, its] political freedom entails ... freedom of all classes, comprised in it, particularly of those who are treated as the servile classes.[37]

So, at one level, Ambedkar was critical of political freedom because it was not complementary to humanizing humanity, which was conceivable once the untouchables were accepted as integral to society. As long as caste prejudices were appreciated by those who mattered in decision making, the goal would remain a distant one. Even a constitutional government was not adequate to accomplish the goal Ambedkar had in mind because a constitutional government was not equal to 'self-government by the people'.[38] Similarly, he also questioned one of the fundamental assumptions of adult suffrage by emphasizing that the introduction of this system of voting guaranteed, under no circumstances, 'a democratic government in the sense of the government by the people and for the people'.[39] At another level, he criticized Gandhi who, always talked about human freedom which was actually a cloak to hide his personalized agenda for securing to the caste Hindus a position of authority and power at the cost of the untouchables. By saying that democracy as it was contemplated in India was deceptive, Ambedkar made a wider point by exposing the inherent limitations of parliamentary democracy based on universal franchise. So, the Congress' affirmation for constitutional democracy of the Western variety did not appear, to Ambedkar, to be useful for his espoused goal of humanizing humanity by completely uprooting the possible sources of dehumanizing humanity. Given the prejudicial objectives, it was not possible for Gandhi and his colleagues to accomplish such a goal because for them 'fight for freedom is for the freedom of nobody except that of the governing class [comprising the caste Hindus] which the Congress put in provinces where they succeeded in winning an electoral majority'.[40] This was illustrative of how the caste Hindu-driven Congress would guide free India in future. Ambedkar's response was categorical. According to him,

> the fight for freedom launched by the Congress has ended in perverting the aim and object of Indian freedom and the Congress itself is a party to such a perversion [and by promoting the caste Hindus] it is no exaggeration to say that they have been the most inveterate enemies of the servile classes, the Untouchables who ... constitute about 80 to 90 per cent of the total Hindu population of India.[41]

Analogous with the above statement are two points to understand how Ambedkar reconceptualized humanizing humanity in contrast with that of Gandhi and Tagore. Despite being aware of the pernicious effect of caste segregation, both of them did not appear to have upheld the view that their first task was to build an opinion against the casteist mindset to the extent Ambedkar did. Perhaps due to their remarkably contrasting existential experiences, they were unable to gauge the prevalent mindset supportive of caste segmentation. Having been subject to humiliation at every stage of his life in India, the feeling that made Ambedkar a crusader against caste being a tool for dehumanizing humanity was almost missing in case of both Tagore and Gandhi; their understanding of deprivation by the untouchables was based on second-hand knowledge or experiences. Hence, their critique of caste system was a little tempered while Ambedkar was far more direct in his attack which was evident when he mentioned that 'if a common man belonging to the servile classes in India is today so fallen, so degraded, so devoid of self-respect, hope of ambition, and so life less, it is entirely due to [the caste Hindus] and their philosophy'.[42] The Congress created a misconception to convey to the rest of the world that political freedom from the British yoke was as good as freedom for all. By insisting that 'democracy and self-government in India cannot be real unless freedom has become the assured possession of all',[43] Ambedkar reiterated an idea which he championed throughout his public career. It was based on his well-nurtured belief that political freedom from British rule was a tool to sustain the hegemony of caste Hindus in perpetuity, which was contrary to freedom in its undiluted sense.

Ambedkar's well-thought-out and articulated points of view were not just a counter to the prevalent mode of humanizing humanity, they also provided inputs in reconceptualizing humanism altogether. Gandhi was persuaded to believe that the processes of dehumanization were rooted in society and hence if processes to the contrary evolved, the sociocultural prejudices were certain to phase out due in course of time. Ambedkar stood in contradiction with the Gandhian approach to the phenomenon, for he was not agreeable to the fact that the actual space for experimenting with various modes of social reform were villages because sociocultural prejudices were largely patronized by the dominant caste there. Tagore's ideas came closer to that of Ambedkar since he also felt that caste was a significant denominator of identity primarily in villages, although he was silent as to whether campaign against caste segregation was likely to succeed if it started from there. In contrast to Gandhi and Tagore, Ambedkar was unambiguous in his views that deliberately engineered state policies were essential for transforming the existent socio-economic context and dominant politico-ideological priorities. This was explicitly stated and firmly argued when he insisted on separate electorate for untouchables. he was firm on his belief that self-government for untouchables was one of the most effective means of building an opinion and a movement against those sociocultural practices nurtured over generations, which were impediments for them to be recognized as 'equal' with others in society. Although, due to Gandhi's vehement opposition, it was not implemented and he was nearly forced to stay away from the demand; but it was the beginning of processes championing the claim that state was a useful instrument to bring about changes as per its preferences. As will be shown in Chapter 6, Ambedkar, by being one of the prime members in the making of the Constitution of India, conceptualized the role of the state as a harbinger of change amidst odds. It was he, who associated the policies for institutional changes with radical social reforms at the grassroots by adopting supportive provisions in independent India's constitution which was adopted in 1949 after decolonization.

Caste as an Impediment to Humanization

Ambedkar was a strong opponent of caste due to his bitter existential experiences of being born as an untouchable and his realization that it was difficult to combat the well-entrenched caste prejudices because they drew nourishment from socioculturally conditioned mindsets. Caste remained a significant feature of the Hindu society primarily because it emerged as a mechanism justifying benefits for a section of humanity at the cost of the majority who were classified as untouchables by the accident of birth. Once one was born in a caste group, one would carry such affiliation till one's death. It was thus divisive and non-alienable: divisive because it was a tool for partitioning human beings on the basis of their birth which means that a child's identity was pre-fixed long before they were born; one's identity was thus non-alienable because the identity was ascriptive in compliance to the age-old rule.

An argument was usually offered that caste was a mode of division of labour as per the ancient Hindu texts. In other words, as caste was based on division of labour there was nothing wrong on according distinctive locations to individuals in society. A surface reading of the theoretical underpinning of the idea is likely to lead one to innocently endorse such a conceptually valid claim. However, a further probe proved otherwise. Here, Ambedkar's intervention is very useful to grasp the actual nature of caste in India. It was a permanent chasm between the caste Hindus and those who belonged to lower castes or untouchables. Hence, it was not,

> merely division of labour, [but a] division of labourers which is unprecedented because in no civilized society is division of labour accompanied by this unnatural division of labourers into water-tight compartments. Caste system is not merely a division of labour, ... it is an hierarchy in which the divisions of labourers are graded one above another.[44]

The argument made by those supportive of caste segregation to define it as an expression of division of labour was, as per Ambedkar, vacuous. The Hindu zealots misled public opinion, seeking to safeguard the interest of the caste Hindus because it was a design to sanction benefit to one section at the cost of another. As caste was a mechanism of segmenting humanity based on birth, it could never be logical. Besides being espoused as a deliberately sustained design to create a permanent fissure among human beings, caste was hardly comparable with division of labour. Labour was based on natural aptitudes, which meant that what was critical here was individuals' capacity and efficiency to be able to accomplish an assigned task. This principle was bypassed in the caste system since it was a ritualistic design prefixing one's assignment based on parental caste identity, instead of following one's capabilities or the required training necessary for a particular task. Fundamental here is the view that caste was *ultra vires* to the core tenets of division of labour as it was practised in colonial India. The historicity of caste leaves a scope to accept the contention that at its origin, it was perhaps linked with division of labour tuned to human needs at a particular juncture of human history. During human development, caste system emerged as an instrument at the disposal of the domineering section of humanity to put the rest under its control. There was another conceptual deficiency in defining caste system as an articulation of division of labour, argued Ambedkar, because he saw the system as violative of the claim since one's caste identity was predetermined and thus provided no choice in deciding which of the castes one preferred. As one's birth was the determining factor, individuals were not allowed to exercise their preferences. Being socially determined, individuals were helpless and thus enslaved to the well-nurtured system of discrimination.

Hinduism and Caste

One of the reasons for Hinduism being an epitome of inequality was caste system. According to Ambedkar, 'inequality is the soul of Hinduism'.[45] While defending this argument, he stated that so long as caste was allowed to survive, inequality remained ingrained in Hinduism which, by upholding the *varna* system consolidated a scheme 'in which the different castes are placed in a vertical series one above the other'. He exonerated Manu, one of the oldest Indian law-maker, who was shown to have devised many inegalitarian mode of human existence in ancient India. He was not charged with the construction of caste system, however, he was held responsible as he was the one who argued persuasively for the continuity of *varna* system. Hence, Ambedkar highlighted that he was charged with being 'the progenitor, if not the author of caste system'.[46] As a result, the Hindu social order was alien to equality and fraternity. Given the justification of caste system, it was obvious that all Hindus were not treated equally; there were social impediments which were maintained by devising a supportive mechanism and concomitant mindsets. So, inequality remained an important ingredient in Hinduism. The question as to why caste system came into being in the first place did not bother Ambedkar, he focused primarily on the distortion of the system whereby it was reduced to a tool of segregating humanity. In other words, he was concerned with the exploration of how caste became an effective instrument in denying a section of humanity of their legitimate rights and place in society. His was a right-based approach which he had adopted at a particular point of India's history when caste discrimination did not seem to have been criticized as vehemently as he expected. His treatises on caste system were thus context-driven and a reading of the philosophy of Hinduism emphasizing why caste gradually became an instrument of oppression.

One of the reasons why caste lost its acceptance was the rise of a group of people who resorted to some concocted explanations for imposing their hegemony to those who did not appear to have been well-grounded in the intricate principles of Hinduism. In other words, Ambedkar attributed the growing importance of caste segregation in India to the lack of education among the majority. Given their failure to have access to the fundamental texts of Hinduism, the masses were at the mercy of the so-called educated persons for comprehending the fundamental tenets of Hinduism. This made it impossible for them to ascertain whether whatever was transmitted to them was in tune with the texts. This was one of the most important factors for Ambedkar to insist on education in his famous slogan—*Educate, Organize and Agitate*—which was an exhortation for guiding movements against caste-based atrocities by those who were with him. His primary concern was to establish equality among the Hindus by being fiercely critical to the sociocultural design contrary to fraternity which, according to him, was complementary to building a foundation for amity and brotherly feelings among human beings. In addition to this, he drew attention to the reasons as to why fraternity was a casualty in India. Broadly speaking, caste was a serious constraint because it led to the development of

> non-social and even anti-social selves' while fraternity is another name for fellow feeling. It consists in sentiments which leads an individual to identify himself with the good of others whereby an individual comes closer to another. It is because of this sentiment of fraternity that the individual does bring himself to think of the rest of his fellow-creatures as struggling rivals with him for the means of happiness, whom he must desire to see defeated in their object in order that he may succeed in his own. It is only fraternity which is contrary to rabid individualism leading to anarchy and social disturbances.[47]

Persuasively argued here are two core points of what constitutes Ambedkar's approach to humanizing humanity. First, he was opposed to mechanically partitioning humanity based on birth regardless of qualities. This was not only unfair, but also illogical, for human beings were capable of accomplishing feats which would have been impossible had they been compartmentalized at their birth. Furthermore, being together was a source of strength. In caste hierarchy, this was forbidden since one's caste identity put one in to a compartment which was un-infringeable because it was socially justified. Secondly, by challenging individualism, he also questioned the fundamental tenets of liberalism which he held so dear while defending many of his assumptions. Implicit here is perhaps his appreciation of an ancient Indian philosophical dictum of *Vasudhaiva Kutumbakam* (the world is my family) which came to Ambedkar via John Stuart Mill's conceptualization of human beings as equal since he quoted Mill's statement extensively in his defence. It is thus not surprising that while supporting his argument for humanizing humanity, he referred to J.S. Mill who suggested that

> society between equals can only exist on the understanding that the interests of all are to be regarded equally. And since in all states of civilization, every person except an absolute monarch, has equals, everyone is obliged to live on these terms with some body; and, in every age some advance is made towards a state in which it will be impossible to live permanently on other terms with anybody. In this way, people grow up unable to conceive as possible to them a state of total disregard of other people's interests.[48]

Based on J.S. Mill's premise mentioned above, Ambedkar developed his ideas in support of equalizing human beings regardless of birth. Of course, the task he had in mind was easier said than done in view of the well-entrenched vested interests being assisted by the unequal practices of caste discrimination. Caste became a source inequality since it upheld hierarchy among Hindus. Castes formed, as per him,

> an hierarchy in which one caste is at the top and is the highest, another at the bottom and its is the lowest and in between there are castes every one of which is at once above some caste and below some castes. The caste system is a system of gradation in which caste except the highest and the lowest has a priority and precedence over some other castes.[49]

Here is another persuasive argument in favour of compartmentalizing Hinduism as 'an exclusive religion [by devising] means of segregation among the Hindus'.[50] As a result, caste ended up making a system by dividing one caste groups from another. It was a design based on in-built sense of differentiation among those belonging to different caste groups. Since one's social esteem was linked with one's caste identity, caste segregation was also a design for humanizing humanity. By setting out a checklist according to one's caste identity, discrimination was socially recognized which Ambedkar decried by arguing that

> caste devitalizes a man. It is a process of sterilization. Education, wealth, labour are all necessary for every individual is to reach a free and full manhood [and] they are interrelated [because] mere education without wealth and labour is barren [and] wealth without education is brutal. So, each is necessary ingredient for human beings to develop with all their qualities.[51]

Explicit here is Ambedkar's understanding of the political economy of Hinduism which is justified with reference to his overall assessment of Hinduism as an impediment for the rise and consolidation of Hindus as a compact collective. By drawing attention to two major limitations of Hindu philosophy, Ambedkar upheld the view that Hinduism was inimical to social equality and individual justice: first, Hinduism never prepared a level-playing field for all, given the critical importance of caste as a system of locating individuals in different categories in terms of their birth with specific ingrained sociocultural identity. This was given and hence, there was no way one was allowed to change one's caste name. Secondly, by resisting inter-mixing, inter-dining, etc., caste system solidified the barrier which was erected at the time of one's birth. Individuals were helpless because the supposed holy texts provided a clear roadmap for each caste groups. Fundamental here was also his point that the boundary which was defined by these texts and was put into practice by evolving a complementary system of behaviour and social practices remained fixed for life for those with specific caste identities. So, the practices which were clearly immoral and also inhuman were not so since they were mentioned in the holy books and pursued by generations of people as axiomatic. One was thus persuaded to argue that the Jeffersonian dictum that men were born equal was repugnant to Hindu social order.

Core to the above discussion was Ambedkar's fundamental point that Hindu social order was bereft of equality and fraternity; instead, it was a mechanism to deliberately create a system of thought by sustaining segregation among human beings for sociocultural and politico-ideological reasons. His new conceptual format reinventing Hinduism as a progenitor of inequality is comprised of three principles: the first is the principle of graded inequality which assumed that due to caste hierarchy, the four castes were vertically divided in terms of their fixed identity from birth. This pronouncement was invincible and unalterable given the spiritual, moral and legal backing. Human minds were accordingly programmed; hence, there was hardly an effective challenge, and occasional outbursts against graded inequality were quelled easily given the support extended by those wielding power and authority due to their apprehension that withering away of caste system meant deprivation of the benefits they were accustomed to. The second principle on which the Hindu social was founded was that of 'fixity of occupation of each and continuance thereof by heredity'.[52] This was also a device to retain the degrading social order because once an individual was assigned a task because of his/her birth, s/he was just like a slave who never had a voice in choosing what s/he preferred to do or whether it was befitting for him/her to carry on the task his/her forefathers continued to discharge, due to inhuman imposition of rigid caste rule. In other words, with caste identity being an exclusive determinant, it left no scope for individual choice and individual inclination, as the dictum was mandatory on him/her given the caste rules. Fixity of one's occupation also involved one's social respectability, argued Ambedkar because there were menial jobs which hardly carried respect in society. So, by deciding the type of job for each caste group, it was also a design to further segregate one section of humanity from another since those working in one area ended up with forming camaraderie among themselves. It also helped to permanently keep the caste groups divided, which was also an impediment for them to join hands together to fight for a common cause. So, it was a political design to clearly disallow unity among human beings. The third principle in this regard was the fixation of people with their respective classes. The point is an expansion of the earlier argument, because the fixation of assignments for each caste groups also created a space for isolation and exclusiveness among them. A healthy society was supposed to develop as per Ambedkar, through togetherness because, there was an underlying thread of unity which got weakened with the application of caste segmentation or, for that matter, any device for secluding one section of humanity from another. Isolation and exclusion made individuals, according to Ambedkar, 'anti-social and inimical towards one another [because] isolation makes for rigidity of class consciousness, for institutionalizing social life and for the dominance of selfish ideals within classes, [and] exclusion leads one to adopt means for maintaining one's exclusivity at any cost'.[53] This principle is meant to consolidate the barrier between caste groups by laying out an institutionalized mode of segregation which was claimed to have drawn on the ancient ritualistic texts. As a result, the system that evolved at one point of time was allowed to continue even in the changed sociocultural and political milieu largely because, as Ambedkar felt, the voice challenging such an inegalitarian system of human existence was too feeble to be muzzled soon.

The discussion detailed above prepares the conceptual background to comprehend the argument Ambedkar made in his widely-publicized text entitled *Annihilation of Caste* (1936) which was, at one level, a powerful attack on the system of segregation of humanity amounting to dehumanization, and, at another level, provided a voice for challenging the system of oppression of those who remained socioculturally and politico-economically peripheral, by the well-off and casteist Hindus. This did not seem to be unusual because the Hindu social order was incongruous with core values of democracy as,

> the tenets of the Hindu social order is that the law by which people are to be governed is already made and is to be found in *Vedas*, *Upanishads*, *Puranas* and the instructions given by the lawgiver, Manu. Nobody has [thus] a right to add to and subtract from it. That being so, a representative assembly of the people is unnecessary. Political liberty which is liberty to frame laws and to make and unmake Government is futility for which there is no place in the Hindu social order.[54]

Being persuaded by his academic mentor at Columbia University (USA), John Dewey, Ambedkar always believed that political liberty was indispensable for humanity to progress. Ambedkar was appalled by the fact that the classical tenets of Hindus were not only opposed to political liberty but, by seeking to rule out the possibility of attack on the vested interests, also helped build a sociocultural milieu in which they did not appear to be contrary to human existence. Therefore, he evolved a new mode of thinking by exposing that Hinduism was a deterrent to the growth of humanity as an indivisible and non-alienable entity. He was aware that the task was difficult, but not insurmountable. His analysis of the Hindu social order was perhaps one of the most persuasive accounts of how Hinduism became an instrument of sociocultural oppression of those belonging to the class of untouchables. With the development of graded inequality in which the status and functions of caste groups were determined and fixed, the system appeared to have struck deep roots in Hindu minds. As a result, the Hindu social order emerged as

> a rigid order [and] no matter what changes take place in the relative position of an individual, his social status as a member of [a caste group] in relations to another [belonging to another caste group] shall, in no way, be affected. The first shall never become the last [and] the last shall never become the first.[55]

Intrinsic here is the point that the Hindu social order, by being inflexible, could never be device for humanizing humanity because of the inherent conceptual and practice-driven limitations. Hinduism was discriminatory. Hence, the idea of democracy was alien to the religious precepts upholding the Hindu social order. To conclude the discourse on Hindu social order from Ambedkar's well-thought-out arguments, one is persuaded to make two points which are elaborated further in the text, *Annihilation of Caste*. Firstly, it is evident that while dissecting the Hindu social order, he appeared to have influenced by his own existential experiences as an untouchable since his birth till he became a dominant voice against discriminatory sociocultural prejudices which were justified as axiomatic by many of those leading the nationalist campaigns in India. Secondly, the writings and guidance of his tutor at Columbia University (USA), John Dewey who, by his clearly articulated views for racial equality in the US, had shown to him the importance of conceptualizing the factors responsible for reinforcing the ideational vision for dehumanizing humanity; otherwise, his battle for humanizing humanity would not have gained salience. What Dewey meant was two-fold: on the one hand, he was keen that Ambedkar prepared an alternative discourse to convey why he felt that the Hindu social order needed to be displaced as it was detrimental to the realization of his humanistic goals; on the other hand, Dewey also inspired Ambedkar to mobilize support not only from among those who were victims of caste oppression, but also from among those like-minded individuals in the nationalist mainstream, to bolster his campaign by spreading its message across the country and also abroad.

The text, *Annihilation of Caste*, is thus a creative amalgamation of ideas which Ambedkar derived from sources which were both internal and derivative. Written as a speech in 1935 on the caste system in India which was to be delivered in the annual convention of anti-caste Lahore-based organization, Jat-Pat-Todak Mondal (society for the break-up of caste system), the text contains a deviant voice because it was meant to challenge the age-old system of segmentation of humanity which did not appear to have been subject before to as fierce a criticism as the text was. There was a plot twist however, the organizers wanted Ambedkar to delete some of the paragraphs which were harsh on Hinduism, especially on the Brahminical hegemony in Hindu social order because they apprehended a counter-attack from the orthodox Hindus. In his response, Ambedkar expressed his reluctance and abstained from the convention. He later published what he wrote with the title, *Annihilation of Caste* in 1936.

Analyzing *Annihilation of Caste* as a Voice for Humanizing Humanity

The text is, as detailed above, a powerful statement on the debilitating sociocultural issues, which were felt by Ambedkar, as required to be highlighted in circumstances in which caste discrimination not only went unchallenged but also inspired many of the caste Hindus to mobilize opinions since his effort was likely to take away their privileges which they had been enjoying over generations. So, the text was, on the one hand, a manifesto for Dalit rights and also a voice for permanently eradicating those discriminatory practices impairing the growth of untouchables as human beings; it was, on the other, an open challenge of an activist who, despite not being integrally connected with mainstream nationalism, helped build a new discourse which did not attract the nationalist ideologues to the extent it was desirable. In fact, it will not be out of place to suggest that his association with the ruling authority was hardly a constraint in evolving his critique of caste-driven Hindu social order, presumably because many of the leading Congressmen, including their supremo, Gandhi felt that despite not being pleasant to many of his colleagues, Ambedkar's views were both persuasive and deserved to be taken seriously. It is also true that Gandhi, who agreed with Ambedkar on almost all points he raised in the text, still wanted him to go slow because he always privileged political independence in preference to any other demands with the apprehension that campaign around them was likely to weaken the nationalist endeavour for India's political emancipation from the British yoke.

The discussion on the text needs to be prefaced by an analytical dissection of the lecture by Ambedkar on the 101 Birth Anniversary of one of the Moderate thinkers, Mahadev Govind Ranade (1842–1901) in 1940. The reason for the discussion of this lecture ahead of the one which was already in public domain since 1936, is linked with the claim that in the 1940 lecture, Ambedkar elaborated the historical context of his ideational vision which was useful to grasp why he conceptualized caste as he did in the context of 1936. In other words, the 1940 tract will be of help in comprehending many of the issues which he referred to in his 1936 text; these issues were not dealt with in detail presumably because his primary aim was to develop those arguments which were effective enough to permanently abolish caste-centric segmentation; one may link Ambedkar being so categorical in his statements in favour of his principal objective with his near surrender to the Mahatma by abdicating the 1935 Communal Award for untouchables which ensured separate electorate for them. The *Annihilation of Caste* was his curt response to Gandhi's defence of *varna* system which was, indirectly, an endorsement of caste differentiation. That Gandhi was also perturbed was evident from the fact that he wrote a rejoinder to Ambedkar's text once it was publicized. By supporting his point of view, Gandhi did not completely reject Ambedkar's views; what he argued was tantamount to persuade Ambedkar to understand the importance of the strengthening of the multicultural political platform that finally evolved to combat the British. Hence, it was not a battle of ideas; instead, it was illustrative of differences of opinion on strategies which, as per Gandhi were governed exclusively by Congress' political priority in preference to Ambedkar's sociocultural aims. Overall, the text, *Annihilation of Caste* and Gandhi's critique reveal that although they did sail through together, their intellectual schism represented important turns in the nationalist voice and vocabulary. Gandhi had his opinion justified with reference to the conceptual universe he preferred while Ambedkar had his own. As liberals, neither of them defended caste system as such although Gandhi prescribed that the required social processes needed to be invented to completely uproots the distortion in the system while Ambedkar preferred the state to act decisively to weed-out the sources of customary discriminatory practices which were justified as they were based on scriptural instructions.

Ranade, Gandhi and Jinnah: Ambedkar's 1940 Speech

This particular speech is of immense importance in tracing the roots of Ambedkar's own conceptualization of humanizing humanity. A relentless campaigner for social reform, M.G. Ranade put his views on ritualistic and well-entrenched customary discrimination in a historical perspective, with reference to the downfall of Brahminic rule in Maharashtra in 1818 after the Battle of Kirkee. Many were happy because with the defeat of the Maratha ruler at the hands of the British, the hegemonic rule of Brahmin Peshwa ended. Ranade was stunned because the decline of the Maratha king also meant loss of freedom and surrender to a foreign race. In other words, once the Marathas were vanquished, they lost to the British their 'most precious possession, namely, freedom'.[56] Upset with the victory of the British, Ranade was keen to explain why it had happened although the Maratha army was equally equipped. He applied his mind to the issue for a persuasive explanation. He realized, as Ambedkar explained, that 'the downfall was due to certain weaknesses in the Hindu social system and unless these weaknesses were removed, the Marathas would never rise again as the most courageous Indians with valour and vigour'.[57] Hence, 'he was passionate about social reform which he carried through meetings, missions, lectures, sermons, articles, interviews, letters ... with unrelenting zeal'.[58] According to him, political campaign against the foreign rulers would result in freedom from a hegemonic alien ruler; but the age-old social customs vertically and horizontally dividing Indians remained one of the most virulent enemies of our society, which needed to be rooted out to bring back India's glory as in the past. In order to bolster his argument, he further added that task did not seem to be easy; in fact, far more difficult than challenging the colonizers because political prisoners were no longer treated as criminals; they were hailed for their selfless contribution to mother India while those combatting the age-old caste driven and religion-centric discriminatory practices were subject to social excommunication which resulted in making them a nobody in society. Ranade thus questioned 'what punishment in the penal code is comparable in its magnitude and severity to excommunication?'[59] A political prisoner on his return after completing jail sentences was always welcomed while those who challenged the established social order were 'loathed and shunned because he [had] the courage to turn upside down the debilitating customary practices weakening the collective mentally, emotionally and also physically'.[60] Hence, Ranade appreciated those who took up social reform as his/her principal aim by saying that

> let it be remembered that he lived in times when social and religious customs however gross and unmoral were regarded as sacrosanct and when ay doubt questioning their divine and moral basis was regarded not merely as heterodoxy but as intolerable blasphemy and sacrilege.[61]

Explicit here was the appreciation for those who were engaged in social reform despite odds, and the disenchantment at the role of those who appeared totally indifferent to its need. According to Ambedkar, political emancipation, unless complemented by the emergence of bonhomie among human beings became futile. Hence, his priority was for radical social reform not only for founding a social order free from segregationist mindsets, but also for laying out a solid foundation for a stable political order. It was a difficult task because many Indians still believed that the system their 'wisest and noblest ancestors … devised was of the most ideal character'.[62] Ranade also held the view that 'the Hindu religious and social is such that you cannot go forward to give its ideal form a reality because ideal is bad; nor can you attempt to elevate the real to the status of the ideal because the real, i.e., the existing state of affairs, is worse than worse could be'.[63] In view of the support of the critical segment of Indian society, the caste Hindus, it was a herculean task to bring about changes in those ritualistic behavioural traits vis-à-vis inter-caste interactions. This was not 'an exaggeration', suggested Ranade because

> the Hindu ideal of society as prescribed by Hindu religion has acted as a most demoralizing and degrading influence in Hindu society; it is Nietzschean [who justified race as a legitimate marker of superior and inferior human beings and concluded that Germans were superior because they were Aryans]. Long before Nietzsche was born, Manu had proclaimed the gospel which Nietzsche sought to preach. [Hinduism] … is a religion which is not intended to establish liberty, equality and fraternity. It is a gospel which proclaims the worship of superman—the Brahmin by the rest of the Hindu society. It propounds that the superman and his class alone are born to live and to rule. Others are born to serve them, and to nothing more. They have no life of their to live, and no right to develop their own personality. This has been the gospel of the Hindu religion.[64]

By drawing attention to Ranade's formulation, Ambedkar brought out the conceptual roots of Nietzsche's ideational vision of racial superiority of Germans. Hinduism was similar to this conceptual format and the sociocultural prejudices were accepted as axiomatic by the Hindu zealots presumably because they were beneficiaries as a result of their continuity. It was Ranade, felt Ambedkar, who, despite upholding nationalism as a rejuvenating ideal, also brought in the public domain those issues which were normally put under the carpet just to avoid social skirmishes. Following this he also defended the claim that 'the caste system is a degenerate form of *Chaturvarnya* which is one of the foundational pillars of Hinduism ... individually and socially, it is a folly and a crime'.[65] It is clear now that Ranade was one of those early nationalists who also felt that political emancipation was not adequate for human emancipation, for which a complete social overhaul was to be done. Although he was aware that the consequences could be disastrous, because the efforts towards altering the prevalent social order meant withdrawal of benefits which the caste Hindus accrued so far due to the salience of divisive social designs. Now, Ambedkar reiterated Ranade's response to the query which he made to find out the defeat of the Marathas by the British. According to him, the Marathas lost to the British because of the lack of unity among them due to differences around many axes. The most devastating division was largely due to the acceptance of caste system as axiomatic. Hence, he stated that 'it is the Brahminic theory of *Chaturvarnya* that has been responsible not only for the defeat but for the decay of Hindu society'.[66] Hindus were demoralized by the zealous endeavour of the privileged caste Hindus for sustaining the caste order of dividing Hindus vertically. This was one of the serious constraints against the rise of Hindus as a compact collective.

A careful analysis of the Ambedkar's assessment of Ranade's contribution as a social reformer suggests that like him, Ranade was also one of the proponents of right-based approaches to humanity. His critique of the system that was perpetuated among the Hindus, enabled him to understand that for the caste Hindus, it was their rights which they were allowed to retain, whereas and for the untouchables, it was their duty to serve the caste Hindus for their well-being. Ranade reinforced that untouchables were deprived of rights in view of the customary practices that evolved and were nurtured for partisan gains, whereas none of his compatriots ever raised their voice for reforming a debased society. By highlighting that 'there were privileges and disabilities—privileges for a few and disabilities for a vast majority, Ranade struggled to create rights', argued Ambedkar.[67] He, Ambedkar further stated, wanted 'to vitalize the conscience of the Hindu society which had become moribund and morbid'.[68] His aim was to lay out the foundation of social democracy which was not possible just by political freedom but by evolving 'a strong moral fiber [because] … he held the view that a nation's moral stamina was more important than mere political freedom'.[69] There are two basic ideas which are reverberated in Ambedkar's *Annihilation of Caste*: first, caste was inimical to freedom per se because it was a design for protecting selfish interests of a select group Hindus at the cost of the majority who were outside the fold; secondly, although he was in favour of annihilating the caste order, he was aware of the difficulties connected with the effort since the well-entrenched vested interests were too strong to be displaced so easily. Ranade was a pathfinder for him since he provided him with some of the ideas which helped in devising an effective strategy in his politico-ideological format. By focusing on relatively lesser-known areas of Ranade's mindset, Ambedkar not only charted a new narrative of empowering the deprivileged, but also helped design a course of action which he felt was appropriate for attaining whatever was achievable in the nationalist context.

Annihilation of Caste: Ambedkar's Manifesto for Empowerment

This part serves to reinforce the claim that this text, by insisting on empowering the deprivileged, not only argues for transforming the nearly-dehumanized, prevalent social order, but also provides critical inputs for delineating ideas for humanizing humanity. The story of how the text was articulated also reveals Ambedkar's firm commitment to social justice. As mentioned above, it was a text which he prepared as a speech to be delivered. Initially, he was reluctant since Jat-Pat-Todal Mandal was led by the caste Hindus because the attitude of the members of the organization 'towards social reform is so different from [his] that [he] found it difficult to pull with them'.[70] Later on, he changed his opinion and agreed to be the chief guest in the annual get-together of the Mandal. The trouble started once the content of the text was made known to them, when Ambedkar sent the text for distribution to the attendees. The organizers felt that the text was not an elaboration of his opinion on how caste was a source of decay in Hindu society; it was also a critique of Hinduism because he identified the text as his 'last speech as a Hindu'.[71] He was attacked further by the organizer by stating that Ambedkar

> unnecessarily attacked the morality and reasonableness of the *Vedas* and other religious books of Hindus … which has absolutely no

> connection with the problem at issue, so much so that some of the passages have become irrelevant and off the point. [Especially] … the last portion which deals with the complete annihilation of Hindu religion and doubts the morality of the sacred books of the Hindus as well as a hint about your intention to leave the Hindu fold does not seem … to be relevant.[72]

At one level, the above letter contained a veiled threat to Ambedkar since his condemnation of Hinduism did not augur well with the organizers led by dominant caste Hindus of Lahore; at another level, it was also an assertion that his views demeaning Hinduism did not elicit support from them since it was contrary to their faith. To defuse the situation, the organizer again insisted that Ambedkar should address them since he was accepted by everyone as a powerful exponent of anti-caste discernments. Ambedkar was invited because, they felt, that he would strengthen their hands by bringing about radical changes in the prevalent mindsets, and, in the process, he would emerge as 'a nucleus in the gigantic effort'.[73] As a born crusader, it was well-anticipated that Ambedkar refused to become a part of such an exercise which was an indirect mode of diluting what he nurtured so far so dearly. In response, while being steadfastly committed to the cause, Ambedkar was equally categorical in his condemnation of the endeavour of the Mandal. While expressing his resentment, he thus argued that

> I did not expect that … the Mandal would be so upset because I have spoken of the destruction of Hindu religion. I thought, it was only fools who were afraid of words. … One cannot have any respect or regard for men who take the position of the Reformer and then refuse even to see the logical consequences of that position, let alone following them out in action.[74]

True to his espoused goal, Ambedkar, by being critical of the Mandal's conceptualization of the destruction of caste system within the Hindu fold, reiterated his arguments, regardless of the consequences. According to him, such an effort was hypocrisy since caste was the product of Hindu society as it developed historically; unless Hindu society was radically transformed, caste which was one of its core pillars, remained as well-entrenched as in the past. Hence, the destruction of caste and destruction of Hinduism in its present form should go in tandem. That he stuck to his point was evident when he declared that he would not allow 'any censorship over [his] address and [this has to be] accepted as it was written by [him] and if the conference so desired, it can adopt a resolution condemning his views as contrary to be objective of this congregation'.[75] The views, Ambedkar expressed were co-terminus with his primary goal. Although one was introduced to the ideas which were likely to have influenced him while writing this seminal text, *Annihilation of Caste*, the exchange of letters between him and the organizers also underlined the dominance of sociocultural prejudices in shaping human minds. Ambedkar was caught by surprise that those who were supportive of the destruction of caste were perturbed when he challenged Hinduism and suggested that unless the foundation of caste was not destroyed, caste was not going to disappear.

The discussion provided not only an introduction to the ideas which figured prominently in the text, but also laid out the perspective in which his arguments were articulated. Broadly speaking, the text has three interrelated components: firstly, it was Ambedkar's endeavour at exposing the inherent limitations of caste which was nothing but a design to keep a large section of humanity in chains for partisan benefits; secondly, it was also a voice, or a manifest of untouchables in organizing an effective campaign for doing away with a system of segregation of humanity on the basis of well-nurtured sociocultural prejudices which were recognized as integral to Hinduism; finally, it was a text to empower and also rejuvenate those who remained peripheral due to a social conspiracy, in which the caste not only took part, but also contributed immensely to the success, despite the adoption of laws favourably disposed to the untouchables; this confirms how difficult it was to weed-out a well-entrenched prejudicial mindset.

Elaboration of the Argument

What is striking in whatever he wrote for defending a particular point, is the clarity in his thought. Two important concerns figured prominently in the texts that he left for the posterity: on the one hand, he pursued his points of view by putting them in the right-based conceptual format which clearly has elements of the Western discourses. His was a critique of the indigenous texts, strong enough to shape human minds because they were detrimental to the realization of the goal for which he intervened politically. On the other hand, his was a voice of protest, a language of rebellion for snatching what was due to the untouchables. As a devout supporter of liberal-constitutionalism, Ambedkar strongly felt that liberal-constitutional governance was an antidote to caste prejudices. There were two interrelated factors which explain why it was so: first, Ambedkar was persuaded to believe out of his own existential experiences of being an untouchable, how atrocious the caste-driven mindsets were, and secondly, he was introduced to the Western liberal world where human beings were treated equally although he remained silent in regard to the racial oppression the African-Americans underwent when he was in the US. Nonetheless, constitutional liberalism continued to remain an important empowering device in so far as Ambedkar was concerned.

Fundamental to the text were Ambedkar's core ideas which he elaborated in other written tracts as well. The underlying theme was however the same, namely how to purge Hindu social order of the obnoxious caste system seeking to dehumanize humanity because it allowed a section to hegemonize the rest of the people. Hence, Ambedkar defined caste as 'a powerful weapon in the hands of the orthodox … for persecuting the reforms and for killing all reform'.[76] The statement had meaningful implications. So long as caste remained a significant determinant of the Hindu social order, it was a deterrent to the rise and consolidation of the liberal values—liberty, equality and fraternity—in Hindu society. As long as they were not allowed to strike roots and prosper, the Hindu social order remained indifferent to the core values of liberalism. For instance, as Ambedkar argued, fraternity which was one of the formidable pillars of democracy was futile since caste order never allowed 'associated living [giving space to] conjoint communication'.[77] Similarly, equality was an anathema among the caste Hindus since the untouchables were already segregated as 'unequals'. Liberty was absent in the sense of free movement and choice of profession by the untouchables just like their caste Hindu counterparts. The denial of basic rights which were admissible in any liberal society was 'a crime and a treason against those who simply demand for their legitimate rights as human beings'.[78] A mere objection to the atrocious practices was not adequate; only by organizing sustained movements against the mindset supportive of caste system, could its roots be eradicated. While elaborating this point, Ambedkar lucidly explained that

> caste is not a physical object like a wall of bricks or a line of barbed wire which prevents the Hindus from co-mingling and which has therefore to be pulled down. Caste is a notion; it is a state of mind. The destruction of caste does not therefore mean the destruction of a physical barrier. It means a notional change.[79]

Notional change here meant an ideational vision which was an aid to the continuity of caste as integral to the Hindu social order. Now, he hurled the salvo by targeting Hindu *shastras* as responsible for the sustenance of such debilitating and dehumanizing practices so far. What was wrong was

> the religion which has inculcated the notion of caste, [and] … if this is correct, then obviously the enemy, you must grapple with, is not the people who observe caste, but the *Shastras* which teach them this religion of caste. [Therefore], criticizing and ridiculing people for not inter-dining or inter-marrying … is a futile method of achieving the desired end. The real remedy is to destroy the belief in the sanctity of the *Shastras*.[80]

This was a revolutionary ideal especially in the nationalist context when the supremo, Gandhi utilized many of the religious precepts for politically mobilizing support for the final battle with the hegemonic British rule. The majority opinion was with Gandhi, which was realized by Ambedkar when he was forced to abdicate separate electorate for the untouchables following the execution of the Poona Pact in 1932. It was also understandable why the Jat-Pat-Todak Mandal objected to Ambedkar's attack on Hindu *shastras,* because it was certain to annoy many of their caste Hindu supporters if he was allowed to present his views which were contrary to theirs. While dwelling on this point, Ambedkar also expressed his resentment against the view that religious transformation of the Hindus was a possible measure because 'religion was not, at all, associated with the idea of change; it is possible only through a revolution, as it happened in the case fifteenth century Crusade which not only developed a powerful critique of Catholicism, but also demolished Pope's authority significantly'.[81] What was thus required was to adopt an appropriate legal system or set of laws creating an ambience contrary to the atrocities against human beings by including both punishment and also reformatory schemes. As 'the idea of law is associated with change',[82] Ambedkar felt, it was perhaps the most effective way to do away with this most obnoxious system of human atrocities. Implicit here was his firm belief in liberal constitutionalism which privileged law as primary to the ascertaining of rights and legitimate due to the individuals as citizens. Being taught by one of the most vocal supporters of liberalism in the West, John Dewey, Ambedkar easily internalized the idea that only with the intervention of a state power, would the artificial design of separating humanity would completely be uprooted. As will be shown in chapter 6, liberal constitutionalism was one of the prime determinants of how he conceptualized the 1949 Constitution of India as the Chairman of the Drafting Committee.

In two specific ways, Ambedkar was indebted to his academic mentor, Dewey: First, he was the one who transmitted to Ambedkar the idea that past trivialities needed to be discarded since it hampered the growth of newer ideas which were context-driven; otherwise, the future of human society was bleak. Second, by emphasizing the importance of past in comprehending the present, Dewey also warned him of not being servile to the past because that was a trap to halt human progress. This was a trap because, by belittling the present and future, the orthodox forces would create a framework of thinking which was 'inimical to progress and is an hindrance to a strong and a steady current life'.[83] Ideationally, Ambedkar followed Dewey in spirit and letters. A careful reading of *Annihilation of Caste* underlines that Ambedkar borrowed many of Dewey's ideas which he propounded in his path-breaking work, *Democracy and Education* (1916). Ambedkar was persuaded to believe that one of the reasons for the untouchables to remain ignorant of the self-fulfilling desires of the caste Hindus was their lack of awareness, which he attributed to lack of education. Hence, his slogan, *Educate, Organize and Agitate* which gained momentum as he rose to prominence as a rebellious voice. It did not require one to go in-depth to understand that the plight of the masses was due to illiteracy which allowed them to be exploited by the orthodox elements by misleading them to believe that whatever they stated were based on their comprehension of the *shastras*. He categorically mentioned this while defending the contention when he adumbrated that 'the masses are too illiterate to know the contexts of the *shastras*. They have believed what they have been told and what they have been told is that the *shastras* do enjoin as a religious duty the observance of caste and untouchability'.[84]

With his relentless efforts, Ambedkar created an environment which led to many of the untouchables going to schools and colleges, because they also realized that by being uneducated, they were not well-equipped to question the views of orthodoxy which were forced on them; once they were capable of comprehending the axiomatic principles, they would easily expose the hypocrisy of the self-proclaimed experts of Hinduism.

Besides rattling the organizers of the convention belonging to Jat-Pat-Todak Mandal, *Annihilation of Caste* also provoked Gandhi to challenge Ambedkar by purportedly showing the inherent limitations of his point of view. First, he was not persuaded to accept Ambedkar's contention that *Vedas, Upanishads, Smritis* and *Puranas*, including *Ramayana* and *Mahabharata* were texts for Hinduism; instead, they were documentary articulation of different phases of humanity in the wake of the progress of human civilization. Here, Gandhi held similar views which Rabindranath

Tagore also propounded. According to him, unlike Christianity, Judaism, among others, the supposed Hindu texts were not, at all, religious in character. They

> do not represent the spiritual experience of one great individual or the greatness of one particular phase of human history, as most of texts of ecumenical religions represent, but [epitomize] a great age of enlightenment which has a complex and collective manifestation, like that of the starry world. [Hence, they are, claimed by Tagore'] not associated with any particular religion, but they have the breadth of a universal soil that supply with living sap all religions which have any spiritual ideal hidden at their core, or apparent in their fruit and foliage.[85]

This was an important ingredient in Tagore and Gandhi's understanding of the so-called Hindu texts. Ambedkar might have failed to understand, given the continuous reference to them while justifying caste discrimination. Gandhi was aware that these noble texts containing humanitarian ideational vision, were distorted by those determined to fulfil their personal interests at any costs. Adherence to caste prejudices was one of them. Hence, Gandhi made a plea to Babasaheb that 'a religion must be judged not by worst specimens but by the best it might have produced. For that and that alone can be used as the standard to aspire to, if not to improve upon'.[86] In his response, Ambedkar not only exposed the weaknesses of Mahatma's argument in defence of the infallibility of caste system. He thus argued that

> the sanctity of caste and *varna* can be destroyed only by discarding the divine authority of the *shastras*. [In order to reinforce his point that the Mahatma failed to understand the logic behind his argument, he further stated that[87]] the questions raised by the Mahatma are absolutely beside the point and show that the main argument of the speech was lost upon him.

Ambedkar was not dissuaded to believe that given his political commitment to caste Hindus, it was expected of the Mahatma to say so. Because, without being supported by these divinely-ordained texts, known as *shastras*, caste Hindus remained helpless in defending their partisan rights of hegemonizing over the rest of society. Hence, Babasaheb questioned the two fundamental features of Hinduism—tolerance and catholicity—as contradictory to each other; one cannot be tolerant by being true to the original tenets of Hindu *shastras* which justified caste segregation even by endorsing what was, evidently, designs of dehumanizing humanity. Such a presentation of the core beliefs of Hinduism was, argued Ambedkar, 'nothing more certifiable than indifference or flaccid latitudinarianism'.[88] What becomes explicit here is his unalloyed belief in the core tenets of liberal-constitutionalism which, he felt, was possibly the most libertarian ideology capable of creating a level playing field for all by denying the sectional claims as contrary to humanity. The target of his challenge was thus the ideal on which Hindu society rested upon. The ideal was drawn on uncritical acceptance of the self-appointed humanistic values propounded by Hindu *shastras* which were misleading and constructed for sectarian benefits. Hence, he categorically stated that

> I should not consent to live in a society which cherishes wrong ideals or a society which having right ideal will not consent to bring its social life in conformity with those ideals. If I am disgusted with Hindus and Hinduism, it is because I am convinced that they cherish wrong ideals and live a wrong social life. My quarrel with Hindus and Hinduism is not over the imperfections of their social conduct. It is much more fundamental. It is over their ideals.[89]

His condemnation of Hindu *shastras* which acted critically in decisively shaping the dominant Hindu mindsets was reiterated here. What was visible in the open in the form of caste discrimination remained so because Hindu *shastras* always came to their aid. So, the argument which he put forward by rejecting the offer of the Jat-Pat-Todak Mandal was repeated here. Ambedkar understood that as long as Hindu *shastras* were determinants of human beings' behaviour towards those compartmentalized as untouchables, the existent sociocultural prejudices could hardly be effectively attacked. Such an understanding allowed him to develop a strategy to combat the well-established caste biases by inspiring the untouchables to be educated, organized and prepared for the battle against the orthodox forces in support of dehumanizing humanity, as well as by inculcating a zeal of defiance to the *shastras* because they were not as axiomatic for humanity as they were projected, *shastras* were not providentially ordained; they were constructed by human beings in accordance with an agenda protective of the interests of the haves at the cost of the have-nots. Caste and class were thus not conceptually incompatible given the fact that the untouchables were also those who were economically peripheral and did not have adequate means to make the two ends meet. In other words, their survival was always at stake because the Hindu social order did not provide any effective mechanism for them to live respectfully just like their caste Hindu counterparts. So, not only were they considered inferior in terms of their caste identity, untouchables always remained at the lower rung of society which made them the most vulnerable section of the Hindu social order.

Concluding Observations

Ambedkar was a rebellious voice indeed. It was, as well, a political voice since one of his principal aims was to radically transform the existing power-relationships between the caste Hindus, and untouchables who constituted a majority of India's demography. He was not a nationalist, but a humanist to the core because by insisting that so long as untouchability continued to remain in the Hindu social order, the claim that the nationalists also fought for humanizing humanity was vacuous. Based on his lived experiences, both as a child and an adult, he realized that the well-nurtured casteist mindset was accountable for this. It was indeed a super-structural component which would lose its force once the base stopped receiving nourishment. It means that the Hindu *shastras* constituted the base of the ideas in support of caste discrimination, and as soon as they were exposed and proved that they were caste-driven exercises, the politico-ideological views in favour of debasing humanity would immediately lose their salience, which also meant that they would no longer remain as effective as in the past. So, Ambedkar defined his task as a social reformer who attributed the decadence of Hindu to the presence and viability of Hindu *shastras* in society.

Along with his endeavour towards intellectually unveiling the limitations of Hindu *shastras*, he also undertook many significant steps to empower the deprivileged untouchables. His slogan—*Educate, Organize and Agitate*—was of great help. As contemporary archival sources suggest, his slogan electrified the socio-economically peripheral sections of the society, not just the untouchables. From this angle, Ambedkar's discourses were not only empowering for the deprivileged but also libertarian in spirit and texture.[90] Hence, the argument that Babasaheb represented an endeavour for liberating the socio-economically and politico-ideologically peripheral sections across the world.

In evolving his well-defined view, the contribution of John Dewey was immensely important. Dewey's views acted decisively in drawing him to liberal constitutionalism which, he also believed, reverberated in the ideas of M.G. Ranade, the Moderate Congressman who also believed that one of the major reasons for decadence among Hindus was the restrictive and dehumanizing sociocultural practices. Ambedkar was persuaded to accept, as argued above, that the defeat of the Marathas by the British in 1818 was primarily due to the failure of Hindus to come together as they were socially segmented in terms of their caste and religion; they were hindrances to the amity which was necessary for conducting an effective operation against a mightier enemy.

Ambedkar's role as an intellectual opponent to Gandhi also helped build an alternative nationalist ideational vision which, however, did not receive adequate attention among the nationalists, including Gandhi. With his rise on India's political scene as an independent voice for the socio-economically peripheral section of humanity, the nationalist discourse became far more enriched than before. Gandhi was aware that untouchability was a grave social problem which needed to be mitigated before it assumed disproportionate significance especially in the context of the consolidation of Muslims as a powerful player in the nationalist campaign. Nonetheless, the Mahatma appeared helpless presumably because he also realized that an attempt on his part to do away with caste system was likely to have massive country-wide repercussions presumably because of the opposition of many of the Congressmen who never felt that caste discrimination was tantamount to dehumanizing humanity. One is tempted to make a comparison here between those who led the independence movement in the US in the late eighteenth century and the Indian nationalists. Like the US freedom fighters who were keen to liberate their country from the European colonizers, their Indian counterparts had also the same objective in mind while being involved in struggles against British colonialism. The claim that neither the US nor the Indian nationalists ever thought of designs for humanizing humanity is since no attempt was made to do away with slavery in the US; similarly, in India, even the nationalist supremo, Gandhi never thought of abdicating his belief in *varnashrama*. The reason does not seem much different; it was a strategic device to sustain the political platform in which those nurturing partisan interests were dominant and the leadership were too scared to confront the difficulties in case any of its decisions weakened the campaign due to horizontal division among those being together for fulfilling the primary politico-ideological goal.

Analogous with his role in seeking to change the prevalent vitiated mindset was also the claim that social reform needed to be accomplished by intentional intervention. Because it was human nature to cling to designs gratifying the partisan interests, it was difficult, if not impossible, to bring about changes if they were left with socially-determined modes of corrective measures. Contrarily, Ambedkar was in favour of targeted intervention because by being habituated of enjoying the fruits of others' labour, caste Hindus could never be persuaded to abjure what they had been accustomed to. s Ambedkar believed that only with state intervention, those enjoying at others' cost would be forced to give up what remained with them illegally, so far. Ideationally, this required a radical change in the prevalent mindset which was not so easy since the vested interests were too well-entrenched to disappear so soon. The state initiatives or legal intervention, as Ambedkar clarified, were necessary to change the prevalent politico-ideological priorities and tune them to humanize humanity, by ruthlessly countering the contrarian attempts based on the *shastric* instructions. Illustrative here was Gandhi–Ambedkar debate that unfolded once Ambedkar released the text, *Annihilation of Caste,* in the public domain. Although the debate was inconclusive since both Gandhi and Ambedkar were clearly tactical in their responses, however, what was critical was the blossoming of ideas in support of their respective views on the Hindu social order and the importance or or lack thereof of *shastras*. The Mahatma triumphed by being the supremo of the nationalist campaign; but, Babasaheb finally succeeded in the establishment of a constitutional structure capable of accomplishing many of the objectives he nurtured since the beginning of his public life. By charting out a specific course of action during the making of the 1949 Constitution, Babasaheb not only complied with liberal constitutional values, but also generated adequate support for them among those who played critical roles in its finalization. The proponents of *shastras* who were the determinants of codifying laws earlier, appeared to have been marginalized in the face of the support Babasaheb received from a well-knit group of his colleagues who also accepted that constitutional liberalism was an empowering and appropriate ideational vision for an independent India.

6

Humanizing Humanity through Constitutional Liberalism

Constitutionalism and constitutionalization are both interrelated and different semantically and conceptually at the same time because the latter is linked with the former and without the former, the latter has no foundational basis. The contrary is also true, for a well-defined constitution was not a guarantee of constitutionalization of a polity and similarly constitutionalization, if not backed by constitutional morality, loses its salience. In other words, a compilation of well-meaning provisions in a constitution does not ensure good governance and is tuned to humanize humanity. History is full examples since time immemorial. An analysis of the role of 'Law-givers' suggests that despite having had a constitution made by one of the most efficient law-givers, Aristotle, Sparta in ancient Greece was unable to seal the growth of forces contrary to the set of laws devised for the city state. Similarly, the Genevan philosopher Jean Jacques Rousseau who was involved in the making of laws for efficient governance, also failed to sustain many of the principalities in Europe. Here is the point that a 'good' constitution was not necessary as an aid for a governance tuned to humanizing humanity, it in turn inhibits the consolidation of processes leading to dehumanizing humanity. What is required is a mindset contributing to the creation of a sociocultural and politico-ideological cosmos which follows the constitutional provisions for the sake of humanity. This is what the famous classicist, George Grote (1794–1871) conceptualized as constitutional morality. While devising this conceptual yardstick, he attributed the success of a constitution to the consolidation of constitutional morality.

Ambedkar played a critical role in constitutionalizing India. He influenced by his academic mentor at Colombia University—John Dewey—along with his colleagues in the Constituent Assembly, carved a new narrative for independent India. One of the reasons for fighting for constitutional liberalism was his belief that it was the only politico-ideological alternative complementary to the fulfilment of his goal of humanizing humanity. Opposed to Hindu caste order, Ambedkar strongly felt that caste discrimination was an anathema to inter-personal relationships drawn on equality. His ideational vision was governed by three interrelated factors: first, in view of the prejudices of the caste Hindus against untouchables, the fundamental human ethos manifested in the ideas of Liberty, Equality and Fraternity remained unrealized so long as caste differentiation was allowed to survive. Secondly, caste prejudices were so internalized that it was difficult to uproot them easily. Ambedkar felt that sociocultural prejudices against the lower castes were products of circumstances in which they were neither deplored nor criticized; instead, they were accepted as axiomatic to Hindus. Hence, victims were forced to endorse the socioculturally justified restrictions and the voices against these practices were very few. Finally, the nationalist campaign appeared to have ignored concerns for human emancipation in its real connotation by privileging political independence. They believed that with the attainment of India's freedom, the task of phasing out sociocultural biases would be easier. Ambedkar rose under these circumstances as he was determined to uproot the sources of caste discrimination for it was not only inhuman but also contrary to the basic tenets of liberalism.

One of the main sources of Ambedkar's ideational vision was John Dewey's commitment to liberal constitutionalism. As the available literature shows, Dewey was one of the most powerful voices against racism in the US; and this had an impact on Ambedkar because he realized that without sustained opposition to human prejudices, it was not possible to create conditions in which human beings were treated equally. Although Ambedkar did not write about racism, there are enough reasons to assume that Dewey inspired him significantly to raise a voice against processes towards dehumanizing humanity. His regular interaction with Dewey on issues of racism showed why racism was a hindrance to the realization of universal humanism.

Ambedkar's stay in the West helped him understand the core values of the Enlightenment philosophy. He accepted that freedom needed to be secured for the individual first; only then, would the collective—comprising these 'free' individuals—would be free. Here is a conceptual point to explain why he differed from the Mahatma. Both fought for freedom: Gandhi accepted that freedom of a collectivity entailed individuals' freedom, meanwhile Ambedkar held opposing views because he was a liberal in his belief and his support to individual was as critical as his support to the collective. Luckily, when he was asked to defend the constitutional provision in the 1949 Constitution for India, neither Gandhi nor any of his vocal supporters opposed the participation of his Congress colleagues in the making of the Constitution. So, the situation was favourably disposed towards Ambedkar because his colleagues in the

Constituent Assembly, barring a few Gandhians, were all supportive of the constitutional scheme that he placed in the Assembly.

Besides his own liberal inclination, many of his colleagues also held similar views. In other words, he was supported by many leading Congressmen with similar ideational priorities while debates centred around the adoption of specific provisions. His task was made easier because the members of the Congress Legislative Party were also tutored by the Congress leadership and their role was charted out long in advance. Apart from the Gandhians who insisted on reorganizing governance in India in accordance with Gandhi's village *swaraj*, the majority of the members of the Assembly acquiesced with Ambedkar and his team.

A perusal of how India's Constitution was made shows that the process was nearly free from skirmishes. The reasons are not difficult to locate. The Assembly was dominated by the members of the Congress and some of the dissenting voices were raised by the Gandhian and those who were baptized politically in Hindu nationalism. Nonetheless, the opposition was never allowed to dominate the proceedings in the Assembly. For instance, the incorporation of Part IV of the Constitution, enumerating Directive Principles was a later development to accommodate the Gandhian demands insisting that Gandhi's model of decentralization should figure in one of the parts of the Constitution.

How did liberalism triumph in India even though Gandhi spearheaded the nationalist campaign? On a careful study of the situation which led to the acceptance of liberalism by majority of the members of the Assembly, one is likely to argue that Gandhi's charm declined and liberalism rose to prominence. Gandhi's absence allowed his disciples, who were trained in the West, to unanimously adopt the Objective Resolutions which were derivative of the fundamental principles of liberalism. Furthermore, the total absence of the Muslim League with the acceptance of India's Partition leading to the dismemberment of the country was of assistance in guiding the majority opinion.

Apart from delving on why liberalism became an ideological priority during the making of the Constitution of a free India, the above paragraph also highlights that it was preferred to strike at the foundation of sociocultural prejudices responsible for sustaining caste system in India. Artificial human division was an antipathy to the core tenets of liberalism, which was a design for humanizing humanity and an ideological tool to effectively combat dehumanization. Moreover, unlike Gandhi, who believed that caste division needed to be tackled by creating a mindset opposed to such prejudices, Ambedkar had no faith in such a conceptual priority. He was in favour of establishing a design of governance to sternly counter these forces practicing caste discrimination and caste-based prejudices.

The aim of this chapter is to understand the constitutionalist Ambedkar who believed that liberalism was a panacea for humanity. By incorporating provisions in independent India's Constitution, he evolved a law-driven design of governance for meaningfully addressing human grievances. Hence, Ambedkar's purpose was to cut out the sources of denial to human beings regardless of their caste, class, and ethnic identities, and put in place a system for humanization.

Foundational Pillars of Ambedkar's Ideational Cosmos

Given the aim of this chapter, it is mandatory to identify the constituents of Ambedkar's visions on why an appropriate system of law was required to eradicate the sources of dehumanizing humanity and to stabilize a polity for ascertaining safety for humanity. This is of great importance for two reasons: first, Ambedkar was raised in an environment where the social mores were more effective in governing human behaviour towards one another, and he strongly felt the importance of laws and an equally capable system of their enforcement; secondly, with his dialectical interaction with liberal states in the US and later in Britain, he realized that compliance with the institutionalized rules and regulations was unlikely to be instinctive, and they needed be inculcated, if necessary, by deploying force. These were the two important considerations which guided Ambedkar in his preference for a constitution with well-defined provisions.

Nationalist Outpouring

An inspection of the nature of Indian nationalism reveals that Indian nationalists who were critical in the campaign were almost all baptized in constitutional-liberalism, largely since they were raised in an India which adopted liberalism as the colonizers derived their ideological priorities from the Enlightenment. This was manifested in the political inclinations of both the opponents and the rulers. There were protests at the behest of the former; but no one was questioning the viability of constitutional governance. Implicit in their acceptance was also the idea that a constitutional governance was accommodative of the 'natives' which steered the rulers in its favour; and, for the nationalists, an endorsement of the importance of constitution was an opportunity to recognize the ruled as integral to administration. In other words, constitution provided a mechanism for 'representation' of the un-represented. Hence, it was an empowering mode of conceptualizing the role of those who remained peripheral in governance in India.

Ambedkar believed that a constitutional government was better than the one guided by mores and values deployed for discriminating one section of humanity from another. Governance in accordance with 'rule of law' meant that citizens were treated equally, both as right-holders and if they violated the law. This assumption had wider implications since it questioned that Ambedkar had not only discriminated against the untouchables, but also against the disprivileged sections of society when he framed free India's Constitution in 1947.

Apart from the environment in which he was raised, he was also guided by the ideational vision of humanity by putting forward the ideas of liberty, equality, and fraternity. He felt that these ideas were critical to humanizing humanity which emerged from his lived experiences as a Dalit. One of the principle reasons which prompted Ambedkar to establish the Independent Labour Party in 1936 was his understanding of politics as a design for transforming the prevalent power-relationships in society. The conceptual premise on which this assumption rested was derivative of his insistence on securing legitimate rights for humanity as a whole and Drawing on this conceptualization, he rightly understood that the presence of rules and enforcement agencies was not adequate to create a society free from discrimination. What was required was to evolve a mindset challenging deviant behaviour of human beings and question those running the state administration. Here comes the criticality of Ambedkar's slogan—*Educate, Organize and Agitate*—that served two purposes: first, the slogan insisted on contacts with the victims which would build a bridge between the organizers and the victims, and secondly, between like-minded individuals. The decisions led to deprivileging one section remained incomprehensible, unless one was equipped to understand the codified decisions for which education was critical. Hence, Ambedkar prioritized 'education' as a component for the empowerment of the deprivileged. There is a similarity between Ambedkar's effort and what Jyotirao Phule did in the late nineteenth century in Maharashtra. One of the reasons for establishing the Satyasadhok Samaj was also to establish schools for Dalits because, like Ambedkar, he also believed that education was indispensable for combatting superstitious mindset.[1] Phule's aim was two-fold: first, with the establishment of schools especially for the socially ostracized untouchables, he created a space for them to be able to acquire the capability of reading, and writing; secondly, schools provided him and his colleagues a bridge of communication with the families of the children.

Democracy

Ambedkar endorsed the view that the first step towards humanizing humanity was the establishment of procedural democracy as it would be easy to identify the violation of laws and the availability of remedies by following well-defined procedures. He emphasized that the constitutional design was a guarantee for human liberty and associated rights. According to him, 'the assertion by individual of his own opinion, and beliefs, his own independence and interest as over against group standards, group authority and group interests is a stepping stone for democracy to strike roots in society'.[2] Caste was a grave impediment to the path of democracy for reasons connected with its rigidity as far as caste-driven rules were concerned. Ambedkar argued that

> caste has an unquestioned right to excommunicate any man who is guilty of breaking the rules of the caste and it is realized that excommunication involves a complete cesser of social intercourse, it will be agreed that that as a form of punishment there is really little to choose between excommunication and death.[3]

It can be asserted that caste was a deterrent to democracy because individuals were governed by strict sociocultural rules that were too internalized to violate for fear of ostracism. Caste system thus took advantage of the helplessness of individuals who remained enslaved to the system. Under these circumstances, the attempt to democratize human behaviour was extremely difficult. The first casualty of caste order was fraternity; because by demarcating one caste group from another, it provided a system of unquestioned division which was of those belonging to different caste groups. For the untouchables, it was a system of denigration; for the caste Hindus, it was a system of accruing benefits based on one's birth.

Democracy was not just a structure of government, but also a philosophy upholding rights of the individuals to be their own rulers, the formation of which varied from one situation to another. In today's context, indirect democracy is perhaps the most acceptable system of public governance where individuals participate in the constitution of the government; here the role of the Constitution was important as it was the template devising appropriate rules for protecting citizen's rights. As a conceptual parameter, Thomas Jefferson's model of democracy in the US was perfect because, according to him and his colleagues who articulated the US Constitution in the 1787 Philadelphia Convention, it was one of the most effective designs for protecting individuals' rights along with their duties. The US Constitution-makers provided adequate guarantee to the citizens against any infringement particularly of their rights, by evolving a police system and other instruments. This was hardly applicable to India, as Ambedkar explained, because 'what is there for the State to police if there are no rights?'[4] The prevalent view was that once individuals acquired rights, laws protected them. Ambedkar however differed, because of his critical understanding of democracy being a sectarian system vis-à-vis specific sections of individuals. He firmly held the view that guarantee by law was not adequate since 'social conscience acts in the preparation of a mindset supportive of laws [and also] … to recognize which of the rights need to be protected and which do not deserve protection'.[5] This means that if the elite community was opposed to accept everyone as eligible to rights, the system was bound to be divided. He drew attention to the fate of African-Americans, the Jews of Germany and the untouchables in India. Social conscience was a significant determinant of whether rights were universal or confined to identified segments of population.

There was one more presupposition required to understand Ambedkar's specific approach to democracy. Built on the assumption that democratic government presupposed a democratic form of society, Ambedkar argued that 'the formal framework of democracy is of no value and would indeed be a misfit if there was no social democracy'.[6] Fundamental here was Ambedkar's critique of institutionalized democracy based on well-defined rules and regulations. If the Constitution had become so significant in governance, the discriminatory policies discrimination the African-Americans in the US would not have been possible. It was attributed to the prevalence of a mindset endorsing racial separation as the norm. To reinforce his argument, he further suggested that 'the politicians never realized that democracy was not a form of Government: it was essentially a form of society. It may not be necessary for a democratic society to be marked by unity, by community of purpose, by loyalty to public ends and mutuality of sympathy'.[7] Primary in the creation of a democratic society was an attitude of mind, an attitude of respect and equality towards their associates, and social organization free from rigid barriers. By being respectful to these two conditions, Ambedkar argued that 'democracy is incompatible and inconsistent with isolation and exclusiveness, resulting in the distinction between the privileged and unprivileged'.[8] While being appreciative of Ranade's effort towards inculcating social democracy, Ambedkar also underlined that he struggled to persuade the Hindu extremists to understand that caste discrimination was inhuman and contrary to the core tenets of democracy. As discussed in Chapter 5, Ranade strongly felt that for the caste Hindus to realize the importance of the universality of rights, the distorted moral fibre which evolved in the wake of the consolidation of caste discrimination by the caste Hindus needed to be abjured first; and, only then, an appropriate milieu would emerge in India.

Ambedkar felt democracy and Constitution were dialectically entwined the former became a structure without substance with the well-defined principles the latter contained. For this dialectical interconnection to be strong and meaningful, the consolidation of 'constitutional morality' which was required which entailed

> habits of paramount reverence for the form of the constitution, enforcing obedience to the authorities acting under and within these forms, yet combined with the habit of open speech, of action subject only to definite legal control, and unrestrained censure of those very authorities as to all their public acts—combined, too, with a perfect confidence in the bosom of every citizen, admits the bitterness of party contest, that the forms of constitution will be not less sacred in the eyes of his opponents than in his own.[9]

Two critical ideas come to the surface which are important to understand Ambedkar's mode of conceptualizing democracy as it evolved in the West. First, he argued that for democracy to succeed, an appropriate mindset helped build constitutional morality. He borrowed this idea from the famous classicist of Greek history, George Grote (1794–1871); it was useful to sustain obedience to the rules and regulations enacted in the constitution. Secondly, he also highlighted that constitutional morality involved universal acceptance of electoral competition which, however bitter it was, should never generate animosity among the political players. Ambedkar raised a fundamental question debating whether this model was universally applicable or acceptable. His response was negative because of these reasons. First, the idea of constitutional morality left no space for the existence of a dominant class, or elites who were destined to rule. Secondly, with the conceptualization of constitutional morality, there was therefore no space to realize that the prevalence of a governing elite was incongruous with democracy and self-government; it further meant that the non-elites remained on the margins as, they were recognized as 'unfit' to govern which allowed the elites to continue. Thirdly, those supportive of constitutional morality failed to understand that given the social milieu, the hegemony of the elites was not an aberration to the system which entailed that rise of the non-elites as rulers was permanently sealed. Fourthly, as Ambedkar felt, the absence of a strong opponent to the governing elites was detrimental to the emergence of a democracy in its real connotation. In practice, the rule of demos was replaced by the rule by the elites, or the chosen few, who were socioculturally privileged. Finally, democracy remained inaccurate so long as it was accompanied by a social conscience opposed to discrimination of human beings around any of the sociocultural and politico-economic axes. It was not easy, given the fact that governing elites were not only well-entrenched in society but also gained enormous political strength by spreading their tentacles across classes, castes, and ethnic groups.[10]

Apart from exposing the inherent limitations of procedural democracy accompanied by constitutional morality, Ambedkar identified another serious gap in the rise and consolidation of hero worship which struck at the root of democracy; this caused irreparable damage to its ethical foundation. By drawing attention to India, he further argued that

> hero worship is not dead in India; it is still par excellence the land of idolatry … [and] … it is a hard if unfortunate fact in India's political life; … it is demoralizing … for the country that reached a stage when alongside the notice boards saying 'beware of pickpockets' we need to have notice boards [Ambedkar sarcastically suggested,] saying 'beware of great man'.[11]

He owed intellectually to Ranade as he helped him comprehend the complex caste order in India, though he did critique him further down the line. He was ready to accept Ranade's assessment, provided he was also convinced that his chosen methods were of utility in the accomplishment of the objective he sought to attain. So, hero worship was not compatible with 'unconditional obedience to the ideas of the hero',[12] argued Ambedkar.

Ambedkar's views were reflected in Part III (Fundamental Rights) of the 1949 Constitution of India. In view of his apprehension, he put a judicial intervention clause in case rights were infringed. The judiciary was empowered to provide the individuals with adequate safety as soon it was approached by the affected individuals. By making the list of fundamental rights as elaborate as possible, Ambedkar appeared to have made the most comprehensive list of constitutional rights in comparison with any other democratic constitution. The list was expansive because Ambedkar was not ready to keep any space for the elites to cheat with this part of the Constitution because their intervention was anything but vicious and harmful from the democratic governance viewpoint. This was an important aspect of Part III of the Indian Constitution; the other critical part relates to the incorporation of groups rights along with individual rights. This was done to strike a balance between individual and collective liberty since they were dialectically interlinked. The purpose was to protect individual rights from being undermined by the collective and vice versa. Conceptually, it was a marriage between individual and group rights and to highlight that the guarantee of one did not automatically protect the other because the possibility of contradiction between them could never be ruled out.

In view of caste hegemony and customary discriminations in India, Ambedkar also provided an elaborate system of limiting beliefs supportive of caste prejudices. Their intervention was as pernicious as that of the well-entrenched state power. Ambedkar emphasized that the agencies for enforcement of individual rights against infringement by any of the sociocultural forces needed to be kept in alert under all circumstances. In a very perceptive speech, he argued that,

> each of these [provisions] protects the individual not just against the state, but against other individuals and against communities [which was based on his apprehension] … that the denial of human dignity, both material and symbolic, is cause not only by public power, but by private power as well—and the task of [the Constitution] is not limited to satisfactorily regulating public power in service or liberty, but extends to positively guaranteeing human freedom even against the excesses of private power.[13]

The purpose was to lay out an elaborate system of restraining those forces, either at the behest of the state, or private individuals, or caste groups, to undermine individual rights. Inherent here was his concern for humanizing humanity, which was likely to be harmed, unless a powerful mechanism was put in place. Based on his ideologies, one is persuaded to make three critical points that are useful to understand Ambedkar's specific narrative for humanizing humanity. First, constitutional guarantee was one of the most critical requirements as far as protection of rights were concerned. As one who also believed in group rights, he paid adequate attention to safeguard collective rights for the collectivity to flourish with their distinct sociocultural attributes. Secondly, he was aware that the claims for individual and collective rights were intermingled. Hence, Part III of the Constitution accorded nearly the same space for both individual and collective rights. In his conceptualization, neither of them prevailed over the other and he was committed to be equally respectful to individual and collective rights. Finally, to settle the difference between individual and group rights, Ambedkar also put in place the judiciary, which would act as a referee who would assess the issues before making a final decision. There was a hint that at the beginning of its journey in independent India, the 1949 Constitution was likely to be restrained temporarily, but this would gradually disappear with the consolidation of an outlook accepting individual and group rights as integral to each other.

Politics of Presence

The main aim of Ambedkar was to recognize the untouchables as integral to humanity. He prepared his debates by drawing upon the arguments on the notion of republican citizenship. It was a model seeking to build a new political design in which justice was conceptualized without 'the fear of illegitimate authorities and corrupt foundations, a space for civic action where the right to belief is available to everyone, liberated from nationalist expectations of reverence and laws of ecclesiastical interference alike'.[14] Linked with this was his idea of democracy which was not procedural but free from fear of being suppressed or/and free from social mores and restrictions. In other words, as long as caste system was allowed to survive, the untouchables would continue to remain 'nobody' because they lacked those attributes to be considered as 'somebody' in society. They did not exist as human beings unless they were linked with the caste Hindus for their survival. Their fate was not likely to change and the attempts for the liquidations of caste would never succeed because

> castes form a graded system of sovereignty, high and low, which are jealous of their status and which know that if a general dissolution came, some of them stand to lose more of their prestige and powers than others do. [Hence, one cannot,] therefore have a general mobilization of the Hindus … for an attack on the Caste System.[15]

Here was the idea that since caste order involved a graded inequality, it was difficult to completely do away with the system because many were reluctant to participate in this campaign for fear of losing benefits and social identity. Furthermore, the demarcation between untouchables and touchables appeared to be axiomatic as Hindu texts suggested that it was for the benefit of those who were born as untouchables. By following Manu's directional instructions 'a Hindu must follow *Veda, Smriti* or *Sadachar*; he cannot follow anything else'.[16] Thus, under no circumstances, was one allowed to question the scriptural directives. As a result, 'rationalism as a canon of interpreting *Vedas* and *Smritis*, is absolutely condemned. [To sustain the command], the same documents also provide punishments in the form of ex-communication for those who fail to accept the dictates justified in accordance with these texts'.[17] In order to further his point Ambedkar added that by being intellectually submissive to these texts, Hindus were deprived of applying their rationality to ascertain whether the claimed 'superiority' was defensible or not; they were always right and Hindus were required to follow because 'even if there is a conflict between *Vedas* and *Smritis* on matter on which they have given a positive solution, the solution is not left to reason [which meant that] there is no scope of judging whether the instructions accord with reason'.[18] Furthermore, in order to dehumanize and derecognize the presence of untouchables in social intercourse, the Hindu system of *varnashrama* justifying *Chaturvarnya* epitomized discrimination based on inequality. The rigidity of the design also revealed that the system to be maintained as it was useful to retain the caste Hindus' hegemony over the untouchables. Given the unquestionable acceptance of structural inequality, the untouchable remained silenced despite being victims of rules and regulations which were contrary to humanity. It was, according to Ambedkar contrived socioculturally with a view to fulfilling a self-driven purpose for the caste Hindus. The untouchables had no option but to be tortured since 'they are condemned to be lowly and not knowing the way to escape, they [thus] became reconciled to eternal servitude, which they accepted as their inescapable fate'.[19] So, *Chaturvarnya* was a degrading system which resulted in the denial of a legitimate space to a large section of humanity; They were systemic deformities which were not easy to do away with because they evolved out of customary practices that were nurtured over centuries. Illustrative here was Ambedkar's description of how caste Hindus were systematically separated from untouchables by creating ghettos for them within the villages, thereby demarcating the latter from the former physically. This was the pattern that emerged in every village. As he described,

> at present, the [caste] Hindus live in the village and Untouchables live in the Ghettoes. [so long as such a divisive social design exists], it is

> difficult to free the Untouchables from the thraldom of the Hindus. Till this system continues, it is impossible for the Untouchables either to free themselves from the yoke of Hindus or to get rid of their Untouchability. It is the close-knit association of the Untouchables with the Hindus living in the same villages which marks them out as Untouchables and which enables the Hindus to identify them as being Untouchables.[20]

The separate settlements represented an exclusive design for dividing the untouchables geographically and territorially. They were allowed to remain in the same village because they were needed for cultivation and other menial jobs. They were landless labourers who were entirely dependent on employment the caste Hindus chose to give them along with low pay. The consequence was disastrous for the untouchables, argued Ambedkar. In the absence of any other sources of livelihood, 'Untouchables continue to remain victims of circumstances in which [by being in Ghetto] they become dependent on the caste Hindus'.[21] The untouchables accepted it as a *fait accompli* or providentially-ordained by God for acts which they committed in their earlier birth. Many accepted the economic exploitation by the caste Hindus as their destiny; there were many, Ambedkar mentioned, who appeared to have risen against such dehumanizing endeavour for selfish benefits at the cost of the majority. The untouchables started a tacit war against the caste Hindus all over the country by challenging such a dehumanizing Hindu code of life which 'gives [caste Hindus] many privileges and heaps upon the Untouchables many indignities which are incompatible with the dignity and sanctity of human life'.[22] The outcome was likely to be unfavourable since the 'caste Hindus are economically and socially strong [which is complemented by] … the support they receive from the police and administration, their counterpart, the Untouchables are handicapped economically and lack the physical power to effectively combat a well-equipped adversary'.[23] The description could not be more accurate than what Ambedkar provided. By dissecting the day-to-day life of the untouchables, he firmly established the roots of dehumanizing humanity although he did not appear to be zealous of the success of the campaign launched by rebellious section of the untouchables because of certain obvious limitations. Nonetheless, he unfolded a new discourse highlighting Dalit intervention in charting out a roadmap for humanizing humanity which was not only inspirational but also conceptually innovative and directional for future activists with identical goals. There are two important inputs here: first, unlike many of his nationalist colleagues who were enamoured by the nationalist campaign for political emancipation, Ambedkar crafted a new mode of conceptualizing humanization of humanity by clearly exposing the limitation of the project since it did not take into account more than half of India's population in view; and secondly, Ambedkar's critique created a space for humanism to be conceptualized differently, and free of socio-political divisions.

Gandhi as a 'Tory'

Ambedkar characterized Gandhi as a tory since he was conservative in his outlook and was never appreciative of the views he offered to put before him about the inherent limitations of the nationalist design for India's political emancipation. The debate that was rooted in their conceptualizations of humanizing humanity is most instructive for more than one reason: first, it was based on two different types of conceptualizations of the political. Gandhi's ideas appeared to be narrow since he was concerned with emancipation from the British rule while Ambedkar, being unable to agree with Gandhi since political freedom was not a guarantee for humanizing humanity, especially liberation of the untouchables from discrimination by the caste Hindus for fulfilling their partisan goals. Secondly, as Gandhi thwarted Ambedkar's attempt to ensure separate electorate, he was convinced that the Mahatma was working for the caste Hindus, presumably because he was also one of the casteists which prevented him from saying what Ambedkar desired while he was vehemently opposing caste-based divisions.

Critical of the nationalist movement that upheld caste and untouchability at the behest of Gandhi, Ambedkar sought to articulate an alternative political ideology by challenging the very foundation of the 'Hinduized' nationalist movement. One of the most significant arguments that Ambedkar made against Hinduism was that caste and untouchability struck at its foundation and it was inherently divisive. Gandhi, by clinging to the basic philosophy of caste never seriously challenged, untouchability in Hinduism. According to Ambedkar, Gandhism was 'a paradox' because 'it stands for freedom from foreign domination [and] at the same time it seeks to maintain a social structure which permits the domination of one class by another on a hereditary basis which means a perpetual domination of one class by another'.[24] To Ambedkar, Gandhi's loyalty to Hinduism amounted to supporting untouchability because it evolved as integrally linked with Hinduism and was considered to be justified. This assumption however stands in contradiction with what the Mahatma sincerely believed. According to him, 'untouchability is not a sanction of religion; it is a device of Satan. There is neither nobility nor bravery in treating the great and uncomplaining scavengers of the nation as worse than dogs to be despised and spat upon'.[25] Ambedkar criticized Gandhi further for having eulogized the Indian villages as illustrative of a unique unit of social, economic and political equilibrium. Ambedkar argued that Indian villages

> represent a kind of colonialism of the Hindus designed to exploit the Untouchables. The Untouchables have no rights. There are there only to wait, serve and submit. They are there to do or to die. They have no rights because they are outside the village republic and because they are outside the so-called republic, they are outside the Hindu fold. This is a vicious circle. But this is a fact which cannot be gainsaid.[26]

For Gandhi, the village was the basis for building a republican society[27] not polluted by colonialism, while for Ambedkar it was 'the black hole' of Indian civilization. Village, for Gandhi, was not just a geographical location where people lived in small settlement drawn on land. For him, the essence it reflected was the essence of Indian civilization. The Indian village had a design, a way of life which had the potential of becoming 'an alternative to the city-based and technology-driven capitalist West'.[28] His conception of village was not anchored 'on the modern notion of development but on the post-modern perspective of quality life'.[29] And, yet for the Dalits, 'the village … could never be an embodiment of justice [since] to remain in village meant remaining tied to the same humiliating occupation that had so far been their fate'.[30] For Ambedkar, the structure of village settlements reflected the basic tenets of Hinduism that never recognized Dalits as its integral part. In other words, village contributed to and sustained the divisive nature of the Hindus society where the untouchables always remained 'outside the fold'. As he eloquently put,

> the Hindu society insists on segregation of the untouchables. The Hindu will not live in the quarters of the untouchables and will not allow the untouchables to live inside the Hindu quarters. … It is not a case of social separation, a mere stoppage of social intercourse for a temporary period. It is a case of territorial segregation and of a *cordon sanitaire* putting the impure people inside the barbed wire into a sort

> of a cage. Every Hindu village has a ghetto. The Hindus live in the village and the untouchables live in the ghetto.[31]

In contrast to Gandhi, Ambedkar conceptualized village as a model of the oppressive Hindu social organization, a microcosm of the circumstance in which Dalits were located. It was 'the working plant of the Hindu social order' where one could see the atrocious nature of Hinduism. Given the role of the villages in sustaining the atrocious social circumstances of the Dalits, Ambedkar never endorsed Gandhi's thoughts about Indian villages because they represented an exclusive domain for the touchables at the cost of the untouchables who were invariably pushed into the margins.

The conflict between Gandhi and Ambedkar on the issue of separate electorate for untouchables and the depressed classes was an articulation of two contrasting perspectives that fundamentally altered the nature of political participation by the Scheduled Castes and Tribes in the British India and its aftermath. Once the separate electorate for the Muslims was conceded by the Congress during the 1935 Government of India Act, Ambedkar argued—on behalf of the Dalits—that they must be allowed to constitute a separate electorate and elect their representatives to the central and provincial legislatures. He further defended the claim by saying that since voting was severely restricted to social class, the geographically disparate depressed classes were unlikely to have any influence in the decision-making process. So, the solution was a separate electorate for them. Ambedkar held the view that untouchables were absolutely separate from Hinduism and hence he tried 'to find a solution to their problem through political separatism'.[32] In order to substantiate his argument, he stated that the Hindus 'had much to lose by the abolition of untouchability, though they had nothing to fear from political reservation leading to this abolition'.[33] As discussed in chapter 5, the debate between Gandhi and Ambedkar on separate electorate was resolved in favour of the former because the latter succumbed to the pressure exerted on him by the nation as the former's 'fast unto death' became a source of concern for the country.

While Gandhi's faith in caste was unquestionable, Ambedkar attributed untouchability to caste and other practices justified in the name of Hinduism. According to Ambedkar, caste system

> is a hierarchy in which the divisions of labour are graded one above the other. This division of labour is not spontaneous, it is not based on natural aptitudes in so far as it involves an attempt to appoint tasks to individuals in advance, selected not on the basis of trained original capacities, but on that of the social status of the parents.[34]

Since the caste system was based on attribution of status by birth, it was inherently exclusive and lost its public-ness. As Ambedkar argued, 'caste has killed public spirit. Caste has destroyed the sense of public charity. Caste has made opinion impossible. [To the Hindus], virtue has become caste-ridden and morality has become caste-bound'.[35] By attacking *Chaturvarnya*, the basic institution holding the caste system in its original form, Ambedkar countered Gandhi's argument that the former was an innocent typology of human beings on *guna* (worth). By dividing the Hindu society into four different categories—Brahmins, Kshatriya, Vaishya and Shudra—based on birth, *Chaturvarnya*,

> sanctions not only a differentiation of persons but also their gradation. [The labels, *Brahmin*, *Kshtriya*, *Vaishya* and *Shudra*] are names which are associated with a definite and fixed notion in the mind of every Hindu. The notion is that of a hierarchy based on birth. So long as these names continue, Hindus will continue to think of the *Brahmin*, *Kashtriya*, *Vaishya* and *Shudra* as hierarchical divisions of high and low, based on birth, and act accordingly. The Hindu must be made to unlearn all this. But how can this happen if the old labels remain and continue to recall to his mind old notions. ... To continue the old name is to make reform futile. To allow this *Chaturvanya*, based on worth to be designated by such stinking labels of *Brahmin*, *Kshtriya*, *Vaishya*, *Shudra*, indicative of social divisions based on birth, is snare. ... To allow this *Chaturvarnya*, based on worth to be designated by such stinking labels of Brahmin, *Kshtriya*, *Vaishya*, *Shudra*, indicative of social divisions based on birth is a snare.[36]

Ambedkar advocated a total rejection of *Chaturvarnya* because of its justification of division within the Hindu society based on birth. Gandhi made his defence in the columns of *Harijan*. Appreciating Ambedkar for his critique of caste,[37] the Mahatma reiterated his faith in Hinduism and its institutions, including the *Chaturvarnya*, to avoid further divisions within the Hindu society. Instead of debating with Ambedkar, Gandhi provided an interpretation of caste and *varnashrama* to defend his point of view in contrast with that of Ambedkar. He believed in *varnashrama* of the *Vedas*, which in his opinion, was based on absolute equality of status, notwithstanding passages in the *Smritis* and elsewhere which were contrary in nature. Defending *varnashrama* as a social arrangement of universally-applicable division of occupation, he thus argued,

> [The four] *Varnas* ... have been sanctioned by the *shastras* [holy books]. Whether or not people are conscious of them, they do exist all over the

> world as we see. There are everywhere these four classes: one to impart knowledge of God for the welfare of the world, another to protect the people against manifold dangers, a third one to carry on the work of farming, etc., to sustain the community and one class to work for these three classes. There is no feeling of high and low to this division.[38]

Gandhi believed that *Chaturvarnya*, which was linked with Hinduism, was

> based on absolute equality of status, notwithstanding passages to the contrary in the *Smritis* [the holy scriptures] and elsewhere. ... There was no prohibition of intermarriage and inter-dining. Prohibition there is of change of one's hereditary occupation for purposes of gain. The existing practice is, therefore, doubly wrong in that it has set up cruel restrictions about inter-dining and intermarriage and tolerates about choice of occupation ... it must be left to the unfettered choice of the individual as to where he or she will marry or dine.[39]

On another occasion, he was critical of the ways caste evolved as a social system governing inter-personal relations by saying 'restrictions as regards inter-marriage and inter-dining which defy reason are very harmful and stand in the ways of the community's progress. It has nothing to do with religion'.[40] He made a distinction between caste and *varnashrama*; while the former was distorted by endorsing various social restrictions, the latter was 'a cooperative society with its members divided into occupational groups, each fulfilling their own functions, but all of equal status';[41] and it was this ideal of caste to which Gandhi adhered to throughout his life. For Ambedkar, this was an attempt to scuttle the contentious issue. Furthermore, Gandhi's critique of the caste system was misleading if it was juxtaposed with his defence for the *Chaturvarnya*, the core of the caste system. This conformed to the endeavours of other Hindu leaders who criticized the practice of caste discrimination to fulfil their political agenda at the cost the Dalits. As Ambedkar argued,

> Hindu leaders became filled with an illicit passion for their belief when any one proposes to rob them of their companionship. The Mahatma is no exception. [He] appears not to believe in thinking. He prefers to follow his saints. ... One must sympathise with him. ... But ... dependence on saints cannot lead us to know the truth. ... In so far as he does think, to me he really appears to be prostituting his intelligence to find the reasons for supporting this archaic social structure of the Hindus. He is the most influential apologist of it and therefore the worst enemy of the Hindus.[42]

Why was Gandhi in favour of the caste system despite its divisive nature? Ambedkar attributed this to Mahatma's narrow political calculations. He shared his views by saying that

> the reason why the Mahatma is always supporting Caste and *Varna* is because he is afraid that if he opposed them he will lose his place in politics. Whatever the source of his confusion the Mahatma must be told that he is deceiving himself and also deceiving the people by preaching Caste under the name of *Varna*.[43]

His attack against Gandhi was articulated in his 1941 speech[44] about 'Ranade, Gandhi and Jinnah'. The speech has two defined parts. First, Ambedkar evolved his critique of Hinduism by drawing extensively on Ranade's view of Hinduism. The second part focuses on his criticism of the role of Gandhi and Jinnah as political leaders of Hindus and Muslims in India. Appreciating Ranade for his critique of Hinduism, Ambedkar stated that Ranade was the first Indian politician who argued that 'there were no rights in the Hindu society, … there were privileges and disabilities, privileges for a few and disabilities for a vast majority'.[45] Furthermore, by citing Ranade's critique of those nationalists who did not realize that one 'cannot be liberal by halves: liberal in politics and conservative in religion',[46] Ambedkar sharpened his criticism of Gandhi, and stated that there was no alternative for the Mahatma but to support Hinduism and caste system simply because 'Mr Gandhi wants the untouchables to remain as Hindus … [n]ot as partners but as poor relations of Hindus'.[47] Characterizing Gandhi as 'a Tory by birth as well as faith'[48] due to his views on social and religious issues, he accused the Mahatma of 'demoralizing' his followers and politics. He attributed the rise of Gandhi rather simplistically to the aid of big business and money magnates. As a result, Indian politics,

> at any rate the Hindu part of it, instead of being spiritualized has become grossly commercialized, so much so that it become a byword of corruption. … Politics has become a kind of sewage system intolerably unsavoury and insanity. To become a politician is like going to work in the drain.[49]

The debate between Gandhi and Ambedkar is significant for two important reasons. First, Ambedkar's sharp critique has not only problematized the twin concepts of justice and freedom by focusing on the Dalit point of view, but it has also posed new social, economic, and political issues involving the peripheral sections of Indian society.

Ambedkar's intervention captured a serious gap in the nationalist socio-political thought. Gandhi, despite being universal in his approach, failed to incorporate Dalit issues while organizing the campaign for freedom. Gandhi represented all regardless of class, caste and creed was based on assumptions inflating the claim of the Mahatma to amicably settle the conflicting socio-political and economic interests of diverse Indian population. Until the 1932 Poona Pact, Gandhi did not effectively negotiate with the Dalits as an emerging and socially formidable constituency of the nationalist politics. Only after this Pact, the Congress leadership formally accorded a legitimate space to the Dalits who had remained peripheral to the struggle for freedom until then. The role of the British government was not insignificant either. By accepting Ambedkar as representative of the Dalits in the 1932 Round Table Conference, the ruling authority deflated Gandhi's claim to represent India as a whole. Gandhi was pushed to the periphery and Ambedkar was brought in because of his success in articulating the issues concerning Dalits which were never adequately addressed either by the nationalist political leadership or by the colonial government. Justice and freedom acquired new connotations in the changed milieu when Dalits had emerged as a politically significant constituency under the stewardship of Ambedkar. It entailed a wide-ranging programme of equality and equity measures seeking to fulfil a wide variety of material and non-material needs of untouchables. It is this total programme of societal transformation that constituted his conception of *swaraj* which was not freedom from colonialism; it was a just freedom.[50] *Swaraj* was not political and economic freedom from colonialism, as conceptualised by Gandhi, but a significant socio-political package striving to amend the conditions of those 'outside the fold'. It would not be wrong to argue that the Gandhi-Ambedkar debate is theoretically innovative and politically crucial in grasping the most volatile phase of Indian nationalism when the Mahatma no longer remained the undisputed leader of the nationalist articulation of freedom struggle. Secondly, it is alleged that Ambedkar manipulated Dalit agenda to undermine the effort of the Indian National Congress to achieve freedom. His 'separatist ideology' caused a fissure in the nationalist campaign. Ambedkar was not persuaded because he regarded 'with great suspicion all attempts, [including that by Gandhi], to portray democratization as a process independent of caste manipulation'.[51] His sustained criticism of Gandhi for supporting the *Chaturvarnya*-based Brahminical social order has wider theoretical implications. According to him, the collusion between Brahminism and colonialism was possible because of the support accorded by Gandhi.

His analogy between a colonial government that drained resources from the colony and a caste ideology that lived off the labour of depriviliged groups are 'consistent with his rhetorical strategy of conflating disparate historical moments within a single frame, in order not only to illuminate the interchangeability of British colonialism and Brahminism, but also to expose the claims of an ideology negated by its own practices'.[52] The debate between Gandhi and Ambedkar is therefore most useful both in grasping relatively non-visible dimensions of Indian reality and conceptualizing the Dalit intervention in the nationalist discourse.

State and Humanization of Humanity

Regarding the role of the state as an instrument in humanizing humanity, Ambedkar differed from Gandhi. The Constituent Assembly witnessed an interesting debate among the liberals and those who upheld Gandhian model of village *swaraj*. A liberal to the core, Ambedkar suggested that, instead of villages, individuals should be the focal point of independent India's constitutional governance. A dissenter of Gandhi's views, he criticized Gandhi's argument for self-dependent village *swaraj* as it was inadequate to rejuvenate India as an independent polity, and it had glaring structural limitations due to caste prejudices in Indian villages. While denouncing the proposal to make the village the basic unit of governance, he argued that,

> it is said that the new Constitution should have been drafted on the ancient Hindu model of a state and that instead of incorporating Western theories the new Constitution should have been raised and built upon village panchayats and district panchayats. ... They just want India to contain so many village governments. The love of the intellectual Indian for the village community is of course infinite if not pathetic. ... I hold that the village republics have been the ruination of India. I am therefore surprised that those who condemn provincialism and communalism should come forward as champions of the village. What is the village but a sink of localism, a den of ignorance, narrow mindedness, and communalism? I am glad that the Draft Constitution has discarded the village and adopted the individual as its unit.[53]

Ambedkar was opposed to the very idea of village being a focal point of governance because he strongly felt that it was a source of oppression. Persuaded by Ambedkar's argument, Nehru too came out in his support by stating that 'a village, normally speaking, is backward intellectually and culturally and no progress can made from a backward environment.

Narrow-minded people are much more likely to be untruthful and violent'.[54] Being supported by Nehru, Patel and other leading Congressmen in the Assembly, it was easier for Ambedkar to persuade the other members. In contrast with Ambedkar's arguments in favour of individual-driven constitution, there were leading Gandhians who built their arguments around Gandhi's ideas. A number of members supported the Gandhian argument in favour of a state constituted of self-sufficient village republics. One of the leading members debating against Ambedkar in the Constituent Assembly was A.C. Guha, who argued that the draft Constitution had 'no trace of Congress outlook, no trace of Gandhian social and political outlook'.[55] He felt that 'the whole Constitution lacks in Congress ideal and Congress ideology particularly'.[56] Insisting that 'the future constitution of India should be a pyramidal structure based on the village *panchayat*', Guha further argues that the idea of village *panchayats* should be respected since it was the Congress ideal. Guha made two arguments in his favour: first, he felt the importance of the constituent units for a strong centre. As he argued,

> we cannot have a strong Centre without strong limbs. If we can build the whole structure on the village *panchayats*, on the willing cooperation of the people, then I feel the Centre would automatically become strong; [hence he urged the Assembly] to incorporate some clauses so that village panchayats may be allowed to play some effective part in the future administration of the country.[57]

Secondly, while critiquing Ambedkar's defence for making individuals as the basic political units, Guha insisted that,

> the villages should be the real basis of the machinery [because] individual is the soul of the whole constitution; given the [fact] that the villages remain the basic units of human settlement in India [they] should be made the basis of the machinery of [India's] administration.[58]

N.G. Ranga, another Gandhian from Madras, appreciated Guha's ideas and critiqued Ambedkar in strong terms; he mentioned that he was

> most unhappy that Dr. Ambedkar should have said what he has said about the village panchayats. All the democratic tradition of our country has been lost on him. If he had only known the achievements of the village panchayats in Southern India over a period of millennium, he would not have said those things. If he had cared to study Indian history with as much care as he seems to have devoted to the history of other countries, he certainly would not have ventured those remarks.[59]

Ranga was critical of centralization of authority which would lead to 'sovietisation and totalitarianism and not democracy', and was in favour of *panchayat*-based governance because it would enable 'the villagers to gain as much experience in democratic institutions as possible in order to be able to discharge their responsibilities through adult suffrage in the new democracy that we are going to establish.'[60] His main concern was to provide an institutionalised space for villagers to enable them to effectively participate in governance. A staunch Gandhian who was committed to decentralization, he saw the *panchayats* as nurseries of democratic governance. Hence, he recommended that,

> it is the duty of the State to establish village panchayats in every village or for every group of villages in order to help our villages to gain training in self-government and also to attain village autonomy in social economic and political matters, so that they will become the foundation stone for the top structure of our Constitution.[61]

Reiterating the argument that they, Guha and his Gandhian colleagues who were disinclined to emulate the Western model of an individual as the core unity of governance, also built a counter argument as they felt that it was ignoring India's deep-rooted social-cultural tradition. The battle was between two incongruous points of view. Ambedkar, who was trained in liberal ethos in the West, preferred a liberal constitution emphasizing the role of state and individual did not seem too inexplicable. His acceptance of the state as an arbitrator was also drawn out of his existential experiences in India, US and Britain. He believed that if the state was made strong by adopting appropriate constitutional provisions, it was easier to purge individuals of their sociocultural prejudices. Once it was established that nurturing and practice of caste discrimination was a criminal offence, Ambedkar believed that the mindset would not only disappear but also create an ambience in which anti-caste ideas would gain momentum. In other words, Ambedkar was keen to introduce state-initiated actions to permanently eradicate sociocultural prejudices for the disprivileged. It was an initiative to create conditions for humanizing humanity, and build persuasive conceptual parameters in its favour.

To review the past, in the Round Table Conference, Ambedkar lost an ideological battle to Gandhi since his demand for a separate electorate for Untouchables was not conceded. Nonetheless, his strong arguments for their electoral protection amidst relentless opposition by the Congress-led caste Hindu leadership, including Gandhi, established Ambedkar's image as a vocal participant who fought against social discrimination in a liberal manner. Ambedkar was aided by a group of intellectually stimulated colleagues in the Drafting Committee for the Constitution, and his role as the chairman of the Committee was most crucial in providing an ideological direction to what finally became the Constitution of India. What is noticeable is the imprint of liberal values in the text of the Constitution which Ambedkar held so dear throughout his life. As shown above, the twin influences of John Dewey and George Grote provided Ambedkar with arguments to defend his distinctive liberal approach to democratic experimentalism in India. The 1950 Constitution of India became a site where the robust sense of Deweyan democracy created an inclusive public space where participation was encouraged, regardless of caste or any other socio-economic denomination,[62] and Grote's constitutional morality acted as a powerful complementary ideological force in the entire exercise. In the face of the opposition from members, Ambedkar stuck to his ideological faith in liberalism, as was evident from the provisions included in the Constitution.[63] His argument against the village republic which Gandhi espoused reveals his unflinching commitment to the fundamental principle of liberalism. In his perception, village was 'but a sink of localism, a den of ignorance, narrow-mindedness and communalism' and he was happy that 'the Draft Constitution has discarded the village and adopted the individual as its unit'.[64] It was possible for him to guide India towards a liberal future since he was aided by other Congress colleagues who, despite being inspired by Gandhi during the nationalist struggle for independence, did not appear to be persuaded by the Gandhian model of village republic.

India's liberal constitution was not adequate to fulfil the ideological mission that Ambedkar sought to achieve because political democracy was futile without social democracy. According to Ambedkar, what deterred India to achieve democracy was the absence of equality and fraternity. By referring to the caste-based social hierarchy, he argued that 'on the social place, we have in India a society based on the principle of graded inequality which means elevation for some and degradation for others; on the economic plane, we have a society in which there are some who have immense wealth as against many who live in abject poverty'. Similarly, fraternity was a remote goal to achieve because 'how can people divided into several thousands of castes [he asked] be one people'.[65] So, the caste system was anti-national, not only because 'it brings about separation in social life … [but also because] it generates jealousy and antipathy between caste and caste [eroding] the foundation of fraternity, and without fraternity, equality and liberty will be no deeper than coats of paint'.[66] Ambedkar was aware that the absence of equality and fraternity meant 'a liquidation' of liberalism in its true form because 'by reason of our social and economic structure, we shall continue to deny the principle of one man one value'.[67] Nonetheless, one can make the argument, of course with hindsight, that the liberal foundational principles of India's constitution set in motion forces that gradually consolidated democracy in India and also the importance of individual as a critical unit in the socio-political and economic processes. This was not a mean achievement given the complex unfolding of circumstances in the presence of 'the hegemonic' Gandhian discourse during the nationalist struggle for freedom and its aftermath. Furthermore, in conceptualizing 'the politics of the era' the obvious hegemonic influence of colonialism cannot be wished away, and Ambedkar, being a product of his time, could not but reflect 'the tension' of a period of history while searching for the most appropriate politico-institutional arrangement to instil values of democratic constitutionalism and equal citizenship. Ambedkar crafted a conceptually-challenging and theoretically-provocative constitutional system of governance based on his creative intermingling of both contextual inputs and derivative intellectual sources.

Post Ambedkar's speech on 4 November 1948 in the Constituent Assembly, two important issues emerged which shaped the processes of constitutionalizing India, first, a strong legally empowered state with appropriate constitutional provisions was required for sociocultural prejudices to be wiped out permanently. There should be a warning here because insistence on a strong state also meant that Ambedkar was in favour of creating a Leviathan state as proposed by Hobbesian. His clarifications are of immense importance here. According to him, the mindset supportive of caste division needed to completely disappear before the idea of India being a democracy was deceptive because humanization of humanity and continuity of divisive mindset were contrarian. The state was entrusted with the duty of securing rights of individuals irrespective of caste, class, and ethnicity; it should also be empowered to adopt stern steps to completely liquidate discriminatory sociocultural designs because they were detrimental to the growth of fraternity among India's citizens. Thus, the state 'exists to usher in conditions conducive for [building a bridge] between the authority of the state and individuals' liberty'.[68] The state was meant to create an environment by being respectful to individuals' rights which needed to protected if there was a threat; either by public authority or by prejudices. As villages were places where caste identity was paramount in determining rights and duties, they were rightfully condemned by Ambedkar as detrimental to humanizing humanity.

Emphasized above are following significant points which are critical to reconceptualize humanizing humanity in contrast with what existed in pre-independent India. Constitutional liberalism was initiated in British India, although it was mechanical since it was just a mode of governance which the colonizers introduced to defuse human wrath against the rulers; by including the loyalists in governance, the rulers established their claim that as far as public administration was concerned, the Indian opinion by the Indian themselves were also decisive. There was a huge gap between what the colonizers promised and what they did for governance. Hence, constitutional liberalism did not unfurl in the real sense of the term. The situation did not seem favourable for constitutional liberalism to strike roots in India which was divided around many sociocultural axes. Religion was a significant divisive force which is evident from Partition; a price for independence. Caste also hindered the growth of fraternity, liberty, and equality since prejudices created a permanent barrier between sections of society. India was fortunate to have Ambedkar as one of the leading members who shaped the 1949 Constitution of India, and by his very intelligent handling of the debates, he succeeded in creating an all-pervasive state by incorporating appropriate legal stipulations. His was a state-centric discourse for constitutional liberalism in its actual semantic and conceptual manifestation. It was based on his beliefs which were an outcome of his experiences in India and in the West. He realized that unless India's moral fabric was replaced by liberal designs for humanity, the future of the efforts towards humanizing humanity did not seem to be as bright as was conceived by those who supported a strong state. Hence, while arguing for a strong state as necessary to remove the debilitating sociocultural practices, he also focused on the importance of democratic ethos and values for acting as a shield against the emergence of a state with draconian features.

Gender Disparity and Dehumanization

Ambedkar's concern for gender parity represents a relatively neglected aspect of his socio-political ideas which deserve careful attention. It is true that his arguments for the Hindu Code Bill were a watershed in the nationalist understanding of the gender question; but his stance for the Hindu Code Bill appears to have been built over the years out of his wider perturbation for human emancipation. By situating Ambedkar's arguments in his broader conceptual universe, the chapter justifies the claim that besides being highly persuasive, his powerful defence for gender justice provides critical inputs to build integra models of social justice and human emancipation.

Convinced that a uniform civil code was one of the most powerful designs for democratizing human existence, Ambedkar introduced the Hindu Code Bill for discussion in the House. B.N. Rau was of great help here since he prepared a draft for him to work on as was the case with the 1950 Constitution of India. Ideologically, he drew on the fundamental tenets of liberalism, liberty, equality, and fraternity, and the belief in the importance of human agency in fulfilling the liberal goal. As he was critical of centrality of religion in human life, he endeavoured hard to create a civil code based on his appreciation of human beings as core to social transformation. He announced before the Constituent Assembly that,

> I personally do not understand why religion should be given this vast, expansive jurisdiction, to cover the whole of life and to prevent the legislature from encroaching upon that field. After all, what are we having this liberty for? We are having this liberty to reform our social system, which is full of inequalities, discrimination, and other things, which conflict with our fundamental rights. It is, therefore, quite impossible for anybody to conceive that the personal law shall be excluded from the jurisdiction of the State.[69]

Here, he was defending his argument for state intervention in the field of personal law as complementary to the attainment of a society of equals. His argument had resonance with K.M. Munshi's statement in its favour. Echoing the sentiment of Ambedkar, Munshi argued,

> we need to divorce religion from personal law, from what may be called social relations or from the rights of parties as regards inheritance or succession. What have these things got to do with religion, I really fail to understand. ... Now, we are in a stage where we must unify and consolidate the nation by every means without being restrained by religious practices. If however religious practices in the past have been so construed as to cover the whole field of life, we have reached a point when we must put our foot down and say that these matters are no religion, they are purely maters for secular legislation.[70]

Conceptually, Ambedkar and Munshi thought alike, that religion had no role to play in personal laws; both were supportive of civic law regarding inheritance or succession, and Munshi appears to have raised an identical voice for liberalism. In a society supportive of prejudicial customs and rituals, theirs was an endeavour to translate their commitments towards liberal values and ethos into practice. This is one aspect of the argument which ran parallel to Munshi's thinking. Ambedkar put forward another technical argument reflective of his legal acumen. He was appalled when there were strong criticisms against the Hindu Code Bill. As he elaborated his point by saying,

> I am surprised at the criticisms for the simple reason that we have in this country a uniform code of laws covering almost every aspect of human relationship. We have a uniform Criminal Code, we have the uniform Law of Transfer of Property, we have a common Negotiable Instruments Acts, which proves that the country has practically a Civil Code, uniform in content and applicable to the whole of the country. … The only province the Civil Code has not been able to invade so far is Marriage and Succession. It is this little corner which we have not been able to invade so far and it is the intention of those who desire to have [an article to that effect] to bring about change.[71]

The Hindu Code Bill was the outcome of a consensus that Jawaharlal Nehru, as independent India's Prime Minister helped build among the Congress legislators. Ambedkar, as India's Law Minister, introduced the bill on 9 April 1948 and clarified that,

> the aim of the bill is to codify the rules of Hindu Law which are scattered in innumerable decisions of the High Courts and of the Privy Council, which form a bewildering motley to the common man and give rise to constant litigation.[72]

It was an attempt to draft a law based on what was already done to ensure gender equality. In other words, it was directed to bring about radical changes in the prevalent system of rules and regulations governing marriage, divorce, and succession. As *Mitakshara* rules were the norm, the laws remained discriminatory; and women were denied being fairly treated by laws in this regard. There were three major features of the bill: first, it sought to codify laws relating to the property rights of a Hindu (either man or woman) who died intestate without a will; secondly, it provided a set of instructions codifying the order of succession among different heirs to the property of a deceased dying intestate; thirdly, the Hindu Code Bill recommended *Dayabhaga* rule—under which property was held by the heir as his personal property with the absolute right to dispose of it either by gift or by will or any other manner that he chose; finally, the Code Bill also stipulated that the wife be allowed to claim separate maintenance from her husband if he wilfully abandoned his wife, and his wife left him and the reasons justified her living separately.

Ambedkar conceptualized Hindu Code Bill within this framework, which was, to him, was a departure from the available arrangement, drawing largely from *Mitakshara* rule. It was persuasive defence, supported by his elaborate arguments which state that The Bill sought to make four changes; first, the widow, daughter, and widow of the predeceased son, all of them were given the same rank as the son in the matter of inheritance; as a result, the number of female heirs recognised now was 'much larger than under either the *Mitakshara* or the *Dayabhaga* systems'; no discrimination was to be made regarding female heirs; whether married or un-married, rich or poor child or no children—would have no relevance whatsoever, and in contrast with the prevalent rules governing inheritance under *Mitakshara* and *Dayabhaga* principles—which preferred the father over the mother to inherit family property—the proposed bill 'alters the system [by putting] the claim of mother over father'.[73] The second important change was regarding the form of marriage; contrary to sacramental marriage which was prevalent, Ambedkar also created provisions for civil marriage, which, by derecognizing the mandatory requirement of stating one's caste, was an attempt to develop a liberal mindset immune from 'narrow and parochial' prejudices. Thirdly, by devising a new set of divorce rules, he sought to create an independent space and voice for women when getting separated from their husbands. There were seven conditions on which divorce was permissible- desertion, conversion to another religion, keeping a concubine or becoming a concubine, incurably unsound mind, virulent or incurable form of leprosy, venereal diseases in communicable form, and cruelty. Justifying divorce as a right for both the partners, Ambedkar further argued that his scheme was 'in no way an innovation [but] a follow-up of what Hindu *shastras* have suggested'.[74] The new customs regarding divorce were created and sustained in a manner which defied the fundamental *shastra*-driven directions. He said that,

> what has happened in this country is that somehow, unfortunately, unnoticed, unconsciously customs [were] allowed to trample upon the text of the *shastras* which were all in favour of the right sort of marital relations. My submission, therefore, to the house is that so far as any new principles have been introduced in the law of marriage and divorce, whatever has been done is both just and reasonable and supported by precedent not only of our *shastra*s but the experience of the world as a whole.[75]

There are other aspects which he highlighted in his speech that correspond to the above points for the conceptual model that he built for gender-parity. The main objective was to have a set of rules for recognizing women as equal partners in matters of marriage, inheritance, and divorce. By reiterating that he drew upon the *shastras* and the prevalent customs, Ambedkar did not appear to have given an entirely new model. He defended that his purpose was to 'repair' the system, since it was an urgency. Quoting the British conservative Edmund Burke, he further pushed that 'those who want to conserve must be ready to repair' … [and] the Bill asks for nothing more than repairing those parts of the Hindu system which are almost dilapidated'.[76] An analytical scan of the above arguments reveals that as a realist Ambedkar resorted to a course which he justified by referring to the prevalent customary practices and the *shastras*. Thus, it was an attempt to bring back the rules and regulations which were complementary to gender-parity. Nonetheless, he was subject to severe criticisms. For instance, Thakur Das Bhargava, a congressman, criticized the Code by saying that it had

> created throughout the whole country a great deal of unpleasantness, restlessness and uneasiness [because] it favours women. As a result, our mothers, sisters and daughters demand that they will not behave properly with their husbands, their brothers and sons. So it will create unnecessary stress in society which is required to be avoided at this stage of our nation.[77]

Bhargava was not alone; there were many of his colleagues who endorsed his point of view. As already shown, those who opposed defended their arguments by suggesting that the Code was likely to be disruptive, as it was strong enough to put men and women in two clearly demarcated compartments.[78] Besides dwelling on the negative outcome of the Code, it was also criticized by a number of legislators, including Rajendra Prasad, who stated that the proposed legislation which would affect 'the entire population by fundamental changes in the personal laws of Hindus', was not sufficiently discussed, circulated and presented for public opinion.[79] But, there were supporters of the Code too. Several women, in their interventions in the debate, endorsed it. G. Durgabai condemned her male colleagues by saying that,

> it will be a great misfortune if at this juncture we fail to enact a Hindu Code within our own borders, in which there will be no discrimination and there will be equality for men and women to move, to develop and to contribute to the re-building of our India. … We have already

> recognized the principle of equality of everyone before law. … We are in the process of passing a uniform civil code. Let us not [therefore] be wanting or halting in having a Code of Hindu Law for ourselves which will prove a great boon to our society.[80]

The Code was hailed by women for being revolutionary and the objective was thus inevitable because it harmed the vested interests of the dominant men. Women were aware that without a strict Code, it would be difficult to bring about gender equality which the Constitution sought to achieve, they also contended that the Code was adequately-equipped to ensure gender-parity. Commenting on the Code, Sucheta Kripalani expressed her concern by saying that despite being 'a wonderfully progressive measure, … the Hindu Marriage Bill … is basically a halting and half-hearted measure'.[81] Nonetheless, there was a note of appreciation that ran through the speeches delivered by women in support of the Code. Being hopeful about the outcome of a Code treating women as equals, they were convinced that once it was codified, the prevalent customs governing marriage, divorce and inheritance would cease to be effective. In his speech endorsing the argument, Gadgil, a minister in Jawaharlal Nehru's interim cabinet, argued that 'it was an appreciative step [since] … now, in the modern world, to talk of custom prevailing over law is a sort of anomaly … and the Hindu Code, by codifying laws [in this regard] will set out a system that cannot so easily be violated'.[82] Those who supported Ambedkar appear to have been inspired by liberal concern for equality, and the critical importance of codified laws and regulations in creating and sustaining a complementary system of governance. For them the Hindu Code Bill was a revolutionary step because it created a space for change for the better, and it devised a design of substantial equality which was not prejudicial to women. In other words, the task that Ambedkar had undertaken was not futile as it led to a new thinking supportive of gender-equality based on Enlightenment values and predispositions. Ambedkar, by privileging the demand for codified laws and regulations, set in motion the processes that helped build a new template for social transformation.

To his distress, the Hindu Code Bill was not approved by the House in its entirety which was a source of disenchantment to Ambedkar. It served as a betrayal which forced him to resign from the cabinet on 27 September 1951. In his letter of resignation, he said 'the Bill was killed and died unwept and unsung [which was also] a great shock and a bolt from the blue'.[83] What was most striking was the drama seeking to shift the blame on those who were responsible for his resignation. Jawaharlal Nehru released a letter he wrote when accepting Ambedkar's request to be relieved, in which he attributed the resignation to the latter being unwilling to carry on because of his ill-health. So, for Nehru, it was a predetermined conclusion because Ambedkar was physically unfit. To the latter, it was a manufactured defence as since illness was the reason he left the cabinet. Charging Nehru of double-talk, Ambedkar clarified that 'how anybody can spell out from those two letters that I resigned because of my health. I am unable to understand. I know that attempts were being made to give such an impression, that is why I wanted to make a statement in the House so that nobody should be under any false impression'.[84] He was not allowed to make an explanatory statement before his colleagues in the House which further confirms that there were reasons beyond what was officially visible. Ambedkar released a press statement stating that 'if the impression which the Prime Minister seems to be desirous of creating by reading the correspondence was the ground of my resignation was my illness, it is not difficult to dispel that conclusion'.[85] Whether Ambedkar resigned due to illness or not does not seem relevant here; what is critical is to ascertain what led Nehru to accept the resignation. There are two arguments that can be underlined: first, there are reasons to believe that the compulsion of the first parliament election in 1952 acted crucially. In fact, Rajendra Prasad, who insisted on the withdrawal of the Bill because it was not adequately discussed in the public domain, gave a clue. As per contemporary evidence, Prasad was reported to have warned Nehru that with general elections round the corner, Nehru, by introducing 'the controversial legislation just then would be taking a gamble on Congress chances in the election'.[86] The purpose was to stall the legislation which was evident when Prasad, in his letter to his colleague Kailash Nath Katju, said, 'I have written as strongly as I could. … I could not have done more'.[87] Despite Ambedkar's efforts in codifying a gender-sensitive code, it was not an easy task since the senior Congress leaders were not favourably inclined—as Prasad's responses indicated. Secondly, the political equations that Ambedkar had with Nehru, given their appreciation for constitutional liberalism, seem to have been disturbed. Apprehending adverse fall out by pushing the Hindu Code Bill, the Prime Minister preferred to go slow and, hence, he was not In favour of passing the Bill in its entirety. As debates progressed in the House, it was clear that most of the legislators did not seem to be favourably disposed to the views that Ambedkar held vis-à-vis gender parity. One of the major points of disagreement between Ambedkar and the Congress legislators was the former's critique of Hinduism being 'an inert' religion and one which was 'inhuman'. This enraged majority of the Congressmen and it was reflected when they expressed their views during the debate to undermine the effort that Ambedkar had undertaken for gender equality. The members of the House were furious with Ambedkar for being so 'abusive and demeaning' of Hinduism, they—as a former legislator Trimbak Raghunath Deogirikar informs—were determined to dampen the passing of the Bill by mobilizing support in its favour.[88] For Ambedkar, it was a lost battle as it was ineffective in garnering the support of his colleagues in the House. Nonetheless, it created a voice in the public domain because of Ambedkar's goal of building an inclusive society free from prejudices around gender axes. It was a mission that remained unrealised, though the voice for gender parity gradually gained momentum in independent India and by 1956, the Indian parliamentarians endorsed the ideological vision that Ambedkar assiduously nurtured. What was accomplished in 1956 can then be said to have rooted in the past when Ambedkar remained a key political player in constitutionalizing India.

Constitutionalizing Gender Parity

Following the growing democratization, issues such as women empowerment and gender rights have gained massive importance in contemporary political discourses in India. Despite having paid adequate attention, the founding fathers did not seem to pursue the matter to the extent it was expected, possibly because they had other pressing priorities. The issue remained unresolved, though it was being continuously raised, especially in the wake of campaigns for democratizing governance. Women were socio-politically exploited was protested, though the roots were hardly touched because of the well-entrenched prejudices against gender-neutral governance. In theoretical terms, it can be explained that patriarchy was hegemonic in relation to the issues of gender. The aim here is to comprehend the complex unfolding of the trajectories leading to the articulation of gender equality as a constitutional goal.

Ambedkar's ideational vision for gender parity was an integral part of how he conceived humanizing humanity. Caste was divisive and did not allow humanity to flourish as one collective. Women were tortured on many counts: a woman hardly had rights in Indian society, and if she belonged to a lower caste, she was further subjected to torture. By conceptualizing women subjugation in a historical perspective, Sharmila Rege, in her path-breaking intervention[89] argued that Buddha should be credited for his initiative to adopt steps to recognise women as capable to their male counterparts by allowing them to be Bhikhunnis or female monks, though under the care of the Bhikhus (male monks). It was a revolutionary step in the context of Indian society which, by being governed by Manu's directions, characterised women as properties who were deprived of executing any function like men. Brahmins debarred women to participate in spiritual deeds which was indicative of their gender prejudices rooted in their privileging Manu's instruction as infallible, argued Rege. As a result, the well-entrenched ideas were allowed to govern gender relationships in India, and the *Manusmriti* remained a determinant in the treatment of women. As per Manu,

> women have no rights to study the *Vedas*. That is why their *sanskars* (rites) are performed without *Vedic mantras*. Women have no knowledge of religion because they no right to know *Vedas*. The uttering of the *Vedic mantras* is useful for removing sin, [and] since women cannot utter *Vedic mantras*, they are as untruth is.[90]

By quoting Manu's understanding of gender issues, Ambedkar pitched his argument for gender parity at two levels, at the wider level of humanity, he attributed gender disparity to a mindset that was based on Manu's defence for women being inferior to men; hence, they were not equipped to read the *Vedic mantras* which made them in equipped to understand what truth was. This was because Manu's ideas were influenced by the Hindu *Dharmashastras*. Secondly, at a specific level, by comparing it with the ideas of Buddha, Ambedkar also put in place one of the most powerful arguments in favour of gender equality. Not only was Manu's claim humiliating and an insult to women, it was a deterrent for women to realizing their full potentials. In contrast, Ambedkar, while presenting the 1951 Hindu Code Bill before parliament for discussion, argued that

> the Hindu Code was the greatest social reform measure ever undertaken by the legislature in this country. No law passed by the Indian legislature in the past or likely to passed in the future can be compared to it in points of its significance. To leave inequality between class and class, between sex and sex, which is the soul of Hindu society, untouched and to go on passing legislation relating to economic problem is to make a farce of our Constitution and to build a palace on a dung heap. I am spreading this message with the hope that this Bill will ultimately bring about a radical social transformation in India.[91]

Once it was decided by the Congress to not pass the Bill, Ambedkar preferred to resign from Nehru's cabinet. Resignation was a temporary setback for him and for those who had great hopes that the acceptance of the Bill would raise a voice against gender discrimination. There were others who talked about gender disparity as detrimental to humanism, but it was Ambedkar, who endeavoured to constitutionalise gender parity by incorporating a specific legislative design at the dawn of India's independence. He was restrained because political compulsions were too strong to be ignored by the Congress leadership, especially just before the first general elections in 1952. One of the factors which guided Ambedkar's colleagues in the cabinet was the apprehension that such a radical legislation reconceptualizing women completely was likely to infuriate the orthodox Congress supporters. So, it was the winnability factor clubbed with political designs which caused Ambedkar's disappointment.

Nonetheless, the Hindu Code Bill was an alternative to the well-established Hindu codes vis-à-vis women. Despite having failed to achieve the goal, Ambedkar was hailed as one who explained each and every paragraph to defend his exclusive opinion on gender equality. It was emphasised that discrimination on any of the sociocultural axes was an impediment towards realizing humanization of humanity. As long as these discriminatory practices were allowed to shape human mind, dehumanization would prevail. Although it was not a novel ideational vision, as many before Ambedkar raised the issue, what was unique in his endeavour was to understand social justice as dialectically linked with the well-entrenched sociological roots of discriminatory practices. By conceptually seeking to capture the roots of deprivation regarding Dalits and women, Ambedkar raised the most critical voice in comprehending the phenomenon in its widest possible sense. In other words, although he devised powerful conceptual designs for understanding discrimination as critical for comprehending dehumanization, the inputs he provided remained useful for grasping its sociocultural roots and manifestation. Implicit here is the claim that despite being deviant from the conventional mode of nationalism, Ambedkar shall continue to be a source of inspiration for rejuvenating humanity not in isolation, but in 'a mode of associated living, of conjoint communicated experience'.[92] Ambedkar thus stands out for his conceptualization of humanism which was contrary to the well-established ideational visions.

Concluding Observations

The chapter is at one level, a reiteration of Ambedkar's argument for humanizing humanity, and, at another level, an attempt to reinvent some of his ideas which do not seem to be as critical to caste and gender, but are stimulating enough to start debates on whether Gandhi's ideational vision had a limited application. This is not a wild claim because Ambedkar, while arguing for associated living and endosmosis as critical to reconceptualise humanism, laid out a new conceptual template which was peripheral in the nationalist thinking. Despite being humiliated by both who mattered in the nationalist campaign and the self-proclaimed custodians of Hinduism, he was hardly dissuaded from his goal, presumably because he internalised that a battle for humanizing humanity could never be as smooth as others. It was a battle between two uneven forces; a powerful segment of society that became invincible by drawing upon historical resources, and those forces which were not only socio-politically peripheral but were disadvantaged on many counts. What perhaps was a source of Ambedkar strength was his steadfast commitment to humanity which was attacked by those in power. So, the struggle for re-establishing humanism amidst adversaries, powerful indeed; could be anything but smooth in nature. As history demonstrates, Ambedkar's plight was no different from his predecessors who also had an agenda for humanizing humanity in a context where it was not just undermined, but was relegated to non-important human sentiments. What Jyotirao Phule experienced in the late nineteenth century in Maharashtra while raising his voice against untouchability was not very different from Ambedkar. Even his successors with the same objectives shall confront these difficulties because the battle for legitimizing the claim of the peripheral sections of society provokes consternation since it will be a threat to the prevalent power relationships.

A careful examination of Ambedkar's role in constitutionalizing India as a prelude to humanizing humanity reveals that besides being influenced by the Western discourses on liberal constitutionalism, he was equally indebted to some of the primary texts of Hinduism for evoking sentiments challenging the fundamental premises on which the discriminatory practices rested. His inclination for liberal constitutionalism was natural since in this ideological discourse, he found theoretical inputs to build his alternative conceptualization in a caste-divided India. Ambedkar evolved his distinct approach to constitutionalizing India based on uncritical acceptance of republicanism because he believed that it was likely to be accepted *en masse* as it was an attack on the notion of denied rights. This was unfair even from the basic humanitarian point of view. So, Ambedkar's protest against such an artificial division came naturally. In fact, it will not be an exaggeration to say that he carried forward a tradition of struggle against these very practices. By his objection, he expressed his indomitable passion to stand for his faith; it did not seem unusual since Ambedkar questioned the mainstream nationalists at every opportunity. In doing so, he was projected as pro-British. But implicit here was also his voice that he articulated by being associated with the ruling authority: he was ideologically compatible with the foundational values on which colonialism was based—the values of constitutional liberalism. He was also convinced that once India was decolonized, there would be need fora republican ideational spirit in the country.

Ambedkar's model of constitutionalizing India was a stepping stone for realizing freedom; his idea of freedom meant non-domination and unfolding of human personality without shackles as was laid out in provisions of the constitution. So, freedom was not for a section of humanity being victims of caste discrimination; freedom was for all which clearly suggests that he was as concerned with the plight of the exploited masses as with those who remained enslaved due to the behavioural traits and activities of a certain section.

By setting out a specific constitutional design for independent India, Ambedkar and his colleagues in the Constituent Assembly charted out a new blueprint for the country in contrast to Gandhi. If the issue is judged independent of the earlier exercises for making the constitution for India, it was a great challenge. Contrary to colonize the colonizers' efforts, which followed constitutional liberalism for obvious reasons, the two major designs prepared by the Congress stalwarts in the past were also derivative of the same ideological faith. The 1928 Motilal Nehru Constitution and the 1943 Constitution charted by a committee chaired by T.B. Sapru drew on constitutional liberalism shows that in view of their politico-ideological baptism in the philosophy of Enlightenment, it did not appear to be intriguing to Ambedkar.

Ambedkar's arguments in favour of liberal constitutionalism were a reaffirmation that inculcation of Enlightenment values were adequate to create a system of constitutional governance which was well-equipped to rush forces discriminating one section from another. They were also a redesigning of the instruments of governance to effectively combat the divisive elements determined to add fuel to the processes of dehumanizing humanity. His was not only a battle for keeping the home in order, but also to disempower forces seeking to weaken human designs for humanizing humanity. Conceptually, Ambedkar evolved a model which was against the casteist mindset, and useful to build a momentous campaign to eradicate activities deviant to humanity from the root.

Conclusion

I

Jean Jacques Rousseau, in his *The Social Contract*, stated that 'Man is born free, and everywhere he is in chains. One thinks himself the master of others, and still remains a greater slave than they'.[1] This is perhaps the most succinct observation of how human beings survived in contemporary world. One must not forget that he wrote these perceptive sentences on the eve of the French Revolution, which popularized the core ideas of humanity—liberty, equality and fraternity; ideas which reconceptualized humanism in a new light. Following this, he reinforced that,

> to renounce liberty is to renounce being a man, to surrender the rights of humanity and even its duties. For him who renounces everything, no indemnity is possible. Such a renunciation is incompatible with man's nature; to remove all liberty from his will is to remove all morality from his acts; … it is an empty and contradictory convention that sets up, on the one side, absolute authority, and, on the other, unlimited obedience.[2]

Three significant points need careful attention here for they highlight the core values of humanism as indivisible and representative of behavioural traits governing human beings regardless of whether they are strong or weak, physically or otherwise. First, being a devout humanist, Rousseau argued that there were certain inalienable rights which should be protected under all circumstances, without which humans ceased to exist. Here, by insisting on the exhortation of liberty, equality, and fraternity, he laid the foundation for humanity to flourish. Secondly, he was aware that in the contemporary world, given the hegemonic presence of individuals seeking to safeguard their exclusive interests, it was difficult to create a system of inclusivity. The context which he had in mind was the pre-French Revolution France when the people were reeling in stark poverty while a miniscule minority was enjoying life at their cost. So, the French society was unevenly segmented. Finally, renunciation of liberty was dangerous for it would lead to the rise and consolidation of absolute authority and unconditional obedience as habit. In other words, if the authority's dictates were complied with by the masses by being helpless due to their apprehension of being tortured or the deployment of coercive measures for obedience, human beings lost their identity as what they were. By implications, Rousseau then meant that unless there was opposition to forces governed solely by the desire of attaining selfish goals, they would remain unshackled. The French Revolution was illustrative of how the disgruntled French citizens rose against the torturous monarch, Louis the XVI which finally culminated in the consolidation of values pertinent to humanity.

The above introductory views are critical to the main theme of the book, namely, humanizing humanity. One should add a warning here. It appears overstretched if we make the argument that it was Rousseau in the eighteenth century who spoke about humanism and suggested how the practice of dehumanizing humanity struck roots in human behaviour. There were many thinkers—long before Rousseau theorized such an endeavour with roots in human society—who not only questioned but also laid their life for the fulfilment of their goal of humanizing humanity. We should keep in mind that the ideas which the thinkers upheld were context-driven. Hence, it does not seem odd when Aristotle justified slavery as the idea of humanity, for it had a very restricted meaning then. For Rousseau, writing in the eighteenth century, the system of allowing ownership of human beings by another section, was not only socially obnoxious but also contrary to the basic tenets of humanity which he articulated by declaring that 'from whatever aspect we regard [this] question, ... the word slave and right contradict each other and are mutually exclusive'.[3] What he meant was that slavery was a cloak to hide the human instinct of exploitation of under-privileged sections.

History is abound with instances of campaigns for humanizing humanity as well as zealous support for tendencies to the contrary to defend the argument that human beings nurtured instinctively values in support of dehumanizing humanity. Illustrative here is how civil rights became civil in its real connotation because of undeterred campaigns by the African-Americans against the white Americans. It is recorded in history that slavery was outlawed after the Civil War in the US, following the promulgation of the 1893 Emancipation Act under the guidance of President Abraham Lincoln. The Act abolished slavery but failed to recognize the African-Americans as equal citizens due to the continuation of the famous Jim Crow Laws, especially in the south. The African-Americans were deprived of voting rights till the Voting Rights Act was accepted by the US Congress in 1965. By denying at least 12 per cent of the total US demography, democracy remained restricted since, under no circumstances, US system of democracy ensured the rule of demos as they denied voting rights to the African-Americans.

Humanization of humanity received another serious jolt with the rise of colonialism which was, as historians have shown, linked with industrialization. To feed industries, the industrialists needed cheap and sustained supply of raw materials and a market for selling the industrially-produced goods. A pure economic interest governed by the zeal to augment wealth at the cost of those who lacked the strength to combat the European powers was one of the prime factors for expansionist strategy which led the Europeans to conquer countries in Asia and Africa. With this control, more than half of the world's population was brought under the hegemony of the Europeans. The obvious consequence was the division between the colonizers and colonized which was a schism between the powerful and the weak. So, it was a perfect milieu for the consolidation of forces for dehumanizing humanity because the colonizers were superior militarily and intellectually. It did not thus seem odd when Edmund Burke (1729–1797), the British parliamentarian, justified British colonialism in India in his many speeches in the House of Lords in the eighteenth century as a necessary intervention for civilizing the barbarians of the East. A new era of dehumanizing humanity was thus ushered in and the self-assigned role of the rulers for civilizing the ruled was neither condemned nor accepted as an aberration in human history.

Humanity is dehumanized not just due to outside intervention; there are instances to demonstrate that dehumanization is also the outcome of prejudiced sociocultural practices upheld by those who are 'superior' to the rest. The caste system in India is a testimony here. Caste discrimination is deep-rooted since it is believed that it is integral to the growth of India as a sociocultural compact. In reality, caste is a deliberately-contrived design of specifying one's location in social hierarchy, determined by birth. As a result, once one is born with a definite caste identity, one continues to remain so regardless of the ways one articulates oneself in future. Traditionally, caste was a means of division of labour, denoting that one's caste identity was decided by one's skill. This is no longer the case, although caste identity becomes a marker of one's sociocultural status in society. Just like racism which continues to figure, directly or indirectly, in the US and South Africa, caste remains an important determinant of power and authority in India. There is no denying that many belonging to the untouchable castes were tortured by the caste Hindus. One of the most vocal spokespersons of equality for all, regardless of caste, was Ambedkar who evolved a powerful critique of caste discrimination in India, which cemented job reservations for the untouchables in the public sector in independent India.

The purpose of the elaboration of the role of caste in justifying dehumanization is to pursue the point that caste discrimination has historical roots in the form of various kinds of divisive designs that human civilization witnessed. It does not seem logical to argue that human beings are instinctively exploitative and thus dehumanized since there are many who always raise their voice against these tendencies in the public domain. So, the argument needs to be qualified by suggesting that under specific circumstances, human beings tend to uphold practices for dehumanizing humanity. As per Rousseau, feudalism in France created a milieu in which the haves did not bother to indulge in practices causing misery and discomfort to have nots. Colonialism was another historical force which, by supporting exploitation of human beings around the world, allowed tendencies for undermining humanity since it privileged the conquerors over the vanquished. In a similar way, caste is also a divisive phenomenon in circumstances when the conventional mindsets are allowed to determine human behaviour which however does not go unchallenged which means that it is neither axiomatic nor a widely-accepted pattern.

Humanizing humanity is a discourse, and so is dehumanizing humanity. The above discussion supports three interrelated reasons: first, both the discourses are linked with the historical stirrings, although it is fair to argue that both of them have also been thoroughly scrutinized in different phases of human civilization; it further means that neither of them has ever been accepted as a determinant of the unfolding of humanity. Secondly, humanization and dehumanization were processes integrally linked with how human society developed over centuries. As argued above, human history was the platform where these two contrarian tendencies fought for hegemony. In some situations, dehumanization appeared to have gained control, and lost to those championing humanizing humanity in others. Are they then alter-egos? The answer is partly yes and partly no—yes, because, as history epitomizes, the consolidation of the processes for humanization are proportionally linked with dehumanization which means that one is a precursor of the other. and no because humanization remains integrally connected with humanity while dehumanization was an aberration of history.

Thirdly, as the documented history of humanity shows, dehumanization struck roots in society presumably because it was never challenged as effectively as it was required. It is true that in today's world, many institutional mechanisms have been devised to remove the roots of dehumanization from human minds by addressing factors instrumental in creating a milieu in society. Can this be adequate? The answer cannot be affirmative since institutional checks are not effective enough to inculcate a mindset opposed to dehumanizing humanity. According to Marxist vocabulary, as long as society is divided in classes, dehumanization will remain integral to human existence; which means that a class-less society is a utopian space when one conceives of humanity which means that the conceptualization of class-less human existence is utopian because it does not seem conceivable so long as human beings are divided around many sociocultural axes.

II

Humanism is not an ideologically segregationist phenomenon. The ideological leanings of those prescribing to humanism is immaterial as they are secondary to their commitment to humanism. This is also a collective and individual goals. For instance, gender disparity is a manifestation of dehumanizing humanity; it can be addressed as a collective concern at the societal level; it is also a matter of individual concern since the practice of gender inequality emerges first in families. Once a viewpoint is consolidated at the individual level, it will be easier to translate it at the collective. So, conceptually, the argument that gender parity can be established by the adoption of laws and their stringent application is not convincing because unless a sense is inculcated to defend the point that women are as essential to society as their male counterparts, the legislative designs appear futile. In her conceptually path-breaking work, the French feminist philosopher Simon de Beauvoir rightfully attributed gender-difference to the prevalent sociocultural practices, which were heavily male-centric. While making the point that one is not born, but rather becomes a woman, she illustrated how male-centric sociocultural practices for centuries made the gender division axiomatic in human civilization. According to her,

> men's economic privilege, their social value, the prestige of marriage, the usefulness of masculine support—all these encourage women to ardently want to please men. They are on the whole still in a state of serfdom. It follows that woman knows and chooses herself not as she exists for herself, but as man defines her. She thus has to be described first as men dream of her since her being-for-men is one of the essential factors of her concrete condition.[4]

One of the most perceptive comments on how women, despite nearly constituting half of the global demography, continue to remain servile to their male counterparts as if they were born to do so. This is a glaring example of dehumanization that society believes men are the custodians of women because they are weak, less intelligent, and unable to shoulder responsibilities and declare themselves as agents of history. The premise on which Simone de Beauvoir grounded her argument was neither based on specific theories nor drawn on scriptural designs, but on a deeper analysis of how humanity passed through various stages. Those championing humanism appeared to have ignored this dimension of history. Even the thinkers who are hailed as bearers of freedom seem to have ignored that there was a biological division in society and women had a significant role in carrying it forward. For instance, Rousseau can easily be charged as a sexist since his treatises were written in an exclusive 'male-format' and he did not refer to women as being integral to human social existence. Carole Pateman, in her *The Sexual Contract* developed this point further by showing that sociocultural customary practices were developed to create a milieu in which women continue to be dehumanized. Sexual difference is 'political difference [because it] is the difference between freedom and subjection [which is justified by] … many theorists [by insisting that] … women naturally lack the attributes and capacities of "individuals"'.[5] She also charges that Rosseau, by excluding half of the population to ascertain patriarchal dominance, defended Social Contract as 'a vehicle through which men transform their natural rights over women into the security of civil patriarchal right'.[6] Hence, women, she further argues, 'are held to be natural subordinates lacking the capacities required to enter into contracts'.[7] The idea is a reverberation of John Stuart Mill, who also believed that

> subordination of wives was inevitable in a gender-divided society because the masters, instead of being happy with mere property, also require something more than actual service, men do not want simply the obedience of women, they want their sentiments. All men, except the most brutish, desire to have, not a forced slave but a willing one, not a slave merely, but a favourite.[8]

Although Mill added a new dimension on the nature of dehumanization of humanity in regard to women, Pateman clarified that women continued to remain a subject of degradation which was socially permissible.

The Western analysis of gender issue runs counter to the *Vedas, Upanishads, Puranas, Smritis,* among others which appeared to have addressed the issue by redefining women as complementary to social progress. Whether it was practised rigidly or not, it certainly identifies a mindset in support of arguments for gender parity. During the nationalist struggle, the mainstream nationalists, especially before the emergence of Gandhi, raised their voice against dehumanizing women since they believed that it was detrimental to their concern for social equality. As history shows, many women came forward to participate in the struggle against the British as they represented a force for dehumanizing humanity by demeaning those who were colonized due to their superior coercive power. For instance, Lala Lajpat Rai, justified gender equality as essential for social well-being because both men and women were complementary to one another. By drawing on one of the ancient texts, *Vishnu Purana*, Rai thus argued that

> Man is *Vishnu*, Woman is *Shri*; she is language, he is thought; she is prudence, he is law; he is reason, she is sense; she is duty, he is right; he is author, she is work; he is patience, she is peace; he is will, she is wish; he is pity, she is gift; he is chant, she is not; she is fuel, he is fire; she is glory, he is sun; she is orbit, he is space; she is motion, he is wind; he is ocean, she is shore; he is owner, she is wealth; he is battle, she is might; he is lamp, she is light; he is day, she is night; he is tree, she is vine; he is music, she is words; he is justice, she is truth; he is channel, she is stream; he is flagship, she is flag; she is beauty, he is strength; she is body, he is soul.[9]

Long before Simone de Beauvoir and Carole Pateman codified their views on gender question, Rai articulated the views which represented the concern of his colleagues as well. The above description of women being complementary to men shows that he was more progressive than many Indians who still held traditional gender views. A careful analysis of Rai's conceptualization of gender issues may suggest that he was not free from patriarchal biases as women were shown to be supportive of men's endeavours; they did not seem to be independent of men as their role was to help men to chart out a course of action. Nonetheless, the fact that Rai—in the early 1920s—raised these issues is a testimony of the claim that Indian nationalists addressed gender questions seriously long before it figured prominently in the Western discourses.

Gender discrimination was one of the critical aspects of dehumanizing humanity. As shown above, both Western discourses and the nationalist approach to women issues attracted adequate attention since this was an integral aspect of the wider concern for humanizing humanity. It is evident that gender disparity is a social phenomenon being nurtured as a system of differentiation bordering on discrimination; this was an outcome of a practice being considered normal in human social behaviour. Despite being challenged regularly, gender disparity did not appear to have been a serious issue in the past; presumably because the prominent social reformers remained nearly indifferent to this aspect of social imbalances. With constitutional guarantees, gender disparity appears to have been conclusively addressed—at least legally, although the dominant mindset appears to be as decisive as was in the past in shaping humanity.

Ambedkar dealt with this while defending the Hindu Code Bill in Parliament in 1951. Despite his persuasive argument for ensuring women their right to parental property, the bill was defeated on the floor of the parliament and he was ultimately forced to resign as what he felt did not augur well with his colleagues who presided over India's destiny following decolonization. This incident was referred to for making the point that gender issues did not appear to have attracted adequate attention in independent India, which also ascertains the critical presence of a mindset opposed to gender equality, notwithstanding the fact that most of those who were decisive in making policies in independent India appeared to have been convinced that gender disparity and dehumanizing humanity were dialectically intertwined. They also realized that mere legislation was ineffective till a supportive mindset emerged, as it needed to be tackled by evolving a counter mindset. In principle, the idea is persuasive. What was a deterrent was that many of the leading nationalists did not seem to have been persuaded which resulted in the end of the 1951 Hindu Code Bill which Ambedkar, as India's first Law Minister, placed before parliament for discussion. One of the major recommendations was the abolition of practices debarring women heirs from inheriting their parental property. As this was discriminatory to women, Ambedkar insisted that the practice should be done away with permanently, to eradicate one of the serious impediments for gender equality.

The Hindu Code Bill raised a wider issue, namely whether recognition of women as legitimate heir was adequate to establish gender parity. The answer is a qualified yes because by legally accepting women as legitimate heirs, the Bill was certainly a significant step in humanizing humanity with the endorsement of the view that their rights were now recognized. This was not enough, as Simone de Beauvoir argued, because what was most critical was to transform the values on the basis of which women were judged. According to her, with economic security, women became empowered in comparison to what they were in the past. But, until 'it brings about the moral, social and cultural consequences it heralds and requires, the new women cannot appear'.[10] Fundamental here is the claim that legislative designs appear futile unless they are backed by sociocultural and moral metamorphosis in society. Only then, 'the slavery of half of humanity is abolished and with it the whole hypocritical system it implies that the division of humanity will reveal its authentic meaning and the human couple will discover its true form'.[11] Analogous with this is also the argument that women liberation is an aid for humanizing humanity since with the rescinding of the mindset defending gender disparity, the forces supporting dehumanizing humanity were certain to be considerably eclipsed. The processes of gender empowerment are thus a significant step towards setting out designs for eradicating disparities in society, both by deliberate legal initiatives and by complementary sociocultural and moral changes. Marching ahead with the objective of humanizing humanity was possible once social circumstances are favourably disposed towards the same.

III

There is a critical conceptual question which is usually asked by those privileging universal humanism as the phenomenon stands in contradiction with nationalism. This query pertains to whether nationalism is congruent with universal humanism or otherwise. A surface reading of the texts of those who opposed nationalism as a conceptual category, primarily because it upholds designs for totalizing human identities, would render humanism as an aspired goal for nationalists, so long as it does not hamper unionization of humanity in terms of selected sociocultural yardsticks cementing a bond among a section of humanity. A blind follower of Western discourses is sure to draw this conclusion. Since the establishment of the 1648 Westphalia Treaty which laid and consolidated the foundation of nation states, the idea that homogeneity is required to be a nation gained momentum. Many European colonizers followed the model once they established their hegemony in countries which were socioculturally and politico-ideologically different. The colonial endeavour led to skirmishes and serious opposition of the colonized towards these efforts. Nonetheless, the colonizers succeeded because they had access to government machineries to quell the opponents. For instance, the introduction of English education in India by the British in 1835, in accordance with the advice by Thomas Babington Macaulay, radically altered the texture of India. By making English as a medium of instruction, the colonizers introduced a *lingua franca* for the country. So, at least, in terms of a mode of teaching and also communication, Indians from different parts of the country became one as they spoke nearly in the same language.

This was vehemently opposed by many in the public domain because they felt that one's holistic growth was determined by their education in their mother tongue. The repercussions of English being forcibly introduced in India by the British, were disastrous for many reasons: not only did it permanently seal the growth of indigenous languages; it was also a serious constraint for those who had no access to English which created a distance between the English educated and the rest. So, it was a divisive design. India was partitioned internally because not only did those with English education look down upon those who did not have it, but they gradually became uprooted from their own traditions and legacies. The fissure that emerged was responsible for generating a sense of superiority among the English educated at the cost of those who were considered to be inferior due to lack of access to the English education. It was a dehumanizing tool since dissociating oneself from one's mother tongue had serious implications in regard to one's personality; they had personalities which were mutilated because they remain disconnected with the sociocultural legacies, which contributed to the evolution of their identity as Indians; they thus became neither truly Indians nor were well-equipped to be like the British rulers.

Nationalism in the Western sense was thus contrary to humanization of humanity since it was inherently divisive and impaired the processes leading to the rise of universal humanism or in other words, humanity being one without being split around any sociocultural, economic and political axes. In contrast, the conceptualization of civilizational unity appeared to be useful in cementing a bond among socioculturally disparate population. This is of theoretical importance for two reasons: on the one hand, it helped build a togetherness among those who were otherwise separate due to contextually relevant reasons; on the other hand, togetherness did not, therefore, entail either surrendering of distinct identities of a collective, or absorptions of values which were clearly alien to them. By advancing such conceptual premises, Gandhi and Rabindranath Tagore upheld the view that for humanity to develop organically, what was required was to create a socio-economic and politico-cultural ambience, in which the tendencies of either subjugating or relegating a community to 'nothing' were combatted as soon as they reared their ugly heads. This is one side of the argument; the other side relates to the role of the foundational sociocultural and politico-ideological preferences which were ingrained in the communities given their belief in those axiomatic texts supportive of humanity as one compact. To be precise, what is hinted here is the critical part that the ancient texts of Indian civilizations—like, *Vedas*, *Upanishads*, among others—played in sustaining the bond, irrespective of frequent intervention from outside. Tagore's argument highlighting that these texts epitomized human experiences in different phases of humanity is persuasive. In other words, he hinted at the fact that the *Vedas*, *Upanishads* and other transcendental texts which are associated with Hinduism are not religious texts in the conventional sense; they are humanistic designs to assist human beings to chart out a context-driven road map for themselves. The argument reinforces the claim that contrary to other major religious texts, like the *Old* and *New Testaments*, the *Quran* and the *Tripitaka*, among others. *Vedas*, *Upanishads* and *Puranas* are not confined to a particular phase of the history of human civilization nor are they the codifications of the heroic deeds of specific Godly human beings; instead, they are an elaboration of how human beings in various phases of their development contributed to the processes of humanizing humanity despite the odds. In other words, in seeking to construct ideational visions, these texts are clearly at variance with the religious texts per se, because they provide critical inputs to understand the past endeavours towards humanizing humanity, by effectively containing the processes of dehumanization of humanity, which are not foreign to human civilization. Significant here is, in other words, the claim that processes of dehumanization and humanization are dialectically interconnected and hence, universal humanism is not just a conceptual category but an endeavour consciously made to take humanity forward as a compact.

IV

It has now been well-established that Western domination, not just physically but intellectually as well, led to the near decimation of humanity as a collective. The uncontrolled march of European powers in Asia and Africa led them to devise a design which they thought was appropriate for the colonized. As a result, while crafting their own mode of governance, they created their own vocabulary by

> privileging some of the values which were of help in their mission and correspondingly downplay or ignore altogether the vicious impact of colonization on the native people, including slavery [to persuasively argue that] Europeans were there for modernizing those parts of the world [which remained] peripheral to the rest of the world.[12]

So, it is fair to argue that colonialism was a tool of dehumanizing humanity since it was meant to contribute to the development of a particular section of humanity located in Western hemisphere of the world. Many analysts illustrated how the European advancement was linked with an unhappy fate for the rest of the world. As is well-known, the inhuman exploitation of the resources in India by the British colonizers contributed to the industrial growth in Britain which implies that without India being a supplier of raw materials and buyers of finished products, it would not have been possible for the former to rise as one of the leading industrial powers in the comity of nations. The heightened racial superiority of the white Europeans caused a permanent fissure among human beings as it led to a division of the world into the ruling and subject races. A partitioned social ontology was thus created to justify the European intervention as appropriate, in that, given their supposed lack of development, the colonized needed the support of the developed Europe. It was ironical that through the conceptualization, by claiming to be superior, the Europeans took onto themselves the responsibilities of civilizing the so-called backward people, who were forcibly brought under their control for the sake of their benefit. In other words, they became self-proclaimed custodians of the so-called peripheral parts of the world, completely ignoring the adverse impact on humanity due to their selfish deeds. Such an endeavour informed many normative and cognitive conceptual designs to support the contention that colonialization was justified by undermining the inevitable adverse impact on humanity. By drawing attention to this aspect of the Western colonial project, Edward Said argued that 'the effort towards colonizing the [so-called] Orient is a political design willed over the Orient because Orient was weaker than the West which elided the Orient's difference with its weakness'.[13] A new discourse or a system of thought was created to conceptually understand 'a heterogenous, dynamic and complex human reality from an uncritical essentialist standpoint [also to support] … what the Europeans did to the weaker sections of humanity'.[14] The outcome is epistemologically prejudicial and restrictive because it was a design seeking to understand the so-called subject races in the derivative cultural images, and it was an effort for justifying the processes at dehumanizing humanity although, for the colonizers, it was not so for obvious reasons.

The tendencies towards dehumanizing and humanizing humanity are as old as human civilization. Colonialism was an outcome of a particular phase of human history; with decolonization, the phase is over, but that does not imply that humanity is no longer dehumanized or the effort towards humanizing humanity has lost its viability. Instead, given the dialectical interconnection between the two contrarian conceptualizations, it is fair to argue that the conceptual parameters that emerged in the West are neither theoretically irrelevant nor intellectually inept. For instance, the Enlightenment model of humanism establishes the claim that the foundation of this human moral world lies in the spontaneous tendency to respond to one another with fellow feeling and with a sense of interrelatedness articulated in the expressions like 'sympathy' or 'empathy'. We are human beings and we are endowed with 'a delicate and generous sensibility which nature has implanted in the hearts of all and whose flowering waits only upon favourable influence of enlightenment and freedom'.[15] Nonetheless, the contemporary research on humanizing humanity also shows that the thinkers espousing Enlightenment principles had applied their ideas of humanity almost exclusively to 'white, able-bodied, gender-conforming makes. ... Any other type was treated as a deficiency and falling-off perhaps falling below the level of human altogether'.[16] This was unfortunately an ingrained tendency among the Enlightenment theorists. David Hume (1711–1776), one of the leading Enlightenment scholars, felt, for instance that 'non-white people were naturally inferior, producing nothing comparable to European creations—no ingenious manufacturers amongst them, no arts, no sciences'.[17] The French Enlightenment theorist, Condorcet (1743–1794) was an exception since he strongly condemned colonialism, racism as well as sexism and 'had a vision of all humanity sharing an enlightened future'.[18] A careful reading of the visions of the ideologues of Enlightenment also reveals that for them, the world was racially divided: the whites and non-whites. The model of conceptualizing humanity in binary terms is both misleading and conceptually vacuous since humanity is multifaceted. Hence, the challenges confronting humanity in different parts of the world are bound to be different and needs to be understood not with reference to grand theories, but by linking them with the prevalent contexts.

The interventions by Tagore, Gandhi and Ambedkar are uniquely textured presumably because their ideas were based on their exposure to the Western discourses along with their existential experiences of being Indian. Being trained in the Western mode of thinking while growing up in colonial India provided them with significant inputs for humanizing humanity. As they were well-acquainted with the indigenous literature, their conceptual designs are useful to fathom the role of colonial authority, and the debilitating sociocultural tendencies crippling humanity from prospering naturally. In other words, their lived experiences at a time when both the Western and indigenous discourses received equal importance in building a relevant conceptual approach to comprehend both humanizing and dehumanizing humanity. In view of the complex intellectual, socio-economic and politico-cultural milieu in which they evolved their unique modes of thinking, they remain pathfinders for reconceptualizing many of the dominant theoretical paradigms which were axiomatic in recent past. By considering the multiple theoretical inputs and the ecosystem which is supportive and otherwise of the tendencies towards humanizing and dehumanizing humanity, the Indian chapter of humanizing humanity is both theoretically innovative and conceptually empowering to the extent of overturning many recognized of ideational discourses.

Notes

Introduction

1 Quentin Skinner, ed., *The Return of Grand Theory in the Human Sciences* (Cambridge: Cambridge University Press, 1985), 3.
2 Questin Skinner, *The Return of Grand Theory in the Human Sciences*, 4–5.
3 Questin Skinner, *The Return of Grand Theory in the Human Sciences*, 5.
4 Karl Popper, *The Open Society and Its Enemies*, Vol. I (London: Routledge, 1995), 1.
5 Karl Popper, *The Open Society and Its Enemies*, Vol. I, 473.
6 Karl Popper, *The Open Society and Its Enemies*, Vol. I, 475.
7 Edward Said, *Orientalism: Western Conceptions of the Orient* (Gurgaon, Harayana: Penguin Books, 2001), 204.
8 Rabindranath Tagore, 'The Philosophy of Our Life', in *The English Writings of Rabindranath Tagore*, ed. Sisir Kumar Das, Vol. 3 (New Delhi: Sahitya Akademi, 1996), 567.
9 Tagore, 'The Philosophy of Our Life', Vol. 3, 567.
10 Tagore, 'The Union of Cultures', Vol. 3, 432.
11 Tagore, 'The Union of Cultures', Vol. 3, 433.
12 Tagore, 'The Union of Cultures', Vol. 3, 435.
13 Tagore, 'The Union of Cultures', Vol. 3, 435.
14 Tagore, 'A Vision of History', Vol. 3, 440–41.
15 Tagore, 'A Vision of History', Vol. 3, 441.
16 Tagore, 'A Vision of History', Vol. 3, 451.
17 Amal Kumar Mukhopadhyay, *Western Political Thought: From Plato to Marx* (Calcutta, West Bengal: KP Bagchi & Company, 1980), 113.
18 Thomas Hobbes, *Leviathan*, ed. J.C.A. Gaskin (London: Oxford University Press, 1996), 86.
19 Hobbes, *Leviathan*, 86.
20 Hobbes, *Leviathan*, 88.
21 Hobbes, *Leviathan*, 88–89.
22 Hobbes, *Leviathan*, 105.
23 Hobbes, *Leviathan*, 109.

24 G.D.H. Cole, 'Introduction', in Jean-Jacques Rousseau, *The Social Contract and Discourses* (1762; repr., London; Everyman, 2001), 33–35.

25 Jean-Jacques Rousseau, 'A Dissertation on the Origin and Foundation of the Inequality of Mankind', in Jean-Jacques Rousseau, *The Social Contract and Discourses*, edited by G.D.H. Cole (London: Everyman, 2001), 49.

26 Cole, Jean-Jacques Rousseau, *The Social Contract and Discourses*, 181.

27 Cole, Jean-Jacques Rousseau, *The Social Contract and Discourses*, 181–96.

28 Cole, Jean-Jacques Rousseau, *The Social Contract and Discourses*, 181–96.

29 Cole, Jean-Jacques Rousseau, *The Social Contract and Discourses*, 203.

30 Cole, Jean-Jacques Rousseau, *The Social Contract and Discourses*, 190.

31 Cole, Jean-Jacques Rousseau, *The Social Contract and Discourses*, 108.

32 Carole Pateman, *The Sexual Contract* (Cambridge: Polity Press, 1988); Charles W. Mills, *The Racial Contract* (Ithaca: Cornell University Press, 1999); Carole Pateman and Charles W. Mills, *Contract and Domination* (Cambridge: Polity Press, 2007).

33 Carole Pateman, *The Sexual Contract* (Cambridge: Polity Press, 1988), 2.

34 Pateman, *The Sexual Contract*, 94.

35 Pateman, *The Sexual Contract*, 118.

36 Pateman, *The Sexual Contract*, 112.

37 Pateman, *The Sexual Contract*, 133.

38 George W. Carey and James McClellan, eds, *The Federalist* (Liberty Fund, Indianapolis: Liberty Fund, 2001), 25.

39 Alexander Hamilton, James Madison and John Jay, *The Federalist Papers* (New York: Mentor Book, 1961), 37.

40 Hamilton, Madison, Jay, *The Federalist Papers*, 37.

41 Hamilton, Madison, Jay, *The Federalist Papers*, 37.

42 Hamilton, Madison, Jay, *The Federalist Papers*, 38.

43 Hamilton, Madison, Jay, *The Federalist Papers*, 38.

Part A: Rabindranath Tagore (1861–1941)

1 Rabindranath Tagore, *My Life in My Words*, ed. Uma Dasgupta (New Delhi: Penguin Random House, 2006), 4–5.

2 Rabindranath Tagore, 'Ram Mohan Roy', in *The English Writings of Rabindranath Tagore*, ed. Sisir Kumar Das, Vol. 3 (New Delhi: Sahitya Akademi, 1996), 667–68.

3 Tagore, 'Ram Mohan Roy', 668.
4 Tagore, *My Life in My Words*, 5.
5 Tagore, *My Life in My Words*, 5.
6 Tagore, *My Life in My Words*, 6.
7 Tagore, *My Life in My Words*, 7.
8 Tagore, *My Life in My Words*, 7.
9 Tagore, *My Life in My Words*, 7.
10 Tagore, *My Life in My Words*, 7.

Chapter 1: Literary Insights and Universal Humanism

1 Rabindranath Tagore, *Ghare Baire*, trans. Radha Chakravarty (New Delhi: Penguin Books, 2011), 670.
2 Tagore, *Ghare Bhaire, 670.*
3 Tagore, *Ghare Bhaire*, 671.
4 Tagore, *Ghare Bhaire*, 671.
5 Tagore, *Ghare Bhaire*, 671.
6 Tagore, *Ghare Bhaire*, 671.
7 Tagore, *Ghare Bhaire*, 671.
8 Tagore, *Ghare Bhaire*, 673.
9 Tagore, *Ghare Bhaire*, 674.
10 Tagore, *Ghare Bhaire*, 674.
11 Tagore, *Ghare Bhaire*, 67.
12 Tagore, *Ghare Bhaire*, 675.
13 Tagore, *Ghare Bhaire*, 715.
14 Tagore, *Ghare Bhaire*, 678.
15 Tagore, *Ghare Bhaire*, 678.
16 Tagore, *Ghare Bhaire*, 687.
17 Tagore, *Ghare Bhaire*, 687.
18 Tagore, *Ghare Bhaire*, 688.
19 Tagore, *Ghare Bhaire*, 689.
20 Tagore, *Ghare Bhaire, 689.*
21 Tagore, *Ghare Bhaire*, 689.
22 Tagore, *Ghare Bhaire*, 689.
23 Tagore, *Ghare Bhaire*, 690.
24 Tagore, *Ghare Bhaire*, 696.
25 Tagore, *Ghare Bhaire*, 704.

26 Tagore, *Ghare Bhaire*, 704.
27 Tagore, *Ghare Bhaire*, 705.
28 Tagore, *Ghare Bhaire*, 707.
29 Tagore, *Ghare Bhaire*, 708.
30 Rabindranath Tagore, foreword to *The Principal Upanishads*, by S. Radhakrishnan (1953, repr., Gurugram, Haryana: HarperCollins Publishers, 2022), 944.
31 Tagore, *Ghare Bhaire*, 747.
32 I elaborated this aspect of the second Partition of Bengal in 1947 in my *Partition of Bengal and Assam, 1932-47: Contour of Freedom* (London: Routledge, 2004).
33 Rabindranath Tagore, *Gora*, trans. Radha Chakravarty (New Delhi: Penguin Books, 2011), 305.
34 Tagore, *Gora*, 306.
35 Tagore, *Gora*, 306.
36 Tagore, *Gora*, 306.
37 Tagore, *Gora*, 306.
38 Tagore, *Gora*, 306.
39 Partha Chatterjee, *The Nation and Its Fragments: Colonial and Postcolonial Histories* (New Delhi: Oxford University Press, 1994), 6–7.
40 Tagore, *Gora*, 314.
41 Tagore, *Gora*, 523–24.
42 Tagore, *Gora*, 524.
43 Tagore, *Gora*, 524.
44 Tagore, *Gora*, 377.
45 Tagore, *Gora*, 377.
46 Tagore, *Gora*, 400.
47 Tagore, *Gora*, 400.
48 Tagore, *Gora*, 400.
49 Tagore, *Gora*, 400.
50 Tagore, *Gora*, 400.
51 Tagore, *Gora*, 401.
52 Tagore, *Gora*, 404.
53 Tagore, *Gora*, 404.
54 Tagore, *Gora*, 502.
55 Tagore, *Gora*, 535.
56 Tagore, *Gora*, 536.

57 Tagore, *Gora*, 567.
58 Tagore, *Gora*, 567–68.
59 Tagore, *Gora*, 575.
60 Tagore, *Gora*, 575.
61 Tagore, *Gora*, 575.
62 Tagore, *Gora*, 575.
63 Tagore, *Gora*, 576.
64 Tagore, *Gora*, 576.
65 Tagore, *Gora*, 576.
66 Tagore, *Gora*, 576.
67 Tagore, *Gora*, 577.
68 Tagore, *Gora*, 577.
69 Abul Mansur Ahmad, a former Congress activist who later became one of the key members of Krishak Praja Party elaborated the historical developments which finally culminated in the formation of Pakistan as an independent state in his *Aamar Dekha Rajnitir Panchas Bachhar* (Politics as I saw in last fifty years), Kitabistan, Dhaka, 1968.
70 Tagore, *Gora*, 297.
71 Tagore, *Gora*, 298.
72 Tagore, *Gora*, 298.
73 Tagore, *Gora*, 299.
74 I dealt with this issue in my *The Three Tagores: Dwarkanath, Debendranath and Rabindranath: India in Transition* (New Delhi: Sage Publications, 2022).
75 The arguments defending gender parity were made earlier in my other books as well. Many of the views are reiteration of what I mentioned in one of my earlier books, entitled *Social and Political Ideas of Rabindranath Tagore* (New Delhi: Sage Publications, 2021).
76 Tagore, *Gora*, 357.
77 Tagore, *Gora*, 357.
78 Tagore, *Gora*, 357.
79 Tagore, *Gora*, 358.
80 Tagore, *Gora*, 358.
81 Tagore, *Gora*, 358.
82 Tagore, *Gora*, 358.
83 Tagore, *Gora*, 377.
84 Tagore, *Gora*, 522.

85 Tagore, *Gora*, 523.
86 Tagore, *Gora*, 523.
87 Tagore, *Gora*, 524.
88 Tagore, *Gora*, 537.
89 Tagore, *Gora*, 575.
90 Tagore, *Gora*, 575
91 Tagore, *Gora*, 576.
92 Rabindranath Tagore, 'Laboratory' in *Rabindra Rachanabali* (Bengali), Vol. 13, Visva Bharati, Kolkata, 1410 (Bangavda), 270.
93 Tagore, 'Laboratory', 271.
94 Tagore, 'Laboratory', 272.
95 Tagore, 'Laboratory', 297.
96 Tagore, 'Laboratory', 276.
97 Tagore, 'Laboratory', 287.
98 Tagore, 'Laboratory', 278.
99 https://webhome.cs.uvic.ca/~mserra/AttachedFiles/PersonalPolitical.pdf, Carole Hanisch, 'The Personal Is Political'.
100 Tagore, *My Life in My Words*, 9.

Chapter 2: Essays Reverberating Concerns for Humanity

1 Ernest Gellner, *Nations and Nationalism* (1983; repr., New Delhi: Select Service Syndicate, 1966), 97.
2 I have dealt with how partition of India was inevitable in my *Partition of Bengal and Assam, 1932-47: Contours of Freedom* (London: Routledge, 2004).
3 Partha Chatterjee in his *The Nation and Its Fragments: Colonial and Post-colonial Histories* (Delhi: Oxford University Press, 1994) argued this point.
4 Rabindranath Tagore, 'Nationalism in the West', in *Nationalism* (1918; repr., Delhi: Macmillan, 1985), 1.
5 Tagore, 'Nationalism in the West', 3.
6 Tagore, 'Nationalism in the West', 4.
7 Tagore, 'Nationalism in the West', 5.
8 Tagore, 'Nationalism in the West', 7.
9 Tagore, 'Nationalism in the West', 8–9.
10 Tagore, 'Nationalism in the West', 9–10.
11 Tagore, 'Nationalism in the West', 10.

12 Tagore, 'Nationalism in the West', 11.
13 Tagore, 'Nationalism in the West', 11–12.
14 Tagore, 'Nationalism in the West', 14.
15 Tagore, 'Nationalism in the West', 15.
16 Tagore, 'Nationalism in the West', 24.
17 Tagore, 'Nationalism in the West', 26.
18 Tagore, 'Nationalism in the West', 26.
19 Tagore, 'Nationalism in the West', 32–33.
20 Tagore, 'Nationalism in Japan', 41.
21 Aurobindo Ghosh, in Vol. 7 of *The Complete Works of Sri Aurobindo* (Pondicherry: Sri Aurobindo Ashram, 2002), 1091–108.
22 Tagore, 'Nationalism in Japan', 44–45.
23 Tagore, 'Nationalism in Japan', 48.
24 Tagore, 'Nationalism in the West', 56.
25 Rabindranath Tagore, 'Nationalism in India', in *Nationalism* (1918; repr., New Delhi: Macmillan, 1985), 67.
26 Tagore, 'Nationalism in India', 68–69.
27 B.R. Ambedkar, Vol. 5 of *Constituent Assembly Debates* (New Delhi: Lok Sabha Secretariat, 2003), 1111.
28 Tagore, 'Nationalism in India', 73.
29 Tagore, 'Nationalism in India', 74.
30 Tagore, 'Nationalism in India', 78.
31 Tagore, 'Nationalism in India', 78.
32 Rabindranath Tagore, 'The Crisis in Civilisation', in Vol. 3 of *The English Writings of Rabindranath Tagore*, ed. Sisir Kumar Das (New Delhi: Sahitya Akademi, 1996), 724.
33 Das, *The English Writings of Rabindranath Tagore*, 725.
34 Das, *The English Writings of Rabindranath Tagore*, 725.
35 Das, *The English Writings of Rabindranath Tagore*, 725.
36 Das, *The English Writings of Rabindranath Tagore*, 725.
37 Das, *The English Writings of Rabindranath Tagore*, 726.
38 Das, *The English Writings of Rabindranath Tagore*, 726.
39 Rabindranath Tagore, 'Institutional Religion', in Vol. 4 of *The English Writings of Rabindranath Tagore*, ed. Nityapriya Ghosh (repr., New Delhi: Sahitya Akademi, 2008), 295–96.
40 Das, *The English Writings of Rabindranath Tagore*, 105.
41 Das, *The English Writings of Rabindranath Tagore*, 120.

42 Das, *The English Writings of Rabindranath Tagore*, 120.
43 Das, *The English Writings of Rabindranath Tagore*, 134.
44 Das, *The English Writings of Rabindranath Tagore*, 134.
45 Das, *The English Writings of Rabindranath Tagore*, 141.
46 Das, *The English Writings of Rabindranath Tagore*, 155.
47 Das, *The English Writings of Rabindranath Tagore*, 157.
48 Das, *The English Writings of Rabindranath Tagore*, 157.
49 Das, *The English Writings of Rabindranath Tagore*, 210.

Chapter 3: Campaigns for Humanizing Humanity

1 Mohandas Karamchand Gandhi, *The Story of My Experiments with Truth* (1929; repr., Ahmedabad: Navajivan Publishing House, 2008), 104.
2 R.K. Narayan, *Waiting for the Mahatma* (1955; repr., Chennai: Indian Thought Publications, 2003), 77–78
3 Mohandas Karamchand Gandhi, 'Satyagraha in South Africa', in Vol. 29 of *The Collected Works of Mahatma Gandhi* (New Delhi: Publications Division, 1999), 38. This discussion is drawn on this tract unless stated otherwise.
4 Mohandas Karamchand Gandhi, in Vol. 3 of *The Collected Works of Mahatma Gandhi* (New Delhi: Publications Division, 1999), 113–14; 119–20.
5 Gandhi, *The Collected Works of Mahatma Gandhi*, Vol. 3, 129.
6 Krishna Kripalani, *Gandhi: A Life* (New Delhi: National Book Trust, 2000), 32.
7 Mohandas Karamchand Gandhi, *The Story of My Experiments with Truth* (1929; repr., Ahmedabad: Navajivan Publishing House, 2008), 177–78.
8 Gandhi, *The Story of My Experiments with Truth*, 178.
9 Gandhi, *Satyagraha in South Africa*, 139.
10 Gandhi, *Satyagraha in South Africa*, 251–52.
11 Gandhi, *Satyagraha in South Africa*, 252.
12 Surendra Bhana and Goolam Vahed, *The Making of a Political Reformer: Gandhi in South Africa, 1893-1914* (New Delhi: Manohar Publishers, 2005), 95.
13 Mohandas Karamchand Gandhi, in Vol. 2 of *The Collected Works of Mahatma Gandhi* (New Delhi: Publications Division, 1999), 6.

14 Gandhi, *The Collected Works of Mahatma Gandhi,* Vol. 2, 6
15 Gandhi, *The Collected Works of Mahatma Gandhi,* Vol. 2, 6
16 Mohandas Karamchand Gandhi, in Vol. 24 of *The Collected Works of Mahatma Gandhi* (New Delhi: Publications Division, 1999), 144.
17 Gandhi, *The Collected Works of Mahatma Gandhi,* Vol. 24, 145–46.
18 Rajendra Prasad, *At the Feet of Mahatma Gandhi* (Bombay: Asia Publishing House, 1961), 7.
19 Jacques Pouchepadass, *Champaran and Gandhi: Planters, Peasants and Gandhian Politics* (New Delhi: Oxford University Press, 1999), 217–18.
20 David Hardiman, *The Nonviolent Struggle for Indian Freedom, 1905-19,* 134.
21 Pouchepadass, *Champaran and Gandhi,* 234.
22 Erik Erickson, *Gandhi's Truth: On the Origins of Militant Nonviolence* (London: Faber & Faber, 1970), 371.
23 Erickson, *Gandhi's Truth,* 378.
24 I have elaborated this aspect Gandhi's politico-ideological vision in my 'Universal Benefit', *Modern Asian Studies* 49, no. 2 (2015).
25 Hardiman, *The Nonviolent Struggle for Indian Freedom, 1905-19,* 157.
26 Jawaharlal Nehru, *An Autobiography* (London: John Lane, The Bodley Head Ltd., 1941), 254–55.
27 Mohandas Karamchand Gandhi, in Vol. 15 of *The Collected Works of Mahatma Gandhi* (New Delhi: Publications Division, 1999), 87–88.
28 Jawaharlal Nehru, *An Autobiography,* 254–55.
29 Gandhi, *The Collected Works of Mahatma Gandhi,* Vol. 15, 155.
30 David Hardiman, T*he Nonviolent Struggle for Indian Freedom, 1905-19* (New Delhi: Oxford University Press, 2021), 11.
31 Michael O'Dyar, 'Manuscript Memoirs' (unpublished manuscript, word file).
32 Ravinder Kumar, ed., *Essays on Gandhian Politics: The Rowlatt Satyagraha of 1919* (Oxford: Clarendon Press, 1971), 337–38.
33 Hardiman, *The Nonviolent Struggle for Indian Freedom, 1905-19,* 173.
34 Gandhi, *The Collected Works of Mahatma Gandhi,* Vol. 15, 155.
35 *Nehru, An Autobiography,* 65–66.
36 Gandhi, *The Collected Works of Mahatma Gandhi,* Vol. 21, 259.
37 Gandhi, *The Collected Works of Mahatma Gandhi,* Vol. 21, 273.
38 Gandhi, *The Collected Works of Mahatma Gandhi,* Vol. 21, 252.
39 Gandhi, *The Collected Works of Mahatma Gandhi,* Vol. 21, 241.
40 Gandhi, *The Collected Works of Mahatma Gandhi,* Vol. 21, 241–42.

41 Sisir Kumar Das, ed., in Vol. 3 of *The English Writings of Rabindranath Tagore* (New Delhi: Sahitya Akademi, 1996), 286.

42 Das, *The English Writings of Rabindranath Tagore,* Vol. 3, 286.

43 Das, *The English Writings of Rabindranath Tagore,* Vol. 3, 287.

44 Judith Brown, *Gandhi's Rise to Power: Indian Politics, 1915-1922* (Cambridge: Cambridge University Press, 1972).

45 Sabyasachi Bhattacharya, ed., *The Mahatma and the Poet: Letters and Debates between Gandhi and Tagore, 1915-1941* (New Delhi: National Book Trust, 1997), 83–84.

46 Bhattacharya, *The Mahatma and the Poet,* 58, 62.

47 Bhattacharya, *The Mahatma and the Poet,* 67–68.

48 Bhattacharya, *The Mahatma and the Poet,* 91.

49 Bhattacharya, *The Mahatma and the Poet,* 65.

50 Because of his involvement in the Swadeshi Movement, Tagore realised, reports Sumit Sarkar, that 'more than 90 per cent of the lower classes have remained entirely indifferent towards the Swadeshi Movement'. Underling the inadequate mass contact, Tagore thus felt 'the need for quiet work in the villages, but few heeded his words of warning and advice [because] young men found constructive work in villages dull and far less attractive than radical politics and eventually terrorism'. Sumit Sarkar, *The Swadeshi Movement in Bengal, 1903-8* (New Delhi: People's Publishing House, 1973), 286.

51 Ranajit Guha, *Dominance without Hegemony: History and Power in Colonial India* (New Delhi: Oxford University Press, 1998), 121.

52 So bitter was Tagore, Guha further reports by quoting from his views, that he hardly concealed his annoyance with the *swadeshi* activists by saying that 'to enforce unity on a person by twisting his neck can hardly be called an action of union; nor, by the same token, can the use of threat or journalistic slander to stop any public airing of disagreement be regarded as working for national unification'. Guha, *Dominance without Hegemony,* 121.

53 Although Tagore had reservations about Gandhi's views on the social and political goal of the Non-cooperation Movement, he appreciated the Mahatma by saying that he 'has won the heart of India with his love; for that we have all acknowledged his sovereignty. He has given us a vision of the *shakti* of Truth; for that our gratitude to him is unbounded'. Bhattacharya, *The Mahatma and the Poet,* 79.

54 Bhattacharya, *The Mahatma and the Poet,* 101–2. On another occasion, Tagore remarked that Gandhi's insistence on *charkha* as complementary to *swaraj* was harmful to the campaign for *swaraj*. In his words, 'a man like the Mahatma may succeed in getting some of our countrymen to make an interest in this kind of uninspiring nature for a time because of their faith in his personal greatness of soul. To obey him is for them an end in itself. To me it seems that such a state of mind is not helpful for the attainment of *swaraj*'. Bhattacharya, *The Mahatma and the Poet,* 119.

55 Bhattacharya, *The Mahatma and the Poet,* 104–5.

56 Bhattacharya, *The Mahatma and the Poet,* 118.

57 Bhattacharya, *The Mahatma and the Poet,* 115.

58 Bhattacharya, *The Mahatma and the Poet,* 118.

59 Bhattacharya, *The Mahatma and the Poet,* 121.

60 Bhattacharya, *The Mahatma and the Poet,* 121.

61 Bhattacharya, *The Mahatma and the Poet,* 123.

62 Bhattacharya, *The Mahatma and the Poet,* 125.

63 Bhattacharya, *The Mahatma and the Poet,* 124.

64 Bhattacharya, *The Mahatma and the Poet,* 125.

65 According to Gandhi, '*khadi* should be linked with liberty. All the time you are spinning, you would not think in terms of your own requirements, but in terms of the requirements of the nation. You will say, "I want to clothe the whole nation that is naked and I must do it non-violently". Each time you draw a thread, say to your selves, "we are drawing the thread of *swaraj*". Multiply this picture million-fold and you have freedom knocking at your door'. Gandhi, *The Collected Works of Mahatma Gandhi,* Vol. 68, 133.

66 Gandhi like the poet also believed in the wider application of *charkha*. In his words, 'Round the *charkha*, that is amidst the people who have shed their idleness and who have understood the value of cooperation, a national servant would build up a programme of anti-malaria campaign, improved sanitation, settlement of village disputes, conservation and breeding of cattle and hundreds of other beneficial activities. Wherever *charkha* work is fairly established, all such ameliorative activity is going according to the capacity of the villagers and the workers concerned'. Bhattacharya, *The Mahatma and the Poet,* 126.

67 Jawaharlal Nehru, *The Discovery of India* (New Delhi: Oxford University Press, 1989), 358–59.

68 Mohandas Karamchand Gandhi, in Vol. 17, *The Collected Works of Mahatma Gandhi* (New Delhi: Publications Division, 1999), 483.

69 Mohandas Karamchand Gandhi, in Vol. 18, *The Collected Works of Mahatma Gandhi* (New Delhi: Publications Divisions, 1999), 483, 489.

70 Judith Brown, *Gandhi's Rise to Power* (Cambridge: Cambridge University Press, 1972), 246.

71 Shahid Amin, *Event, Metaphor, Memory: Chauri Chaura, 1922-1992* (New Delhi: Oxford University Press, 1995), 16.

72 Mohandas Karamchand Gandhi, in Vol. 43 of *The Collected Works of Mahatma Gandhi* (New Delhi: Publications Divisions, 1999), 117.

73

> (1) total prohibition; (2) reduction of the rupee ration to 1s 4d; (3) reduction of land revenue by at least 50 per cent and making it subject of legislative control; (4) abolition of the salt tax; (5) reduction of the military expenditure by at least 50 per cent; (6) reduction of the salaries of the highest grade service to one half or less so as to suit the reduced revenue; (7) imposition of protective tariff on foreign cloth; (8) passage of the Coastal Tariff Reservation Bill; (9) discharge of all political prisoners save those condemned for murder, withdrawal of all political prosecutions and abrogation of Section 124-A, Regulation III of 1818 and the like and permission of all Indian exiles to return; (10) abolition of the CID or its popular control and (11) issue of licenses to use firearms for self-defence, subject to popular control.

Mohandas Karamchand Gandhi, in Vol. 48 of *The Collected Works of Mahatma Gandhi* (New Delhi: Publications Division, 1999), 404–5.

74 Nehru, *An Autobiography*, 210.

75 India Office Records, L/PJ/1930-193, Irwin to the Secretary of the State, Wedgewood Benn, 3 May 1930.

76 Nehru, *An Autobiography*, 215.

77 Mohandas Karamchand Gandhi, in Vol. 23 of *The Collected Works of Mahatma Gandhi* (New Delhi: Publications Division, 1999), 127.

78 Mohandas Karamchand Gandhi, in Vol. 48 of *The Collected Works of Mahatma Gandhi* (New Delhi: Publications Division, 1999), 427

79 Mohandas Karamchand Gandhi, in Vol. 50 of *The Collected Works of Mahatma Gandhi* (New Delhi: Publications Division, 1999), 279.

80 India Office Records, Halifax Papers, Mss. Eur, C 152 (25), Tej Bahadur Sapru to Irwin, 19 September 1930.
81 Mohandas Karamchand Gandhi, in Vol. 51 of *The Collected Works of Mahatma Gandhi* (New Delhi: Publications Division, 1999), 74.
82 Gandhi, *The Collected Works of Mahatma Gandhi,* Vol. 51, 74.
83 Gandhi, *The Collected Works of Mahatma Gandhi,* Vol. 48, 429.
84 I have dealt with this aspect of the collaboration between Gandhi and the African-American Gandhians in my *Confluence of Thought: Mahatma Gandhi and Martin Luther King Jr.* (New York, NY: Oxford University Press, 2013).
85 Mohandas Karamchand Gandhi, in Vol. 83 of *The Collected Works of Mahatma Gandhi* (New Delhi: Publications Division, 1999), 156.
86 Gandhi, *The Collected Works of Mahatma Gandhi,* Vol. 83, 198.
87 Gandhi, *The Collected Works of Mahatma Gandhi,* Vol. 86, 19.
88 Gandhi, *The Collected Works of Mahatma Gandhi,* Vol. 83, 200.
89 Nehru, *The Discovery of India,* 475.
90 Tottenham, *Congress Responsibility*, 68
91 Tottenham, *Congress Responsibility,* 62.
92 Gandhi, *The Collected Works of Mahatma Gandhi,* Vol. 83, 197.
93 Gandhi, *The Collected Works of Mahatma Gandhi,* Vol. 83, 197–98, 403. Gandhi, *The Collected Works of Mahatma Gandhi,* Vol. 83, 403.
94 India Office Records, L/PO/6/1O2A, Viceroy to the Secretary of State, 9 August 1942.
95 India Office Records, 9 August 1942.
96 India Office Records, 9 August 1942.
97 India Office Records, 9 August 1942.
98 Martin Luther King Jr., 'Love, Law and Civil Disobedience', in *A Testament of Hope* (New York: HarperCollins, 1986), 47.
99 Martin Luther King Jr, *Stride Towards Freedom: A Montgomery Story* (New York: HarperCollins, 1958), 102.
100 King Jr., 'Love, Law and Civil Disobedience' 47.
101 Martin Luther King Jr., *Stride Towards Freedom: A Montgomery Story* (New York: HarperCollins, 1958), 171–72.
102 Mohandas Karamchand Gandhi, in Vol. 77 of *Collected Works of Mahatma Gandhi* (New Delhi: Publication Division, 1999), 73.
103 Mohandas Karamchand Gandhi, in Vol. 49 of *The Collected Works of Mahatma Gandhi* (New Delhi: Publications Division, 1999), 17.

104 Gandhi, *Hind Swaraj or Indian Home Rule*, 44.

105 Gandhi, *Hind Swaraj or Indian Home Rule*, 44.

106 Gandhi, *Hind Swaraj or Indian Home Rule*, 44.

Chapter 4: Conceptualizing Humanizing Humanity

1 I have dealt with this aspect of Gandhian mode of opposition in my *Local Politics and Indian Nationalism: Midnapur, 1919-1944* (New Delhi: Manohar Publishers, 1997).

2 Mohandas Karamchand Gandhi, in Vol. 21 of *The Complete Works of Mahatma Gandhi* (New Delhi: Publications Division, 1999), 133.

3 David Hardiman, *The Nonviolent Struggle for Indian Freedom, 1905-19* (Gurgaon: Penguin Books, 2018), 168.

4 Hardiman, *The Nonviolent Struggle for Indian Freedom*, 168.

5 Gandhi, in Vol. 21 of *The Complete Works of Mahatma Gandhi,* 134.

6 Gandhi, in Vol. 21 of *The Complete Works of Mahatma Gandhi*, 134–35.

7 Mohandas Karamchand Gandhi, 'Ahimsa or Love', vol. IV of *The Selected Works of Mahatma Gandhi: The Basic Works* (1968; repr., New Delhi: Publications Divisions, 1994), 218.

8 Mohandas Karamchand Gandhi, vol. 15 of *The Collected Works of Mahatma Gandhi* (New Delhi: Publications Divisions, 1999), 254.

9 Mohandas Karamchand Gandhi, vol. 21 of *The Collected Works of Mahatma Gandhi* (New Delhi: Publications Divisions, 1999), 135.

10 Gandhi, *The Collected Works of Mahatma Gandhi,* Vol. 15, 317.

11 Mohandas Karamchand Gandhi, *My Experiments with Truth* (Ahmedabad: Navajivana Publications, 1927), 83.

12 Gandhi, *My Experiments with Truth,* 82.

13 Gandhi, *My Experiments with Truth,* 83.

14 These ideas are collated from Gandhi's own assessment of Raychandbhai which he articulated in his *Autobiography*. Gandhi, *My Experiments with Truth,* 188–95.

15 Gandhi, *My Experiments with Truth,* 127.

16 Gandhi, *My Experiments with Truth,* 274–75.

17 Gandhi, *My Experiments with Truth,* 4.

18 Gandhi, *My Experiments with Truth,* 83.

19 Gandhi, *My Experiments with Truth,* 83.

20 Mahadeva Desai, *Mahadev Desai's Diary*, Vol. VII (1953; repr., Varanasi, Uttar Pradesh: Sarva Seva Sangh Prakashan, 2019), 236.

21 Mahadeva Desai, *Mahadev Desai's Diary*, Vol. VIII (1953; repr., Varanasi, Uttar Pradesh: Sarva Seva Sangh Prakashan, 2019), 48.
22 Leo Tolstoy, 'A letter to Hindu', *Free Hindustan*, 14 December 1908.
23 Gandhi, *My Experiments with Truth,* 274.
24 Gandhi, *My Experiments with Truth*, 275.
25 Mohandas Karamchand Gandhi, Vol. 34 of *The Collected Works of Mahatma Gandhi* (New Delhi: Publications Division, 1999), 399.
26 Edward Carpenter, *Civilization: Its Cause and Cure and Other Essays* (1889; repr., Charleston, South Carolina: Bibliobazaar, 2008), 181.
27 Edward Carpenter, *Civilization: Its Cause and Cure and Other Essays* (London: Swan Sonneschein & Co, 1889), 33.
28 Carpenter, *Civilization,* 49.
29 Gandhi, *My Experiments with Truth,* 31.
30 Gandhi, *My Experiments with Truth,* 63.
31 Gandhi, *My Experiments with Truth,* 31.
32 Mohandas Karamchand Gandhi, Vol. 9 of *The Collected Works of Mahatma Gandhi* (New Delhi: Publications Division, 1999), 337.
33 Mohandas Karamchand Gandhi, *Hind Swaraj* (Ahmedabad: Navajivan Publications, 2006), 45.
34 Gandhi, *Hind Swaraj,* 45.
35 With a remarkable clarity of vision, Rabindranath Tagore succinctly wrote about his views on nation in a rather small piece, entitled *Nation Ki* (Bengali). During his lecture tour in America, 1916–1917, he elaborated some of these points, including his views on nationalism in India, see Rabindranath Tagore, *Nationalism* (1917; repr., New Delhi: Rupa Publications, 1994), 77–79.
36 Tagore, *Nationalism,* 89.
37 Sabyasachi Bhattacharyya, ed., *The Mahatma and the Poet: Letters and Debates between Gandhi and Tagore, 1915–1941* (New Delhi: National Book Trust, 1997), 172.
38 Ashis Nandy, *The Illegitimacy of Nationalism* (New Delhi: Oxford University Press, 1994), 89.
39 Tagore, *Nationalism,* 90.
40 The Congress dismissed Jinnah's demand for parity because 'in numerical terms this meant the equation of minority with majority which was both absurd and politically impossible'. To this Jinnah retorted that 'the debate was not about numbers nor even about communities but

about Nations. Nations were equal irrespective of the size'. For details of Jinnah's argument, see Diana Mansergh, ed., *Independence Years: The Selected Indian and Commonwealth Papers of Nicholas Mansergh* (New Delhi: Oxford University Press, 1999), 227–30.

41 Jinnah's Presidential address in the 1940 Lahore session of the All India Muslim League. Syed Sharifuddin Pirzada, ed., *Foundations of Pakistan*, Vol. II (Karachi: National Publishing House, 1970), 337.

42 Ayesha Jalal, 'Nation, Reason and Religion; Punjab's Role in the Partition of India', in *Economic and Political Weekly* (1998): 2185.

43 Paul Brass, *Ethnicity and Nationalism: Theory and Comparison* (New Delhi: Sage Publications, 1991), 94.

44 Mohammad Ali Jinnah, 'MA Jinnah's Press Statement', *The Dawn*, 1 August 1946, 7.

45 Nirmal Kumar Bose and P.H. Patwardhan, *Gandhi in Indian Politics* (Mumbai: Asia Publishing House, 1967), 7.

46 Rabindranath Tagore was critical of the nationalist leaders for having not defined the concept of *swaraj* in a meaningful way. In his words, 'our political leaders have refrained from giving us a clear explanation of what is *swaraj*'. Sabyasachi Bhattacharya, ed., *The Mahatma and the Poet: Letter and Debates between Gandhi and Tagore, 1915-1941* (New Delhi: National Book Trust, 1997), 114.

47 Barrington Moore, Jr., *Social Origins of dictatorship and Democracy: Lord and Peasant in the Making of the Modern World* (Boston: Beacon Press, 1966), 373–74.

48 Mohandas Karamchand Gandhi, Vol. 42 of *The Collected Works of Mahatma Gandhi* (New Delhi: Publications Division, 1999), 469.

49 Anthony Parel, ed., *Hind Swaraj and Other Writings* (Cambridge: Cambridge University Press, 1997), 90.

50 Bipan Chandra et al., *India's Struggle for Independence* (New Delhi: Viking Press, 1988), 92.

51 Chandra, *India's Struggle for Freedom*, 96.

52 Bipan Chandra, *Nationalism and Colonialism in Modern India* (New Delhi: Orient Longman, 1979), 110.

53 Chandra *India's Struggle for Independence*, 94.

54 Chandra, *India's Struggle for Independence*, 96–98.

55 Philosophically, Gandhi drew on 'methodological individualism' where individual is a relevant unit of account because it is individuals who

reason, have moral sense and exercise choice. As Gandhi believed that 'if the individual ceases to count what left of society' he had little sympathy with the holistic notion 'that society is ontologically prior to the individual'. Ajit Dasgupta, *Gandhi's Economic Thought* (London: Routledge, 1996), 182–83.

56 Chandra, *India's Struggle for Independence,* 100.

57 Chandra, *India's Struggle for Independence,* 547.

58 Bal Ram Nanda, *The Moderate Era in Indian Politics* (New Delhi: Oxford University Press, 1983), 14.

59 Nanda, *The Moderate Era in Indian Politics,* 4–5.

60 Joginder Singh Dhanki, ed., *Perspectives on Indian National Movement: Selected Correspondence of Lala Lajpat Rai* (New Delhi: National Book Organization, 1998), 119.

61 Dhanki, *Perspectives on Indian National Movement,* 120.

62 Bipin Chandra Pal, *Swadeshi and Swaraj* (Calcutta: Dasgupta & Company, 1954), 117–18. This volume contains Pal's 1907 Madras speeches entitled 'the new movement, 'the gospel of *swaraj*', and '*swaraj*'.

63 Aurobindo Ghose, *Bande Mataram,* 11 May 1907, 7.

64 Thomas Pantham and Kenneth L. Deutsch, eds, *Political Thought in Modern India* (New Delhi: Sage Publications, 1986), 114.

65 Pantham and Deutsch, *Political Thought in Modern India,* 116.

66 Raghavan Iyer, ed., *The Moral and Political Writings of Mahatma Gandhi,* Vol. iii (Oxford: Clarendon Press, 1986), 275.

67 Mohandas Karamchand Gandhi, Vol. 51 of *The Collected Works of Mahatma Gandhi* (New Delhi: Publications Division, 1999), 220.

68 Gandhi, *The Collected Works of Mahatma Gandhi,* Vol. 23, 71–72.

69 Gandhi, *Hind Swaraj,* 73.

70 Ramchandra Gandhi, 'The Swaraj of India', *Indian Philosophical Quarterly* 11, no. 4 (1984): 461.

71 Guha, 'The Swaraj of India', 461.

72 Guha, 'The Swaraj of India', 462.

73 Krishna Chandra Bhattacharya, 'Swaraj in Ideas', *Indian Philosophical Quarterly* 11, no. 4 (1984): 383.

74 Bhattacharya, 'Swaraj in Ideas', 385–86.

75 Anthony J. Parel, ed., *Gandhi, Freedom and Self-rule* (New Delhi: Vistaar, 2000), 17.

76 Fred Dallmayr, 'What is Swaraj? Two Conflicting Visions', ed. Anthony J. Parel, *Gandhi, Freedom and Self-rule* (New Delhi: Vistaar, 2000), 111.

77 Parekh, *Gandhi*, 81.

78 Mohandas Karamchand Gandhi, Vol. 69 of *The Complete Works of Gandhi* (New Delhi: Publications Division, 1977), 333–34.

79 Mohandas Karamchand Gandhi, in Vol. 69 of *The Complete Works of Mahatma Gandhi* (New Delhi: Publications Divisions, 1999), 334.

80 Mohandas Karamchand Gandhi, Vol. V of *The Selected Works of Mahatma Gandhi, Selected Letters* (1968; repr., Ahmedabad: Navajivan Publishing House, 1995), 298.

81 Nehru, *A Bunch of Old Letters,* 43.

82 Gandhi, *The Selected Works of Mahatma Gandhi, Selected Letters,* Vol. V, 362.

83 Chatterjee, *Gandhi's Religious Thought,* 181.

84 Chatterjee, *Gandhi's Religious Thought,* 181.

85 Gandhi, *My Experiments with Truth*, 31.

86 Gandhi, in Vol. 21 of *The Collected Works of Mahatma Gandhi,* 241.

87 Gandhi, in Vol. 21 of *The Collected Works of Mahatma Gandhi,* 241.

88 Gandhi, in Vol. 21 of *The Collected Works of Mahatma Gandhi,* 241.

89 Sibnarayan Ray, Vol. II of *Selected works of MN Roy* (New Delhi: Oxford University Press, 2000), 101.

90 Mohandas Karamchand Gandhi, Vol. 21 of *The Collected Works of Mahatma Gandhi* (New Delhi: Publications Division, 1999), 134–35.

91 Gandhi, in Vol. 21 of *The Collected Works of Mahatma Gandhi,* 459.

92 Judith Brown, *Nehru: A Political Life* (New Delhi: Oxford University Press, 2004), 223.

93 Brown, *Nehru,* 223.

94 Brown, *Nehru*, 223.

95 Anthony Parel makes this point while explaining the meaning which Gandhi attributed to *swaraj* in a monograph that included Gandhi's *Hind Swaraj*. Parel, *Hind Swaraj and Other Writings*, 73.

96 Ruth Harris, *The Life and Legacy of Vivekananda* (Cambridge, Massachusetts: Harvard University Press, 2022), 382.

97 Akhandananda, *Service of God in Man* (Chennai: Sri Ramkrishna Math, 2013), 62.

98 Harris, *The Life and Legacy of Vivekananda*, 389.

99 Harris, *The Life and Legacy of Vivekananda*, 401.

100 Dennis Dalton, *No Violence in Action: Gandhi's Power* (1995; repr., New Delhi: Oxford University Press, 1998), 16–17.
101 Parel, *Hind Swaraj and Other Writings*, 7.
102 Ashis Nandy, *The Intimate Enemy: Loss and Recovery of Self under Colonialism* (New Delhi: Oxford University Press, 1983).
103 Parel, ed., *Hind Swaraj and Other Writings,* 39–41.
104 Nandy, *The Intimate Enemy,* 48.
105 Mohandas Karamchand Gandhi, *Hind Swaraj or Indian Home Rule*, (1929; repr., Ahmedabad: Navajivan Publishing House, 2006), 107.
106 Gandhi, *Hind Swaraj or Indian Home Rule,* 111.
107 Gandhi, *Hind Swaraj or Indian Home Rule*, 108.
108 Partha Chatterjee, *Nationalist Thought and the Colonial World: A Derivative Discourse* (New Delhi: Oxford University Press, 1986), 87.

Chapter 5: Reconceptualization of Humanizing Humanity

1 Gyanendra Pandey, *A History of Prejudice: Caste and Difference in India and USA* (New York: Cambridge University Press, 2013), 26.
2 Pandey, *A History of Prejudice,* 16.
3 Bhikhu Parekh, 'The Intellectual and Political Legacy of BR Ambedkar', in Vol. I of *BR Ambedkar: The Quest for Justice,* ed. Aakash Singh Rathore (New Delhi: Oxford University Press, 2021), 3.
4 Bhimrao Ramji Ambedkar, 'The Indian Ghetto—The Centre of Untouchability: Outside the Fold', comp., Vasant Moon, Vol. 5 of *Dr. Babasaheb Ambedkar Writings and Speeches* (1979; repr., Mumbai: Education Department, Government of Maharashtra, 2014), 25.
5 Ambedkar, 'The Indian Ghetto', Vol. 5, 26.
6 Bhimrao Ramji Ambedkar, 'Untouchability and Lawlessness', comp.,Vasant Moon, Vol. 5 of *Dr. Babasaheb Ambedkar Writings and Speeches* (1979; repr., Mumbai: Education Department, Government of Maharashtra, 2014), 55.
7 Bhimrao Ramji Ambedkar, 'The Hindu and his Belief in Caste', comp., Vasant Moon, Vol. 5 of *Dr. Babasaheb Ambedkar Writings and Speeches* (1979; repr., Mumbai: Education Department, Government of Maharashtra, 2014), 102.
8 Bhimrao Ramji Ambedkar, 'Problems of Discrimination', comp., Vasant Moon, Vol. 5 of *Dr. Babasaheb Ambedkar Writings and Speeches* (1979; repr., Mumbai: Education Department, Government of Maharashtra, 2014), 111.

9 Bhimrao Ramji Ambedkar, 'The Untouchables: Untouchability among Hindus', comp., Vasant Moon, Vol. 5 of *Dr. Babasaheb Ambedkar Writings and Speeches* (1979; repr., Mumbai: Education Department, Government of Maharshtra, 2014), 266.

10 Ambedkar, 'The Untouchables', Vol. 7, 266.

11 Ambedkar, 'The Untouchables', Vol. 7, 266–67.

12 Bhimrao Ramji Ambedkar, *Mr. Gandhi and Emancipation of Untouchables* (Jalandhar: Bheem Patrika Publications, 1943), 196–67.

13 Bhimrao Ramji Ambedkar, 'I Have No Homeland', comp., Vasant Moon, Vol. 17 (part 1) of *Dr. Babasaheb Ambedkar Writings and Speeches* (1979; repr., Mumbai: Education Department, Government of Maharashtra, 2014), 53–54.

14 Bhimrao Ramji Ambedkar, 'Slaves and Untouchables', comp., Vasant Moon, Vol. 5 of *Dr. Babasaheb Ambedkar Writings and Speeches* (1979; repr., Mumbai: Education Department, Government of Maharashtra, 2014), 18.

15 Bhimrao Ramji Ambedkar, 'Untouchability', comp., Vasant Moon, Vol. 3 of *Dr. Babasaheb Ambedkar Writings and Speeches* (1979; repr., Mumbai: Education Department, Government of Maharashtra, 2014), 105.

16 Bhimrao Ramji Ambedkar, 'What Congress and Gandhi Have Done to the Untouchables: A False Charge', comp., Vasant Moon, Vol. 9 of *Dr. Babasaheb Ambedkar Writings and Speeches* (1979; repr., Mumbai: Education Department, Government of Maharashtra, 2014), 168.

17 Ambedkar, 'What Congress and Gandhi Have Done to the Untouchables', Vol. 9, 168.

18 Ambedkar, 'What Congress and Gandhi Have Done to the Untouchables', Vol. 9, 169.

19 Ambedkar, 'What Congress and Gandhi Have Done to the Untouchables', Vol. 9, 89.

20 Ambedkar, 'What Congress and Gandhi Have Done to the Untouchables', Vol. 9, 291.

21 Ambedkar, 'What Congress and Gandhi Have Done to the Untouchables', Vol. 9, 312.

22 Ambedkar, 'What Congress and Gandhi Have Done to the Untouchables', Vol. 9, 317.

23 Ambedkar, 'What Congress and Gandhi Have Done to the Untouchables', Vol. 9, 119–20.

24 Ambedkar, 'What Congress and Gandhi Have Done to the Untouchables', Vol. 9, 190–91.
25 Ambedkar, 'What Congress and Gandhi Have Done to the Untouchables', Vol. 9, 191.
26 Ambedkar, 'What Congress and Gandhi Have Done to the Untouchables', Vol. 9, 412.
27 Ambedkar, 'What Congress and Gandhi Have Done to the Untouchables', Vol. 9, 413.
28 Ambedkar, 'What Congress and Gandhi Have Done to the Untouchables', Vol. 9, 414.
29 Bhimrao Ramji Ambedkar, 'Dr. Babasaheb Ambedkar: Writings and Speeches', comp., Vasant Moon, Vol. 9 of *Dr. Babasaheb Ambedkar Writings and Speeches* (1979; repr., Mumbai: Education Department, Government of Maharashtra, 2014), 419.
30 Ambedkar, *Dr. Babasaheb Ambedkar*, Vol. 9, 419.
31 Ambedkar, *Dr. Babasaheb Ambedkar*, Vol. 9, 420.
32 Ambedkar, *Dr. Babasaheb Ambedkar*, Vol. 9, 420.
33 Ambedkar, *Dr. Babasaheb Ambedkar*, Vol. 9, 430–31.
34 Ambedkar, *Dr. Babasaheb Ambedkar*, Vol. 9, 31.
35 Bhimrao Ramji Ambedkar, 'Mr. Gandhi and the Emancipation of the Untouchables', comp., Vasant Moon, Vol. 9 of *Dr. Babasaheb Ambedkar Writings and Speeches* (1979; repr., Mumbai: Education Department, Government of Maharashtra, 2014), 431.
36 Ambedkar, 'Mr. Gandhi and the Emancipation of the Untouchables', Vol. 9, 431–32.
37 Bhimrao Ramji Ambedkar, 'What Congress and Gandhi Have Done to the Untouchables: A Plea to the Foreigner', comp., Vasant Moon, Vol. 9 of *Dr. Babasaheb Ambedkar Writings and Speeches* (1979; repr., Mumbai: Education Department, Government of Maharashtra, 2014), 444.
38 Ambedkar, 'What Congress and Gandhi Have Done to the Untouchables', Vol. 9, 444.
39 Ambedkar, 'What Congress and Gandhi Have Done to the Untouchables', Vol. 9, 444.
40 Ambedkar, 'What Congress and Gandhi Have Done to the Untouchables', Vol. 9, 467.
41 Ambedkar, 'What Congress and Gandhi Have Done to the Untouchables', Vol. 9, 467.

42 Ambedkar, 'What Congress and Gandhi Have Done to the Untouchables', Vol. 9, 468–69.

43 Ambedkar, 'What Congress and Gandhi Have Done to the Untouchables', Vol. 9, 488.

44 Bhimrao Ramji Ambedkar, *Annihilation of Caste,* comp., Vasant Moon Vol. 1 of *Dr. Babasaheb Ambedkar: Writings and Speeches* (1979; repr., Mumbai: Education Department, Government of Maharashtra, 2014), 47.

45 Bhimrao Ramji Ambedkar, 'Philosophy of Hinduism', comp., Vasant Moon in Vol. 3 of *Dr. Babasaheb Ambedkar: Writings and Speeches* (1979; repr., Mumbai: Education Department, Government of Maharashtra, 2014), 87.

46 Ambedkar, 'Philosophy of Hinduism', Vol. 3, 25.

47 Ambedkar, 'Philosophy of Hinduism', Vol. 3, 44.

48 Bhimrao Ramji Ambedkar, 'JS Mill and Equality', comp., Vasant Moon in Vol. 3 of *Dr. Babasaheb Ambedkar: Writings and Speeches* (1979; repr., Mumbai: Education Department, Government of Maharashtra, 2014), 44–45.

49 Ambedkar, 'Philosophy of Hinduism', Vol. 3, 45.

50 Ambedkar, 'Philosophy of Hinduism', Vol. 3, 65.

51 Ambedkar, 'Philosophy of Hinduism', Vol. 3, 68–69.

52 Ambedkar, *Annihilation of Caste,* Vol. 3, 111.

53 Ambedkar, 'The Hindu Social Order', Vol. 3, 111.

54 Ambedkar, 'The Hindu Social Order', 115.

55 Ambedkar, 'The Hindu Social Order', Vol. 3, 115.

56 Bhimrao Ramji Ambedkar, 'Ranande,Gandhi and Jinnah', comp., Vasant Moon, Vol. 1 of *Dr. Babasaheb Ambedkar: Writings and Speeches* (1979; repr., Mumbai: Education Department, Government of Maharashtra, 2014), 216.

57 Ambedkar, 'Ranade, Gandhi and Jinnah', Vol. 1, 217.

58 Ambedkar, 'Ranade, Gandhi and Jinnah', Vol. 1, 217.

59 Ambedkar, 'Ranade, Gandhi and Jinnah', Vol. 1, 217.

60 Ambedkar, 'Ranade, Gandhi and Jinnah', Vol. 1, 218.

61 Ambedkar, 'Ranade, Gandhi and Jinnah', Vol. 1, 218.

62 Ambedkar, 'Ranade, Gandhi and Jinnah', Vol. 1, 218.

63 Ambedkar, 'Ranade, Gandhi and Jinnah', Vol. 1, 218.

64 Ambedkar, 'Ranade, Gandhi and Jinnah', Vol. 1, 218–19.

65 Ambedkar, 'Ranade, Gandhi and Jinnah', Vol. 1, 219.

66 Ambedkar, 'Ranade, Gandhi and Jinnah', Vol. 1, 219.
67 Ambedkar, 'Ranade, Gandhi and Jinnah', Vol. 1, 223.
68 Ambedkar, 'Ranade, Gandhi and Jinnah', Vol. 1, 223.
69 Ambedkar, 'Ranade, Gandhi and Jinnah', Vol. 1, 223.
70 Ambedkar, *Annihilation of Caste,* Vol. 1, 27.
71 Vasant Moon, comp., Vol. 1 of *Dr. Babasaheb Ambedkar: Writings and Speeches* (1979; repr Mumbai: Education Department, Government of Maharashtra, 2014), 31.
72 Moon, *Dr. Babasaheb Ambedkar,* Vol. 1, 31.
73 Moon, *Dr. Babasaheb Ambedkar*, Vol. 1, 31.
74 Moon, *Dr. Babasaheb Ambedkar*, Vol. 1, 31.
75 Moon, *Dr. Babasaheb Ambedkar*, Vol. 1, 34.
76 Ambedkar, *Annihilation of Caste,* Vol. 1, 66.
77 Ambedkar, *Annihilation of Caste,* Vol. 1, 67.
78 Ambedkar, *Annihilation of Caste,* Vol. 1, 67.
79 Ambedkar, *Annihilation of Caste,* Vol.1, 68.
80 Ambedkar, *Annihilation of Caste,* Vol. 1, 68.
81 Ambedkar, *Annihilation of Caste,* Vol. 1, 76.
82 Ambedkar, *Annihilation of Caste,* Vol. 1, 76.
83 Ambedkar, *Annihilation of Caste,* Vol. 1, 79.
84 Moon, *Dr, Babasaheb Ambedkar,* Vol. 1, 87.
85 Rabindranath Tagore, 'Institutional Religion', ed., Nityapriya Ghosh, Vol. 4 of *The English Writings of Rabindranath Tagore* (New Delhi: Sahitya Akademi, 2008), 295–96.
86 Moon, *Dr. Babasaheb Ambedkar,* Vol. 1, 83–84.
87 Moon, *Dr. Babasaheb Ambedkar,* Vol. 1, 87.
88 Moon, *Dr. Babasaheb Ambedkar,* Vol. 1, 91.
89 Moon, *Dr. Babasaheb Ambedkar,* Vol. 1, 94.
90 Aishwary Kumar pursued this argument in his *Radical Equality: Ambedkar, Gandhi and the Risk of Democracy* (Stanford: Stanford University Press, 2015).

Chapter 6: Humanizing Humanity through Constitutional Liberalism

1 Rasalind O'Hanlon, *Caste, Conflict and Ideology: Mahatma Jotirao Phule and Low Caste Protest in Nineteenth Century Western India* (Cambridge: Cambridge University Press, 1985), 189–254.

2 Bhimrao Ramji Ambedkar, *Annihilation of Caste,* comp., Vasant Moon, in Vol. 1. of Dr. *Babasaheb Ambedkar Writings and Speeches* (1979; repr., Mumbai: Education Department, Government of Maharashtra, 2014), 56.

3 Ambedkar, *Annihilation of Caste,* Vol. 1, 56.

4 Bhimrao Ramji Ambedkar, 'Ranade, Gandhi and Jinnah', comp., Vasant Moon, in Vol. 1. of Dr. *Babasaheb Ambedkar Writings and Speeches* (1979; repr., Mumbai: Education Department, Government of Maharashtra, 2014), 221.

5 Ambedkar, 'Ranade, Gandhi and Jinnah', Vol. 1, 222.

6 Ambedkar, 'Ranade, Gandhi and Jinnah', Vol. 1, 222.

7 Ambedkar, 'Ranade, Gandhi and Jinnah', Vol. 1, 222.

8 Ambedkar, 'Ranade, Gandhi and Jinnah', Vol. 1, 222.

9 Bhimrao Ramji Ambedkar, 'Ranade, Gandhi and Jinnah', comp., Vasant Moon, in Vol. 9. of Dr. *Babasaheb Ambedkar Writings and Speeches* (1979; repr., Mumbai: Education Department, Government of Maharashtra, 2014), 202.

10 Ambedkar, 'What Congress and Gandhi Have Done to the Untouchables: A Plea to the Foreigners', Vol. 9, 203–4.

11 Ambedkar, 'Ranade, Gandhi and Jinnah', Vol. 1, 230.

12 Ambedkar, 'Ranade, Gandhi and Jinnah', Vol. 1, 231.

13 Bhimrao Ramji Ambedkar, in Vol. 5. of *Constituent Assembly Debates* (New Delhi: Lok Sabha Secretariat, 2003), 975.

14 Aishwary Kumar, *Radical Equality: Ambedkar, Gandhi and the Risk of Democracy* (Stanford: Stanford University Press, 2015), 224.

15 Ambedkar, *Annihilation of Caste,* Vol. 1, 72.

16 Ambedkar, *Annihilation of Caste,* Vol. 1, 72.

17 Ambedkar, *Annihilation of Caste,* Vol. 1, 72.

18 Ambedkar, *Annihilation of Caste,* Vol. 1, 72–73.

19 Ambedkar, *Annihilation of Caste,* Vol. 1, 63.

20 Bhimrao Ramji Ambedkar, 'State and Minorities', comp., by Vasant Moon in Vol. 1 of *Dr. Babasaheb Ambedkar: Writings and Speeches* (1979; repr., Mumbai: Education Department, Government of Maharashtra, 2014), 425.

21 Ambedkar, 'State and Minorities', Vol. 1, 426.

22 Ambedkar, 'State and Minorities', Vol. 1, 426.

23 Ambedkar, 'State and Minorities', Vol. 1, 426.

24 B.R. Ambedkar, "Gandhism" in *The Essential Writings of BR Ambedkar*, ed. Valerian Rodrigues (New Delhi: Oxford University Press, 2002), 165.

25 Mohandas Karamchand Gandhi, 'The Sin of Untouchability', in *What is Hinduism* (New Delhi: National Book Trust, 2001), 115.

26 BR Ambedkar, 'Outside the Fold', in *The Essential Writings of BR Ambedkar*, ed. Valerian Rodrigues (New Delhi: Oxford University Press, 2002), 331.

27 Gandhi's idea of village *swaraj* is that

> it is completely republic, independent of its neighbours for its own vital wants, and yet interdependent for many others in which dependence is a necessity. Thus, every villager's first concern will be to grow its own food crops and cotton for its cloth. ... The government of the village will be conducted by a panchayat of five persons, annually elected by the adult villagers, male and female, possessing minimum prescribed qualifications.

Mohandas Karamchand Gandhi, in Vol. 83 of *The Collected Works of Mahatma Gandhi* (New Delhi: Publications Division, 1942), 308–9.

28 Surinder S. Jodhika, 'Nation and Village: Images of rural India in Gandhi, Nehru and Ambedkar', *Economic and Political Weekly*, 10 August 2002.

29 T.K. Oommen, 'Gandhi and Village: Towards a Critical Appraisal', in *Economic and Social Principles of Mahatma Gandhi*, ed. Subrata Mukherjee and Sushila Ramaswamy (New Delhi: Deep & Deep, 1998), 226.

30 Gauri Viswanathan, *Outside the Fold: Conversion, Modernity and Belief* (New Delhi: Oxford University Press, 1998), 238.

31 B.R. Ambedkar, *The Untouchables: Who Were They? And Why They Became Untouchables*? (New Delhi: Amrit Book Company, 1948), 21–22.

32 Judith Brown, 'The Mahatma and Modern India', *Modern Asian Studies*, 3, no. 4 (1969): 331.

33 Upendra Baxi, 'Emancipation as Justice: Babasaheb Ambedkar's Legacy and Vision' (paper presentation, Babasaheb Ambedkar Centenary Celebration, Tamil Nadu, 5 March 1991).

34 Bhimrao Ramji Ambedkar, *Annihilation of Caste,* in *The Essential Writings of BR Ambedkar*, ed. Valerian Rodrigues (New Delhi: Oxford University Press 2002), 262.

35 Rodrigues, *The Essential Writings of BR Ambedkar,* 275.

36 Ambedkar, *Annihilation of Caste,* Vol. 1, 59.

37 Mohandas Karamchand Gandhi, 'Dr. Ambedkar's indictment,' in *What is Hinduism* (New Delhi: National Book Trust, 2001), 119–20.

38 Mohandas Karamchand Gandhi, in Vol. 70 of *The Collected Works of Mahatma Gandhi* (New Delhi: Publications Division, 1936), 142–43.

39 Mohandas Karamchand Gandhi, in Vol. 70 of *The Collected Works of Mahatma Gandhi* (New Delhi: Publications Division, 1935), 121–22.

40 Mohandas Karamchand Gandhi, in Vol. 70 of *The Collected Works of Mahatma Gandhi,* 142.

41 Brown, 'The Mahatma and Modern India,' *Modern Asian Studies* 3, no. 330.

42 Bhimrao Ramji Ambedkar, 'Reply to the Mahatma,' in *The Essential Writings of BR Ambedkar*, ed. Valerian Rodrigues (New Delhi: Oxford University Press, 2002), 318.

43 Rodrigues, *The Essential Writings of BR Ambedkar,* 316.

44 M.G. Ranade (1842–1901) was a liberal politician who also became a member of the House of Commons. He was known for his critique of Hindu society, based on his understanding of the practices of Hinduism in contemporary India. Born in 1842 at Biphad in Nasik district of Bombay presidency in a Chitpavan Brahmin family, M.G. Ranade was influenced by the pure monotheism of the *Upanishads*. He was famous for his views deprecating the caste system and untouchability. As a true liberal, he championed the cause of women and favoured widow-marriage. He was an ardent supporter of also industrialization, emancipation of the *ryot* (cultivators holding land from the landlord on certain conditions) from the moneylender. As an editor of an Anglo-Marathi daily from Bombay, *Induprakash* (1864–1871), Ranade published his view on social reform. A founder member of the Indian National Congress, Ranade was characterized as a 'modern *rishi*' (saint) by his Congress colleagues. He articulated his views in *Revenue Manual of the British Empire in India, Essays in Indian Economics* and *Rise of the Maratha Power.* He also wrote *A Theist's Confession of Faith* in which he attempted to create an ideological basis for the *Prarthana Samaj*, a Poona-based reformist organization. S.P. Sen (ed.), Vol. III. of *Dictionary of National Biography* (Calcutta: Institute of Historical Studies, 1973–1974), 479–81.

45 Ambedkar, 'Ranade, Gandhi and Jinnah,' Vol. 1, 223.

46 Ambedkar, 'Ranade, Gandhi and Jinnah', Vol. 1, 223.
47 Madhav Sadashiv Gore, *The Social Context of an Ideology: Ambedkar's Political and Social Thought* (New Delhi: Sage Publications, 1993), 166.
48 Rodrigues, *The Essential Writings of BR Ambedkar,* 124.
49 Rodrigues, *The Essential Writings of BR Ambedkar,* 129.
50 Upendra Baxi, 'Emancipation as Justice: Babasaheb Ambedkar's Legacy and Vision (paper presentation, Babasaheb Ambedkar Centenary Celebration, Tamil Nadu, 5 March 1991).
51 Gauri Viswanathan, *Outside the Fold: Conversion, Modernity and Belief* (New Delhi: Oxford University Press, 1998); Viswanathan, *Outside the Fold,* 216.
52 Viswanathan, *Outside the Fold*, 237.
53 Bhimrao Ramji Ambedkar, Vol. VII of *The Constituent Assembly Debates* (New Delhi: Lok Sabha Secretariat, 2003), 38–39.
54 Letters from Jawaharlal Nehru to Gandhi. 508.
55 Bhimrao Ramji Ambedkar, Vol. VII of *The Constituent Assembly Debates* (New Delhi: Lok Sabha Secretariat, 2003), 255.
56 Ambedkar, *The Constituent Assembly Debates,* Vol. 7, 255.
57 Ambedkar, *The Constituent Assembly Debates,* Vol. 7, 256.
58 Ambedkar, *The Constituent Assembly Debates,* Vol. 7, 256.
59 Ambedkar, *The Constituent Assembly Debates,* Vol. 7, 350.
60 Ambedkar, *The Constituent Assembly Debates,* Vol. 7, 350.
61 Ambedkar, *The Constituent Assembly Debates,* Vol. 7, 351.
62 Keya Maitra, 'Ambedkar and the Constitution of India: A Deweyan experiment', *Contemporary Pragmatism* 9, no. 2 (2012): 301–20.
63 Granville Austin, *The Indian Constitution: The Cornerstone of a Nation* (New Delhi: Oxford University Press, 1999), 39–41.
64 Ambedkar, *The Constituent Assembly Debates,* Vol. 7, 39.
65 Bhimrao Ramji Ambedkar, in Vol. X of *The Constituent Assembly Debates* (New Delhi: Lok Sabha Secretariat, 2003), 979.
66 Ambedkar, *The Constituent Assembly,* Vol. X, 980.
67 Ambedkar, *The Constituent Assembly,* Vol. X, 979.
68 Shailaja Menon, 'The Fractured Society of the Republic', in Vol. II of *BR Ambedkar: The Quest for Justice*, ed. Aakash Singh Rathore (New Delhi: Oxford University Press, 2021), 161.
69 Bhimrao Ramji Ambedkar in Vol. 2 of *Constituent Assembly Debates,* (New Delhi: Lok Sabha Secretariat, 2003), 781.

70 Ambedkar, Vol. 2, *Constituent Assembly Debates*, 547.
71 Ambedkar, Vol. 2, *Constituent Assembly Debates*, 550–51.
72 Moon, *Dr. Babasaheb Ambedkar Writings and Speeches*, Vol. 14 (part 1), 5.
73 Moon, *Dr. Babasaheb Ambedkar Writings and Speeches*, Vol. 14 (part 1), 5–6.
74 Moon, *Dr. Babasaheb Ambedkar Writings and Speeches*, Vol. 14 (part 1), 269.
75 Moon, *Dr. Babasaheb Ambedkar Writings and Speeches*, Vol. 14 (part 1), 270.
76 Moon, *Dr. Babasaheb Ambedkar Writings and Speeches*, Vol. 14 (part 1), 283.
77 Moon, *Dr. Babasaheb Ambedkar Writings and Speeches*, Vol. 14 (part 1), 315.
78 Reba Som provided details of the critics and their points which they put forward in their defence in her 'Jawaharlal Nehru and the Hindu Code: A Victory of Symbol over Substance', *Modern Asian Studies* 28, no. 1 (1994): 172–73.
79 Durga Das, ed., Vol. VI of *Sardar Patel's Correspodence, 1945-1950* (Ahmedabad: Navajivan Press, 1972), 213.
80 Moon, *Dr. Babasaheb Ambedkar Writings and Speeches*, Vol. 14 (part 1), 403.
81 Moon, *Dr. Babasaheb Ambedkar Writings and Speeches*, Vol. 14 (part 1), 399.
82 Vasant Moon, comp., Vol. 14 (part 2) of *Dr. Babasaheb Ambedkar Writings and Speeches* (1979; repr., Mumbai: Education Department, Government of Maharashtra, 2014), 1029–30.
83 Bhagwan Das, ed., Vol. I, of *Selected Speeches of BR Ambedkar* (Mumbai, Maharashtra: Bheem Patrika Publications, 1969), 71.
84 Moon, *Dr. Babasaheb Ambedkar Writings and Speeches*, Vol. 14 (part 1), 404.
85 Vasant Moon, comp., Vol. 17 (part 1) of *Dr. Babasaheb Ambedkar Writings and Speeches* (1979; repr., Mumbai: Education Department, Government of Maharashtra, 2014), 404.
86 K.M. Munshi, ed., Vol. I of *Indian Constitutional Documents* (Bombay: Bharatiya Vidya Bhawan, 1967), 87.
87 Balmiki Chowdhury, ed., Vol. 10 of *Dr. Rajendra Prasad: Correspondence and Select Documents*, (New Delhi: Allied Publishers, 1988), 218.
88 T.R. Deogirikar, *Twelve Years in Parliament (Democracy in Action)*, (Poona, Maharashtra: Chitrashala Prakashan, 1964), 211–18.
89 Sharmila Rege, *Against the Madness of Manu: BR Ambedkar's Writings on Brahminical Patriarchy* (New Delhi: Navayana, 2013).
90 Rege, *Against the Madness of Manu*, 121.

91 Rege, *Against the Madness of Manu*, 241–42.
92 Ambedkar, *Annihilation of Caste*, Vol. 1, 57.

Conclusion

1 Jean Jacques Rousseau, *The Social Contract and Discourses* (1762, repr; Vermont: Everyman, 2001), 181.
2 Rousseau, *The Social Contract and Discourses*, 186.
3 Rousseau, *The Social Contract and Discourses*, 189.
4 Simone de Beauvoir, *The Second Sex* (1949, repr; London: Vintage Books, 2013), 159.
5 Carole Pateman, *The Sexual Contract* (Cambridge: Polity Press, 1988), 6.
6 Pateman, *The Sexual Contract*, 6.
7 Pateman, *The Sexual Contract*, 179.
8 John Stuart Mill, 'The Subjection of Women', in A.S. Rossi (ed.), *Essays in Sex Equality* (Chicago, Illinois: University of Chicago Press, 1970), 141.
9 Lajpat Rai, *Unhappy India* (Calcutta: Banna Publishing Co, 1928), 173.
10 Beauvoir, *The Second Sex*, 777.
11 Beauvoir, *The Second Sex*, 782.
12 Charles W. Mills, *The Racial Contract* (Ithaca, NY: Cornell University Press, 1997), 33.
13 Edward Said, *Orientalism* (1978; repr., Gurgaon, Haryana: Penguin Books, 1995), 204.
14 Said, *Orientalism*, 333.
15 Sarah Bakewell, *Humanly Possible: Seven Hundred Years Humanist Freethinking, Inquiry and Hope* (New York: Penguin Books, 2023), 132–33.
16 Bakewell, *Humanly Possible: Seven Hundred Years Humanist Freethinking, Inquiry and Hope*, 162.
17 Bakewell, *Humanly Possible: Seven Hundred Years Humanist Freethinking, Inquiry and Hope*, 178.
18 Bakewell, *Humanly Possible: Seven Hundred Years Humanist Freethinking, Inquiry and Hope*, 179.

Bibliographical Notes

As this is a study of humanizing humanity, the text draws on the ideas of three major nationalist thinkers who, in their specific fashions, evolved models for realizing the objective. What is striking, despite the fact that these thinkers were raised in nearly the same sociocultural milieu and likely to have imbibed the same politico-ideological visions, is that they ended up creating different models which, they found, were appropriate for the goals they espoused. The explanation for such divergences is hardly difficult because they saw the prevalent context and internalized the prevalent ideas in accordance with their own priorities. What was however common in their perception was their compatible concerns for humanity. Gandhi preferred political independence as it was complementary to the achievement of his goal; Rabindranath Tagore insisted of sociocultural amity among people irrespective of caste, religion and ethnicity as integral to his ideational vision; Ambedkar had faith in liberal constitutionalism as a panacea for the downtrodden who were so due to sociocultural reasons and economic disparities.

The paragraph above is useful to understand the logic that is followed in preparing this bibliography. As mentioned above, the purpose is to conceptualize/reconceptualize an idea which is not novel, since many thinkers, regardless of their locations, remain concerned with humanizing humanity and ,thus they designed their models as an antidote to the processes of dehumanizing humanity since they are incongruent with the former, and yet, an essential component for realizing the ultimate goal for sustaining humanity. There should be a caveat here because, despite being drawn on different intellectual sources, they were born and nurtured in an environment when colonialism reached its zenith and was the most brutal, presumably because there was very little force to effectively combat the colonial rulers.

It is matter of great advantage to the author if the thinkers codified their ideas in various written sources with the primary purpose of spreading their views. Fortunately, with the availability of collected works of these thinkers, it is easier for me to articulate their ideas with reference to how they evolved them in many of their written tracts. The Government of India published more than 100 volumes of Gandhi's Collected Works; the Government of Maharashtra collated B.R. Ambedkar's writings in seventeen volumes which are easily available; and Visva-Bharati, with the publication of seventeen volumes, allowed access to Rabindranath Tagore's creative literary writings and other critical essay. Furthermore, the Sahitya Akademi, New Delhi printed many of Tagore's texts in English in four volumes. These sources provide critical inputs to dwell on how they conceptualized the phenomenon of humanizing humanity.

As is true of Bibliographies per se, it is difficult to include all the written texts on the theme in a single bibliography; so, it is usually a select bibliography of relevant texts and written interventions by many authors who examined their ideas from different perspectives. It is possible that this bibliography may have missed some of the important texts according to some authors who found them useful for building their arguments. Hence, it is claimed here that the books and essays which figure in this bibliography are chosen by the author himself and according to his prerogative. Hence, this bibliography may not be useful to those who raise different questions or dwell on different issues.

This bibliography is just a pathfinder for the researchers who plan to work on issues of political thought which was critical to understand how humanization and/or dehumanization are conceptualized/reconceptualized in the nationalist context, and, also on how the prevalent socio-economic and politico-ideological contexts play critical roles in shaping thoughts of these creative thinkers. This bibliography is also an aid to understand the role of specific intellectual inputs in shaping an ideational vision of a thinker, and also as to why they might not be as critical as they are, in regard to another thinker. The bibliography is just a list of books, essays, and other written interventions which are pertinent to the conceptualization of the principal theme of this book.

Selected Bibliography

Alavi, Hamza. 'Misreading Partition Road Signs.' *Economic and Political Weekly* (November 2002): 2–9.

———. 'Social Forces and Ideology in the Making of Pakistan.' *Economic and Political Weekly* (October 2002): 21.

Ambedkar, B.R. 'Thoughts on Pakistan.' In Inventing *Boundaries: Gender, Politics and Partition of India*, edited by Mushirul Hasan. New Delhi: Oxford University Press, 2000.

Ambedkar, B.R. *What Congress and Gandhi Have Done to the Untouchables.* Bombay: Thacker & Co., 1946.

Amin, Shahid. 'Gandhi as Mahatma: Gorakhpur district, eastern UP, 1921-22'. In *Subaltern Studies: writings on South Asian Studies*, Vol. III, edited by Ranajit Guha. New Delhi: Oxford University Press, 1984.

———. *Event, Metaphor, Memory: Chauri Chaura, 1922-92*. New Delhi: Oxford University Press, 1995.

Ananthanathan, A.K. 'The Significance of Gandhi's Interpretation of Gita.' *Gandhi Marg*, 13, no. 3 (October 1991).

Austin, Granville. *The Indian Constitution: The Cornerstone of a Nation*. New Delhi: Oxford University Press, 1966.

Benedict, Anderson. *Imagined Communities: Reflections on the Origin and Spread of Nationalism*. London: Verso, 1991.

Bagchi, Amiya. *Private Investment in India, 1900–39*. Cambridge: Cambridge University Press, 1972.

Bakshi, Rajni. *Bapu Kuti: Journeys in Rediscovery of Gandhi*. New Delhi: Penguin Books, 1998.

Bandyopadhyay, Sekhar. *From Plassey to Partition: A History of Modern India*. New Delhi: Orient Longman, 2004.

Bandyopadhyaya, Jayantanuja. *Social and Political thought of Gandhi*. Bombay: Allied Publishers, 1969.

Bera, Sadananda and Narayan Chandra Sau. *Rabindranath O Rajniti: Eekhan O Thakhan*. Kolkata: Kallol, 2013.

Berlin, Isaiah. *The Sense of Reality: Studies in Ideas and Their History*. New York: Farrar, Straus and Giroux, 1996.

Bhabha, Homi K. *The Location of Culture*. London: Routledge, 1994.

Bhalla, Alok, ed. *Stories About the Partition of India*. New Delhi: Penguin Books, 1994.

Bhattacharya, Sabyasachi, ed. *The Mahatma and the Poet: Letters and Debates between Gandhi and Tagore, 1915-1941*. New Delhi: National Book Trust, 1997.

———. *Vande Mataram: The Biography of a Song*. New Delhi: Penguin Books, 2003.

Bhattacharyya, Buddhadeva. *Evolution of the Political Philosophy of Gandhi*. Calcutta: Calcutta Book House, 1969.

Bilgrami, Akeel. 'Gandhi, the Philosopher.' *Economic and Political Weekly* 38, no. 39 (2003).

Birla, G.D. *In the Shadow of Mahatma: A Personal Memoir*. Calcutta: Orient Longman, 1964.

Bondurant, Joan V. *Conquest of Violence: The Gandhian Philosophy of Conflict*. Princeton: Princeton University Press, 1958.

Bose, N.K. *My Days with Gandhi*. Calcutta: Orient Longman, 1974.

Bose, Nirmal Kumar. *Studies in Gandhism*. Calcutta: India Associated Publishing Co., 1962.

Bose, Subhas Chandra. *The Indian struggle, 1920-42*. London: Asia Publishing House, 1964.

Bose, Sugata. 'Nation, Reason and Religion: India's Independence in International Perspective.' *Economic and Political Weekly* (August 1998).

Bose, Sugata and Ayesha Jalal. *Modern South Asia: History, Culture, Political Economy*. New Delhi: Oxford University Press, 1998.

Brown, Judith. 'The Mahatma and Modern India.' *Modern Asian Studies* 3, no. 4 (1969).

———. *Gandhi and Civil Disobedience: The Mahatma in Indian politics, 1928-1934*. Cambridge: Cambridge University Press, 1977.

———. *Gandhi: Prisoner of Hope*. New Delhi: Oxford University Press, 1990.

———. *Gandhi's Rise to Power: Indian Politics, 1915-1922*. Cambridge: Cambridge University Press, 1972.

———. *Modern India: The Origins of An Asian Democracy*. New Delhi: Oxford University Press, 1985.

———. *Nehru: Political Life*. New Delhi: Oxford University Press, 2004.

Chakrabarty, Bidyut, ed. *Communal Identity in India: Its Construction and Articulation in the Twentieth Century*. New Delhi: Oxford University Press, 2003.

———. 'Peasants and the Bengal Congress, 1928–38.' *South Asia Research* 5 (May 1985).

———. 'BR Ambedkar and the History of Constitutionalizing India.' *Contemporary South Asia* 2, no. 24 (2016).

———. 'BR Ambedkar: A "Rebel" Liberal in the Gandhian Universe.' *Indian Historical Review* 23, no. 2 (2016).

———. 'Religion, Colonialism and Modernity: Relocating "Self" and "Collectivity"'. *Gandhi Marg* 23, no. 3 (2002).

Chakrabarty, Bidyut. *Biplabi : A Journal of the 1942 Open Rebellion*. Kolkata: KP Bagchi & Co, 2002.

———. *Local Politics and Indian Nationalism: Midnapur, 1919-1944*. New Delhi: Manohar Publishers, 1997.

———. *Subhas Chandra Bose and Middle Class Radicalism: A Study in Indian Nationalism, 1928–40*. New Delhi: Oxford University Press, 1990.

———. *The Partition of Bengal and Assam, 1932-47: Contour of Freedom*. London: Routledge, 2004.

Chakrabarty, Dipesh. 'Friendships in the Shadow of Empire: Tagore's Reception in Chicago, circa, 1913-1932.' *Modern Asian Studies* 48, no. 5 (2014).

———. *Provincializing Europe: Postcolonial Thought and Historical Difference*. New Delhi: Oxford University Press, 2000.

———. 'Nation and imagination', *Studies in History* 15, no. 2 (1999).

Chatterjee, Kalyan. 'Gora: Tagore's Paradoxical Self', *Indian Literature* 49, no. 3 (May–June 2005).

Chatterjee, Margaret. *Gandhi's Religious Thought*. London: Macmillan, 1983.

Chatterjee, Partha. 'Gandhi and the Critique of Civil Society.' In *Subaltern Studies: Writings on South Asian Studies*, Vol. III, edited by Ranajit Guha. New Delhi: Oxford University Press, 1984.

———. 'Gandhi Please Stand Up?'. *Illustrated Weekly of India* (January 1984).

———. 'The Fruits of Macaulay's Poison Tree.' In *The Present History of West Bengal*. New Delhi: Oxford University Press, 1997.

———. 'The Nation in Heterogeneous Time', *Indian Economic and Social History Review* 38, no. 4 (2001).

———. *A Princely Impostor? The Kumar of Bhawal and the Secret History of Indian Nationalism*. New Delhi: Permanent Black, 2002.

———. *The Nation and Its Fragments: Colonial and Postcolonial Histories*. New Delhi: Oxford University Press, 1994.

———. *The Politics of the Governed: Reflections on Popular Politics in Most of the World*. New Delhi: Permanent Black, 2004.

Chatterjee, Partha and Ira Katznelson, eds. *Anxieties of Democracy: Tocquevillean Reflections on India and United States*. New Delhi: Oxford University Press, 2012.

Chaube, Shibanikinkar. *Constituent Assembly of India: Springboard of Revolution*. New Delhi: Manohar Publishers, 2000.

———. *The Making and Working of the Indian Constitution*. New Delhi: National Book Trust, 2009.

Chaudhuri, Nirad C. *The Autobiography of an Unknown Indian*. Berkeley, California: University of California Press, 1968.

———. *Thy Hand Great Anarch: India, 1921–52*. London: Chatto and Windus, 1987.

Chaudhuri, Rosinka. 'Hemchandra's Bharat Sangeet (1870) and the Politics of Poetry: A Pre-history of Hindu Nationalism in Bengal?', *Indian Economic and Social History Review* 42, no. 2 (2005).

———. 'The Flute, Gerontion, and Subalternist Misreadings of Tagore', *Social Text* 78, no. 1 (2004).

Chaudhuri, Sukanta, ed. *The Cambridge Companion to Rabindranath Tagore*. Cambridge: Cambridge University Press, 2020.

Chiriyankandath, James. 'Creating a Secular State in a Religious Country: The Debate in the Indian Constituent Assembly.' *Commonwealth and Comparative Politics* 38, no. 2 (2000).

Chopra Pran. *The Supreme Court versus the Constitution: A Challenge to Federalism*. New Delhi: Sage Publications, 2006.

Choudhury, Khaliquzzaman. *Pathway to Pakistan*. Lahore: Longmans, 1961.

Chowdhruy, Sujit, Madhav Khosla and Pratap Bhanu Mehta, eds. *The Oxford Handbook of the Indian Constitution*. New Delhi: Oxford University Press, 2016.

Cohn, B. *Colonialism and Its Forms of Knowledge: The British in India*. Princeton: Princeton University Press, 1996.

Conniff, James. 'Burke and India: The Failure of the Theory of Trusteeship.' *Political Research Quarterly* 46, no. 1 (1993).

Dalton Dennis. *Non-Violence in Action: Gandhi's Power*. New Delhi: Oxford University Press, 1998.

Darling, Malcolm Lyall. *At Freedom's Dawn*. London: Oxford University Press, 1949.

Das, Durga, ed. *Vallabhbhai Patel Correspondence, 1945–50*, Vol. IV. Ahmedabad: Navajivan Publishing House, 1972.

Dasgupta, Ajit K. *Gandhi's Economic Thought*. London: Routledge, 1996.

Dasgupta, Jyotirindra. *Language, Conflict and National Development*. Berkeley, California: University of California Press, 1970.

Dasgupta, Sandipto. 'A Language Which is Foreign to Us: Continuities and Anxieties in the Making of the Indian Constitution.' *Comparative Studies of South Asia, Africa and the Middle East* 34, no. 2 (2014).

Dasgupta, Subrata. *The Bengal Renaissance: Identity and Creativity—from Rammohun Roy to Rabindranath Tagore*. Ranikhet: Permanent Black, 2007.

Dasgupta, Uma. *Rabindranath Tagore: A Biography*. New Delhi: Oxford University Press, 2004.

Datta V.N. 'Iqbal, Jinnah and India's Partition'. *Economic and Political Weekly* (December 2002).

Dhulipala, Venkat. *Creating a New Medina: State Power, Islam and the Quest for Pakistan in Late Colonial North India*. Cambridge: Cambridge University Press, 2016.

Dirks, Nicholas. *Castes of Mind: Colonialism and the Making of Modern India*. Princeton: Princeton University Press, 2001.

Doke, Joseph J. *MK Gandhi: An Indian Patriot in South Africa*. London: Read Books, 2008.

Doniger, Wendy and Martha C. Nusbaum, eds. *Pluralism and Democracy in India: Debating the Hindu Right*. New York, NY: Oxford University Press, 2015.

Dutt, R. Palme. *India today*. London: Victor Gollancz Ltd., 1940.

Dutta, Krishna and Andrew Robinson. *Rabindranath Tagore: The Myriad-minded Man*. New York, NY: St. Martin's Press, 1995.

Dutta, Pradip Kumar. *Rabindranath Tagore's 'The Home and the World': A Critical Companion*. London: Anthem Press, 2004.

Dworkin, R. *A Matter of Principle*. Boston, Massachusetts: Harvard University Press, 1986.

———. *Freedom's Law*. Boston, Massachusetts: Harvard University Press, 1986.

———. *Law's Empire*. Boston, Massachusetts: Harvard University Press, 1986.

———. *Taking Rights Seriously*. New Delhi: Universal Law Publishing House, 1999.

Elangovan, Arvind. 'Constitutionalism, Political Exclusion, and Implications for Indian Constitutional History: The Case of Montague-Chelmsford Reforms (1919).' *South Asian History and Culture* (2016).

———. 'Provincial Autonomy, Sir Benegal Narsing Rau, and an Improbable Imagination of Constitutionalism in India, 1935-38.' *Comparative Studies of South Asia, Africa and the Middle East* 36, no. 1 (2016).

———. 'The Making of the Indian Constitution: A Case for A Non-Nationalist Approach.' *History Compass* 12, no. 1 (2014).

———. 'The Road Not Taken: Sir Benegal Narsing Rau and the Indian Constitution.' In *Decolonization and the Politics of Transition in South Asia*, edited by Sekhar Bandyopadhyay. New Delhi: Orient Blackswan, 2016.

Elmhirst, Leonard K. *Poet and Plowman*. Kolkata: Visva-Bharati, 2008.

———. *Rabindranath Tagore: Pioneers in Education*. London: John Murray, 1960.

Erickson, E. *Gandhi's Truth: On the Origins of Militant Non-violence*. New York, NY: Faber & Faber, 1970.

Ferguson, Niall. *Empire: The Rise and Demise of the British World Order and the Lessons for Global Power*. New York, NY: Basic Books, 2002.

Fisher, Louis. *Gandhi: His Life and Message for the World*. New York, NY: New American Library, 1982.

———. *The Life of Mahatma Gandhi*. New York, NY: Harper and Row, 1981.

Fox, Richard. *Gandhian Utopia: Experiments with Culture*. Boston, Massachusetts: Beacon Press, 1989.

Frank, Andre Gunder. 'Gandhi, the Philosopher.' *Economic and Political Weekly* 38, no. 43 (2003).

Freitag, Sandria B. *Collective Action and Community: Public Arenas and the Emergence of Communalism in North India*. New Delhi: Oxford University Press, 1990.

Gaikwad, S.M. 'Ambedkar and Indian Nationalism.' *Economic and Political Weekly* (March 1998).

Gajendragadkar, P.B. *Law, Liberty and Social Justice*. Bombay: New Age Printing Press, 1965.

Galanter, Marc. 'Who are the Backward Classes?' *Economic and Political Weekly* (October 1978).

Galanter, Marc. *Competing Equalities: Law and the Backward Classes in India.* New Delhi: Oxford University Press, 1984.

———. *Law and Society in Modern India.* New Delhi: Oxford University Press, 1997.

Ghose, Benoy. *Iswar Chandra Vidyasagar.* New Delhi: Publication Division, Ministry of Information and Broadcasting, Government of India, 1971.

Ghosh, Sachindralal. *Raja Rammohun Roy: Pathmaker of Modern India.* New Delhi: National council of Education, Research and Training, 1970.

Gier, Nicholas. 'Gandhi, Ahimsa and Self.' *Gandhi Marg* 15, no. 1 (1993).

———. 'Gandhi, Pre-modern, Modern or Post-modern?', *Gandhi Marg* 18, no. 3 (1996).

Godrej, Farah. *Cosmopolitan Political Thought: Method, Practice, Discipline.* New York: Oxford University Press, 2011.

Gopal, S. ed. *Jawaharlal Nehru.* 3 vols. London: Jonathan Cape, 1973–1984.

Gordon, L. 'Mahatma Gandhi's Dialogue with Americans.' *Economic and Political Weekly* 37, no. 4 (2002).

Gore, M.S. *The Social Context of an Ideology: Ambedkar's Political and Social thought.* New Delhi: Sage Publications, 1993.

Griffiths, Percival. *To Guard My People: The History of the Indian Police.* London: Ernest Benn, 1971.

Gudavarthy, Ajay. *Maoism, Democracy and Globalization: Cross-currents in Indian Politics.* New Delhi: Sage Publications, 2014.

Guha, Chinmoy, ed. *Bridging East & West: Rabindranath Tagore and Roman Rolland correspondence (1919-1940).* New Delhi: Oxford University Press, 2018.

Guha, Ranajit. *Dominance without Hegemony: History and Power in Colonial India.* New Delhi: Oxford University Press, 1998.

———. *History at the Limit of World History.* New York, NY: Columbia University Press, 2002.

Guru, Gopal. 'Ethics in Ambedkar's Critique of Gandhi', *Economic and Political Weekly* (April 2017).

Haksar, Vinit. *Rights, Communities and Disobedience: Liberalism and Gandhi.* New Delhi: Oxford University Press, 2001.

Haque, Azizul. *A Plea for Separate Electorate in Bengal.* Calcutta: Ministry of Culture, 1931.

Hardiman, David. *Gandhi in His Times and Ours*. New Delhi: Permanent Black, 2003.

———. *Peasant Nationalists of Gujarat: Kheda district, 1917-34*. New Delhi: Oxford University Press, 1981.

Hardy, P. *The Muslims of British India*. Cambridge: Cambridge University Press, 1972.

Hasan, Mushirul, ed. *India Partitioned: The Other Face of Freedom*, vol. 1. New Delhi: Roli Books, 1995.

———. ed. *Inventing Boundaries: Gender, Politics and the Partition of India*. New Delhi: Oxford University Press, 2000.

———. *Legacy of a Divided Nation: India's Muslims since Independence*. New Delhi: Oxford University, 1997.

Hasan, Zoya, E. Sridharan and R. Sudarshan, eds. *India's Living Constitution: Ideas, Practices, Controversies*. Ranikhet: Permanent Black, 2002.

———. *Politics of Inclusion: Castes, Minorities and Affirmative Action*. New Delhi: Oxford University Press, 2009.

Hashim, Abul. *In Retrospection*. Dhaka: Mowla Brothers, 1974.

Hayek, F.A. *The Constitution of Liberty*. Chicago, Illinois: University of Chicago Press, 1978.

Henningham, S. 'The Social Setting of the Champaran Satyagraha: The Challenge of an Alien Rule.' *Indian Economic and Social History Review* 13, no. 1, 1976.

Hodson, H.V. *The Great Divide: Britain–India–Pakistan*. London: Hutchinson, 1969.

Horsburgh, H.J.N. *Non-Violence and Aggression: A Study of Gandhi's Moral Equivalent of War*. London: Oxford University Press, 1968.

Iyer, Raghavan, ed. *The Moral and Political Writings of Mahatma Gandhi*. 3 vols. Oxford: Clarendon Press, 1986–1987.

Jaffrelot, Christophe. *Analyzing and Fighting Caste: Ambedkar and Untouchability*. New Delhi: Permanent Black, 2005.

Jangam, Chinnaiah. *Dalits and the Making of Modern India*. New Delhi: Oxford University Press, 2017.

Jayal, Niraja Gopal. *Citizenship and Its Discontents: An Indian History*. Ranikhet: Permanent Black, 2013.

Jha, Sadan. 'Charkha, "Dear Forgotten Friend" of Widows: Reading the Erasures of Symbols.' *Economic and Political Weekly* 39, no. 28 (2004).

Jinnah, Muhammad Ali. *Speeches*. Karachi: Pakistan Publications, 1963.

Jones, Kenneth W. *Socio-religious Reform Movements in British India*. Cambridge: Cambridge University Press, 1994.

Juergensmeyer, Mark. *Fighting with Gandhi*. San Francisco, California: Harper and Row, 1984.

———. *Gandhi's Way: A Handbook of Conflict Resolution*. New Delhi: Oxford University Press, 2003.

Kalekar Commission. *Report of the Backward Classes Commission*. New Delhi: Government of India, 1956.

Kamath M.V. and V.B. Kher. *The Story of Militant but Non-violent Trade Unionism: A Biographical and Historical Study*. Ahmedabad: Navajivan Trust, 1993.

Karunakaran, K.P. *New Perspectives on Gandhi*. Shimla: Indian Institute of Advanced Studies, 1969.

Kashyap, Subhash C. *Our Constitution: An Introduction to India's Constitution and Constitutional Law*. New Delhi: National Book Trust, 2015.

———. *The Indian Constitution: Conflicts and Controversies*. New Delhi: Vitasta Publications, 2010.

Kaviraj, Sudipta. 'Tagore and Transformation in the Ideals of Love', in *Love in South Asia: A Cultural History*, edited by Francesca Orsini. Cambridge: Cambridge University Press, 2006.

Keer, Dhananjay. *Dr. Babasaheb Ambedkar: Life and Mission*. Mumbai: Popular Prakashan, 2012.

Khilnani, Sunil. 'Gandhi and History,' *Seminar*, no. 461 (January 1998).

———. *The Idea of India*. London: Hamish Hamilton, 1997.

Khosla, Madhav. *The Indian Constitution*. New Delhi: Oxford University Press, 2012.

King, Robert D. *Nehru and the Language Politics of India*. New Delhi: Oxford University Press, 1997.

Kolge, Nishikant. *Gandhi Against Caste*. New Delhi: Oxford University Press, 2017.

Kopf, David. *The Brahmo Samaj and the Shaping of the Modern Indian Mind*. New Delhi: Archives Publishers Pvt. Ltd., 1988.

Kripalani, Krishna. *Gandhi: A Life.* New Delhi: National Book Trust, 1968.

———. *Rabindranath Tagore: A Biography.* New Delhi: UBS Publications, 2008. First published 1962 by Literary Licensing (Whitefish).

Kripalani, Sucheta. *An Unfinished Biography.* Ahmedabad: Navjivan Publishing House, 1978.

Krishnaswami, Sudhir. *Democracy and Constitutionalism in India: A Study of the Basic Structure Doctrine.* New Delhi: Oxford University Press, 2009.

Kumar, Aishwary. *Radical Equality: Ambedkar, Gandhi and the Risk of Democracy.* California: Stanford University Press, 2015.

Kumar, Ravinder. *Essays on Gandhian Politics: The Rowlatt Satyagraha of 1919.* Oxford: Clarendon Press, 1971.

———. 'Gandhi, Ambedkar, and Poona Pact, 1932', *South Asia: Journal of South Asian Studies* 8, no. 1 (1985).

Kumarappa, J.C. *Gandhian Economic Thought.* Mumbai: Vora and C, 1951.

Kymlicka, Will. *Multicultural Citizenship: A Liberal Theory of Minority Rights.* Oxford: Clarendon Press, 1995.

———. *Politics in the Vernacular.* Oxford: Oxford University Press, 2001.

Larson, Gerald. 'Mandal, Mandir, Masjid: The Citizen as an Endangered Species in Independent India', in *Religion and Law in Independent India,* edited by Robert D. Baird. New Delhi: Manohar Publishers, 1993.

———. *Religion and Personal Law in Secular India: A Call to Judgment.* Bloomington: Indiana University Press, 2001.

Legg, Stephen, 'Dyarchy: Democracy, Autocracy and the Scalar Sovereignty of Interwar India', *Comparative Studies of South Asia, Africa, and the Middle East* 36, no. 1 (2016).

Mahajan, Gurpreet. *Identities and Rights: Aspects of Liberal Politics in India.* New Delhi: Oxford University Press, 1998.

Mahajan, Sucheta. *Independence and Partition: The Erosion of Colonial Power.* New Delhi: Sage Publications, 2000.

Mahalanobis, Prasanta Chandra. *Prasange Rabindranath.* Kolkata: Mahalanobis Trust, 1985.

———. *Rabindranath.* Kolkata: Ananda, 2002.

Manor, J., ed., *Nehrus to the Nineties: The Changing Office of Prime Minister in India.* London: Hurst, 1994.

Mansergh, Diana, ed., *Independence Years: The Selected Indian and Commonwealth Papers of Nicholas Mansergh.* New Delhi: Oxford University Press, 1999.

Markovits, Claude. *The Un-Gandhian Gandhi: The Life and Afterlife of the Mahatma.* New Delhi: Permanent Black, 2003.

Mehrotra, S.R. and Dinyar Patel, eds, *Dadabhai Naoroji: Selected Private Papers.* New Delhi: Oxford University Press, 2016.

Mehta, Uday Singh. *Liberalism and Empire: India in British Liberal Thought.* New Delhi: Oxford University Press, 1999.

Mehta, V.R. *Foundations of Indian Political Thought.* New Delhi: Manohar Publications, 1992.

Menon, Dilip. 'Religion and Colonial Modernity: Rethinking Belief and Identity', *Economic and Political Weekly* (April 2002).

Menon, V.P. *The Transfer of Power in India.* Madras: Orient Blackswan, 1993. First published 1957 by Orient Longman (Hyderabad).

Metcalf, Thomas R. *Ideologies of the Raj.* Cambridge: Cambridge University Press, 1998.

Mitra, Ashok. *The New India, 1948-1955: Memoirs of an Indian Civil Servant.* Mumbai: Popular Prakashan, 1991.

Moon, Penderel, ed., *Wavell: The Viceroy's Journal.* Oxford: Oxford University Press, 1973.

Moon, Penderel. *The British Conquest of Dominion of India.* London: Duckworth, 1989.

Moore, Barrington Jr. *Social Origins of Dictatorship and Democracy: Lord and Peasant in the Making of the Modern World.* Boston: Beacon Press, 1966.

Morris-Jones, W.H. 'Mahatma Gandhi: Political Philosopher', *Political Studies* 8 no. 1 (February 1960).

Muhammad, Ali Chaudhuri. *The Emergence of Pakistan.* New York: Columbia University Press, 1967.

Mukherjee, Hiren. *Gandhi: A Study.* New Delhi: People's Publishing House, 1991. First published 1958 by National Bookv Agency (New Delhi).

Mukherjee, Kedar Nath. *Political Philosophy of Rabindranath Tagore.* New Delhi: S. Chand & Company Ltd, 1982.

Mukherjee, Mithi. 'Justice, War and Imperium: India and Britain in Edmund Burke's Prosecutorial Speeches in the Impeachment Trial of Warren Hastings', *Law and History Review* 23, no. 3 (Fall 2005).

Mukherjee, Ramkrishna. *The Rise and Fall of the East India Company.* Monthly Review Press, 1974.

Mukherjee, Rudrangshu. *The Penguin Gandhi Reader.* New Delhi: Penguin Books, 1993.

Mukherjee, Subrata and Sushila Ramaswamy, eds. *Economic and Social Principles of Mahatma Gandhi.* New Delhi: Deep & Deep, 1998.

———. eds. *Ethics, Religion and Culture.* New Delhi: Deep & Deep, 1998.

———. eds. *Non-Violence and Satyagraha.* New Delhi: Deep & Deep, 1998.

———. eds. *Political Ideas of Mahatma Gandhi.* New Delhi: Deep & Deep, 1998.

Mukherjee, Subrata. *Gandhian Thought: Marxist Interpretation.* New Delhi: Deep & Deep, 1997.

———. *The Political Ideas of Rabindranath Tagore: Reflections of a Public Intellectual.* New Delhi: Rupa Publications, 2020.

Mukhopadhyay, Amartya. *Politics, Society and Colonialism: An Alternative Understanding of Tagore's Responses.* New Delhi: Foundation Books, 2010.

Namboodiripad, E.M.S. *The Mahatma and the Ism.* New Delhi: People's Publishing House, 1959.

Nanda, B.R. *Gandhi and His Critics.* New Delhi: Oxford University Press, 1985.

———. *In Search of Gandhi: Essays and Reflections.* New Delhi: Oxford University Press, 2004.

———. *Mahatma Gandhi: A Biography.* New Delhi: Oxford University Press 1996. First published 1989 by Oxford University Press (Delhi).

———. *The Nehrus: Motilal and Jawaharlal.* London: George & Allen, 1962.

Nandy, Ashis. 'Nationalism: Genuine and Spurious: Mourning Two Early Post-nationalist Strains, *Economic and Political Weekly* 41, no. 38. (2006).

———. *The Illegitimacy of Nationalism: Rabindranath and the Politics of Self.* New Delhi: Oxford University Press, 1994.

———. *The Intimate Enemy: Loss and Recovery of Self under Colonialism.* New Delhi: Oxford University Press, 1983.

Naoroji, Dadabhai. *Poverty and Un-British Rule in India.* London: S. Sonnenschein, 1901.

Narayan, R.K. *Waiting for the Mahatma*. Chennai: Indian Thought Publications 2003. First published 1955 by Michigan State University Press (Michigan).

Nayar, Sushila. *Mahatma Gandhi's Last Imprisonment: The Inside Story*. New Delhi: Har-Anand, 1996.

Nehru, Jawaharlal. *An Autobiography*., London: John Lane the Bodley Head, 1941.

———. *The Discovery of India*. New Delhi: Oxford University Press, 1989. First published 1946 by Signet Press (Calcutta).

Neogy, Ajit K. *Santiniketan and Sriniketan*. New Delhi: National Book Trust, 2015.

Newbigin, Eleanor. 'Personal Law and Citizenship in India's Transition to Independence', *Modern Asian Studies* 45, no. 1 (2011).

Noorani, A.G. *Constitutional Questions in India: The President, Parliament and the States*. New Delhi: Oxford University Press, 2000.

O'Hanlon, Rosalind. *Caste, Conflict, and Ideology: Mahatma Jotirao Phule and Low Caste Protest in Nineteenth-century Western India*. Cambridge: Cambridge University Press, 1985.

Omvedt, Gail. *Cultural Revolt in a Colonial Society: The Non-Brahmin movement in Western India, 1873-1930*. Scientific Socialist Educational Trust (1976).

———. *Dalits and the Democratic Revolution: Dr Ambedkar and Dalit Movement in Colonial India*. New Delhi: Sage Publications, 1994.

Orwell, George. 'Reflections on Gandhi', *Partisan Review* (January 1949).

Pandey, Gyanendra. *Hindus and Others: The Question of Identity in India Today*. New Delhi: Viking, 1997.

———. *Remembering Partition: Violence, Nationalism and History in India*. Cambridge: Cambridge University Press, 2001.

Pantham, Thomas and Kenneth L. Deutsch. *Political Thought in Modern India*. New Delhi: Sage Publications 1986.

Pantham, Thomas. 'Gandhi: *Swaraj*, *Sarvadaya* and *Satyagraha*', in *Political Theories and Social Reconstruction: A Critical Survey of the literature on India*. New Delhi: Sage Publications, 1995.

———. 'Habermas' Practical Discourse and Gandhi's Satyagraha', in *Political Discourse: Explorations in India and Western Political Thought,* edited by Bhikhu Parekh and Thomas Pantham. New Delhi: Sage Publications, 1987.

Pantham, Thomas. 'Thinking with Mahatma Gandhi: Beyond Liberal Democracy', *Political Theory* 11, no. 2 (1983).

Parekh, Bhikhu. 'Nehru and the National Philosophy of India', *Economic and Political Weekly* 26 no. 182 (1991).

———. *Colonialism, Tradition, and Reform: An Analysis of Gandhi's Political Discourse.* New Delhi: Sage Publications, 1999.

———. *Debating India: Essays on Political Discourse.* New Delhi: Oxford University Press, 2015.

———. *Gandhi.* Oxford: Oxford University Press, 1997.

———. *Gandhi's Political Philosophy.* Notre Dame: University of Notre Dame Press, 1989.

Parel, Anthony J., ed. *Gandhi, Freedom, and Self Rule.* New Delhi: Vistaar, 2000.

———. ed. *Hind Swaraj and Other Writings.* Cambridge: Cambridge University Press, 1997.

Petit, Philip. *Republicanism: A Theory of Freedom and Government.* Oxford: Oxford University Press, 1999.

Philips, Anne. *The Politics of Presence.* Oxford: Clarendon Press, 1995.

Philips, C.H. *The East India Company, 1784-1834.* Manchester: Manchester University Press, 1961.

Pirzada, S.S., ed. *Foundations of Pakistan: All India Muslim League Documents*, Vol. II. Karachi: National Publishing House, no date.

Poddar, Arabinda. *Tagore: The Political Personality.* Kolkata: Indiana, 2004.

Pouchepadas, Jacques. *Champaran and Gandhi: Planters, Peasants and Gandhian Politics.* New Delhi: Oxford University Press, 1999.

Prasad, Bimal. *Pathway to India's Partition: A Nation within a Nation, 1877-1937,* Vol. II. New Delhi: Manohar, 2000.

Prasad, Ganesh. 'Whiggism in India'. *Political Science Quarterly* 86 (1966).

Pylee, M.V. *Constitutional Government in India.* London: Asia Publishing House, 1965.

Pyralal, Mahatma. *Gandhi: The Early Phase*, 2 Vols. Ahmedabad, Gujarat: Navajivan Publishing House, 1958.

Radhakrishnan, Sarvepalli, ed. *Mahatma Gandhi: Essays and Reflections.* Mumbai: Jaico, 2003.

Ramnath, Kalyani. 'We the People: Seamless Webs and Social Revolution in India's Constituent Assembly Debates', *South Asia Research* 32 no. 1 (2012).

Rao, Shiva. *The Framing of India's Constitution*. 5 Volumes. New Delhi: Universal Law Publishing Company, 1968.

Rathore, Akash Singh. *Indian Political Theory: Laying the Ground Work for Swaraj*. Oxford: Routledge, 2017.

Ray, Bhrati. 'New Woman in Rabindranath Tagore's Short Stories: An Interrogation of Laboratory', *Asiatic* 4 no. 2 (December 2010).

Ray, Rajat K. ed. *Mind, Body and Society: Life and Mentality in Colonial Bengal.* Calcutta: Oxford University Press, 1995.

———. *Exploring Emotional History: Gender, Mentality and Literature in the Indian Awakening.* New Delhi: Oxford University Press, 2001.

Rege, Sharmila. 'Introduction' to *Against the Madness of Manu: BR Ambedkar's Writings on Brahmanical Patriarchy*. New Delhi: Navayana Publishing Pvt. Ltd., 2013.

Richards, G. *The Philosophy of Gandhi: A Study of His Basic Ideas.* Surrey: Curzon Press, 1982.

Rodrigues, Valerian, ed. *The Essential Writings of BR Ambedkar.* New Delhi: Oxford University Press, 2004.

———. 'Ambedkar as a Political Philosopher', *Economic and Political Weekly* 15 (April 2017).

———. 'Reading Texts and Traditions; the Ambedkar-Gandhi Debate', *Economic and Political Weekly* (January 2011).

Rolland, Romain. *Mahatma Gandhi.* London: Allen & Unwin, 1924.

Roover, Jakob De. *Europe, India and the Limits of Secularism.* New Delhi: Oxford University Press, 2015.

Rosenfeld, Michel. *Affirmative Action and Justice: A Philosophical and Constitutional Enquiry.* New Haven: Yale University Press, 1991.

Roy, Anupama. *Citizenship in India*. New Delhi: Oxford University Press, 2016.

———. *Mapping Citizenship in India.* New Delhi: Oxford University Press, 2010.

Roy, M.N. *India in Transition*. Bombay: Nachiketa Publications, 1971.

Roy, Ramashray. *Self and Society: A Study of Gandhian Thought.* New Delhi: Sage Publications, 1985.

Roy, Satyendranath. *Rabindranather Samajchinta*. Calcutta Granthalaya, 1985.

Roy, Srirupa. *Beyond Belief: India and the Politics of Postcolonial Nationalism.* Durham: Duke University Press, 2007.

Rudolph, Lloyd and S.H. Rudolph. *The Modernity of Tradition: Political Development in India.* Chicago, Illinois: The University of Chicago Press, 1967.

———. *The Realm of the Public Sphere: Identity and Policy.* New Delhi: Oxford University Press, 2008.

Saez, Lawrennce. *Federalism with a Centre.* New Delhi: Sage Publications, 2002.

Sen, Amartya. 'Tagore and his India', *New York Review of Books* 44, no. 12 (1997).

———. *Identity and Violence: The Illusion of Destiny.* London: Allen Lane, 2006.

———. *The Argumentative India: Writings on Indian History, Culture and Identity.* New York, NY: Picador, 2005.

———. *The Idea of Justice.* New York, NY: Allen Lane, 2009.

Sen, Ashok. *Rajnitir Pathakrame Rabindranth.* Calcutta: Visva Bharati Granthan Bhivag 2004.

Sen, Sachin. *The Political Thought of Tagore.* Calcutta: General Printers and Publishers Ltd., 1947.

Sen, Sarbani. *The Constitution of India: Popular Sovereignty and Democratic Transformations.* New Delhi: Oxford University Press, 2007.

Seth, Sanjay. 'Rewriting Histories of Nationalism: The Politics of 'Moderate Nationalism' in India', *American Historical Review* 104, no. 1 (February 1999).

Sethi, J.D. *Gandhi Today.* Durham: Carolina Academic Press, 1978.

Settar, S. and Indira B. Gupta, eds. *Pangs of Partition: The Human Dimension,* Vol. II. New Delhi: Manohar, 2002.

Shaikh, Farzana. 'Muslims and Political Representation in Colonial India: The Making of Pakistan', *Modern Asian Studies* 20, no. 3 (1986).

Shani, Ornit. 'Making India's Democracy: Rewriting the Bureaucratic Colonial Imagination in the Preparation of the First Elections', *Comparative Studies of South Asia, Africa and the Middle East* 36, no. 1 (2016).

Sharma, Brij Kishore. *Introduction to the Constitution of India.* New Delhi: Prentice-Hall of India, 2005.

Singh, Anita Inder. *The Origins of Partition of India, 1936–47*. New Delhi: Oxford University Press, 1987.

Sinha, Diksit. *A Poet's Experiment in Rebuilding Samaj and Nation: Sriniketan's Rural Reconstruction Work, 1922-1960*. Bolpur, West Bengal: Birupjatio Sahitya Sammiloni, 2019.

Sitaramayya, B. Pattabhi. *History of the Indian National Congress*, Vol. II, (1935–47). New Delhi: S. Chand & Co, 1969.

Skaria, Ajay. *Unconditional Equality: Gandhi's Religion of Resistance*. Minneapolis: University of Minnesota Press, 2016.

Smith, D.E. *Nehru and Democracy: The Political Thought of an Asian Democrat*. Calcutta: Orient Longman, 1958.

Som, Reba. 'Jawaharlal Nehru and the Hindu Code: A Victory of Symbol over Substance?', *Modern Asian Studies* 28, no. 1 (1994).

Somanathan, Rohini. 'Assumptions and Arithmetic of Caste-based Reservations', *Economic and Political Weekly* (June 2006).

Southard, Barbara. 'The Feminism of Mahatma Gandhi', in *Economic and Social Principles of Mahatma Gandhi*, Vol. 3, edited by Subrata Mukherjee and Sushila Ramaswamy. New Delhi: Deep & Deep Publications, 1998.

Sowell, Thomas. *Affirmative Action around the World: An Empirical Study*. New Haven: Yale University Press, 2004.

Spear, Percival. *The Oxford History of Modern India, 1740–1947*. Oxford: Clarendon Press, 1965.

Stokes, Eric. *The English Utilitarians and India*. Cambridge: Cambridge University Press, 1959.

Suradkar, Santosh. 'Mukti Kon Pathe: Caste and Class in Ambedkar's Struggle', *Economic and Political Weekly* (December 2017).

Sutherland, Lucy. *The East India Company in Eighteenth-century Politics*. Oxford: Clarendon Press, 1962.

Tai, Yong Tan and Gynesh Kudaisya. *The Aftermath of Partition in South Asia*. London: Routledge, 2000.

Taneja, Anup. *Gandhi, Women and the National Movement, 1920-47*. New Delhi: Har-Anand, 2005.

Tarchek, Ronald J. *Gandhi: Struggling for Autonomy*. New Delhi: Vistaar, 1998.

Teltumbde, Anand. 'Introuction' to *BR Ambedkar: India and Communism*. New Delhi: Leftworld, 2017.

Tendulkar, D.G. *Mahatma: The Life of MK Gandhi*. New Delhi: Ministry of Information and Broadcasting, Government of India, 1961.

Thompson Edward, Palmer. *Rabindranath Tagore: Poet and Dramatist*. London: Macmillan, 1926.

———. *Alien Homage: Edward Thompson and Rabindranath Tagore*, New York,NY: Oxford University Press, 1993.

———. 'Introduction' to *Rabindranath Tagore's Nationalism*. New Delhi: Rupa Publications, 1992.

Tirmizi, S.A.I., ed. Vol. 1 of *The Paradoxes of Partition, 1937–47*. New Delhi: Centre for Federal Studies, Jamia Hamdard, 1998.

Topdar, Sudipa. 'Duties of a "Good Citizen": Colonial Secondary School Textbook Policies in Late Nineteenth-century India', *South Asian History and Culture* (2015).

Tripathi, P.K. 'Free Speech in the Indian Constitution: Background and Prospect', *Yale Law Journal* 67, no. 3 (1958).

Upadhyaha, Prakash Chandra. 'The Politics of Indian Secularism', *Modern Asian Studies* 26, no. 4 (1992).

Vajpayi, Ananya. *Righteous Republic: The Political Foundation of Modern India*. Cambridge: Harvard University Press, 2012.

Van der Veer, Peter. *Religious Nationalism: Hindus and Muslims in India*. New Delhi: Oxford University Press, 1996.

Varshney, Ashutosh. 'Contested Meanings: India's National Identity, Hindu Nationalism and the Politics of Anxiety', *Daedalus* 122, no. 3 (1993).

———. *Ethnic Conflict and Civic Life: Hindus and Muslims in India*. New Haven: Yale University Press, 2002.

Venkatesan, Venkatasubramanian. *Constitutional Conundrums: Challenges to India's Democratic Process*. Gurgaon,Haryana: LexisNexis, 2014.

Verma, Vidhu. *Non-discrimination and Equality in India: Contesting Boundaries of Social Justice*. Oxford: Routledge, 2012.

Vundru, Raja Sekhar. *Ambedkar, Gandhi and Patel: The Making of India's Electoral System*. New Delhi: Bloomsbury, 2018.

Weber, Thomas. *Conflict Resolution and Gandhian Ethics*. New Delhi: The Gandhi Peace Foundation, 1991.

Weiner, Myron. 'The Political Consequences of Preferential Policies: A Comparative Perspective', *Comparative Politics* 16, no. 1 (1983).

Weiner, Myron. 'The Struggle for Equality: Caste in Indian Politics', in *The Success of India's Democracy*, edited by Atul Kohli. Cambridge: Cambridge University Press, 2001.

Williams, Melissa. *Votes, Trust and Memory: Marginalized Groups and the Failings of Liberal Representation*. Princeton: Princeton University Press, 1998.

Willinson, Steven. *Votes and Violence: Electoral Competition and Ethnic Riots in India*. Cambridge: Cambridge University Press, 2004.

Wolpert, S. *Nehru: A Tryst with Destiny*. New York, NY: Oxford University Press, 1996.

Zachariah, Benjamin. *Developing India: An Intellectual and Social History, c. 1930-50*. New Delhi: Oxford University Press, 2005.

Zaidi, A.M. *The Encyclopedia of the Indian National Congress*, Vol. 12, edited by S.G. Zaidi. New Delhi: S. Chand & Co., 1981.

Zeillot, Eleanor. *From Untouchable to Dalit: Essays on the Ambedkar Movement*. New Delhi: Manohar, 1996.

———. *Ambedkar's World: The Making of Babasaheb and the Dalit Movement*. New Delhi: Navayana, 2003.

Index

About the Author

Bidyut Chakrabarty was Vice Chancellor, Visva-Bharati, Santiniketan, West Bengal, India from 2018 to 2023.